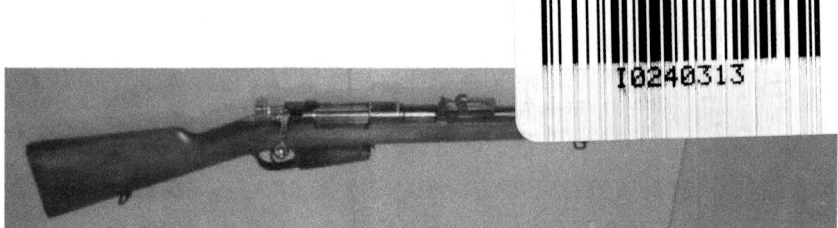

# America's Crossroads
## The Public Record

## Kevin Barr

Title: America's Crossroads, The Public Record

Copyright © 2023 by Kevin Barr

Cover design by Kevin Barr

*All rights reserved.
No part of this book may be reproduced in any form or by any electronic or mechanical means including information storage and retrieval systems, without permission in writing from the author. The only exception is by a reviewer, who may quote short excerpts in a review.
Printed in the United States of America*

―

*Change-Maker Net LLC*

―

*First Printing: 2023*

*ISBN 979-8-218-23527-7*

## Table of Contents

**America's Crossroads**
**The Public Record**
**Why The Interest**
**Richard Case Nagell The Man Who Knew Too Much**
**Terre Haute Police Report**

Hotel Registration Card and Phone Log

San Antonio Police Report

FBI Reports from the National Archives

FBI Report

More FBI Reports from the National Archives

FBI Report

Letter to the Honorable Chief Justice Earl Warren

Internal Government Memo
    Perhaps an Important Discovery

Letter from J. Lee Rankin, General Counsel
    Warren Commission

Three and one half years later, 1967 Press Release

Three FBI Reports following the Press Release

Report from LBJ Library

FBI Report, Jack Ruby – Young Communist League

Telephone Conversation, Researcher Larry Haapenen

Perry Russo Transcript

Record Recovery

Welcome to the Twilight Zone

Appearance Counts

Points To Be Made and Question That Arise

Luisa Calderon

Any CIA Interest in Luisa Calderon Prior to the Assassination?

The Hunt for the Rifle

The Assassination Rifle

More than one assassin and more than one patsy?
    Jack Ruby and a Young Man

Terre Haute

Terre Haute and the CIA

William King Harvey, America's James Bond

James Jesus Angleton
Berlin
Return To Washington
Prior To The Bay of Pigs Invasion
President Kennedy is Elected
The Bay of Pigs
The Bay of Pigs Aftermath
The Problem With Castro
ZR/RIFLE
Bill Harvey's & Jim Angleton's Relationship 1961
Operation Mongoose
The Cuban Missile Crisis
Finishing Harvey
The Big Fat Question Is
Rome, Italy
Fair Play For Cuba Committee
Philby!
The Martin and Lewis Affidavit (Supplemented)
In The Period Prior to the Assassination
   544 Camp Street
   CIA Activity
   Tracy Barnes
   David Athlee Phillips
   E. Howard Hunt
   George Joannides
   Robert Maheu
President John Kennedy's Assassination
We Have Recovered 3 Bullets
Parkland Hospital, Nurse Phyllis Hall
Alek James Hidell Anagram: Jailed Leak Helms
North by Northwest

The Backchannel
The Alleged Khrushchev - Kennedy Agreement
Any Evidence of Past CIA KGB Cooperation?
A Joint CIA – KGB Operation
AM/LASH
Lansdale Involved Or Set Up?
JM/WAVE's History
Otto Skorzeny, QJ/WIN
A Glimpse Of CIA Headquarters Activity
More on the Terre Haute House Records
FBI Division Five
Who Would Have Been Important Enough to Shoot in Terre Haute?
Terre Haute's Ray Cline
Ray S. Cline and William King Harvey
Harry Power And/Or The Rifle, Either One Significant?
Questions
Who Was James Jesus Angleton?
Who Placed Bill Harvey in the Public Record
House Select Committee's Interest
William King Harvey, Post Assassination
Harvey's and Rosselli's Post Assassination Activity
Harvey Alludes To Rumors
Who Was Bill Harvey?
The Dark Forces
So, What Could Have Motivates Them?
   The Period Leading Up To World War II
   Germany Lost The War, But Did The Nazis Lose?
   Dealing with Berlin
   Nazis Seriously? Didn't They Lose The War?
   Hints and Glimpses

**Allen Dulles, James Jesus Angleton, & Richard Helms**
**So, what's your interest in it?**
**Citations**

# AMERICA'S CROSSROADS
## The Public Record

On August 24, 2006 at 7:21 pm, some 43 years after the Kennedy assassination, Harry L. Power said to me: "the circumstances involving my appearance are so, so far from the truth that the wrong people that might have gotten that information could have railroaded my ass, because they wanted somebody and they needed somebody, and if that information would have been pursued at the time they would have had him."

"They would have had me and hence I would have become the second shooter on the knob and all of my affiliations with the communist agents in Cuba, they would have had almost a slam dunk proving that I was affiliated. I associated with Oswald and I was sent to Terre Haute to knock off this CIA guy and just another proof of the fact that I supposedly was a member of the Young Communist League and that kind of stuff. They would have had a patsy made, that's it."

---

On November 22, 1963, the 35th President of the United States, John Fitzgerald Kennedy, was assassinated in Dallas, Texas by a twenty-four-year-old assassin named Lee Harvey Oswald. Almost immediately the Dallas Police discovered a rifle on the sixth floor of the Texas School Book Depository, they first identified the rifle as a German Mauser rifle.

Three days later November 25, 1963, a young twenty-year-old named Harry L. Power walked into the Terre Haute House, in Terre Haute, Indiana. He had no luggage, although he did carry a long paper package. He registered at the hotel giving an address in San Antonio, Texas. Two days later the maid found that his bed had not been slept in and he had left behind a 7.65 Argentine German Mauser Rifle, Model 1891.

This is the untold story of Terre Haute, Indiana and its many possible connections to the Kennedy assassination.

This story begins with the Terre Haute House. The Terre Haute House was a hotel at the corner of 7$^{th}$ and Wabash Avenue in Terre Haute, Indiana. How appropriate, or ironic, that this story centers around 7$^{th}$ and Wabash Avenue, because there is this sign at this historic intersection that proclaims 7$^{th}$ and Wabash Avenue, "The Crossroads of America." It is here that the old National Road, which opened the west, from east coast to west coast, crosses old U.S. 41, the once major North South highway running from Chicago to Florida. This story is not only centered around a geographic crossroads for the Nation, but a psychological crossroads for the Nation, the time when many American citizens began to mistrust their government. Thus, the name of this book: "*America's Crossroads*".

As this story unfolds it will be clear that if I had not been in Terre Haute, I would not have been in a position to see some of the pieces of the puzzle.

I almost never watch the local news. I have come to believe that it was fate back in 1995 when I turned on the TV and heard Mark Edwards, a local TV reporter say "The

Kennedy Assassination and Terre Haute, Indiana. Was there a Conspiracy at The Crossroads?"

Here is a transcript of Mark's presentation on WTWO from 1995:

*"Terre Haute, Indiana and the Kennedy Assassination, was there a connection?"*

*"For those of us over the age of 40 this headline of November 22nd, 1963 'President is Assassinated, Dallas Scene of Shooting' is forever burned into our memories. The unthinkable happened and our lives have never been the same. Much has been written about that black Friday in Texas, and whispers of conspiracy, and second gunmen, and endless mysteries continue to haunt our lives."*

*"A few months ago, a friend of mine, Jane Robertson of Terre Haute told me about another book about the Kennedy assassination. And on page 572 the author made reference to an obscure incident in Terre Haute that I'd never heard of before."*

*"I spoke to Dick Russell, the author of the book, The Man Who Knew Too Much. A book in which former military intelligence agent Richard Case Nagell is the primary subject."*

*"Richard Case Nagell was a former intelligence agent. Nagell indicated in correspondence that it was important to follow up on a fellow from San Antonio, who after the assassination stayed in a hotel in Terre Haute, Indiana, and left behind a rifle. A rifle which was quite similar to the one said to have been Lee Harvey Oswald's, which was found in Dallas following the assassination of President Kennedy."*

Mark Edwards: *"When I first began this probe several months ago, I was naturally skeptical. Skeptical about whether this event had ever occurred in Terre Haute, in the first place. But as the witnesses mounted and the evidence began to pile up, I was faced with a mystery and a troubling question. Could there have* been a Conspiracy at the Crossroads of America?"

"I found it hard to believe that virtually no one in Terre Haute had ever heard the strange story of this mysterious man from Texas who checked into the Terre Haute House within days of the President's murder."

"The former hotel manager Dick Van Allen was surprised that anyone would be asking about the weapon left in room 705, after nearly 32 years. But he did remember the incident."

"Normally," said Van Allen, "the maids when they would find something a little out of the ordinary, such as gun, or excess money, or maybe a ring, or a pin, or something like that, well, they would normally come down and we would look into the situation, to see what it was all about. In this case, umm, when I looked at it, it was a rifle of course, so I called the police."

Police Detective Eugene Butts appears on the screen and says, "because of the type of rifle that it was, the detectives and I, we talked about the significance of the rifle and the possibility of its having been involved in the Kennedy thing in Dallas. Because it was a day or two after Kennedy was killed, why we assumed that it was important."

Van Allen continued: "All of us were quite alarmed about the whole situation. I know the police and the FBI were too. Things began popping."

The reporter Mark Edwards reappeared on the screen with a 1960's picture of the lobby of the Terre Haute House in the background. "On November 25th, 1963, the lobby of the Terre Haute House looked a lot like this. Most of the nation was watching the President's funeral on TV, while at the front desk of the Terre Haute House appeared a young man calling himself Harry L. Power. He signed a registration card for room 705 and took the elevator to the seventh floor of the Terre Haute House. Few people actually saw the mysterious man from San Antonio,

Texas."

"According to official police reports, when Harry Power entered the Terre Haute House he had no luggage, but he did carry a rifle in a paper package, it was a German Mauser rifle. When he left the Terre Haute House this rifle was all that was left behind."

"What happened to that rifle is an interesting story."

"The rifle was packed up and turned over to the FBI. The original police report indicates that the rifle that was given to the FBI back in 1963 was a high-quality German Mauser rifle serial number U8686."

Police Detective Butts then appears on the screen to verify that he remembers it being a Mauser.

Edwards continued: "What former police detective Butts told me is confirmed by this letter, sent by the Terre Haute Police Department to the attention of Earl Warren of the Warren Commission. Which leaves this burning question: Why isn't this incident ever mentioned in the Warren Report?"

Dick Russell, author of The Man Who Knew Too Much appears on the screen: "Well, the Warren Commission overlooked many things, and many things were withheld from the commission by the FBI and the CIA."

Detective Butts, "It's troubled me. I know that it, even way back then, why it troubled other officers on the Terre Haute Police Force. The fact that nothing was ever done with it."

"Another question is why isn't the incident better known in Terre Haute? Professor Larry Haapanen Ph.D now lives in Idaho, but in 1967 he visited Terre Haute to research the Harry Power story."

Professor Larry Haapanen: "I talked to Walt Sawyer the editor of the Terre Haute Star and, he mentioned that in 1963 after this happened the local news media knew about what had happened, *but they kept it quiet. And that was the reason, or that explains why there wasn't any public knowledge of it until 1967 when the chief of police went public with it in a story to the Associated Press."*

*"Something even more curious is Harry Power's behavior. Police knew he tried to sell the rifle and/or the scope and tried to purchase ammunition at a local gun shop before leaving it in his room for the maid to find."*

*"After much searching and leg work," said Edwards, "I was able to find the man who sold a bus ticket for St. Louis, to the mysterious man from Texas. But even after 32 years he is uncomfortable talking on camera about a bizarre incident that occurred here at the Terminal and asked that his identity be kept confidential."*

*"Police reports show that Power bought a bus ticket for St. Louis. The last anyone saw of the man who called himself Harry Power was here at the bus terminal, nearly 32 years ago. The ticket agent told police that when the bus for St. Louis was called out over the loudspeaker, Power jumped up from his seat, ran out this back door, and disappeared down the alley into the night."*

*Dick Russell: "Harry Power may be a pseudonym, or alias, for someone else. What is on record about him is that he had been in the service, as had Oswald. That he was a very good marksman and like Oswald he professed to be very left wing. Nagell told me that Power was either a Trotskyite or a Maoist type who had been seen with Oswald in Texas on more than one occasion."*

*Professor Larry Haapanen: "I think, Harry L. Power did exist and, may very well yet be alive. So, it's just a case of perhaps publicizing this and seeing if he steps forward."*

*"It may turn out that the name Harry L. Power is actually a real person's name, now whether that is the same person that was in Terre Haute, we don't know."*

*Dick Russell: "If you or someone else can find Harry L. Power, if he is still alive. I think we may very well get some very interesting answers as to who really assassinated President Kennedy."*

*"So," said Mark Edwards, "I've joined the handful of researchers who are searching for the man from Texas and the secrets only he can reveal. And while I have some intriguing leads as to whom Harry Power really is. The question of why he left the rifle in the Terre Haute House and why the Warren Commission ignored him, will likely be forever hidden behind the curtain of time."*

## WHY THE INTEREST

Because I have lived in Terre Haute all my life and am in fact third generation Terre Haute, and because I have a certain loyalty to Terre Haute, all of this made me particularly interested in and excited about this story. So much so, that I have spent a considerable amount of time since 1995, researching what might have happened. Imagine that Terre Haute, Indiana, "The Crossroads of America," holding the key to one of the greatest mysteries in history? Does Terre Haute, Indiana hold the key to the Kennedy Assassination?

I kept thinking about this story. I thought about how the stranger from San Antonio, Texas reportedly had no luggage, like he had left somewhere in a hurry. How the rifle was the same make as the one the Dallas Police first identified as being Lee Harvey Oswald's on the sixth floor of the Texas School Book Depository on the day of the assassination. And of the bizarre and conspicuous behavior, of jumping up and running out of the bus station when the bus was called out over the loudspeaker.

For the next year I turned the story over and over in my mind asking myself such questions as: Why Terre Haute? Why leave the rifle where it would be found? Why not ditch the rifle in the Wabash River just a few blocks away? Was there a reason for leaving the rifle where it would be recovered, or discovered? This Harry L. Power character, according to reports didn't have any luggage. Did he leave somewhere in a hurry and not have time to pack? If he did decide to leave in a hurry, then it would appear to be while he was in possession of a rifle. Why did he try to sell the rifle? Having failed to sell the rifle why would he try to buy ammunition? Was Harry L. Power his real name or an alias? Was Harry

L. Power significant? Was the rifle significant? Was Terre Haute significant? Was there someone significant in Terre Haute to shoot? Was leaving the rifle behind intended to put what was going on in the Public Record? If so, it sure did. Why Terre Haute? Why Terre Haute? Why Terre Haute?

In 1996, a year after hearing this story I decided to pursue this story about the stranger from San Antonio, Texas. I remembered most of the story from a year earlier, but I needed to know some important facts, like the name of the mysterious stranger, which I couldn't remember. So, I called the TV station and asked for Mark Edwards. I was told that Mark Edwards no longer worked at the station, so I asked for the Production Manager, Andy Alderton. I asked for Andy because just prior to the story airing on TV in 1995 I had been out to WTWO and worked with Andy on the editing of a videotape that I created about the Internet. In 1995, web browsers and web pages were cutting edge and I ended up making and marketing a videotape about the Internet to some forty-eight local businesses, which became their introduction to the Internet. The only reason I mention Andy Alderton is because amazingly and again as fate would have it, Andy plays multiple major roles later in this story. Anyway, I talked to Andy at WTWO and said, "do you remember me, you worked with me on the Internet tape?" Andy did remember me, and he gave me Mark's phone number.

Mark Edwards turned out to be a very nice person and very interesting to talk to. Mark ended up giving me copies of the videotape of his news story, a copy of the Terre Haute Police report, a copy of a letter to Chief Justice Earl Warren from the Terre Haute Police Department, and a copy of the hotel registration card that Harry L. Power had filled out and signed.

Mark obtained the police reports, the registration card, and the letter to Earl Warren through researcher and professor Larry Haapanen. I spoke with Dr. Larry Haapanen and he had obtained these documents from the National Archives way back in the late 60's.

This story is a collection of what I have discovered, in roughly the order that I discovered it.

For those of you too young to remember the assassination of President John F. Kennedy, let me bring you quickly up to speed with a paraphrased version of the original official United States Government version, so that you may follow along. On November 22, 1963, President Kennedy was shot to death while riding in a motorcade through Dallas, Texas. Within hours, a man named Lee Harvey Oswald was taken into custody inside a movie theater in Dallas, Texas. Two days later the nation and the world witnessed on television Lee Harvey Oswald being shot to death in the basement of Dallas Police Headquarters by a man named Jack Ruby (real name Jack Rubinstein). The former Vice President of the United States, Lyndon Baines Johnson, now having assumed the Office of the President, appointed a Commission within days of the murder to investigate the matter. The Commission became known as the Warren Commission, named after the head of the Commission who was at the time the Chief Justice of the Supreme Court, his name was Earl Warren. The commission found that Lee Harvey Oswald was the lone gunman, and that Jack Ruby was supposedly motivated to kill Oswald in order to save Mrs. Kennedy from the ordeal of Lee Harvey Oswald's prosecution in a court of law. That's it. End of story. Case closed. However, I should point out that the majority of Americans do not believe this "official version."

There have, however, been follow-up government investigations. Most notable was the House Select Committee on Assassinations of the U.S. House of

Representatives (HSCA). One of their findings says: "The committee believes, based on the evidence available to it, that President John F. Kennedy was probably assassinated as a result of a conspiracy. The committee is unable to identify the other gunman or the extent of the conspiracy."

I was eight years old and in $3^{rd}$ grade at Meadows School in Terre Haute, when President Kennedy was assassinated. I can remember standing in line at school, just after lunch. Suddenly the teachers, looking very concerned, became excited, and began rushing from all over the school to the teacher's lounge. This was not normal to see teachers hurrying through the hallways and we all sensed something was going on. Someone said President Kennedy had been shot. It was a very sad and disturbing time. I will never forget it.

# RICHARD CASE NAGELL THE MAN WHO KNEW TOO MUCH

The book *The Man Who Knew Too Much*, by Dick Russell, triggered Mark Edward's report on WTWO Terre Haute. The book was written about a former military intelligence agent named Richard Case Nagell.

Note to reader: When you see a paragraph like the paragraph immediately below followed by something like: HSCA 1801002510111 you can assume that this text is pretty much verbatim as written by one of the government investigative committees, or as found in an FBI report. In this case the paragraph immediately below this is a quote from the HSCA, the House Select Committee on Assassinations. Any comments that I might have added are enclosed in ( ) parentheses.

The history of Richard Case Nagell is important. Nagell was a member of U.S. Military Counterintelligence in Tokyo and dealt with vital (classified) information. HSCA 1801002510111

Mid 1963, the CIA sent Richard Case Nagell to 544 Camp Street in New Orleans to investigate the activities of Lee Harvey Oswald, Guy Banister, Clay Shaw, and David Ferrie. Tracy Barnes, the CIA officer who sent Nagell, was allegedly familiar with Oswald, having used him as an informant in the Soviet Union. Barnes wanted Nagell to **determine if Oswald was still working for the FBI** and to establish a relationship with the group in New Orleans. Nagell quickly learned that the group was planning to assassinate President Kennedy. He tried to warn the authorities, but his warnings were ignored. [1]

In September 1963, Richard Case Nagell sent a registered letter to the FBI Director J. Edgar Hoover, warning that Lee Harvey Oswald was planning to assassinate President John F. Kennedy. Nagell also listed two of Oswald's aliases, including Alex Hydell.

Nagell became concerned when he didn't get a response from the FBI. Afraid that he might be made to look like he had a hand in the assassination with Oswald, he decided to take himself out of play by getting himself arrested. So, on November 21, 1963, Nagell walked into a bank in El Paso, Texas pulled out his Colt .45 and fired two shots into the ceiling of the bank. (I like to say: "He deposited two bullets in the bank.") Nagell then went outside, waiting to be arrested. The bank guard ran right past him, and Nagell had to yell at him to come back. [2]

This is what is said in a House Select Committee on Assassinations (HSCA) document 180100251011 about Richard Case Nagell:

The plot began in March 1962; the parties did not meet [in Mexico City] until July 1963. Parties included in the plot were Alex Hydell, otherwise known as Lee Harvey Oswald; a female attorney who is a well-known Communist in Los Angeles, blond, about 35 years age at that time; hotel headwaiter, Frity, first name unknown, who owned a launch believed to be shuttling between Mexico and Cuba. Also believed to be involved – Warren Brogie, hotel chain manager; and Richard Case Nagell, former Captain, U.S. Army, associated with Counterintelligence in Japan in 1959. HSCA 1801002510111

In the Warren Report there is a short FBI report dated December 20, 1963, in which Nagell says: "For the record he would like to say that his association with Oswald was purely social and that he had met him in Mexico City and in Texas."

FBI 124-10169-10081

Nagell, "the conspiracy I was cognizant of, I'm not saying is the same one that resulted in the president's death, although I'm sure the same people were involved." [3]

Nagell indicated in correspondence that it was important to follow up on the fellow from San Antonio, who after the assassination stayed in a hotel in Terre Haute, Indiana, and left behind a rifle. A rifle which was similar to the one said to have been Lee Harvey Oswald's. [4]

Nagell, stated, "this man [Harry L. Power] had known Lee Harvey Oswald and had been seen with him…" Nagell wrote in May 1976: "I know little about the fella who once resided in San Antonio. I think he was a Trotskyite or Maoist type." [5]

# TERRE HAUTE POLICE REPORT

The Terre Haute Police Department report dated 4/7/1964, filed by Detectives Schoffstall and Eaton was sent to the attention of Chief Justice Earl Warren, of the Warren Commission, and it says:

---

–

> On November 27, 1963, the undersigned officers were assigned by Chief of Detectives John O'Leary to investigate a gun, which had been found in room 705 at the Terre Haute House Hotel, 7$^{th}$ & Wabash in this City.
>
> At approximately 2:30 P/M November 27$^{th}$, 1963, the undersigned Detectives arrived at the Terre Haute House Hotel where we talked to Mr. Van Allen, manager of the Hotel, and who showed us to the room which had been occupied by one Harry L. Power, who gave an address of 127 N. University Ave. San Antonio, Texas. In our investigation of the room, we found a German Mauser 7.65-mm torn apart lying across the arms of a chair, this gun had been cleaned and well taken care of, serial # U-8686. Mr. Van Allen then gave these officers the registration card and the phone calls made by this subject in the two days that he was at the Hotel. We then called for the Technician, in order to try to get what fingerprints that we could, however we found that the maid had already cleaned the room and everything had been wiped clean. We also called the F.B.I. office and advised them of what we had found, they in turn sent F.B.I. Agent Ken Phelps to make an investigation of this matter. On November 26, 1963, Harry L. Power made a phone call from the Hotel to Poff's Gun Shop located in Twelve Points, this City, and

in checking with this Gun Shop we found that Power was trying to sell this gun, and when he could not get the price that he thought that the gun was worth he tried to purchase ammunition for it. We were also advised, by Chief of Police Riddle that he thought that he had seen this subject in the American Sports building and at that time Power was trying to purchase ammunition but was unable to get it. We also learned that this subject had no baggage or clothing other than what he was wearing, which was a Dark Blue Suit, and a description was given as follows: FAIR COMPLECTED, STOCKY BUILD, SANDY OR LT. BRN. HAIR, 22 to 23 years of age, 5'6" W/M, NEATLY DRESSED, COMBED HAIR STRAIGHT BACK.

On November 28, 1963, the undersigned Detectives sent a letter to the Police Department San Antonio, Texas asking them for a complete character check on Harry L. Power, which came back stating that no arrest or criminal data could be found with the Department.

On December 7, 1963, Assistant Chief of Detectives Eugene Butts wrote a letter to Emil Peters, Inspector, San Antonio, Texas Police Department, which included a little more information concerning this case, since we had not received any word on the letter sent by the undersigned.

On Dec. 10, 1963, Capt. Butts received a letter from inspector Peters stating that Detective T.T. Fenley had been assigned to the case and would send a complete report on his finding.

In the meantime, investigation by the undersigned revealed that this subject had been in the Bus Terminal where we talked to one Don Locker who stated that this subject came into the Terminal on Monday Nov. 25, 1963, and purchased a ticket to St. Louis, Mo. At 5:45 PM, that night, when Locker called out over the microphone that *this bus was ready to leave, this subject got up and ran out the door and down the alley. It was revealed through correspondence that Harry L. Power resided at 108 N. University Avenue, San Antonio, Texas, and worked for Acme Neon Company in that City. He was employed by that company for about one year, and left the Company on December 12, 1962, and left a forwarding address of Gen. Delivery ~~Luftberry~~ [Taftberry] Manila, West Virginia. He was born 4/5/43, 5'10" 180 lbs., and has a current Iowa driver's license. We also learned that a Roger Drisch [Dresch] had worked with Harry Power and knew that he owned a rifle such as was found here.*

*Through correspondence to the National Rifle Association, we learned that they could not find anything in their files in reference to the German Mauser U-8686 found in the Terre Haute House Hotel in this City on Nov. 26, 1963.*

*This case is still under investigation by the undersigned Detectives.*

---

–

# HOTEL REGISTRATION CARD AND PHONE LOG

The name on the registration card dated Nov. 25, 1963, is shown as Harry L. Power, his address is given as 127 N. University Ave., San Antonio, Texas.. He checked into room 705 of the Terre Haute House, the cost of the room, $5.00 a day.

The following day, Nov. 26$^{th}$ the hotel logged a phone call from room 705 to Poff's Sporting Goods Store.

The rifle was a German Mauser rifle 7.65-mm, serial number U8686. On the day of the assassination, the Dallas Police identified the rifle on the 6$^{th}$ floor of the School Book Depository as a 7.65-mm German Mauser rifle, within twenty-four hours the Dallas Police changed their story and announced that the rifle found on the 6th floor was an Italian Mannlicher-Carcano rifle.

According to the police report, Power's unusual behavior at the bus station occurred on November 25$^{th}$. The hotel logged a second phone call coming from room 705 on the 26th; it was made to the Bus Station. So here we have Harry Power calling the bus station the day after he supposedly made enough of a scene that it was noticed and later reported to the police. It seems unusual that a person would contact, or return to a place, where they had recently created a scene. It makes me wonder if someone was impersonating Harry in an attempt to call attention to Harry Power and at the same time trying to associate Harry with the St. Louis destination for some reason. This brings to mind the allegations that others may have impersonated Lee Harvey Oswald in an effort to make him look a certain way.

# SAN ANTONIO POLICE REPORT

San Antonio Police report dated 12/9/1963, 3:30 PM, T.T. Fenley #90 filed the following report (paraphrased):

---

—

The San Antonio Police report, which was sent back to the Terre Haute Police Department said that the address given by Harry Power at the Terre Haute House was not correct. They found that 127 University, should have been 108 University.

San Antonio reports that July 1962 Harry L. Power tried to get a driver's license. But he failed the test and did not apply again. Although, as a result, the license bureau was able to tell the San Antonio Police that Power is 5' 10," 180 pounds, date of birth 4/5/1943. Harry gave his place of employment as Acme Neon Co. The San Antonio Police discovered that Power already had a valid driver's license from Iowa, at the time that he reportedly tried to get a Texas driver's license. (It would appear that the whole reason for this little exercise was to establish Harry's height, weight, date of birth and place of employment, being as Harry already had a valid driver's license in Iowa. I suspect that this wasn't Harry who went to the licenses bureau, but someone posing as Harry.)

The report goes on to say that Harry is a painter by trade. San Antonio Police talked to Don McNay who owns the Acme Neon Company. McNay said that Power left his company on September 12, 1962, that he was a smart aleck type person and a troublemaker. He said Power left owing a lot of bills. McNay also told the police that one of his workers Roger Dresch, who is an artist and who used to work for him, had told him that Power carried a card for the "YCL," The Young

Communist League. Dresch said the card looked real and had Power's name on the front along with the words "Young Communist League." On the back of the card was some kind of oath.

McNay said the last time he had heard from Power was when Power wrote for his W2 forms from this address: General Delivery, Taftberry, Manila W. VA.

The San Antonio Police then went to Roger Dresch's current place of work, to talk to him. Dresch said that Power was an odd sort of person. That he had a warped outlook on life. That he felt the world owed him a living and that there was nothing wrong with Communists. He spoke freely about Communists and about our type of Government. He doesn't remember Power saying anything about doing any harm to any Official. His outlook was to go back to W. VA and take his rifle and go into the hills and stay there for the rest of his life. He was a top marksman going to the rifle range at least 2 or 3 times a week. The card that he carried was cream colored with dark blue or black letters.

The San Antonio Police next went to Harry's old address of 108 University and learned that Power was married to a woman in the Air Force and that he was an ex-Army man [ex-Air Force] and that they seemed to have a lot of family trouble and that Power moved out around September 1962.

Harry appears to have moved from San Antonio in September of 1962. Where was Oswald Sept 1962? Oswald moved to Dallas Oct. 8, 1962, and worked for Jagger-Stovall-Chiles, and met a man named George de Mohrenschildt, who was a white Russian perhaps an intelligence operative and who was allegedly a spy for the Nazis in this country during World War II. (A white Russian was a member of the White Army, or was the opposition to the Bolsheviks/communists, or the Red Army in the Russian Civil War of 1918 to 1921.)

In the "President's Commission on the Assassination Vol. 16, Page 53," there is a page shown from Oswald's address book. Under the title Jagger-Chiles Stovall, Oswald wrote "micro dots." (Microdots were used in the spy-trade and are photographic images that have been reduced in size, so as to be undetectable, as a microdot can appear to be simply a period in a line of text in a document.)

According to the Warren Report, "on the application for [post office] box No. 6225, Oswald gave an incorrect street number, though he did show Beckley Avenue, where he was then living." Harry Power did the same thing at the Terre Haute House when he registered for a room. He put as an address, 127 University, when the address he had previously lived at was 108 University.

Harry Power seems to be documented in the "Public Record" much the same as Lee Harvey Oswald was portrayed. Let us contrast the two. Harry is 20. Oswald is 24. Oswald does not drive and does not have a driver's license. Harry had a valid driver's license in Iowa but decided to apply for a driver's license in Texas and flunked the test. Harry is allegedly a member of the Young Communist League; Oswald is portrayed as being a member of the Fair Play for Cuba Committee in New Orleans. Harry is said to be ex-Army [ex-Air Force]. Oswald is an ex-Marine. Both are alleged to have voiced some support for communism. Harry is depicted as a hermit who wants to head for the hills. Oswald is supposedly a loner. Both are supposed to be good riflemen, and both seem to have family problems. Both have a problem giving the correct street address. Both had problems boarding buses!

With the information provided by Mark Edwards I was able to go out on the Internet and searched the National Archives for Harry L. Power and Terre Haute. I found thirteen FBI reports that referenced Harry Power in their title and one that referenced Terre Haute. The way the National Archives worked, back when I went looking was, the titles of the documents are searchable on the internet, but if you want to read the document, such as an FBI report, you must contact the National Archives and request a copy.

If you wish to follow one of my first steps in this process you can go to the Internet and search for "Harry Power" or "Terre Haute" in the National Archives, JFK Assassination Records at http://www.archives.gov/research/jfk/

# FBI REPORTS FROM THE NATIONAL ARCHIVES

There are 10 documents in the National Archives/ JFK Assassination System that were generated in 1963 concerning Harry L. Power and the rifle that was left in Terre Haute.

<u>Agency: FBI, Record # 124-10266-10116, and Agency File # 100-14205-2</u>

*Subject: JFK, Suspect, Harry L. Power*
*From: Indianapolis*
*To: FBI Director*
*Date: 12/10/1963*

*Text: On 12/10/63, Chief of Detectives JOHN O'LEARY (NA), Terre Haute PD, Terre Haute, Indiana, advised the following:*

*On 11/27/63, in the late afternoon his department received a call from the Terre Haute House Hotel Manager, stating that a person had rented a room on the night of 11/25/63, had apparently **left without paying for the room**, and a maid had discovered a rifle abandoned in the room.*

*Detective SCHOFFSTALL determined the following: On **11/25/63, at approximately 10:58 PM**, a person **registering as HARRY L. POWER**, 127 North University Avenue, San Antonio, Texas, rented a room at the Terre Haute House Hotel **On 11/26/63, POWER made two local calls, one to Poff's Gun Store and one to the bus terminal** Also, on 11/26/63, POWER went to Poff's Gun Store and **attempted to sell a 7.65 caliber German Mauser Rifle, SN***

U8686. POWER would not give his name or address and the manager of Poff's Gun Store did not buy the rifle.

Power returned to the hotel on 11/26/63 and **had the rifle wrapped in newspaper. The only luggage, which POWER had,** other than the rifle, **was a small leather zipper case containing shaving supplies.** POWER was last seen at the Hotel on 11/26/63 at about 6:00 PM when he asked the Bell Captain where he might do some laundry.

**On 11/27/63, the maid noted that the bed in POWER'S room had not been used,** and the **rifle** which POWER had, was **disassembled, and lying on a chair.** POWER was described as a white male, age 22, 5'8", stocky build.

O'LEARY stated inquiry was made by Assistant Chief of Detectives EUGENE BUTTS, of his department, to determine if possibly POWER was wanted in San Antonio. He stated **it was not believed the rifle indicted any possible attempt of murder in Terre Haute** and it would be impossible to see the Republican or Democratic City Headquarters from the room, which POWER had rented at the hotel. Furthermore, since the city elections have been over for about one month, the Republican and Democratic City Headquarters are no longer in operation.

No further investigation being conducted by Indianapolis. For information San Antonio, the rifle taken from the hotel is in possession of the Terre Haute PD.

---

–

Note the date and time that Harry checked into the Terre Haute House was 11/25/63, at approximately 10:58 PM (per the report immediately above). Harry allegedly ran from the bus station earlier the same night at 5:45 PM, Monday, Nov. 25, 1963 (per the first Terre Haute Police report above). The bus station and the Terre Haute House are one block apart, on the same side of the street, on the same alley. Harry could have run from the bus station to the Terre Haute House, where he checked in. However, it does not take five hours and 13 minutes to run this distance. A young twenty-year-old should be able to cover the distance in under a minute.

The description of what Harry had with him when he checked in seems detailed. It is said that not only did he not have any luggage, but also it says that he had a small leather zipper case containing shaving supplies and a package wrapped in newspaper. Not only did they notice that he had a shaving kit, but they reportedly noticed it was made of leather.

# FBI REPORT

Agency: FBI, Record # 124-10266-10117, and Agency File # 100-14205-3 (Shortened Version)

*Bureau files show **Harry L. Power, born 4/5/43 at LaSalle, Illinois, was subject of Interstate Transportation of Stolen Property investigation in 1960, Omaha file 87-6489**. Omaha furnished pertinent background information regarding subject to Indianapolis.*

---

–

I requested the Omaha file 87-6489, but was told that it had been destroyed, old records.

# MORE FBI REPORTS FROM THE NATIONAL ARCHIVES

<u>Agency: FBI, Record # 124-10266-10119, and Agency File # 100-14205-5 (Shortened Version)</u>

*Harry L. Power passed a bad check in the amount of $75.00 in Iowa.*

*On the endorsement of the check, POWER gave his address as Kessler [Keesler] AFB, Biloxi, Mississippi, Squad 3404. Leads were set out in this communication for the New Orleans Office to determine if HARRY L. POWER was a member of Squadron 3404 and if the above-described check was a **true-name** check.*

*FBI checked with Keesler Air Force Base Mississippi, advised that Harry L. Power, AF 16 66 2539, arrived at Keesler AFB from Lackland AFB on 5/23/60 and that he was assigned to Squadron 3404. It was pointed out that by Special Order J-765, paragraph 2, dated 7/8/60, that Power was **dropped from the rolls effective 7/4/60 AWOL**.*

*In view of the fact that investigation by the Chicago, New Orleans and Omaha Divisions revealed **checks written by subject to be true name**, no investigation was conducted by the Omaha Office.*

---

We have now established that Harry L. Power is a real person passing bad checks, not an alias. We have also learned that Harry is AWOL from the military and that he was stationed in Biloxi, Mississippi at Keesler Air Force Base in 1960. Keesler Air Force Base is an hour and a half away from New Orleans.

In *"The House Select Committee on Assassinations, HSCA,"* deposition of Marina Oswald (widow on Lee Oswald, now Mrs. Porter), August 9, 1978, it says:

> Question: Were there any other groups that he [Oswald] spoke about?
> Answer: That is all that I can recall.
> Question: Did he ever mention Keesler Air Force Base in Mississippi?
> Answer: What?
> Question: Keesler Air Force Base, which is in Mississippi.
> Answer: No
> Question: He never discussed friends from the Air Force base?
> Answer: Well, I didn't know that he had anything to do with the Air Force.
> Question: Well, they are people he [Oswald] may have known who were in the Air Force.
> Answer: I don't know. <u>HSCA</u> Vol. 12, Page 394-395

Other than documents related to Harry Power and the text above related to Oswald, I haven't seen any other reference in the Warren Commission, or the House Select Committee documents that reference Keesler Air Force Base. Lee Harvey Oswald was posted at Keesler Air Force Base from May 3, 1957, through July 8, 1957, and Harry Power; according to the FBI report above was apparently posted at Keesler in 1960.

Jack Martin who is thought to have been an intelligence operative reported to the FBI that Thomas Edward Beckham "age seventeen…was in California allegedly passing fraudulent checks on his father's account," and in 1959 he had been "subject of an interstate transportation of stolen property investigation." FBI 124-10058-10072, HQ,

62-109060-4618 Feb. 20, 1967. (Sounds a lot like Harry. Jack Martin, who you will hear more about later, appeared to have been tasked with making Thomas Edward Beckham appear to be just another patsy.)

# FBI REPORT

<u>Agency: FBI, Record # 124-10266-10118, and Agency File # 100-14205-4</u>

Subject: JFK, Suspect, Harry L. Power
From: San Antonio
To: Director FBI
Date: 12/13/1963

Text: There is enclosed for the Indianapolis Division nine copies of an FD 302 reflecting information obtained from ROGER DRESCH, 2630 Hackamore, San Antonio.

For the information of the Bureau, DRESCH advised that **subject told him during the summer of 1961 that he was a member of the Young Communist League, and he exhibited a card, which subject stated was his membership card in this organization.** DRESCH does not recall any wording on the card. **DRESCH described POWER as anti-KENNEDY administration and an enthusiastic hunter.**

*[Person's name blacked out]* (T symbol), **who has some knowledge of communist activities in the San Antonio Area, on 12/13/63 advised that to his knowledge there is no Young Communist League group in San Antonio nor was there in 1961.**

---

—

Harry was allegedly a member of the Young Communist League in San Antonio, yet an FBI informant reports there was no Young Communist League in San Antonio. Similarly, Oswald was supposedly a member of the Fair Play for Cuba Committee, but there was no such committee in New

Orleans, unless you count Oswald as a committee of one.

There is evidence that Lee Oswald was showing a "Communist Party" and a "Fair Play for Cuba" card at the Cuban Embassy in Mexico City. Cuban Consul in Mexico City, Eusebio Azcue Lopez, testified, "He [Oswald] exhibited, or produced, documents such as one attesting to his membership in the 'U.S. Communist Party.' Also, another indicating that he is a member of the 'Fair Play for Cuba Committee.'" _HSCA_ Vol. 3, Page 130-131

Alfredo Mirabal Diaz of the Cuban Embassy, Mexico City, testified, "In fact, I noticed that he [Oswald] presented a card or credentials as belonging to the 'Communist Party of the United States.' I understand, or it is also my understanding, that the 'Communist Party of the United States' stated that he [Oswald] never belonged to the party. I was surprised by the fact that the card seemed to be a new card."
_HSCA_ Vol. 3, Page 176

"I must say [said Diaz] that I also have been a Communist for a number of years and that generally <u>we do not use credentials, or a card</u>, to identify ourselves as members of the party. I was surprised by his unusual interest in using identification as a Communist." _HSCA_ Vol. 3, Page 176

---

–

# LETTER TO THE HONORABLE CHIEF JUSTICE EARL WARREN

Back in 1963 the Terre Haute Police contacted the FBI, the San Antonio Police Department, and now comes the following letter to Chief Justice Earl Warren of the Warren Commission on April 9, 1964. You can't say the Terre Haute Police Department didn't try.

---

—

*April 9, 1964*

*Honorable Chief Justice Earl Warren*
*United States Supreme Court*
*Washington, D.C.*

*Dear Sir:*

*Enclosed find case records from my department concerning an incident in our city, which may interest your Commission regarding investigation of the assassination of President Kennedy* **and/or attempt on the life of General Walker**.

*You will note by the reports that there is a rifle involved in this investigation. This weapon is in the possession of the Terre Haute Police Department at this time and is available to your Commission at any time.*

*Respectfully yours,*
*Frank Riddle*
*Chief of Police*

---

—

General Walker was a leader of the radical right, a real right-winger. In 1961, the Kennedys relieved him of his command in West Germany because he was espousing his views to his troops. General Walker ended up moving to Dallas, Texas.

Apparently, the Terre Haute Police had gotten the impression that Harry L. Power had been investigated in relation to an assassination attempt that was made on General Walker, in Texas. In a Treasury Department, Secret Service report dated 12/26/63, Marina Oswald (Lee's wife) alleged that General Walker was the head of a fascist organization in the U.S. She also stated that when her husband returned home late one night, he was very nervous and finally told her that he shot Walker with his rifle and that it was best for everybody that he got rid of him." *HSCA* 180-10110-10289

The shot ended up just missing General Walker as it was slightly deflected off a cross piece in the window frame.

**The Assassinations Committee speculated, "That if it could be shown that Oswald had associates in the attempt on General Walker, they would be likely candidates as the grassy knoll gunman."**

Walter Kirk Coleman, age 15, Dallas, Texas, lived near General Walker and heard a blast on the evening of April 10, 1963. Coleman ran immediately to the fence, which separates the property where he resides and that of the Mormon Church parking lot. Coleman stepped up on a bicycle, which put him in a position to look into the parking lot.

Coleman observed two men. No. 1 hurried towards the driver's side of this car. The car was parked headed towards Turtle Creek Boulevard with the motor running and the headlights on. No. 2 was about ten yards behind No. 1.

No. 1 got into the 1950 Ford and drove off at a normal rate

of speed. He did not notice if No. 1 was carrying anything in his hands. He was a white male, 19 or 20 years old, 5'10," 130 pounds, dark, bushy hair, thin face, large nose, real skinny.

No. 2 observed at the driver's side of the Chevrolet. He had the door open, and the front seat pushed forward. He was leaning through the car door and into the back seat area of this car. Cars were a 1950 Ford and a 1958 Chevrolet. <u>National Archives and Records Administration, NARA</u> 201-2892-8

## INTERNAL GOVERNMENT MEMO

The following handwritten memo concerns the Warren Commission's response back to the Terre Haute Police Department following receipt of the Terre Haute Police Department's Police report and letter to Chief Justice Earl Warren:

---

—

*Internal Government memo dated 4/21/1964,*
*From: Mr. Redlich*
*To: Mr. Rankin and Mr. Willent.*

*Written in cursive:* **My recommendation is that we acknowledge and take no further action.** *If both of you agree, please return and I'll write the letter.*

J.L.R. writes I agree. Willent wrote so that I can't read it. Both apparently agreed because we have the letter of response below.

---

—

"Acknowledge and take no further action." What? Are we missing something here? We must be. Why wouldn't you want to at least investigate a little further? After all this is the President of the United States we are talking about here.

# PERHAPS AN IMPORTANT DISCOVERY

I had assumed that the handwritten note above from a Mr. Redlich was a note from the FBI to Mr. Rankin and Mr. Willent of the Warren Commission staff. But then the thought occurred to me that the FBI always types their memos, reports and correspondence, so I checked the Internet to see who Mr. Redlich was and found this:

In 1963 Norman Redlich was a 38-year-old professor of law at New York University and was appointed special assistant to Warren Commission staff director J. Lee Rankin. Redlich was a workaholic, who wrote his opinions and reworked the labors of the other lawyers on the staff seven days and nights a week. Hoover, the Director of the FBI, ordered that Redlich's past be investigated. Hoover discovered that Redlich was on the Emergency Civil Liberties Committee, **an organization considered by Hoover to have been set-up to "defend the cases of Communist lawbreakers."** Redlich had also been critical of the activities of the House Committee on Un-American Activities.

This information was leaked to a group of right-wing politicians. On 5th May 1964, Ralph F. Beermann, a Republican Party congressman, made a speech claiming that Redlich was associated with the **Fair Play for Cuba Committee.** Beermann called for Redlich to be removed as a staff member of the Warren Commission. He was supported by Karl E. Mundt who said: **"We want a report from the Commission which Americans will accept as factual, which will put to rest all the ugly rumors now in circulation and which the world will believe. Who but the most gullible** would believe any report if it were written in part by persons with Communist connections?"

Gerald Ford led the attack as he called for Redlich to be dismissed. However, Earl Warren and J. Lee Rankin both supported Redlich and he retained his job.

Norman Redlich was a special assistant to the Warren Commission and was given the responsibility of reading every document submitted to the Commission and he was the one who decided who would receive each document. This gave Redlich a great deal of power, as he controlled the flow of information to the Commission. Redlich was also a key figure in writing the Warren Report as he was responsible for drafting many of the key sections of the report.[6]

As you and I now know, Mr. Redlich recommended "no further action" on Harry Power an alleged card-carrying communist on 4/21/64, just 14 days before Mr. Redlich's objectivity was called into question on 5/5/64, concerning Communism, but was cleared enough to continue to serve the Warren Commission.

Was the information provided to the Warren Commission, by the Terre Haute Police, enough to warrant an investigation? The Warren Commission staff had the following information: that it was the Terre Haute Police Department's impression that Harry had been investigated for the shooting at General Walker, that the rifle was the same make as the rifle first announced on the day of the assassination, and that Harry had allegedly shown a Young Communist League Card.

Ironically Mr. Redlich was asked the following question concerning a different incident, however the question and the answer by Mr. Redlich seem to fit the Terre Haute incident. Redlich who worked for the Warren Commission was asked: Would knowledge of [           ] have made a difference? "I think it would have affected it, …" he replied. "I think that an important fact like that might have led to additional inquiry … It is possible that this additional fact might have led to additional inquiry."

# LETTER FROM J. LEE RANKIN, GENERAL COUNSEL

Warren Commission
Letter dated 4/22/1964, copies to Mr. Rankin, Mr. Willent, and Mr. Redlich.

---

*Mr. Frank Riddle*
*Chief of Police*
*Terre Haute, Indiana*

*Dear Mr. Riddle:*

*Chief Justice Warren has asked me to reply to your letter of April 19, 1964, which was accompanied by records from your department concerning the incident involving a rifle occurring shortly after the assassination of President Kennedy.*

*We do not feel that there is any need for the Commission to examine the rifle at this time, but we thank you for your cooperation in calling this matter to our attention.*

*Sincerely,*
*J. Lee Rankin*
*General Counsel*

---

We know that J. Lee Rankin, General Counsel, Warren Commission knew about Harry L. Power and Terre Haute, because he signed the letter above responding back to the

Terre Haute Police Department (letter immediately above). One would assume that Earl Warren might have known about this, being as the letter from the Terre Haute Police was originally addressed to him, but we do not know for sure if the Chief Justice was ever informed concerning the police report and the letter. We only have J. Lee Rankin's claim in a letter that he is speaking for Chief Justice Earl Warren. I haven't seen any indication that members of the Warren Commission, including Earl Warren, had knowledge about Harry L. Power, nor have I seen any evidence that the FBI provided the Warren Commission, or its staff, with its reports on Harry L. Power. We do know that the Terre Haute Police did their job and attempted to notify the Warren Commission.

## THREE AND ONE HALF YEARS LATER, 1967 PRESS RELEASE

Three and a half years after President Kennedy's assassination an interview was conducted by the Associated Press with retired Police Chief Frank Riddle where Riddle talked about the rifle being left in Terre Haute. This press release dated 4/3/67, was a good thing, because it triggered three more law enforcement reports, as shown below. There is some incorrect information in the Associated Press, press release. The rifle was not a 6.5-millimeter Italian Mannlicher-Carcano. Secret Service agents did not take the rifle. The stranger from San Antonio was not a salesman, but a sign painter.

The following three reports were generated when a Mr. Marvin Watson in the White House contacted the FBI in 1967, saying President Johnson wanted to know more about this AP story, the rifle, and this mysterious stranger from San Antonio, Texas.

# THREE FBI REPORTS FOLLOWING THE PRESS RELEASE

Agency: FBI, Record # 124-10057-10354 & 180-10020-10456, Agency File # 62-109060-5018

Subject: ***JFK, Disparaging Remark***, Harry L. Power
From: Indianapolis
To: FBI Director
Date: 4/4/67

Text: Following is a shortened version of FD 302 interview of Roger Dresch by an FBI Agent, San Antonio, Texas, Dec. 12, 1963.

Roger Dresch visited in Power's home on several occasions and had lunch with him many times during the early part of 1961 until Power left San Antonio in the fall of 1961. He stated that he knew Power about seven or eight months and **in conversation with him determined that he was anti-Kennedy Administration and also, he expressed enthusiasm concerning hunting. On one occasion he exhibited a rifle with a scope, which he was going to sight in on a range**, but Dresch did not know whether he was the owner of this rifle.

While eating lunch during the summer of 1961, **Power told Dresch that he was a member of the Young Communist League. He then pulled out of his billfold a cream-colored card, rectangular in shape, wallet size with some lettering on it and stated that this was his membership card in the Young Communist League.** He stated that this is **the only time that Power ever mentioned the Young Communist League and as far as he recalls he never mentioned the**

Communist Party.

Power claimed that his father was an alcoholic and he [Harry] served as a paratrooper in the U.S. Air Force. **He 'griped' a great deal about his position in life and occasionally talked about going into some isolated place and living the life of a hermit.**

---

Agency: FBI, Record # 124-10057-10355 & 180-10020-10457, Agency File # 62-109060-5019

Subject: JFK, Suspect, Harry L. Power
From: Indianapolis
To: FBI Director
Date: 4/4/67

Text: Concerning press release by Ex Chief of Police, Terre Haute, Ind., concerning man in possession of rifle in Terre Haute at time of assassination.

Info concerning this matter previously furnished Bureau in San Antonio and Indianapolis reports both captioned **"Harry L. Power, SM-C,"** which reflects man registered at Terre Haute House Hotel as Harry L. Power, Nov. 25, 1963, and departed Nov. 27, 1963, leaving in hotel room disassembled seven point six five caliber German Mauser rifle, SN U Eight Six Eight Six. Power had attempted unsuccessfully to sell this rifle to gun store at Terre Haute on Nov. 26, 1963. In 1961 he told a coworker in San Antonio that he was a member of Young communist League.

No other info concerning above incident in Indianapolis files. **Rifle mentioned above is currently in the custody of the Terre Haute, Ind., PD.**

Agency: FBI, Record # 124-10057-10356 & 124-10057-10357, Agency File # 62-109060-5020

Subject: Assassination of President Kennedy
From: A. Rosen, FBI
To: Mr. DeLoach, FBI
Date: 4/4/67

Text: Mr. Marvin Watson at the White House called April 3, 1967, concerning Associated Press Release No. 41, relating to a rifle of the same model as the one named as the gun used in the assassination of President Kennedy, being found in a Terre Haute, Indiana, hotel three days after the President's slaying. This release out of Putnamville, Indiana, was attributed to Frank Riddle, a retired Chief of Police, who said the 6.5-millimeter Italian Mannlicher-Carcano rifle was traced to a salesman in San Antonio, Texas. He also said his information about the rifle was turned over to the Warren Commission and the rifle was taken by Secret Service agents. Riddle said San Antonio authorities informed him the salesman had no criminal record, was a member of the Young Communist League, and an expert rifle marksman. He refused to name the salesman.

Based on the information available, it was not possible to identify any information in Bureau files with this Associated Press release. Mr. Tom Kelley, Assistant Director in Charge of Investigations, Secret Service, was telephonically contacted concerning this matter and he advised that **Secret Service first learned of this incident in 1965 when James Rowley, Director of Secret Service, was in Terre Haute, Indiana, making a speech**. Mr. Kelley furnished the name of the individual as Harry L. Power and advised the information received was to the effect that the *individual had left the hotel without paying his bill and had left a German Mauser rifle in the hotel room. Kelley stated they had attempted to locate this individual in San Antonio without success. Kelley advised that* **Secret Service did not pick up this rifle from the Terre Haute Police Department.**

*Bureau files reflect a* **Security Matter – C** *file on one Harry L. Power and that the San Antonio Police Department advised the San Antonio Office [of the FBI] on 12/9/63 of an inquiry from the Terre Haute Police Department concerning Power on November 25, 1963, indicating Power had abandoned a German-made rifle, caliber 7.65, Serial No. U8686 [U8686] on the 7*$^{th}$ *floor of the Terre Haute Hotel. The San Antonio Police Department stated their inquiry showed that Power had been employed with Acme Neon Company approximately one year, until September 12, 1962, when he left San Antonio, furnishing a forwarding address of General Delivery, Taftberry, Manila, West Virginia. An associate worker, Roger Drisch [Dresch], advised he observed Power with a Young Communist League membership card in his possession. No further information was available according to the San Antonio Police Department.*

*On subsequent interview of Roger Dresch by Bureau Agents, he advised Harry L. Power told him during the summer of 1961 that he was a member of the Young Communist League and exhibited the card, which Power stated was his membership card. Dresch described Power as anti-Kennedy administration and had no further information concerning Power or Communist activities in San Antonio.*

**<u>No further action was taken by the Bureau concerning this matter inasmuch as the rifle in question was not identical to the rifle, which was believed to have been in the possession of Oswald at the time of the assassination</u>**

*of President Kennedy, it being a 6.5-millimeter model 91/38 Mannlicher-Carcano rifle, Serial No. C2766. In addition, Power appeared to have no connection of any kind with events, which occurred in Dallas relative to the assassination.*

*A check with the Terre Haute, Indiana, Police Department revealed that the German Mauser abandoned in the hotel room was still in custody of the Terre Haute Police Department as of April 3, 1967.*

*ACTION: In view of Mr. Watson's call concerning this matter, there is attached a blind memorandum setting forth information relative to this rifle.*

At the bottom of this document, I believe it was **J. Edgar Hoover** who **wrote: "OK. They certainly pay a lot of attention to trivia,"** and then it is signed "H."

---

—

**The FBI didn't continue to investigate Harry, simply because "the rifle was not identical with the rifle which was believed to have been in the possession of Oswald at the time of the assassination."** This is brilliant police work. This statement precludes the possibility that there may have been more than one assassin and thus more than one rifle. And, what about the fact that the rifle in Terre Haute is the same make and model, as the rifle identified by the Dallas Police on the sixth floor of the School Book Depository immediately following the assassination, before they changed its description to something else?

It was not until January 15, 2005, that I finally went out on the Internet to see what "SM-C", or **"Security Matter C"** meant. **"C" stands for Communist. The FBI had Harry L. Power classified in their files as a "Communist!"**

# REPORT FROM LBJ LIBRARY

This report was restricted, but they reviewed it and released it to the author.

<u>Agency: NARA, Record # 179-30003-10234, Agency File # (none)</u>

*Subject: RE Rifle Found in Terre Haute, Indiana
Came from the LBJ Library
Date: 4/4/67*

Author's description of report: two pages total. The first page is basically the same as <u>Agency: FBI, Record # 124-10057-10356 & 124-10057-10357, Agency File # 62-109060-5020,</u> shown above except the following text is a little different in the following paragraph:

*"Inasmuch as the rifle abandoned by Power at the Terre Haute Hotel was a German-made rifle and not of the type owned by Lee Harvey Oswald, it being a 6.5-millimeter Model 91/38 Mannlicher-Carcano rifle, no further inquiries were made in 1963 concerning this matter."*

---

The interesting thing about this document from the LBJ Library is what someone has written on the bottom of the page in cursive. It says: "For Report on Robert Clayton Buick, see individual file on Buick." Why this is interesting is because (a) Robert Clayton Buick is not referenced anywhere in the text on the two pages that I have from the LBJ Library and (b) upon seeing this I requested all the information listed in the National Archives on Robert Clayton Buick. Last time I checked, six documents in the National Archives have still not been released concerning Robert Buick. Robert Clayton Buick was an intelligence informant, who allegedly met Oswald and Richard Case Nagell at the Hotel Luma in Mexico City in 1963. You remember Richard Case Nagell, he is the one that walked into an El Paso bank and deposited two bullets. Buick was also later incarcerated in the same jail cell with Nagell, in 1966. What a coincidence that they would end up in the same cell? Speculation is that Nagell's and Buick's conversations were recorded, while they were incarcerated in the same cell. Being as someone wrote on this FBI report that concerned Harry Power, "see Report on Robert Clayton Buick," it would be interesting to see if Harry L. Power is referenced in Robert Clayton Buick's file. Why did someone think the file on Robert Clayton Buick was relevant to Harry Power? I don't know the answer.

# FBI REPORT, JACK RUBY – YOUNG COMMUNIST LEAGUE

I searched the National Archives on the Internet for "Young Communist League." I found an FBI report dated December 10, 1963. It says:

> Agency: HSCA, Record # 1801002710253, Agency File # 105-82555-754

> Subject: Lee Harvey Oswald, Fernando Penabaz, Fair Play for Cuba Committee, Jack Rubenstein, Young Communist League
> From: FBI, Lionel E. Belanger
> Date: 12/10/63

> "On 12/5/63 Fernando Penabaz, former professor of English, Cuban Ministry of Education and holder of government posts in Costa Rica and Nicaragua, interviewed by WESH-TV, Orlando, Florida."

> "Penabaz cited facts concerning one Jack Rubenstein, one of the founders of the Revolutionary Youth, which he characterized as a Marxist organization. Penabaz also said that one **Jack Rubenstein was cited as a member of the National Executive Committee of the Young Communist League (YCL)**."

> "Penabaz went on to state that he had obtained facts from reports of public hearing of the "DIES" Committee of August 17, 1938 **that a Jack Rubenstein had been one of the founders of Revolutionary Youth, a Marxist Organization in 1930** and also in volume I of these hearings he had been one of the leaders in 1929 of the Lowstone phonetic – Gitlow phonetic group of the Communist Party, USA

(CPUSA). It was reported further in hearings on December 2, 1939, that a Jack Rubenstein attended a CPUSA caucus in 1929."

"Another reference to Jack Rubenstein was in the 80$^{th}$ Congress House Report in which a cable, made public, **referred to COMRADE JACK RUBENSTEIN a member of the Bureau of the National Executive Committee of the Young Communist League**.

---

–

The Young Communist League. This is the organization whose membership card Harry Power was alleged to have shown to his co-worker. Could this be a link, the proverbial smoking gun, between Harry L. Power, the guy that came to Terre Haute, and Jack Rubenstein, more commonly known as Jack Ruby? Jack Ruby of course shot and killed Oswald in the Dallas Police Station after the assassination.

Please note the date of the FBI report is 12/5/63. Bear in mind that the incident in Terre Haute and Harry L. Power's alleged association with the "Young Communist League" was not publicly known at that time and is not publicly well known to this day and yet here we have a Cuban exile, Dr. Penabaz, thirteen days after the assassination and just eight days after Harry left the rifle, alleging that Jack Ruby is a member of the National Executive Committee of the "Young Communist League!"

Did Jack Ruby know Harry L. Power? Were they both supposedly members of the "Young Communist League?" Harry L. Power lived in Chicago up until around seventeen years of age. Jack Ruby lived in Chicago at this time. Did Harry know Jack Ruby, when Harry was growing up?

This FBI report from Penabaz obviously makes Jack Ruby out to be a communist, as a member of a communist organization, just like Oswald and Harry Power allegedly were, or were to be perceived as being. Was Harry a participant, or a possible second patsy with implied, or possible links to Ruby and Oswald? Remember what Nagell said, "it is important to follow up on a fellow from San Antonio, who after the assassination stayed in a hotel in Terre Haute, Indiana, and left behind a rifle."

# TELEPHONE CONVERSATION, RESEARCHER LARRY HAAPENEN

The following is a November 14, 1970, memo of a telephone conversation between Kennedy researcher and Professor Dr. Larry Haapanen and Don McNay [owner of Acme Sign Co.], of San Antonio, Texas (shortened version):

> *McNay asked me if the police report said Power was a pretty good boy? McNay confirmed that Roger Dresch was an employee of his, and said, Harry showed Roger a card that had YCL on it and Dresch said Harry was really proud of it, and so I told the San Antonio Police about it." I told McNay the Young Communist League went out of existence in 1943.*
>
> *McNay said, "Harry was a very nice kid." But he also said that Power was something of a troublemaker, going around to the other employees and telling them they weren't getting paid enough. McNay said he seemed to recall that **Power was from Chicago**, and that his father had a restaurant there.*
>
> *McNay said that before Power left San Antonio, he went to different jewelry stores, saying he had worked there [at Acme] for eight months, and bought $400-$500 worth of jewels on credit. McNay said he supposed Power couldn't have gotten more than $80 for them if he tried to dispose of them.*
>
> *McNay said, "**Harry was a pretty smart boy. He was a fast thinker**."*
>
> *McNay said Power was good looking, with "blond hair, and he liked to comb it with a curl in it." He said Power had a wife who was "a WAF sergeant out at Lackland."*

# PERRY RUSSO TRANSCRIPT

I found a transcript out on the Internet. It represents what Perry Russo said when the New Orleans District Attorney Jim Garrison put Russo under hypnosis and truth serum. You may remember a party being portrayed in the Oliver Stone movie JFK. We know about the party in 1963 because of Perry Russo. Perry Russo was an insurance salesman, and a friend of David Ferrie. Russo was supposedly present at a party in New Orleans when talk turned from assassinating Castro to assassinating President Kennedy, by triangulated crossfire. The thinking was that President Kennedy's assassination could be made to look like Castro had done it, giving the U.S. an excuse to invade Cuba. Allegedly present during this conversation, an individual by the name of Leon Oswald, David Ferrie, and Clay Shaw (alias Clay Bertrand). Additionally, while under truth serum and hypnosis Perry Russo also indicated there were others at this party. He said: "There were a couple of boys that looked American to me, and we shook hands with two or three, and there is Joe and **Harry**."

Here we have a young boy who looks American and whose name is Harry at the party in New Orleans where the possibility of the assassination of President Kennedy was discussed. Then again, this could have been any Tom, Dick, and Harry.

# RECORD RECOVERY

In 2004 the City of Terre Haute announced that they had arranged with the owners of the Terre Haute House to take construction companies on tours to see if anyone would be interested in restoring the old hotel. I contacted Steve Witt, the Director of the Department of Redevelopment, whom I knew, and was able to tag along on one of the tours. There were six of us on the tour: Steve Witt and Mike Case from the Redevelopment Office, two contractors: Kyle and David Beaver, Dave Adams representative for the owners and me.

The date was November 30, 2004. We were told to meet outside of the hotel's main door on $7^{th}$ Street at 10:00 am. I went about ten minutes early because I didn't want to miss getting in the building. Being as it was November in Indiana and brutally cold that day I stood inside the front door of the Federal Building, which was just across the street from the Terre Haute House, now Indiana State University's College of Business. The Federal Building was also where the FBI office was located back in 1963. To my knowledge the FBI had been in the Federal Building forever. So, it must have been very convenient for the FBI back on November 27, 1963, when the rifle was discovered just across the street, and everyone came running.

As I stood there waiting and looking at this large twelve story, 250 room hotel, last used in the late sixties I told myself to keep my emotions in check and not get too excited. I thought the odds were not good of finding the records showing who all was in the hotel at the same time as Harry. And even if we did find the records, I wondered: Would they let me have them? On the other hand, I felt at this point that this whole experience seems to have been directed from outside of myself. What were the odds that so many things had fallen into place and worked out for me as I investigated this story? I had to smile, I didn't necessarily believe in fate before, but I had come to believe in fate at this point. It was almost like those who had gone before, beyond the grave, want this story told.

I told Dave Adams, as we assembled, that I was interested in this guy that left a rifle in the Terre Haute House back around the Kennedy assassination and I was wondering if the hotel still had any records. I wanted to see who else might have been at the hotel at the same time as Harry. Dave told me there was a whole closet full of records in the basement and that we could go down there toward the end of the tour.

The entire tour was conducted in the warm glow of flashlights, as there wasn't any electricity until we got to the basement where there was a string of lights strung in the hallway. Even then, when we got to the closet, it was mainly a flashlight operation.

The closet was literally waist high, full of records, which were falling out of the closet and spilling into the hallway. The closet was lined with shelves on both sides, full of boxes and stacks of record. I knew that I was looking for cards that the hotel guests signed in on because I had a photocopy of the card that Harry L. Power had signed in on. Harry's signature card was found in the National Archives along with the letter to Earl Warren and the Terre Haute Police report.

The individual cards at the base of this stack of records, that were falling out of the closet and were scattered on the floor at my feet, were dated 1962. I stood there stunned. I said, okay we are looking for November 1963. Dave Adams climbed up and was walking on top of the records. Steve Witt started looking in the boxes on the shelves just inside the door on the right. I stood there for a couple of reasons, one

I think I was praying and hoping, afraid that this was going to take more time to find than anyone on the tour would be willing to spend and secondly, there was only so much room for people in the closet.

I stood and watched as Steve, holding the flashlight in one hand ripped open a box that had been labeled with a marker "1963." The box was at eye level on the shelf just inside and to the right of the doorsill. Steve began pulling out whole stacks of cards held together by numerous rubber bands, and all tied up in twine. Each stack represented about a half a month's worth of cards.

With a flashlight in one hand and alternating stacks of cards in his other, he began reading the date on the top card, "1963!" It took us four minutes! Four minutes, to find two stacks of cards for November 1963!

We now know who was in the Terre Haute House in 1963. The Signature cards for November 1963 were retrieved on November 30, 2004, about ten months prior to the hotel's demolition. I believe the hotel was last used as a hotel in 1968 and the hotel sat there all that time patiently waiting to give up these precious, moldy, smelly records. Dave Adams said that I was welcome to keep them. There is one thing I can tell you for sure, the famous bandleader Louis Armstrong was not involved in the assassination of President Kennedy on November 22, 1963, because he and his band signed in for a stay at the Terre Haute House on that fateful day.

Above records waist deep in closet and signature

cards tied up in twine and rubber banded.

Finding the hotel registers, well that's another story. In the records closet, in the basement, I saw just a couple of hotel registers, one was from 1955, none were from 1963. When I got the signature cards home, sorted, and listed them on a spreadsheet I found that three cards were missing in addition to Harry's. Based upon the fact that the cards are numbered in consecutive order it appeared that the three cards closest in time to Harry's were missing. I figured that due to their proximity in time to Harry's signing into the hotel, that perhaps the three missing cards had also been turned over to the FBI or taken by the Terre Haute Police. I wanted to know who might have come in with Harry and I figured that the hotel register would display their names.

The representative of the owners of the Terre Haute House, Dave Adams, was kind enough to let me back in to look for the registers. The first time I was left to roam around for a couple of hours, I didn't find any registers. I wondered if the hotel manager might have taken them home. Unfortunately, the hotel manager, Mr. William Van Allen had passed away. Well as it turns out, or as fate would have it, I knew Mr. Van Allen's daughter Susan Van Allen Eisman. Susan married one of my ATO fraternity brothers, so I had known Susan from the mid 1970s.

I called Susan up to ask if perhaps her dad had kept the registration books. Susan said no, but if I could get her in the Terre Haute House, she could show me where her dad's office had been. Well, I hated to call Dave Adams back up again to get in the hotel one more time, but I couldn't turn around and just say to Susan, "no, that's all right, but thanks anyway."

February 28, 2005, at 3:45 PM, Dave, Susan and I meet at the 7$^{th}$ Street door. As we walked in Susan immediately led us over behind the registration desk. Susan said, "I talked to my sister Zonnie last night and she said that there is a room behind the registration desk where they used to keep the registration books." If you looked closely, you could see the slight outline of a door cut into the very nice wood paneled wall behind the registration desk. As we opened the door, Dave declared, "I didn't know there was a door there!" The room was very small, only large enough for a toilet on the right side and a four-drawer filing cabinet on the left-hand side. I held my breath and slowly pulled open the file drawers one at a time. The only thing I found was an empty coffee cup in the second drawer. But, beside the file cabinet, all lined up on the floor approximately two feet wide were the registration books from 1961 through 1968. Somewhere in the middle we found the two registration books for 1963.

One of the most important pieces of information that I was able to extract from the hotel's signature cards and hotel register is that Harry L. Power is shown in the registration book as indicating that he would be staying until November 29$^{th}$. As we know Harry ended up leaving November 27$^{th}$, two days earlier than apparently first planned.

Based upon the hotel records, I count fifteen (15) people who stayed in the Terre Haute House from November 25$^{th}$ through November 27$^{th}$ indicating to me that perhaps there was a meeting taking place. The norm for a stay in the Terre Haute House seemed to be just one night, per the records, people seemed to be just passing through on their way to somewhere else.

What might the purpose of this meeting be? I am guessing that if the intent was to rouse the American people up, to call for an invasion of Cuba, well you are going to need war material and logistics. We have a Lt. Col. Leon Corcos from DSAPSO, Columbus, Ohio registered in the Terre Haute House from the 25$^{th}$ to the 27$^{th}$. The name DSAPSO has changed over the years, but the address hasn't. Defense Industrial Security Command on East Broad St. Columbus, OH Security Div of NASA Police & Espionage Agency for US munitions makers. Now the Defense Logistics Agency Defense Supply Center, Columbus, Ohio the largest suppliers of weapon systems spare parts, meeting the readiness needs of America's Warfighters.

According to the book, *The Torbitt Document: NASA, Nazis and the JFK Assassination*, "The killing of President Kennedy was planned and supervised by Division Five of the Federal Bureau of Investigations (FBI), whose usual duties are espionage and counter-espionage activities. FBI Division Five is a highly secret police agency." The FBI's Division Five is located at this same address in Columbus, Ohio!

By leaving the rifle behind on the 27$^{th}$, might this have been an attempt by Harry, or his handlers, to call attention to a meeting that had, or was occurring from the 25$^{th}$ to the 27$^{th}$, in the Terre Haute House?

We will go into more detail on the FBI's Division Five and what the *Torbitt Document* has to say later in this book, after you have become more acquainted with some of the possible characters involved with Division Five. There are also at least three other card/registration entries that you might find interesting. I will also touch on them later.

My intent is to publish an inexpensive complimentary e-book called: *Documentation Supplement America's Crossroads*, that will contain: scanned copies of the Terre Haute Police reports, San Antonio Police's reply to the Terre Haute Police Department, Terre Haute Police's letter to Earl Warren of the Warren Commission, Norm Redlich's Warren Commission memo, FBI reports on Harry L. Power, Signature cards from Terre Haute House for 11/23/1963 to 11/30/1963, the Terre Haute House Registration Book pages for November 1963 and a spreadsheet that I put together listing information from the cards and registration book. Perhaps you will find things that I missed.

## WELCOME TO THE TWILIGHT ZONE

Now the following is too weird! Welcome to the *Twilight Zone*. I searched the Internet on February 24, 2009, for the name Paul Grinstead, which is the name of a person who stayed at the Terre Haute House on November 30, 1963. I searched on Paul Grinstead, up popped this web site: http://fusionanomaly.net/doppelganger.html.

Doppelgänger is the very large title at the top of the page.

The web page goes on to describe "Doppelgänger" as: The frightful image seen at the window, or staring back from the mirror, could be your own-double, or doppelgänger (from the German for "double goer"), the sight of which could foretell your own imminent demise. Sometimes described as the soul embodied, sometimes an astral projection or aura, the double most often presented itself as a warning.

Doppelgänger or doppelganger (dòp´el-gàng´er, dôp´el-gèng´er) noun, a ghostly double of a living person, especially one that haunts its fleshly counterpart. [German, a double: doppel, double (from French double). DOUBLE + Gänger, goer (from Gang, a going, from Middle High German ganc, from Old High German).]

Then this web page goes on to feature pictures and descriptions of a *Twilight Zone* episode #21 called "Mirror Image." In this episode a young twenty-five-year-old women named Millicent Barnes is waiting on her bus **in a bus station as she detects that a double of herself seems to have previously appeared to others such as the ticket agent.** (Bus station, ticket agent, sound familiar?) Later as the bathroom door swings open and shut, she sees reflected in the bathroom mirror her double sitting on a bench in the bus station wearing the exact same outfit, but by the time she can get to the door and open it her double has gone.

A businessman named **Paul Grinstead** strikes up a conversation with Millicent and she relates the strange things that have been happening to her. Finally, Millicent's bus arrives and Paul Grinstead walks her to her bus. Suddenly Millicent screams and runs from the bus and back into the bus station, having witnessed her double sitting on the bus. Paul rushes off after her as the camera pans over to Millicent's double, who is seated on the bus.

Paul and Millicent decide to wait for the next bus, which is not until morning. Millicent ends up falling asleep on a bench and when she wakes, she tells Paul about her dream. Millicent describes how there are different planes of existence and how everybody has a counterpart. But by some kind of freakish accident, sometimes a counterpart finds its way into this world. For the counterpart to survive, it must take over and replace the original.

Paul excuses himself, telling Millicent that he is going to call a friend, but instead he calls the police after discussing the situation with the nosy ticket agent. The police come and take Millicent away. Later Paul leaves his bag by the bench and goes over to the water fountain. Turning he sees someone **running out of the bus station** with his bag. Paul pursues the man as they **run out of the bus terminal down the alley and into the night (sound familiar?)**. While they are running Paul Grinstead discovers that he is chasing a double of himself.

This episode aired on February 26th, 1960, some three years and nine months prior to Harry Power's alleged incident at the Terre Haute bus station. I would say this is life imitating art, or to coin a phrase, a doppelgänger episode, a double goer. What evil genius, or warped perverted sense of humor could have possible brought this about? Provided that this is not just a coincidence. You have Harry's double goer (an imitator) gaining the attention of the ticket agent, not getting on the bus, and running from the bus station, down the alley and into the night. Taken in the context of that moment in time and borrowing from the definitions above: this seems to have "presented itself as a warning" which could be "foretelling Harry's imminent demise," had not the plan changed.

I have read that the CIA had, back in those days, had on file a large collection of movies and films serving as a source of ideas and inspiration. It seems to me that someone may have had a warped sense of humor or was inspired to recreate in life what had been created in the *Twilight Zone,* some three years and nine months earlier.

## APPEARANCE COUNTS

The definition of a patsy is, "one who is duped or victimized." It probably isn't hard to dupe a twenty-year old, or anyone, if they don't know the whole picture, or the ramifications of seemingly innocent acts. Acts like perhaps showing a card and claiming to be something you might not be or leaving a nice rifle behind in a hotel room.

Harry may not be guilty of anything, but it may be important to look and see how Harry L. Power appears, or was made to appear in the public record. Is it just coincidence that Harry L. Power and Lee Harvey Oswald had so many things in common in the public record, or was this part of a plan?

Let's take a moment to look at what was placed in the public record concerning these two:

- Harry was 20. Oswald was 24.

- Harry was AWOL from the military. Oswald defected to the Soviet Union.

- The Terre Haute Police had the impression that Harry L. Power had been investigated for the shooting at General Walker. Lee Harvey Oswald was said by his wife Marina to have shot at General Walker.

- Harry supposedly was a Young Communist League member. Oswald was supposedly a Fair Play for Cuba Committee member.

- Harry supposedly displayed a "Young Communist League Card."  Two witnesses say that Oswald displayed a "Communist Party" and a "Fair Play for Cuba" card.

- Harry supposedly wanted to be a hermit. Oswald was supposedly a loner ("loner," page 6, Warren Report).

- Harry allegedly carried his rifle wrapped in newspaper. The conclusion that the Warren Commission reached, pages 130-134, was that "Oswald carried a rifle to work in a long paper bag, and that, 'a handmade bag of wrapping paper and tape was found in the southeast corner of the sixth floor alongside the window from which the shots were fired.'"

- Harry didn't own a car. Oswald didn't own a car.

- Harry had a driver's license in Iowa, but supposedly failed to pass the license exam in Texas and did not try again. Oswald went twice to the license branch to get a driver's license, once on Nov. 11, 1963, the license branch was closed for election-day, and once on Nov. 16, 1963, just six days before the assassination, but gave up because the line was too long (source the Warren Report, page 740).

- When Harry registered at the Terre Haute House, he put down the correct street name in San Antonio where he had once previously lived, but he put down the wrong street address number. Oswald, when he applied for a post office box, did the same thing, he gave an incorrect street number, though he did show the correct street name of Beckley Avenue, where he was then living (source the Warren Commission).

- Depending on what time of the day it was on Nov. 22, 1963, Harry Power had a German Mauser rifle that matches the description of the rifle found on the sixth floor of the Texas School Book Depository. Oswald's rifle alleged to be an Italian Mannlicher-Carcano rifle, also matched the description of the rifle found on the sixth floor of the Texas School Book Depository, just later in the day, or the next day.

- Harry Power was reported as a member of the Young Communist League. Jack Rubenstein, or Jack Ruby was said to have been a member of the National Executive Committee of the "Young Communist League" (YCL) as told to the FBI by Cuban exile Dr. Fernando Penabaz. This seems to link Harry to Ruby more than Oswald ever was. Being as Oswald was never reported to be associated with the Young Communist League, nor was Jack Ruby ever reported to have been a member of the Fair Play for Cuba Committee.

- Harry Power is alleged to have said, "that there was nothing wrong with Communists." "He spoke freely about Communists and about our type of Government." Oswald is reported to have done and said these same kinds of thing.

- In the San Antonio Police report Harry Power was portrayed as an odd sort of person. That he had a warped outlook on life. Oswald is alleged to have been this way.

- Harry Power was alleged to have professed anti-Kennedy administration feelings. Oswald didn't.

- Harry was reported in the San Antonio Police report as a

top marksman going to the rifle range at least 2 or 3 times a week. Oswald is reported to have been seen at rifle ranges and was alleged to be a good marksman.

- Harry is reported to be an ex-Army man or Air Force and he seemed to have a lot of family trouble. Oswald was an ex-Marine with supposedly a lot of family problems.

- In the San Antonio Police report, Harry Power was said to have felt the world owed him a living.

- Both reportedly showing membership cards. Harry, a "Young Communist League" card. An FBI report disputes the fact that the YCL existed in San Antonio at the time Harry was showing a membership card. Oswald, a "Fair Play for Cuba Committee" card, which the Warren Commission, page 728 says, "Oswald was in fact the only member of the 'New Orleans branch,' which had never been chartered by the National Fair Play for Cuba Committee."

- Both may have allegedly missed buses. Harry allegedly missed the bus in Terre Haute. Then later that same evening at approximately 10:58 PM, Harry Power checked into the Terre Haute House. According to the Warren Report, page 736, when Oswald was in Mexico, "the manifest for bus No. 340, leaving Mexico City for Monterrey and Nuevo Laredo, contains the name 'Oswald', in any event, Oswald did not take bus 340."

- There may be some evidence that others impersonated both Harry Power and Lee Oswald. Harry Power may have been impersonated in the bus station incident.

- Both are said to be practicing with their rifles. Quoting an FBI report about Harry, "he exhibited a rifle with a scope which he was going to sight in on a range." Quoting the Warren Commission page 192, "According to George de Mohrenschildt, Oswald said that he went target shooting with the rifle." "Marina Oswald testified she observed Oswald sitting with the rifle on their screened porch at night, sighting with the telescopic lens and operating the bolt."

- The Warren Commission asked Marina Oswald if Lee Oswald knew people from Keesler Air Force Base where Harry Power had been stationed and these two references to Keesler are the only references to Keesler that I have seen in the whole assassination story.

- Both Lee and Harry appear to have been suspects in shooting at General Walker.

# POINTS TO BE MADE AND QUESTION THAT ARISE

The public record on Harry L. Power resembles Oswald's. As it stands, the public record on Harry L. Power would not have been created had Harry Power not left the rifle in the hotel in Terre Haute, Indiana. Leaving the rifle, at the very least, put Harry Power on the record and left the door open for some potential future use or purpose.

The most that Harry L. Power may be guilty of is showing some sort of card and having had in his possession a rifle that seems to fit as a piece to a puzzle. On the other hand, the least that Harry may be guilty of is showing some sort of card and having had in his possession a rifle that seems to be significant.

The real question is: Was Harry Power significant to events as they were unfolding in the United States? Apparently, the Terre Haute Police thought that Harry Power was significant and the only information that they had initially was the rifle, the fact that the assassination had occurred only three days before, and the fact that Harry had indicated that he was from Texas.

Why, if Harry was involved in anything, would Harry register at the hotel under his real name and then leave behind a potentially significant weapon, in a room registered under his real name? You would think that he wouldn't. Unless Harry Power didn't realize just how significant he might look in the public record. According to the hotel register, **when Harry registered, he indicated that he was planning on staying in the hotel from the 25$^{th}$ to the 29$^{th}$. The rifle was discovered on the 27$^{th}$; two days sooner than**

**Harry had originally indicated that he planned to check out.** What was going on in the Terre Haute House two days later? Stay tuned.

What was it the FBI said about Harry? They didn't say anything about Harry, instead they rendered an opinion about Harry's rifle saying, "No further action was taken by the Bureau concerning this matter inasmuch as the rifle in question was not identical to the rifle which was believed to have been in the possession of Oswald at the time of the assassination of President Kennedy." Had I taken this approach I would have spent many years of my life doing something else.

It's almost as if someone wanted the rifle to emerge in Terre Haute, Indiana. Perhaps someone did.

# LUISA CALDERON

I discovered the following in December 2004. It literally brought tears to my eyes and gave me cold chills. I can always tell when I think that I have found something significant, because I have had this physical reaction a couple of times while researching this story.

**In the Investigation of the Assassination of President John F. Kennedy, Vol. 11 (House Select Committee on Assassinations HSCA) it says:**

> *The Committee devoted considerable attention to the following memorandum that was obtained as a result of a review of the Oswald file:*
>
> Comments on **Luisa Calderon** Carralero
> *1. A reliable source reported that on 22 November 1963, several hours after the assassination of President John F. Kennedy, Luisa Calderon Carralero, a Cuban employee of the Cuban Embassy in Mexico City and believed to be a member of the Cuban Directorate General of Intelligence (DGI) [DGI – Cuba's Intelligence, or spy network], discussed news of the assassination with an acquaintance. Initially, when asked if she had heard the latest news,* **Calderon replied, in what appeared to be a joking manner, "Yes of course, I knew almost before Kennedy."** <u>HSCA</u> *Vol. 11 Page 494*
>
> *Says the HSCA: Standing by themselves, Luisa Calderon's cryptic comments may not have merited serious attention. Her words may indeed have indicated foreknowledge of the assassination but may equally be interpreted without such a sinister implication. Nevertheless, the committee [the House Select Committee on Assassinations] determined that Luisa Caldron's case merited serious attention in the months*

*following the assassination. HSCA Vol. 11 Page 494*

Luisa Calderon's name first surfaced in connection with the assassination, on November 27, 1963, in a cable sent by then-Ambassador Mann to the State Department. <u>HSCA</u> Vol. 11 Page 495: The CIA turned around on the same day Nov. 27$^{th}$ and sent Mann's communiqué to the White House, State Department, and the FBI. *CIA 104-10054-10142*

In that cable, Mann stated: ...Washington should urgently consider feasibility of requesting Mexican authorities to arrest for interrogation: Eusebio Azcue, **Luisa Calderon**, and Alfredo Mirabal. The two men are Cuban national and Cuban consular officers. Luisa Calderon is a secretary in Cuban Consulate here. <u>HSCA</u> Vol. 11 Page 495

This cable did not state the basis for arresting Calderon. Nevertheless, the CIA's copy of this cable bears a handwritten notation on its routing page. That notation states: "Info from Ambassador Mann for Secretary Rusk re: [...] persons involved with Oswald in Cuban Embassy." Ambassador Mann went on to state in urgent terms: "They may all quickly be returned to Havana in order to eliminate any possibility that Mexican government could use them as witnesses." <u>HSCA</u> Vol. 11 Page 495

According to CIA files, Calderon made reservations to return to Havana on Cubana Airlines on December 11, 1963, less than 4 weeks after the assassination. She left Mexico City for Havana on 15 December 1963. <u>HSCA</u> *Vol. 4*, Page 221 and <u>HSCA</u> Vol. 11 Page 495

Calderon, Azcue, and Mirabal were not arrested nor detained for questioning by the Mexican Federal Police. Nevertheless, Silvia Duran, a friend and associate of Calderon's and the one person believed to have had repeated contact with Oswald, while he was in Mexico City, was arrested and questioned by the Mexican police on two separate occasions. <u>HSCA</u> Vol. 11

Page 495

The information regarding Duran's interrogation was passed by CIA to the Warren Commission on February 21, 1964, more than 2 months after Calderon had returned to Cuba. HSCA Vol. 11 Page 495

During May 1964, **(six months after the assassination) information from a Cuban defector tying Luisa Calderon to the Cuban Intelligence apparatus was reported to the CIA. The defector, [AMUG-1 or A-1], was** himself **a Cuban intelligence officer** who supplied valuable and highly reliable information to the CIA regarding Cuban intelligence operations. The CIA's Joseph Langosch, Chief of Counterintelligence for the Special Affairs Staff (for Cuban operations), debriefed the Cuban defector, [A-1]. Langosch's memorandum stated that [A-1] had no direct knowledge of Lee Harvey Oswald or his activities.

[A-1] was asked if Oswald was known to the Cuban intelligence services before November 23, 1963. (It is public knowledge he was in Mexico during the period 9-26-63 to 10-3-63.) [A-1] told Langosch: **Prior to October 1963, Oswald visited the Cuban Embassy in Mexico City on two or three occasions. Before, during, and after these visits, Oswald was in contact with the** Direccion General De Intelligencia (**DGI**), **specifically with Luisa Caldron**, Manuel Vega Parez, and Rogelio Rodriguez Lopez. This would appear to mean that one or more contacts were made after Oswald returned to the United States i.e., between 10-3-63 and 11-22-63. HSCA Vol. 11 Page 495-496 and HSCA Vol. 4 page 165

Langosch thereafter wrote that Calderon's precise relationship to the DGI was not clear. As a comment on this statement, he set forth the CIA cable and dispatch traffic that recorded her arrival in Mexico during January 1963 and departure for Cuba within 1 month after the assassination. *HSCA* Vol. 11 Page 496

April 26, 1965, in a CIA document, subject Luisa Rodriguez Calderon, source [clearly A-1] identified a photograph of Luisa Rodriguez Calderon and said that she had been connected with the Direccion General de Inteligencia (General Directorate of Intelligence – DGI) and the former secretary of the **Young Communists** in the Cuban Ministry of Exterior Commerce. *CSCI* 316/01783-65 page 1

AMMUG-1 or A-1 reported that Luisa Calderon Carralero was also known as Luisa Rodriguez Calderon. [Born in 1940, Luisa would have been 23 years old in 1963]. Luisa CALDERON was transferred directly from her position in the Ministry of Exterior Commerce to a post in Mexico, a matter of surprise to the Source [A-1]. She arrived in Mexico on 16 January 1963. *HSCA* Vol. 4 page 164 and 221, *HSCA* 180-10143-10159, *CIA* Agency #28-16-03 and from *HSCA* 180-10083-10210

On May 7, 1964, Langosch recorded additional information he had elicited from [A-1] regarding Oswald's possible contact with the DGI. Paragraph 3 of this memorandum, stated in part: Luisa Calderon, since she returned to Cuba has been paid a regular salary by the DGI even though she has not performed any services. Her home is in the Vedado section where the rents are high. Source [A-1] has known Calderon for several years. Before going to Mexico, she was the **Secretary General of the Communist Youth** [or Young Communists] in the Ministry of Exterior Commerce in the department, which was known as the "Empresa Transimport." *HSCA* Vol. 11 Page 496

On May 8, Langosch further disclosed [A-1's] knowledge of the Oswald case. He paraphrased [A-1] knowledge of Calderon as follows: I thought that Luisa Calderon might have had contact with Oswald because I learned about 17 March 1964, shortly before I made a trip to Mexico, that **she had been involved with an American in Mexico**. The information to which I refer was told to me by a DGI case officer named Norberto HERNANDEZ de Curbelo. I had commented to (him) that it seemed strange that Luisa Calderon was receiving a salary from the DGI although she apparently did not do any work for the Service. Hernandez told me that hers was a peculiar case and that **he himself had investigated her and believed that she had been recruited in Mexico by the Central Intelligence Agency although Manuel Pineiro, the Head of the DGI, did not agree**. As I recall, **Hernandez had investigated Luisa Calderon. This was because, during the time she was in Mexico, the DGI had intercepted a letter to her by an American who signed his name OWER (phonetic) or something similar**. As you know, the pronunciation of Anglo-Saxon names is difficult in Spanish so I am not sure of how the name mentioned by Hernandez should be spelled. As I understand the matter, **the letter from the American was a love letter, but indicated that there was a clandestine professional relationship between the writer and Luisa Calderon**. I also understood from Hernandez that **after the interception of the letter she had been followed and seen in the company of an American. I do not know if this could have been Oswald**... *HSCA* Vol. 11 Page 496-497 and *HSCA* Vol. 4 Page 168

This is what brought tears to my eyes and **to my knowledge this is something that no one else has put together. You put a "P" in front of "OWER" and you of course have "POWER." As in Harry L. Power. OWER sounds a lot closer to Power, than Oswald!** This of course does not prove that the love letter was from Harry Power. The letter could have come from someone else whose name sounds like "Ower." Nevertheless, the pieces do seem to fit in this story better than in the Oswald story, or any other part of the assassination story. Interesting that they spelled this phonetically in the CIA reports as "Ower," as opposed to "Our." It works for me; it may have worked for them also. Much easier to put a "P" in front of "ower," than to put a "P" in front of "our," that would be Pour.

[A-1] also recalled something else in relation to Luisa receiving the letter from an American: Source further recalled something about an American student who visited Cuba and who was alleged to have made a recruitment pitch to Luisa Rodriguez Calderon or was associated in some way with a pitch made to her. The Cuban government, according to a source, thought that the United States Government had recruited Calderon while she was in Mexico, and she was recalled to Cuba. CSCI – 316/01783-65 page 1. Could Harry have been the young American trying to recruit Luisa for the U.S. of A.?

On 11 December 1963, Luisa Calderon made reservations to return to Cuba on Cubana Airlines. Calderon said that she would not be returning to Mexico. _CSCI_ 316/01783-65 Page 2.

**The May 8 memorandum is significant, (so says the HSCA), because [A-1] indicated that [not only he, but] a second Cuban Intelligence officer believed Calderon to be a CIA operative.** _HSCA_ Vol. 11 Page 498

On May 11, 1964, Rocca (Angleton's right-hand man at the CIA, Angleton was in charge of counterintelligence and of the CIA portion of the assassination investigation) wrote a memorandum to Richard Helms (the DDP, Deputy Director of Plans CIA) regarding the information Langosch had elicited from [A-1]. **Rocca proposed that: The DDP** in person, or via a designee, preferably the former, **discuss the [A-1] situation on a very restricted basis with Mr. Rankin** [of the Warren Commission] **at his earliest convenience**, either at the

Agency or at the Commission headquarters. Until this takes place, it is not desirable to put anything in writing. <u>HSCA</u> Vol. 11 page 497

On **May 15, 1964, Helms wrote Mr. Rankin of the Warren Commission** regarding [A-1's] information about the DGI, indicating its sensitivity and operational significance. Attached to **Helms' communication was a paraphrased account** of Langosch's May 5 memorandum. **In that attachment, the intelligence associations of two Cuban diplomatic employees, Manuel Vega Perez and Rogelio Rodriguez, were set forth. Nevertheless, that attachment <u>made absolutely no reference whatsoever to Luisa Calderon</u>**. <u>HSCA</u> Vol. 11 Page 497

According to Joseph Langosch, CIA Chief of Counterintelligence, Special Affairs Staff: AMMUG/1 [or A-1] was of significant value to the Agency concerning information on CUIS [Cuban Intelligence] because prior to A-1's defection, CIA information on CUIS was quite meager. He also said the A-1's bona fides were firmly established. A-1 was considered reliable, and the CIA had confidence in his abilities. <u>HSCA</u> 180-10143-10159 – <u>CIA</u> Agency #28-16-03

Howard Willens of the Warren Commission requested access to the questions used in Langosch's interrogation of [A-1]. On June 18, 1964, Rocca's [and Angleton's] Counterintelligence Research and Analysis people responded. The only mention of Calderon that Willens found in the May 5 memorandum was as follows: "The precise relationship of Luisa Caldron to the DGI is not clear. She spent about six months in Mexico from which she returned to Cuba early in 1964. Willens was not shown Langosch's memoranda of May 7 and May 8, 1964, that contained much more detailed information on Luisa Calderon, including [A-1's] report of her possible association with Lee Harvey Oswald and/or American intelligence.

*HSCA* Vol. 11 Page 497

**The evidence indicates that the CIA did not provide a report of Calderon's conversation of November 22 to the Warren Commission.** Consequently, even though the Warren Commission was aware that Calderon reportedly had connections to intelligence work, as did other Cuban Embassy officers, the vital link between her background and her comments was never established for the Warren Commission by the CIA. **The agency's omission** in this regard may have foreclosed the Commission's actively pursuing **a lead of great significance.** *HSCA* Vol. 11 Page 497

**The HSCA wrote in their report: The Warren Commission was never given the information by which it could evaluate Luisa Calderon's significance to the events surrounding President Kennedy's assassination. Had the Commission been expeditiously provided with this evidence of her intelligence background**, association with Silvia Duran, **and her comments following the assassination, it may well have given more serious investigative consideration to her potential knowledge** of Oswald **and the Cuban Government's possible involvement in a conspiracy to assassinate President Kennedy.** *HSCA* Vol. 11 Page 498

**The CIA failed to provide the Warren Commission with all information in its possession pertaining to Luisa Calderon**, a Cuban consulate employee in Mexico City suspected of having ties to the Cuban intelligence service. Calderon, who was alleged in 1964 by a Cuban defector to have been in contact with an American who might have been Oswald during the period of time of Oswald's visit to Mexico City, engaged in a conversation approximately 5 hours after the assassination in which she indicated possible foreknowledge of the assassination. *HSCA Report* Page 254

**"Calderon's comments were not reported [by the CIA] to

**the Warren Commission**, apparently an agency oversight." *HSCA* 180-10142-10056 (That is generous.)

Two difficult issues remain that were raised by the evidence. First, why did the Agency not provide the Calderon conversation to the Warren Commission? Second, why did the Agency not reveal to the Warren Commission its full knowledge of Calderon's intelligence background, her possible knowledge of Oswald and her possible connection to the CIA? *HSCA* Vol. 11 Page 498

The HSCA wrote: In most instances, the evidence indicates that the CIA acted in a responsible and professional manner. Nevertheless, **the evidence does show at least three separate instances of deficiencies by the CIA in the reporting of information to the Warren Commission.** *HSCA* Vol. 11 Page 499

The first instance—**the Agency's failure to report the anti-Castro assassination plots** to the Warren Commission... The evidence, however, shows that these plots were in fact highly relevant and should, therefore, have been reported to the Warren Commission. *HSCA* Vol. 11 Page 499

The second instance—stemming from the CIA's legal responsibility to protect its sources and methods. *HSCA* Vol. 11 Page 499

Finally, [the third instance] the evidence shows that **Luisa Calderon's comments expressing possible foreknowledge of President Kennedy's assassination should have been reported to the Warren Commission.** Her known association with Cuban diplomatic personnel in Mexico City and reported association with the DGI add to the force of the facts. Had her comments been reported to the Warren Commission, they might have merited the Commission's serious attention? In this regard, the Commission did not have the opportunity to make its own judgment. *HSCA* Vol.

11 Page 499

Isn't this interesting? Two, if not all three instances, touch on the Terre Haute story: the first the assassination attempts on Castro, which you will later see have a very definite tie into Terre Haute and secondly Luisa Calderon's relationship with a young American, possibly Harry "P"ower. Perhaps all roads do lead to Terre Haute, the Crossroads of America? Perhaps Terre Haute is the key to the Kennedy assassination?

The House Select Committee on Assassinations obtained a CIA document verifying that all three of Oswald's alleged Cuban contacts in Mexico City were DGI (Cuban Intelligence).

**The CIA creates a 201 file when a person is of interest.** As many as fifteen years after the assassination, a document dated September 27, 1978, shows that the CIA still wanted to keep Luisa Calderon out of the picture as the CIA's Scott Breckinridge, wrote to the HSCA: "We [CIA] would prefer no reference in an unclassified report to what is in the Calderon 201 file."

The House Select Committee on Assassination **(HSCA) asked to interview Fidel Castro and Louisa Calderon. They were able to interview Fidel Castro, however they were not permitted to interview Louisa Calderon, the reason [excuse] given, "due to illness."** *Report of the Select Committee on Assassinations* Page 123

Apparently, the House Select Committee on Assassinations was not aware of the FBI reports on Harry L. Power, or they missed connecting the dots. Ower sounds like Power, not Oswald, in my opinion.

# ANY CIA INTEREST IN LUISA CALDERON PRIOR TO THE ASSASSINATION?

Yes, the CIA did show interest in Luisa Calderon prior the assassination: On June 22, 1963 [exactly five months before the assassination of President Kennedy] the CIA, Western Hemisphere Division sent a dispatch to their Chief of Station [Ted Shackley], JM/WAVE, concerning Luisa Calderon Carralero. [The information is the kind of information we would expect the CIA to pay attention to, such as the fact that Luisa worked in the Cuban Embassy in Mexico City as of Jan. 16, 1963, her date of birth: 1940, her passport number, etc.] A picture of Luisa Calderon is also attached. <u>CIA</u> #104-10052-10132

CIA communications June 28, 1963, Carlos Blanco a delegate in Mexico of the Association of Anti-Communist Foreign Service Officials and Employees in Exilo, created a background report for the CIA on personnel in the Cuban Embassy in Mexico. It gives information on everyone identified with the embassy, including Ana Luisa Calderon, it says, "Ana Luisa Calderon, Secretary of the Commercial Office Cuba. Report pending."

July 15, 1963, JM/WAVE (the CIA's station for anti-Castro operations) in Miami requested from Chief of Station (COS) Mexico City, Chief, SAS and Chief, Western Hemisphere, biographic data on personnel in the Cuban Embassy in Mexico City. It says, please card all names and return a set of index cards to JM/WAVE. <u>HSCA</u> 180-10144-10211

According to the CIA's Russell Holmes, when interviewed by a Congressional investigator, the CIA had placed in Oswald's

201 file a memo concerning a taped phone conversation July 19, 1963, between Louisa Calderon and an American who was about to move to Dallas. This memo was placed in the file after Oswald supposedly traveled to Mexico City and before the assassination of President Kennedy.

On July 31, 1963, the CIA Chief, Special Affairs Staff (for Cuban operations) sent to the Chief of Station, Mexico City [Win Scott] a dispatch that says: "[L-9] reported that **Luisa Calderon has a sister residing in Texas, married to an American of Mexican descent. Luisa may go up to the border to visit her sister soon** [or her mother may make the trip – details not clear]. If [L-9] can further identify the sister, our **domestic exploitation** section might be in a position to follow up on this lead. Please levy this requirement on L-9 at the next opportunity. _CIA_ 104-10069-10266 (Judging from this, the CIA was looking to possibly "exploit" Luisa Calderon, as we might expect them to, approximately four months before the assassination.)

In the days following the Kennedy assassination, the CIA originally assigned the job of investigating what happened to John Whitten. Whitten wrote a document casting doubt on the possibility that Oswald was a Soviet agent who would have been permitted by the Soviets to make open visits and phone calls to the Soviet Embassy in Mexico.

James Jesus Angleton, CIA - Counterintelligence was promoting the idea that the Soviets had a hand in the assassination. The Whitten document appears to have been finished and submitted to Angleton on December 13, 1963. However, there is a second copy very similar yet different in significant ways and submitted to Rocca [Angleton's right-hand man] on December 10. In the paragraph above where Whitten says it is quite unlikely Oswald was a Soviet agent, in the Rocca document it allows for the possibility. [7]

Then at the end of the Rocca document there is a small, and in my opinion a very important paragraph, it says:

At 1445 hours on 22 November, the Yugoslav Ambassador to Mexico, Gustav VLAHOV telephoned and insisted on speaking to Soviet Ambassador to Mexico BAZAROV. In a conversation concerning news of President Kennedy's assassination, VLAHOV said, **"I knew he was wounded even before the Americans." Both then laughed.**

See how the lines supposedly spoken by two different people, Louisa in one conversation and Vlahov in a completely different conversation, are so nearly identical. It appears that the words are coming from the same source, like the words were orchestrated **by the same source**:

**At the end of the Rocca/Angleton version of this transcript it says:**
"I knew he was wounded even before the Americans." Both then laughed.

Calderon...in...a joking manner, "Yes of course, I knew almost before Kennedy."

My point is that these words seem to have been composed by and coming from the same source. **Being as we know that this modified report resided in Rocca's office, right-hand man to James Jesus Angleton in the CIA's Counterintelligence division, this may be the evidence needed to show that the conspiracy to assassinate President Kennedy was being orchestrated in part by James Jesus Angleton, the CIA's Counterintelligence Chief.** As you will also soon see, Whitten ends up being replaced by Rocca as the CIA's interface to the Warren Commission!

Years later in a CIA document dated 5/23/75 the CIA's Raymond Rocca, right hand man to CIA Counterintelligence Chief James Jesus Angleton, admitted that Luisa Calderon was Cuban intelligence saying, "Luisa Calderon – as a member of the DGI unit in Mexico City – could very well have known something that would make what she said to her unidentified caller less a matter of boastful self-indulgence than was assumed at the time. *CIA* 104-10103-10271

In 1975 a participant in the Rockefeller Commission wrote about Luisa Calderon's possible knowledge of the Kennedy assassination, "Latin hyperbole?  Boastful ex post facto suggestion of foreknowledge."  *HSCA* 180-10142-10056 They may be right about the hyperbole; Rocca may have written words into Luisa's mouth. On the other hand, they hadn't made the possible "OWER," "Power" connection, now had they?  My instincts tell me that the odds are pretty high that there might be a connection. Remember Luisa was working in the Communist Youth area back in Cuba. Harry L. Power was allegedly showing a Young Communist League card back in San Antonio around 1962 and his co-worker said he acted quite proud of it.  Then again, the letter sent to Calderon might not have been sent by Harry, but rather by someone trying to set Harry up. Or again this might be a coincidence and Harry wasn't involved at all.

The CIA's David Athlee Phillips told the anti-Castro Cuban Antonio Veciana that "a news story was circulating immediately after the assassination that Oswald had met a couple on the Mexican border while on his way to Mexico City, prior to the assassination.  In the CIA document 104-10069-10266 above we were told that "[L-9] reported that Luisa Calderon has a sister residing in Texas, married to an American of Mexican descent. **Luisa may go up to the border to visit her sister soon**." Pure speculation, but interesting to think about: Could this couple meeting Lee Oswald at the Mexican border possibly have been Luisa Calderon and Harry L. Power? Might the original intent have been to tie these three together in the public record? Would this fit what might seems to have been the original intent to make the assassination of President Kennedy appear to have been the work of Fidel Castro, what with Luisa's ties to Cuban intelligence, Lee's supposed ties to the Fair Play For Cuba Committee, Harry's supposed connection to the Young Communist League and with Harry and Luisa's possible relationship all documented in a love letter from a guy who's last name sounds like "Ower'?

My personal opinion is that the planners of the assassination, up until the decision was made to leave the rifle, fully intended to use Harry Power as perhaps a patsy for a second shooter, as backup in case the line on Lee Harvey Oswald fell through, or as additional proof that there had been a conspiracy by Castro, or the Communists, to assassinate President Kennedy **and perhaps others of importance in the United States**. For some reason it was decided to just cut things off at Oswald and it appears that it was determined by the powers that be that they didn't want to go there, when it came to Luisa Calderon, in Mexico City and Harry L. Power, in Terre Haute, Indiana. However, they did leave their options open by leaving the rifle behind. This was enough to put Harry Power in the public record, just in case another line of investigation was needed, maybe?

## THE HUNT FOR THE RIFLE

I called retired Terre Haute Police Detectives Butts and George Schoffstall. When I called Butts about the rifle, he said the rifle was packaged up and given to the FBI by Schoffstall. When I called Schoffstall, he said that the last time he saw the rifle it was at police headquarters, and he said he did not package up the rifle and give it to the FBI.

I understood from talking to Terre Haute Police Officers Butts and Schoffstall that they recalled the Mauser rifle left in Terre Haute as being sporterized (shortened) and that it was a German Mauser, Argentine 1891 rifle.

I contacted then Police Chief Joe Newport at the Terre Haute Police Department in 1998. They searched for old files, but didn't have anything on it, and had not heard about the rifle, or the story.

Mark Edwards told me later that Detective Butts had told him that at some point back in the 60s or 70s Butts had made his way out to Hollywood and had actually had a few small parts in some movies. Detective Butts told Mark that he had taken the Terre Haute Police files with him to Hollywood, thinking this would make a good movie. Unfortunately, Butts's car was stolen while he was in California and the files were in the vehicle.

Rifle left in Terre Haute looked like this:

## 7.65 Argentine German Mauser Rifle, Model 1891

The Warren Commission investigated a report that, during the first two weeks of November 1963, just before the assassination, Oswald had a telescopic sight mounted and sighted in on a rifle at a sporting goods store in Irving, Texas. Dial Ryder and his employer, Charles W. Greener, believed that they never worked on an Italian Mannlicher-Carcano rifle.

I had noticed in different books, about the assassination, that Dial Ryder had said that he was sure that he hadn't drilled three holes and mounted a scope on an Italian rifle, because Dial Ryder said that he had never worked on an Italian rifle in his life. But I hadn't ever seen what Dial Ryder thought he had worked on until I was going through the microfilm that I acquired from the New Orleans Library that contained documents from District Attorney Garrison's investigation. I found the following: "Dial Ryder 11/465 7/224 (written in the numbers 26-376) 22/54 RE 11/24 11/235 22/523 **Ryder thinks Oswald may have brought in an Argentine Rifle** (read Mauser) **about two weeks before 11/22[4]**. This text brought tears to my eyes. Dial Ryder believed that he had worked on an Argentine, I assume, Mauser rifle.

In a House Select Committee document dated 3/12/79 a staff member says, "I recognize the name Interarmco in Alexandria, Virginia." Mark Flanagan says his team was told by several sources that Interarmco is a CIA front, which sells arms to selected organizations. *HSCA* 180-10120-10006 Additionally, I had picked up on information that Interarmco was owned by a former CIA agent, so I went out on the internet searching for the words Interarmco and Mauser.

I found an article by Daniel Reynolds, entitled *"Mauser History,"* on the web site, www.carbinesforcollectors.com. On the internet Dan says: "Interarmco imported large numbers of brand new and excellent M1891 rifles around 1961. They cut down many into Mannlicher style carbines with 22" barrels and a newly fabricated nose cap which many people today mistake for original carbines. These conversions were rumored done in a shop in Puerto Rico, but could have been done at the large facility Interarmco maintained outside London in the tax-free zone at Heathrow."

Guess how long the longest part of a modified, sporterized, Mauser rifle is when it is disassembled? **The longest part, the barrel to the receiver, is 22"**.

Here is a picture of an unmodified 7.65-millimeter caliber Model 1891, Argentine Mauser rifle. Notice how the wood stock extends to the end of the barrel. The barrel is obviously longer than a sportsterized version, however the length is hard to compare looking at my two different pictures.

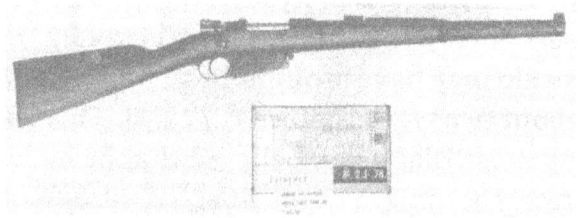

FIGURE 25.—A 7.65-millimeter caliber Argentine Mauser rifle, Model 1891.

I obtained this picture, of all places from page 399, volume 7 of the *Select Committee on Assassinations of the U.S. House of Representatives, Investigation of the Assassination of President John F. Kennedy* (HSCA). I was thrilled to find it for a number of reasons. First, I was wondering how I was going to get a picture of an unmodified 7.65 Argentine 1891 Mauser rifle. Second, it is easy to compare this picture with the picture of a rifle that resembles the one that was left by Harry in Terre Haute. Note how the wood stock and the barrel are shorter on the modified Mauser. Also notice how the metal band around the wood stock and the rifle barrel no longer exists on the modified Mauser. The barrel of the modified rifle is thus easily removed from the wood stock by simply unscrewing two screws. The maximum length of the modified Mauser disassembled is 22 inches. This makes it much shorter than an unmodified Mauser rifle and much shorter than Oswald's alleged Italian Mannlicher-Carcano rifle.

I found it curious and quite a coincidence that the Select Committee selected a 7.65 Argentine German Mauser rifle, model 1891 rifle, as representative of what a Mauser rifle looks like. I found it curious for two reasons, first, it is the exact same make and model as the rifle left in Terre Haute. Second, Mausers are identified by the country that contracted with the German-based company to produce each version of the Mauser rifle. Thus there are Argentine, Austrian, Belgium, Bolivian, Brazilian, Chilean, Chinese, Colombian, Costa Rican, Czechoslovakian, Danish, Dominican Republic, Ecuadorian, El Salvadorian, Estonian, Ethiopian, French, German, Greek, Guatemalan, Haitian, Honduran, Iraqi, Irish, Japanese, Latvian, Liberian, Lithuanian, Luxembourg, Manchurian, Mexican, Moroccan, Netherlands, Nicaraguan, Norwegian, Paraguayan, Persian/Iranian, Peruvian, Polish, Portuguese, Romanian, Saudi Arabian, Serbian/Yugoslavian, Slovakian, South African, Spanish, Swedish, Thailand, Turkish, Uruguayan, Venezuelan, and Yemenite (German made or licensed) Mauser rifles. Not only are there at least 52 countries identified with, and on these rifles, but there have also been many different models produced throughout the years, beginning around 1871.

## THE ASSASSINATION RIFLE

On the day of the assassination, on the sixth floor of the Texas School Book Depository, the Dallas Police first identified the rifle as a 7.65mm German Mauser rifle. But then later, within twenty-four hours, the Dallas Police said, in effect, oops, we misidentified the rifle; it is now an Italian Mannlicher-Carcano rifle. A long brown paper package and three rifle cartridges were also found near the alleged sniper's nest.

Quoting CBS's Walter Cronkite on November 23, 1963: "Definite identification has been made of the type of rifle used in the assassination of President Kennedy. It was not a Mauser as was reported throughout yesterday and most of today, but an Italian Mannlicher Carcano rifle." <u>Video on YouTube</u>

According to the *Warren Report*, page 235: The rifle found on the sixth floor of the Texas School Book Depository Building was initially identified as a Mauser 7.65 rather than a Mannlicher-Carcano 6.5."

Attorney, Mark Lane, before the Warren Commission said, "Now, in reference to the rifle, there is an affidavit sworn to by Officer Weitzman, in which he indicates that he discovered the rifle on the sixth floor of the Book Depository Building at, 1:22 p.m., on November 22, 1963." <u>President's Commission on the Assassination</u> (Warren Commission) Vol. 2 Page 46

"Now **in this affidavit, Officer Weitzman swore that the murder weapon which he found on the sixth floor was a 7.65 Mauser**, which he then went on to describe in some detail, with reference to the color of the strap, et cetera."

*President's Commission on the Assassination* Vol. 2 Page 46

Mark Lane continued, "**A German Mauser is nothing at all like an Italian carbine. I think almost any rifle expert will indicate that that is so**. I have been informed that almost **every German Mauser has stamped upon it the caliber, as does almost every Italian carbine**." *President's Commission on the Assassination* Vol. 2 Page 46

"If I were permitted to cross-examine Mr. Wade and Officer Weitzman, **I would seek to find out how the most important single element in this case or any other murder case, physical evidence, the murder weapon, how [they] could be so completely in error about this**." *President's Commission on the Assassination* Vol. 2 Page 46

"**I would like to know how [they] could have been so wrong about something so vital**." *President's Commission on the Assassination* Vol. 2 Page 47

Mr. Rankin: Let the record show that at this time the Commission is giving Mr. Lane an opportunity to examine the rifle known as Commission Exhibit No. 139.

Mr. Lane. Thank you. May I comment upon the examination?

The Chairman. Yes, you may; if you saw anything of any significance there you may state it.

Mr. Lane. Yes. I would like to call to the attention of the Commission the affidavit signed by a police officer, Seymour Weitzman, dated the 23$^{rd}$ day of November 1963, the original of which was at one time in the office of the district attorney of Dallas. In that document, Officer Weitzman states he found, along with another person—a deputy sheriff, the alleged murder weapon, on the 22$^{nd}$ day of November 1963, on the sixth floor of the Book Depository Building. *President's Commission on the Assassination* Vol. 5 Page 560-561

And in that affidavit Mr. Weitzman—Officer Weitzman—swears that the murder weapon, which he found on the floor, was **a Mauser 7.65** millimeter. A Mauser, of course, is a German weapon. The rifle which is before the Commission, and which is, I assume, allegedly now the murder weapon, is, of course, not a German Mauser 7.65 millimeter, but is an Italian carbine, 6.5 millimeter. *President's Commission on the Assassination* Vol. 5 Page 560-561

**Although I am personally not a rifle expert, I was able to determine that it was an Italian carbine because printed indelibly upon it are the words "Made Italy" and "caliber 6.5." I suggest it is very difficult for a police officer to pick up a weapon, which has printed upon it clearly in English "Made Italy, Cal 6.5," and then the next day draft an affidavit stating that that was in fact a German Mauser, 7.65 millimeter.**

The Chairman. Very well. Anything further? We will take a short recess then. *President's Commission on the Assassination* Vol. 5 Page 560-561

Roger Craig and Seymour Weitzman discovered a 7.65 Mauser on the sixth floor of the schoolbook depository. In a video on *YouTube*, Roger Craig, Dallas Deputy Sheriff said: **"We weren't any more than 6 or 8 inches from the rifle and stamped right on the barrel of the rifle was 7.65 Mauser."**

KBOX's news report from Dallas, Friday afternoon, November 22, 1963: **A rifle found in a staircase on the fifth floor** of the building on which the assassin is believed to have shot the President of the United States. Sheriff's deputies **identify the weapon as a 7.65 Mauser**, a German made Army rifle with a telescopic sight. It had one shell in the chamber. Three spent shells were found nearby. *President's Commission on the Assassination* Vol. 26 Page 599

The following is from the: *President's Commission on the Assassination* Vol.19 Page 507 County of Dallas, Sheriff's Department, dated Nov 22, 1963.

To: Mr. Decker,

I was assisting in the search of the **6th floor** of the Dallas County Book Depository at Elm and Houston St. proceeding from the east side of the building. Officer Whiteman [Weitzman?] DPD and I were together as we approached the Northwest corner of the building. The rifle was partially hidden behind a row of books with two (2) other boxes of books up against the rifle. **The rifle appeared to be a 7.65mm Mauser** with a telescope sight on the rifle. Capt. Fritz was called to the scene and also someone from the ID. Pictures were taken and then Capt. Fritz picked up the rifle. I first saw the rifle at 1:22pm date.

Signed: E.L. Boone

Testimony of Mr. E.L. Boone: I got a battery-powered light and went over to the Texas School Book Depository to help with the search of the building. I proceeded to the sixth (6th) floor of the building to search for the rifle. In the northwest corner of the building approx. three (3) feet from the east wall of the stairwell and behind a row of cases of books was the rifle, what appeared to be a **7.65mm Mauser** with a telescopic site. The rifle had what appeared to be a brownish, black stock and blue steel metal parts. *President's Commission on the Assassination* Vol. 19 Page 508-509

Mr. Ball. Who referred to it as a Mauser that day?

Mr. Boone. I believe Captain Fritz. He had knelt down there to look at it, and before he removed it, not knowing what it was, he said that is what it looks like. We were just discussing it back and forth. And **he said it looks like a 7.65 Mauser**. *President's Commission on the Assassination* Vol. 3 Page 295

Mr. Ball. In the statement that you made to the Dallas Police Department that afternoon, you referred to the rifle as a 7.65 Mauser bolt action.

Mr. Weitzman. In a glance, that's what it looked like. I thought it was one.

Mr. Ball. Are you familiar with rifles?

Mr. Weitzman. Fairly familiar because I was in the sporting goods business for a while. *President's Commission on the Assassination* Vol. 7 Page 108

It is my understanding that a 7.65 German Mauser rifle is a very accurate and well-made weapon and that there is a significant difference in the quality of the German Mauser rifle as compared to an Italian Mannlicher-Carcano rifle.

At one time, bolt-action rifles like the German Mauser, the **Argentine Mauser** (which is made in Germany) and the Mannlicher-Carcano were the standard military weapons of most counties. *Select Committee on Assassinations, U.S. House of Representatives, HSCA* Vol. 7 Page 372

On the day of the assassination, Frank Ellsworth was present in Dallas, Texas, an agent of the U.S. Alcohol, Tobacco and Firearms (ATF) Division. Immediately after the assassination, which occurred at 1:30 P.M., Frank Ellsworth actively participated in the search of the Texas School Book Depository. As **per Ellsworth's account, the Italian Mannlicher-Carcano rifle**, believed to be connected to the crime, **was actually located on a floor lower than the sixth floor.** Ellsworth remembered a detective from **the Dallas Police Department discovered the Italian rifle on the fourth floor** of the Texas School Book Depository. **Based on various reports, it appears that a German Mauser rifle was found on the sixth floor.** [8]

There is no mention in the FBI, or Terre Haute Police report of a scope being a part of the disassembled rifle that was left in Terre Haute. According to *Select Committee on Assassinations, U.S. House of Representatives, HSCA* Vol. 7 Page 373: "It is the opinion of this panel that an individual could attain better accuracy using the iron sights than the scope under the circumstances involved in Dealey Plaza."

From the *President's Commission on the Assassination*:
Mr. Ball. I noticed you have a screwdriver there. Can you assemble it without the use of a screwdriver? Mr. Cortland Cunningham (Special Agent of the FBI concerning the Italian rifle) Any object that would fit the slots on the **five screws** that retain the stock to the action [could be used]. *President's Commission on the Assassination* Vol. 2 Page 252. (Modified Mausers like the one left in Terre Haute have the advantage of two screws, three fewer screws equals less time required to assemble and disassemble.)

Buell Wesley Frazier was 19 years old and lived with his sister, in Irving, Texas, and they lived just a few doors down from Mrs. Paine's house. Oswald's wife Marina and their daughters were staying with Mrs. Paine. Frazier and Oswald both worked at the Texas School Book Depository. Buell Frazier would give Oswald a ride back and forth to work when Lee came out to stay at Mrs. Paine's house. Buell Wesley Frazier gave Oswald a ride to work the morning of the assassination and got a good look at the brown paper package Lee Harvey Oswald was carrying on the morning of the assassination. Here is some of what was said in his Warren Commission testimony: "I asked Lee what's in the package? And he said, 'Curtain rods." Paraphrasing: The package was brown like the paper sacks you get at the grocery store. Three times Frazier said in his testimony before the Warren Commission that: "The package was roughly around 2 feet," or around 24 inches. I would point out that this is much too short to be a Mannlicher-Carcano rifle, which is 34 inches long, when broken-down. Frazier testified that the package Lee carried into the Texas School Book Depository only extended from Lee's right hand, which was cupped, up to Lee's arm pit. If Lee Oswald was carrying a Mannlicher, Frazier would have most certainly noticed, as the package would have visibly extended above Lee's shoulder.[9]

Mr. Frazier.  When I got in the car, I have a kind of habit of glancing over my shoulder and so at that time I noticed there was a package laying on the back seat, I didn't pay too much attention and I said, "What's the package, Lee?" And he said, "Curtain rods," and I said, "Oh, yes, you told me you were going to bring some today."

Mr. Ball.  What did the package look like?

Mr. Frazier.  Well, I will be frank with you, I would just, it is right as you get out of the grocery store, just more or less out of a package, you have seen some of these brown paper sacks you can obtain from any, most of the stores, some varieties, but it was a package just **roughly about two feet long**.

Mr. Frazier.  ... **around two feet, give and take a few inches**.

Mr. Ball.  How wide would you say that would be?

Mr. Frazier.  Oh, say, **around 5 inches**, something like that. **5, 6 inches**. _President's Commission on the Assassination_ Vol. 2 Page 226

(Walking into the School Book Depository, Oswald walked ahead of Frazier)
Mr. Ball. You say he had the package under his arm when you saw him?
Mr. Frazier. Yes, sir.
Mr. Ball. You mean one end of it under the armpit?
Mr. Frazier. Yes, sir; he had it up just like you stick it right under your arm like that.

Mr. Ball. And he had the lower part---
Mr. Frazier. The other part with his right hand.
Mr. Ball. Right hand?
Mr. Frazier. Right.
Mr. Ball. He carried it then parallel to his body?
Mr. Frazier. Right, straight up and down.
<u>President's Commission on the Assassination</u> Vol. 2 Page 228

Mr. Ball. But the right hand was it on the end or the side of the package?
Mr. Frazier. No. He had it cupped in his hand.
Mr. Ball. Cupped in his hand?
Mr. Frazier. Right.
<u>President's Commission on the Assassination</u> Vol. 2 Page 239

(Frazier was shown the bag recovered from the Texas School Book Depository)
Mr. Ball. Will you take a look at it as to the length? Does it appear to be about the same length?
Mr. Frazier. No, sir.
Mr. Ball. Was the bag about that width or a different width?
Mr. Frazier. Well, I would say it appears to me it would be pretty close, but it might be **just a little bit too wide. I think it is, because you know yourself you would have to have a big hand with that size but like I say he had this cupped in his hand** because I remember glancing at him when he was walking up ahead of me.
<u>President's Commission on the Assassination</u> Vol. 2 Page 239

The rifle that was owned by Oswald she [Marina] had seen many times. She recalled specifically seeing it when they lived on Neeley Street, and she knows that Oswald had the rifle in the garage at the Paine residence. **She advised she did not know that the rifle had a scope on it.** <u>President's Commission on the Assassination</u> Vol. 23 Page 413

Mrs. Ford was a part of the informal group of friends

who were a part of the Russian immigrant population in Dallas, Texas who had tried to help the Oswalds out given the Oswald's desperate economic situation and Marina's inability to speak English. At one point after Lee Oswald had apparently beaten his Russian born wife Marina, Marina had taken their daughter and went to stay with the Fords at their house. Mrs. Ford would end up translating some documents and conversations for Marina Oswald following the assassination, as Marina's English at that time was nearly nonexistent.

On March 13, 1964, Mrs. Ford testified before the Warren Commission, page 321, that she was present just prior to the arrival of the FBI for another interview, this interview was concerning the alleged shooting by Lee Oswald at General Walker. Mrs. Ford told the Warren Commission in her sworn testimony that **Marina's attorney** Mr. William McKenzie **said to Marina, "They will ask you if there were two guns, you tell them there was one gun that was used."** (The Warren Commission, from what I can determine, failed to question Mr. McKenzie concerning the question of Lee Oswald possibly having more than one rifle.)

Marina Oswald stated that on November 22, 1963, she had been shown a rifle in the Dallas Police Department, reportedly found at the Texas School Book Depository, and **was unable to positively identify it** as the same one she had observed in the above-mentioned garage. She stated that it was a dark color like the one she had seen, but **she did not recall the sight**. *President's Commission on the Assassination* Vol. 23 Page 384

When asked about Lee Oswald's rifle Marina Oswald said, "**It had a hump, or elevation, but there was no scope, no telescope.**" *Peter Gregory transcript* File 344 (Perhaps the hump was an iron site folded down.)

Mr. Rankin: When you saw the rifle assembled in the room, did it have the scope on it?

Marina Oswald: **No, it did not have a scope on it**. _President's Commission on the Assassination_ Vol. 1 Page 13

The Warren Commission, page 119, says that the Klein's Sporting Goods Company received an order for a rifle in March 1963, on a coupon clipped from the February 1963 issue of the American Rifleman magazine'. The only problem with this is the February 1963 issue does not show this particular Italian Mannlicher-Carcano rifle for sale in that particular issue. Obviously in a murder case establishing a link between the murder weapon and the murderer is critical. In this case evidence linking Lee Harvey Oswald, also known as A. Hidell, to an Italian Mannlicher-Carcano rifle is at best shaky, if not unproven.

Attorney Mark Lane testified to the Warren Commission that Mr. Klein of Klein Sporting Goods, the mail-order house where Oswald allegedly bought his rifle, said—"The FBI warned me to keep my trap shut." _President's Commission on the Assassination_ Vol. 2 Page 49

_President's Commission on the Assassination_ Vol. 22 Page 531 – 546. "United States Department of Justice, Federal Bureau of Investigation," dated May 18, 1964:

RAY JOHN, [TV news correspondent] Channel 8, WFAA-TV, advised that he recalls that on the afternoon of Sunday, November 24, 1963, following the shooting of LEE HARVEY OSWALD, that he received a telephone call sometime between 3:00 and 3:30 P.M. of that day from an anonymous male caller, who stated that he believed "OSWALD" had had a rifle sighted at a gun shop located in the 200 block on Irving Boulevard in Irving, Texas. He [John] asked the anonymous caller where he obtained this information, the caller declined to elaborate. *President's Commission on the Assassination* Vol. 22 Page 531 - 546

John advised that he decided to offer this information to law enforcement for whatever it might be worth, and he, called the office of J. WILL FRITZ, Captain, Homicide and Robbery Division, Dallas Police Department, at about 3:45 P.M. and furnished this information to Detective FAY TURNER of that Division. *President's Commission on the Assassination* Vol. 22 Page 531 - 546

At 6:30 P.M. on November 24, 1963, an anonymous male caller telephonically advised a Special Agent of the FBI at Dallas, Texas, that at about 5:30 P.M. he learned from an unidentified sack boy at Wyatt's Supermarket, Plymouth Park Shopping Center, Irving, Texas, that LEE HARVEY OSWALD, on Thursday, November 21, 1963, had his rifle sighted at the Irving Sports Shop, 221 East Irving Boulevard, Irving, Texas. He said he could furnish no further details concerning this matter and does not know if it is true or how the boy found out this information. *President's Commission on the Assassination* Vol. 22 Page 531 – 546

The above anonymous male caller sounded as if he were a normal, stable individual, but said he did not desire to identify himself. *President's Commission on the Assassination* Vol. 22 Page 531 - 546

Mr. Dial Ryder [of the Irving Sport Shop] stated that he definitely had not talked to any representative of any newspaper or other news service prior to being contacted by a Special Agent of the Dallas Office of the Federal Bureau of Investigation on November 25, 1963. He stated he found the Irving Sports Shop repair tag bearing the name "OSWALD" as customer on November 23, 1963, but had not told anyone, other than his wife, about finding the tag prior to being interviewed by the Special Agent of the FBI on November 25,

1963. *President's Commission on the Assassination* Vol. 22 Page 531 - 546

On November 25, 1963, a Special Agent of the Dallas Office of the FBI proceeded to Irving, Texas, and found the Irving Sports was closed. Neighborhood inquiry revealed that the owner of the Irving Sports Shop was a WOODROW GREENER, who was reportedly then visiting at an unknown address in East Texas. In GREENER's absence, an employee, DIAL D. RYDER, 2028 Harvard, Irving, Texas, was contacted at his home, at which time he stated that he had, on November 23, 1963, found a repair tag bearing the name "OSWALD". RYDER and the Agent then proceeded to the Irving Sports Shop, where the Agent examined the pertinent repair tag and the interview continued. *President's Commission on the Assassination* Vol. 22 Page 531 – 546

The FBI checked with all of the individuals listed in the immediate area of Texas with the last name of Oswald but found no Oswald who had been to the Irving Sports Shop.

Mr. RYDER said he first noticed repair tag number 18374, which bears the name of "OSWALD" as the owner of the gun to be repaired, on Saturday, November 23, 1963. He stated that on that occasion he, RYDER, was cleaning off his workbench, it being cluttered with various tools, and repair tags, and it was during this cleaning up that he noticed the tag bearing the name "OSWALD." He pointed out that the tag attracted his attention as the name "OSWALD" had been mentioned frequently in the news on November 22 and 23, 1963. *President's Commission on the Assassination* Vol. 22 Page 531 – 546

Mr. RYDER said he usually prepares repair tags in pen as he carries a ballpoint pen in his shirt pocket but does recall that on one occasion on an unrecalled date during the first two weeks of November 1963, he had used a pencil during the greater part of a day. He recalled that on the date he had used a pencil [the day] he made a trip to Cullum and Boren Company, Dallas, Texas, and picked up some items. *President's Commission on the Assassination* Vol. 22 Page 531 - 546

On May 4, 1964, Cullum and Boren Company made available for review invoices that reflect sales to Irving Sport Shop signed by DIAL RYDER. Invoices were signed by Dial Ryder in pencil on November 6$^{th}$, 12$^{th}$, and 13$^{th}$. *President's Commission on the Assassination* Vol. 22 Page 531 – 546

Mark Lane: "Of course one must zero in a rifle in order to be even fairly accurate with it. One must practice with the specific weapon which one is going to use, in order to have any accuracy, in any event." *President's Commission on the Assassination* Vol. 2 Page 48

Mark Lane: "Now, I spoke with Dial M. Ryder, who is a gunsmith in Irving, Tex., at the Irving Sport Shop, and he told me that he mounted a telescopic sight on a rifle for a man named Oswald during October 1963." *President's Commission on the Assassination* Vol. 2 Page 48

"Unfortunately, this was around deer season and a lot of people were getting rifles fixed, or repaired, or sights mounted, and he does not recall what this gentleman named Oswald looked like." *President's Commission on the Assassination* Vol. 2 Page 48 (What Dial Rider might have meant, or even said, was that he didn't recognize a picture of Oswald as having been the same person as the person who brought in the rifle to be worked on. You would think that the FBI would have shown Rider a picture of Oswald and said it this the guy?)

"But he does know that a rifle was brought to him by someone whose name now appears in this record as Oswald, and that he drilled three holes in the rifle for a mount, a telescopic mount. **He said he did not attach a telescopic sight to the Italian carbine, because he would have only drilled two holes.**" *President's Commission on the Assassination* Vol. 2 Page 48

Mr. GREENER [owner of the Irving Sports Shop] was asked if there is any question in his mind that a gun represented by the repair tag bearing the name "OSWALD" was brought into the store. Mr. GREENER said it is his opinion that the repair tag represents a bona fide transaction, pointing out that DIAL RYDER has been employed by him, GREENER, for the past six years, and during that period he has found RYDER to be a good, steady, reliable employee and he has never known of RYDER doing anything wrong; therefore, he has every confidence in RYDER. He said he, GREENER, goes away and leaves the entire business in RYDER's care and "I never worry a minute about the business." *President's Commission on the Assassination* Vol. 22 Page 531 - 546

Mr. Dial D. Ryder, 2023 Harvard stated he is employed as Service Manager, Irving Sport Shop, 221 South Irving Boulevard. **Mr. RYDER viewed a photograph of the gun used to assassinate President KENNEDY after which he stated he did not sell the mount on that gun, as that is not the type of mount handled by Irving Sport Shop and does not recall the gun.** *President's Commission on the Assassination* Vol. 22 Page 523 "Commission Exhibit 1325, Federal Bureau of Investigation," dated 11/25/63.

Mr. RYDER located Irving Sport Shop repair tag number 18374, which is undated and contains the name "OSWALD" as the owner of the gun being repaired. The tag reflects the work as being "drill and tap $4.50" and "bore sight $1.50" for a total of $6.00. The tag contains no additional information, is prepared in pencil, is not dated and Mr. RYDER stated this is the only record in existence of this transaction. RYDER said the tag was prepared by himself. He pointed out that as there is no record of sale of mounts or other items, this would reflect that customer OSWALD brought in the gun, scope and mounts with only work being performed which was drill and tap and bore sight. Mr. RYDER stated that the work for OSWALD was performed between November 1 and 14, 1963. *President's Commission on the Assassination* Vol. 22 Page 523

Mr. RYDER stated he has no recollection of mounting a side mount of the type on the gun used to assassinate President KENNEDY ... *President's Commission on the Assassination* Vol. 22 Page 523

Mr. Liebeler. You based that **statement, that you had not mounted the scope on that particular kind of rifle, is that correct? Mr. Ryder. Right, on this Italian rifle---I never worked on them. I [have] seen them, but as far as doing any physical work [on them], I haven't done none, even to this date, I haven't [ever] worked on any of them.** Mr. Liebeler. You are absolutely sure about that? Mr. Ryder. **I am positive on that, very positive.** *President's Commission on the Assassination* Vol. 11 Page 226. (**Another point Dial Ryder made is that the picture of the Italian Mannlicher-Carcano rifle alleged to be Oswald's shows just two screws holding the mount of the scope on, whereas the repair ticket indicated three holes were to be drilled and tapped on the rifle that matched up with the Oswald repair tag.**) *President's Commission on the Assassination* Vol. 11 Page 226. **The rifle found on the sixth floor of the Texas School Book Depository had two holes in it bored for the installation of a scope** prior to shipment to Oswald in March 1963. *The Warren Report* Page 646

Mr. RYDER viewed a photograph of LEE HARVEY OSWALD, taken August 9, 1963, after which he stated that he cannot be positive that OSWALD had been a customer in the Irving Sport Shop but is quite sure that he has seen and/or talked to OSWALD probably in the store. **He stated that he associates**

**OSWALD's picture with that of an individual who brought in an Argentine made rifle about two weeks ago and he, RYDER, attached a scope on that gun.** <u>President's Commission on the Assassination</u> Vol. 22 Page 523

Following the assassination and upon seeing a picture of Lee Oswald on TV, Mrs. Edith Whitworth and Mrs. Gertrude Hunter reported that Lee Harvey Oswald came into the Whitworth's furniture store on either November 6, 7, or 8, 1963 looking to have a rifle repaired. He had mistaken the furniture store for a sporting goods store, as the previous proprietor had left a sign on the front of the building that read "Guns." Mrs. Whitworth gave Oswald directions to the Irving Sports Shop down the road. Oswald proceeded to get into a 1956 or 1957 two-tone blue and white Ford or Chevrolet and ended up heading the wrong direction on a one-way street and had to turn the vehicle around. <u>President's Commission on the Assassination</u> Vol. 22 Page 455 and 531 – 547

It seems obvious that the witnesses from the Furniture Store tend to validate the possibility that Lee Harvey Oswald did in fact bring a rifle into Dial Ryder at the Irving Sport Shop. It also seems clear that the rifle was not an Italian rifle and according to Dial Ryder's recollection it was an Argentine rifle. Here is what Mr. Liebeler of the Warren Commission had to say about this:

Mr. Liebeler. As we discussed briefly off the record before we started, it appears that there are three possibilities concerning this [repair] tag. One, in view of the fact that Mr. Ryder is quite clear in his own mind that he never worked on an Italian rifle similar to the one that was found in the Texas School Book Depository, **we can conclude either that the Oswald on the tag was Lee Oswald and he brought a different rifle in here, or it was a different Oswald who brought another rifle in** here, or that the tag is not a genuine tag, and that there never was a man who came in here with any gun at all. *President's Commission on the Assassination* Vol. 11 Page 249

If this repair tag represents a transaction with Lee Harvey Oswald, **not only does it mean that Lee Harvey Oswald owned another rifle, but according to Dial Ryder it was an Argentine rifle.** I probably don't need to remind you of this coincidence, but the rifle that was left in Terre Haute was a "German Mauser 1891 Argentine" rifle.

Mr. Ryder: "I [talked with] a lady with the Washington press. She called Klein's and found out the rifle [alleged to be Oswald's, the Italian Mannlicher-Carcano] had already been drilled and tapped. In other words, he had bought the scope and rifle from Klein's, and they were shipped together." President's *Commission on the Assassination* Vol. 11 Page 228 - 229

The Dial Ryder story seriously calls into question the theory that the Italian Mannlicher-Carcano rifle was the rifle of choice for Lee Harvey Oswald on the day of the assassination. Here we have evidence that Lee Oswald had a rifle, but according to Dial Ryder it was not an Italian rifle, but an Argentine rifle. Dial Ryder was certain it was not an Italian rifle because he said he had never worked on an Italian rifle in his life. He did say that if he mounted a scope on a rifle for a guy named Oswald, which he did do according to the repair tag, then he mounted it on an Argentine rifle. Not only that but combine this with the very credible account from the ladies located just down the street in the furniture store and it seems very likely that Lee Harvey Oswald actually did bring in another kind of rifle, an Argentine rifle, not an Italian rifle, which Dial Ryder proceeded to work on. Either that or, someone was posing as Oswald when they stopped in the furniture store and then proceed on to the Irving Sports Shop to have a scope mounted on an Argentine rifle using the name of Oswald. I would point out that the ladies at the furniture store said that Oswald proceeded to get in a car and drive away. Only problem, Lee Oswald didn't have a driver's licenses and did not have a car, so this would indicate that this might have been someone else impersonating Oswald.

Mark Lane was an attorney, who was retained by Mrs. Oswald, Lee's Oswald's mother, to represent her and her dead son's interests. Mark Lane testified before the Warren Commission:

Mr. Lane: "When I spoke with Mr. Klein, he indicated that he did not want to discuss any aspect of this matter with me. I asked him if that was because he was told not to talk with anyone about this case, and he said yes. I said who told you that? He said, 'The FBI agents told me, ordered me not to discuss this case.' I pointed out to him that in our democratic society, the FBI cannot order anyone not to discuss a case. So, he did." *President's Commission on the Assassination* Vol. 2 Page 49

Mark Lane: "I talked to Milton Klein, who is the owner of Klein's sporting goods store in Chicago—Klein's Sporting Goods is the name of the establishment, in Chicago. And he told me that—he runs the mail-order house which sent the carbine, Italian carbine, to Dallas, not to Oswald, but to A. Hidell, and that he sent that out with the holes already bored in the Italian carbine, and equipped with a telescopic sight, which was already attached to the rifle." *President's Commission on the Assassination* Vol. 2 Page 48 (It is interesting that the Italian rifle shipped with the scope already attached, however, Marina Oswald said, that the rifle that she saw "had a hump, ... but there was no scope..." This would indicate that Marina might have seen another rifle.)

Mark Lane: "He told me that he mailed this rifle with the holes already bored and with the telescopic sight already mounted to someone named A. Hidell. He also said that 'No ammunition was purchased from [him] by Hidell at that time or since.'" *President's Commission on the Assassination* Vol. 2 Page 49

Marina Oswald in testimony before the Warren Commission stated that Lee Oswald's rifle was left lying on the floor, wrapped in a blanket, in Mrs. Paine's garage. (Not a very good way to care for a rifle, especially one that is supposed to have a scope mounted on it, as scopes can easily get jarred out of alignment. Mrs. Paine is the lady whom Marina Oswald lived with in Texas in the time leading up to the assassination.) Marina also indicated that the garage had two doors, one inside door leading to the kitchen, and a second door that opened to the outside. There is no indication whether the outside door was locked. *President's Commission on the Assassination* Vol. 1 Page 26 & 52

Marina testified that Ruth Paine told her the morning of the assassination that she had worked in the garage the previous evening and knew that she had turned the light off, but that the light was on in the morning. And she guessed that Lee was in the garage. If so, Marina said that she didn't see it. (The point is that someone is thought to have been in the garage and left the light on. It was assumed that Oswald did it. Again, anyone could have entered the garage through the outside door, locked or not.)

Mark Lane: "Since it has been alleged that the rifle was in the garage during the entire period of time, of course—that was in Irving, Tex., and he was in Dallas, Tex.—it would have been impossible for him to practice during the week while he was in Dallas, **with that particular rifle**." *President's Commission on the Assassination* Vol. 2 Page 48

Mark Lane: "But here we have Oswald going home to get an inferior rifle, which rifle is the only rifle in the whole world which can be traced to him, which rifle **he is going to leave behind as a calling card after the assassination is complete**." <u>President's Commission on the Assassination</u> Vol. 2 Page 52. **(We might consider thinking the same thing about the rifle left in Terre Haute, was it left as a "calling card?")**

Mark Lane: "And so he goes home to Irving, Tex., and he gets this rifle, and he wraps it up in paper, we are told, and brings it into the Book Depository Building. Now, the rifle can be broken down. But it would be not much shorter if it were broken down—perhaps 6 or 7 inches shorter." <u>President's Commission on the Assassination</u> Vol. 2 Page 52

This is from a Secret Service Interview with Mrs. Marguerite Oswald (Lee Oswald's mother) recorded on November 25, 1963:

Question: "In these past two or three days we talked about this rifle that Lee had in the garage over at the Paine residence and in Irving. Now, you have expressed your opinion that someone else might have gotten a hold of this rifle. Now, would you go into that a little bit, what you feel like did happen or could have happened?"

Mrs. Oswald: "Of course, this is just speculation, when Marina told me yes, Lee had a rifle. Lee liked to hunt, he always liked to hunt, and the statement was made in the paper when he defected. And he had a rifle a long time. And that FBI man asked when she was picked up about the rifle and she told the FBI man, "Yes, Lee has a rifle." They showed her a big rifle. **She says no she don't think that is the same rifle that Lee had.** She says I told the FBI man because Lee has rifle, she says, but **she didn't think it was the same rifle that the FBI man showed her.** So, since they did not have a home of their own and they lived in this house, and **Marina told me that Lee kept the rifle in the garage, anyone could have access to the rifle, so even though it would be Lee's**

**rifle, to me doesn't necessarily mean that Lee used it since it was just in the garage."** <u>President's Commission on the Assassination</u> Vol. 16 Page 741

Page 81 of the *"Warren Report"* says the rifle is a bolt-action, clip-fed rifle found on the sixth floor of the Depository, inscribed with various markings, including "MADE ITALY," "CAL. 6.5," "1940" and the [serial] number C2766.

(Robert A. Frazier, firearms expert with the FBI)
Mr. Eisenberg. "Have you measured the dimensions of this rifle assembled, and disassembled?"
Mr. Frazier. "Yes, I have."
Mr. Eisenberg. "Could you give us that information?"
Mr. Frazier. "The overall length is **40.2 inches**. It weighs 8 pounds even. With the scope. **The stock length is 34.8 inches**, which is the wooden portion from end to end with the butt plate attached. **The barrel** and action from the muzzle to the rear of the tang, which is this portion at the rearmost portion of the metal, is **28.9 inches**. The barrel only is 21.18 inches. The tang is the rear of the receiver of the weapon into which the rear mounting screw is screwed to hold the rearmost part of the metal action of the weapon into the wooden stock. From the end of that portion [the tang] to the muzzle of the weapon is 28.9 inches. **The entire metal part is then a total of 28.9 inches, because the metal tang does not detach from the metal barrel.**"
Mr. Eisenberg. "And **the length of the longest component when the rifle is dissembled**, Mr. Frazier?"
Mr. Frazier. "**34.8 inches, which is the length of the stock, the wooden portion**."
Mr. Eisenberg. "Can you describe to us the telescopic sight on the rifle?"
Mr. Frazier. "It is a four-power telescopic sight employing crosshairs in it as a sighting device, in the interior of the scope. It is stamped "Optics Ordinance Incorporated,

Hollywood California," and under that is the inscription "Made in Japan." It is a very inexpensive Japanese telescopic sight. The mount attached to it was also made in Japan."

Mr. Eisenberg. "Have you removed the mount?"

Mr. Frazier. "Yes, I have."

Mr. Eisenberg. "How many holes did you find drilled into the receiver?"

Mr. Frazier. "There are two holes in the receiver. In the sight itself there normally are three holes, two of which have been enlarged to accommodate the two mounting screws presently holding the mount to the rifle."

(To determine if Klein's Sporting Goods in Chicago mounted the sight on the rifle)

Mr. Frazier. "We contacted the firm, Klein's Sporting Goods in Chicago, and asked them concerning this matter to provide us with a similar rifle mounted in the way in which they normally mount scopes of this type on these rifles and forward the rifle to us for examination. When we received the rifle, we examined the mount and found that two of the holes had been enlarged, and that screws had been placed through them and threaded into the receiver of the rifle. The third hole in the mount had not been used. We also found that an identical scope to the one on the Commission's rifle was present on the rifle."

Mr. Eisenberg. "Were the screws used in mounting the scope on the rifle as those used in mounting the scope on [Oswald's] rifle?"

Mr. Frazier. "Yes, sir."

Mr. Eisenberg. "And the holes were the same dimensions?"

Mr. Frazier. "Yes, they are. And the threads in the holes are the same."

*President's Commission on the Assassination* Vol. 3 Page 395 – 397

Mr. Eisenberg. "Could you briefly explain the operation of

this rifle, the bolt action and the clip-feed mechanism?"
Mr. Frazier. "Yes, sir; the weapon is loaded by turning up the bolt handle, drawing the bolt to the rear, and inserting the clip from the top of the weapon, after the clip has been loaded with the number of rounds you desire to load. The maximum number of rounds the clip holds is six. However, the weapon can be loaded with a clip holding 5,4,3,2, or 1 round. The weapon will hold a maximum of seven. (6 in the clip and one, which can be manually placed in the chamber.)"
<u>President's Commission on the Assassination</u> Vol. 3 Page 398

(Result of the test firing of the Italian Mannlicher-Carcano)
Mr. Eisenberg. Mr. Frazier, could you tell us why, in your opinion, all the shots virtually all the shots, are grouped high and to the right of the aiming point?
Mr. Frazier. Yes, sir. **When we attempted to sight in this rifle at Quantico, we found that the elevation adjustment in the telescopic sight was not sufficient to bring the point of impact to the aiming point. In attempting to adjust and sight-in the rifle, every time we changed the adjusting screws to move the crosshairs in the telescopic sight in one direction it also affected the movement of the impact or the point of impact in the other direction. That is, if we moved the crosshairs in the telescope to the left it would also affect the elevation setting of the telescope. And when we had sighted-in the rifle approximately, we fired several shots and found that the shots were not all landing in the same place but were gradually moving away from the point of impact**. This was apparently due to the construction of the telescope, which apparently did not stabilize itself--- that is, the spring mounting in the crosshair ring did not stabilize until we had fired five or six shots. (Author: In other words when the sight's crosshairs were adjusted from side to side it would also move the horizontal crosshair up or down, or the reverse, adjust the horizontal and the vertical crosshair would move out of position and the crosshairs

moved around on their own and would not stay where they were originally intended. The sight on the Italian rifle was defective, moved around, and did not work. Just what one might expect of a rifle that was kept lying on the floor of a garage with only a blanket for protection). *President's Commission on the Assassination* Vol. 3 Page 405

Testimony of Ronald Simmons, Chief of the Infantry Weapons Evaluation Branch of the Ballistics Research Laboratory of the Department of the Army.
Mr. Eisenberg. ...any difficulties with sighting the weapon in?
Mr. Simmons. Well, they could not sight the weapon in using the telescope and no attempt was made to sight it in using the iron sight. We did adjust the telescopic sight by the addition of two shims, one, which tended to adjust the azimuth, and one, which adjusted an elevation. The azimuth correction could have been made without the addition of the shim, but it would have meant that we would have used all of the adjustment possible, and the shim was a more permanent means of correction.
Mr. Eisenberg. By azimuth, do you refer to the crosshair, which is sometimes referred to as the windage crosshair?
Mr. Simmons. Yes. *President's Commission on the Assassination* Vol. 3 Page 443 - 444

In a murder case, of course, one of the most important elements is to connect the weapon to the murderer. In the case of the Italian Mannlicher-Carcano rifle and Lee Harvey Oswald there is some controversy as to whether that proof was ever established. Part of the problem arose because the Dallas Police turned over the Italian rifle to the FBI for processing on November 22, 1963, the day of the assassination, but they didn't tell the FBI until a whole four days later that they had lifted a palm print from the rifle.

The Warren Report says, "On November 22, before

surrendering possession of the rifle to the FBI Laboratory, Lieutenant Day of the Dallas Police Department had 'lifted' a palm print from the underside of the gun barrel 'near the firing end of the barrel about 3 inches under the wood stock, when I took the wood stock loose.' *Warren Report* Page 123

In the TV series, on the History Channel, *"The Men Who Killed Kennedy, The Patsy,"* they charged: that the authorities were never able to prove that the rifle, found in the School Book Depository, was Oswald's rifle. However, a smudged palm print had been discovered on the weapon just hours after a mysterious visit to the funeral home, where Oswald's body had been taken by mortician Paul Groody. Paul Groody: "In the early-early morning, around one a.m. agents came, they, um, fingerprinted. They carried a satchel and equipment and asked if they might have the preparation room to themselves and after it was all over, we found ink on Lee Harvey's hands, showing that they had finger printed him and palm printed him." *The Men Who Killed Kennedy, The Patsy*

The FBI's crime lab technician, Sebastian Latona testified that the poor finish of the K-1 rifle made it absorbent and not conducive to getting a good print. He also said that none of the other prints on the rifle could be identified because they were of such poor quality. *HSCA* Page 218

Lt. Day of the Dallas Police maintained in testimony that after the lift he could still see traces of the print under the barrel. Mr. Latona of the FBI testified with the respect to the lift of the palm print, that "evidently the lifting had been so complete that there was nothing left to show any marking on the gun itself as to the existence of such—even an attempt on the part of anyone else to process the rifle." *HSCA* Page 218

The staff of the Warren Commission were so suspicious that they wrote a memo on August 28, 1964, saying, "We suggest that additional investigation be conducted to determine with greater certainty that the palm print was actually lifted from the rifle as Lt. Day has testified. The only evidence we presently have on that print is the testimony of Lt. Day himself. *HSCA* Page 218

It is pretty amazing that such a critical piece of evidence, like a palm print, in such an important case, would be so slowly communicated by the Dallas Police to the FBI.

The question is: did Lee Harvey Oswald have in his possession a German Mauser Argentine 1891 rifle?

The Dallas Police did not find any rounds for the Italian 6.5 Mannlicher-Carcano rifle among Oswald's possessions following his arrest, neither on his person, nor where he was staying. (Harry Power apparently didn't have as much ammunition as he would have liked either.)

The CIA continued to refer to the rifle used in the assassination as a Mauser. In a CIA report, dated November 25, 1963, 3 days after the assassination it states, "On November 22, 1963, Lee Harvey Oswald shot President Kennedy, while the President was riding in an open automobile on a Dallas Texas street. The rifle used was a Mauser..."

Then there is this testimony of Warren Caster in the Warren Commission, Volume VII page 386-388. This is not the full testimony, just portions. The authorities learned about this incident in the School Book Depository from Lee Oswald who mentioned it when he was being questioned by Captain Will Fritz of the Dallas Police and FBI Special Agent James Hosty and James Brookhout. Oswald stated that he had observed a Mr. Truly, a supervisor at the Texas Schoolbook Depository on November 20, 1963, display a rifle to some individuals in his office. *Warren Report* Page 612:

Mr. Ball. Will you state your full name, please?

Mr. Caster. Warren Caster.

Mr. Ball. What is your business?

Mr. Caster. Textbook publishing.

Mr. Ball. Are you with some company?

Mr. Caster. Yes, I am assistant manager for Southwestern Publishing Co. with offices at 411 Elm Street.

Mr. Ball. You have offices in the Texas School Book Depository Building?

Mr. Caster. Yes

Mr. Ball. Did you ever bring any guns into the School Book Depository Building?

Mr. Caster. Yes, I did.

Mr. Ball. When?

Mr. Caster. I believe it was on Wednesday, November 20, during the noon hour.

Mr. Ball. And what kind of guns were they?

Mr. Caster. One gun was a Remington, single-shot, .22 rifle, and the other was a .30-06 **sporterized Mauser**. I left the Depository during the noon hour and had lunch and, while out for the lunch hour, I stopped by Sanger-Harris Sporting Goods to look for a rifle for my son's birthday—I beg your pardon, Christmas present—son's Christmas present, and while I was there I purchased the single-shot .22—and at the same time was looking at some deer rifles. I had, oh, for several years been thinking about buying a deer rifle and they happened to have one that I liked, and I purchased the .30-06 while I was there.

Mr. Ball. And then you went back to work, I guess?

Mr. Caster. Yes ... I entered the Texas School Book Depository Building on my way up to the buying office, I stopped by Mr. Truly's office, and while I was there, we examined the two rifles that I had purchased.

Mr. Ball. Who was there besides you and Mr. Truly?

Mr. Caster. I think Mr. Ball, and Mr. Shelley was there—and Mr. Roy Truly.

Mr. Ball. And what did you do with them after that?

Mr. Caster. I left at the end of the working day, oh, around 4 o'clock and took the guns in the cartons and carried them and put them in my car and carried them home.

Mr. Ball. Did you ever have them back in the Texas School Book Depository Building thereafter?

Mr. Caster. They have never been back to the Texas School Book Depository Building since then.

Mr. Ball. Where were those guns on November 22, 1963?

Mr. Caster. The guns were in my home.

The only point I am making here is that I found it interesting that the rifle was a sporterized Mauser. From what I can gather the term sporterized is like saying that the rifle has been modified. Sporterizing a rifle can include shortening the barrel and the wood stock. Thus, the rifle that came to Terre Haute would be considered a sporterized Mauser.

FBI document dated 11/27/63, says: "On November twenty last, the Dallas Police sighted **two** unknown **men sighting in a rifle near the scene of where the President was later assassinated**. Rifle being sighted in at two silhouette targets. An old model car was seen in the vicinity of the men. Police circled to contact they men and they disappeared. *HSCA* 180-10005-10017

From Wikipedia on the internet: Ricky White (the son of Roscoe White, who was a Dallas policeman) claims that his father's diary clearly showed that he was part of a three-man assassination team in Kennedy's murder. The diary stated that there were six shots fired — two by his father. The diary also said that Mauser rifles were used in the assassination. Ricky White remembers his father giving him two rifles after the assassination in Dallas. One was an **Argentinean rifle and the other was a 7.65 Mauser**. The Senate Intelligence Committee located (in 1976) a third photograph of Oswald with a backyard pose that was different from the previous ones exhibited by the Warren Commission. The photo introduced in 1976 was found by the widow of Dallas Police Officer Roscoe White, amongst his belongings.

In 1995 the Assassinations Record Review Board released an FBI envelope labeled: "FBI Field Office Dallas 89-43-1A-122" and it was dated 12/2/1963. The contents of the envelope, a 7.65 mm rifle shell. The shell was found in Dealey Plaza on 12/2/63 following the assassination, the release of this information was the first that anyone had ever heard about a 7.65 rifle shell connected to Dealey Plaza. The 7.65 mm rifle shell is missing from the envelope. Researcher Anna Marie Kuhns-Walko was the first to discover and reported about the envelope. The envelope had the following label: "7.65 shell found in Dealey Plaza on 12/02/1963 ... determined of no value and destroyed."

Harry L. Power's German Mauser Argentine 1891 rifle used a 7.65 mm round. What a shame, or crime, that this shell casing was destroyed.

## DOES THE TERRE HAUTE RIFLE SEEM TO FIT?

Do the pieces fit? Please keep in mind that nowhere was the model of the German Mauser rifle ever officially declared to be an Argentine model but notice how the word Argentine keeps coming up and notice how the possibility seems to exist for a rifle with features that are different from the Italian rifle. Out of a minimum 52 possible Mauser models, just one model the Argentine model keeps surfacing.

- The rifle in Dallas was first identified as a 7.65-mm Mauser rifle (7.65 Mauser matches the rifle in Terre Haute), then later in the day Mr. Wade (Dallas prosecuting attorney) identified the rifle in Dallas as a German Mauser rifle, ultimately it became an Italian Mannlicher-Carcano rifle.

- Maximum length of the modified German Mauser Argentine 1891 rifle like the one in Terre Haute, when disassembled and sportsterized, 22 inches. Buel Wesley Frazier said the length of the paper package carried by Oswald was "roughly about two feet long." That would be 24 inches, including the brown paper bag. Not even close to the "length of the longest component, when the Italian rifle was disassembled, which was 34.8 inches."

- Dial Ryder said that he worked on an Argentine rifle and had never worked on an Italian rifle. The possibility of Oswald having a rifle worked on by Dial Ryder is reinforced by the testimony of the ladies in the furniture store who identified Lee Oswald and his family, as having been in their store and they said that they had directed Oswald to the Irving Sporting Goods Store. True, unless this was an Oswald look-alike.

- It would be interesting to see someday if the rifle that was left in Terre Haute shows any signs of having had a scope, which would apparently be indicated by holes having been drilled and tapped to mount a scope.

- The House Select Committee on Assassinations somehow managed to feature an Argentine 1891 German Mauser rifle in their twelve-volume report. What is amazing about this is that the Argentine model is just one of at least 52 other countries that had models that could have been selected and still have been called a Mauser. Then in addition to that, the model 1891 represents just one of more than a few time period possibilities.

- There is evidence that a salesman brought into the Texas School Book Depository a sporterized Mauser just two days prior to the assassination. As previously mentioned, I understood from talking to Terre Haute Police Officers Butts and Shoffstall that they recalled The Mauser rifle left in Terre Haute as being sporterized (shortened) and that it was a German Mauser, Argentine 1891 rifle.

- There could have been more than one 7.65 Argentine German Mauser at play in the assassination. Oswald might have had a sight mounted on one; there might have been another with just an iron sight. The Warren Commission rifle experts said that for such a small area, an iron sight would have been preferable.

- Marina Oswald's attorney Mr. McKenzie hinted that there might be questions as to Lee Harvey Oswald having had a second rifle. McKenzie said to Marina, "They will ask you if there were two guns, you tell them there was one gun that was used."

- The Terre Haute incident has always been an obscure

event and neither the Terre Haute Police report, nor the FBI reports say what model of Mauser was left in the Terre Haute House. They don't say that it was an Argentine model, nor an 1891 model, nor a modified rifle, nor a rifle with just an iron sight. The reports do give the serial number and reported that the rifle was a German Mauser rifle. And yet there are references and even a picture of an Argentine 1891 model in the HSCA Report, a reference to a sporterized Mauser rifle in the School Book Depository, a preference expressed by the Warren Commission rifle experts for the use of an iron sight in such a small area, the size of the rifle as described by Buel Wesley, Dial Ryder's reference to a Argentine rifle, and Ricky White's reference to both an Argentine and a 7.65 Mauser rifle, description all of which according to Butts and Schoffstall, match up with the rifle in Terre Haute.

- The Dallas Police, searching through Oswald's possessions after his arrest, found no rounds for a 6.5 Mannlicher-Carcano rifle and the clip for loading multiple rounds was never found in the School Book Depository, to my knowledge.

- Apparently Lee Oswald had two rifles: Marina's attorney advised her, "They will ask you if there were two guns, you tell them there was one gun that was used." Marina testified that Lee's rifle did not have a scope. The Italian rifle that was supposedly shipped to Lee Oswald already had a scope mounted on it at the time of shipment. It would therefore seem that the rifle, as seen by Marina, was not the Italian rifle, but another rifle.

A 7.65 shell found in Dealey Plaza just days after the assassination on 12/2/1963 and is of the same caliber as that of the rifle that was left in Terre Haute, Indiana.

Based on the Dial Ryder story, does it seem as if Lee Harvey

Oswald, or someone posing as Oswald, might have had possession of a German Mauser Argentine rifle? Dial Ryder stated that, "he associates Oswald's picture with that of an individual who brought in **an Argentine** made **rifle**." Dial Ryder had a service ticket on which he had written the name Oswald. Dial Ryder also indicated that he had never worked on an Italian rifle in his life.

Oswald's rusty old Italian rifle with the scope that never lined up and jumped around when fired was stored on the floor of a garage. Questions were raised during the Warren Commission investigation as to just how secure the garage was. With an outside entrance to the garage, someone other than Oswald could have easily retrieved the rifle from the garage floor.

I would, however, point out that the Argentine rifle might have been the most common, or most popular, German Mauser rifle model, and that this might help to explain the many Argentine coincidences. Just because Harry Power had a German Mauser rifle, does not mean that he was involved in the assassination. It only means that Harry Power's rifle does seem to fit with what is in the public record concerning rifles that may be linked to the assassination.

## MORE THAN ONE ASSASSIN AND MORE THAN ONE PATSY?

If there was a planned conspiracy, then I would assume the planners would recognize that the probability of success would be greatly enhanced if they had more than one sniper. And if they were paying attention to the details, then they would probably want to have more than one patsy. What if the second patsy, and/or assassin, got away?

Some fifty people in Dealey Plaza that day claimed that shots came from the grassy knoll. How much more believable the assassination story would have been had there been a second patsy for fifty some witnesses to point at?

Dealey Plaza is an open area, dissected by three streets, surrounded by buildings, with a grassy knoll on one side. On top of the grassy knoll was a picket fence and a line of trees. Immediately behind the fence was a parking lot and across the parking lot there was a railroad-switching yard and a Railroad Switching Control Tower.

Is there evidence of another sniper, in addition to the possibility of Oswald? Yes, I think there is:

## JACK RUBY AND A YOUNG MAN

Julia Ann Mercer was driving toward the overpass on Elm Street in Dealey Plaza around an hour before the assassination, when she got caught in traffic and was stuck behind a pickup truck that was stalled, had its hood up, and was sitting at the base of the grassy knoll. <u>HSCA</u> Vol. 12, Page 16-17

Julia Ann Mercer sat behind the pickup truck and watched as a young man, whom she described as being a white male around 20 years old, reached over the tailgate of the pickup and removed what appeared to be a brown gun case. The young man then proceeded to walk up the grassy knoll, and as he did so, the end of the gun case was caught momentarily on something on the ground. She later described the man as having the same general build, size, and age as Oswald, but she could not identify Oswald as being the young man she saw walk up the hill. The 20- to 24-year-old man was wearing a gray jacket, brown pants, and **a plaid shirt**. He also wore a wool stocking cap with a tassel on it. <u>HSCA</u> Vol. 12, Page 16-17

Julia Ann Mercer also got a good look at the second man who remained in the pickup truck slouched over the wheel. She described this second man as heavy-set, middle aged, with light brown hair, and wearing a green jacket. Julia Ann Mercer said she was "able to look right in the man's face" as she eased her way around to the side of the pickup truck. As a result, on November 23$^{rd}$ the day after the assassination and the day before Jack Ruby shot Oswald in the Police Station, Julia Ann Mercer was able to select Jack Ruby's photograph out of photographs shown to her by the Dallas Police Department. **She knows it was Jack Ruby**'s photograph because the police turned over the picture and the name Jack Ruby was written on the back. The next day, November 24$^{th}$ as Julia Ann Mercer sat watching the transfer of Oswald from Dallas Police custody to the Sheriff's Department, she again recognized Jack Ruby as he shot and killed Lee Harvey Oswald on TV. *HSCA* Vol. 12, Page 16-17

Lee E. Bowers Jr., at the time of the assassination on November 22, was located in the Union Terminal Railroad Control Tower, which was located across a parking lot, which was behind the picket fence, which was atop the grass knoll. Bowers noticed two men standing within 10 or 15 feet of each other [behind the picket fence]. Bowers said the two men were directly in his line of vision toward the mouth of the underpass and appeared to be watching the progress of the motorcade. One of the men was middle aged, heavy set, and was wearing white shirt and dark trousers. The other man was in his **mid-twenties**, wearing either a **plaid shirt** or a plaid jacket. Bowers said he saw the man in the white shirt standing there at the time of the shots, but that he could not see **the younger man in the plaid clothing** because of the trees, which made him harder to distinguish. At the time of the shots, Bowers watched as a motorcycle cop ran up the incline toward the trees in the general area where the two men were standing; Bowers said there was some kind of commotion at that place, but that he did not know what had happened. *HSCA* Vol. 12, Page 12-13

Apparently, some young man in his 20's or 30's was seen by Julia Ann Mercer reaching over the tailgate of a pickup truck to retrieve a rifle case, which he then walked up the grassy knoll while Jack Ruby sat waiting in a pickup truck. Julia Ann got a better look at the young man than she did the driver, yet she did not identify the young man as Lee Harvey Oswald, but she did identify Jack Ruby as the driver of the pickup truck. I would draw from this only that the young man was not Lee Harvey Oswald and apparently there was another young man involved with Jack Ruby and the pickup truck at the base of the grassy knoll just an hour before the assassination and he was wearing a plaid shirt. Then Lee Bowers reports seeing a young man in his twenties wearing a plaid shirt, or plaid jacket behind the picket fence atop the grassy knoll at the time of the assassination. Lee Bowers died in a mysterious car crash not too long after the assassination.

Forty to fifty people in Dealey Plaza said that shots came from the grassy knoll.

Jean Hill, who was the closest spectator to the presidential limousine reported in her book "*The Last Dissenting Witness*" that she saw a rifleman behind the picket fence at the top of the knoll. She also saw someone running immediately after the assassination from the corner of the School Book Depository over to the end of the picket fence. Two days later she identified that person as Jack Ruby when he appeared on TV as he shot Lee Harvey Oswald. Jesse C. Price, who was on the roof of the Terminal Annex Building, saw someone running from the picket fence over to the railroad siding and he had something in his hand. <u>HSCA</u> Vol. 12, Page 12. Dallas police officer Tom Tilson was off duty in his squad car when he heard over the police radio that the President had been shot. He saw a man "slipping and sliding" down the embankment of the railroad yard overpass and because of his speed, the man rammed against the side of a "dark" car, which was parked there. Tilson said he then saw the man do something at the rear door of the car, like "throw something inside," then he jumped behind the wheel and took off at a high rate of speed. Officer Tilson was able to make a U-turn and catch up with the driver, who he identified as Jack Ruby, whom he knew. <u>HSCA</u> Vol. 12, Page 15-16

Rumor had it that J.D. Tippit; the Dallas police officer shot immediately after the assassination and Jack Ruby knew each other and were good friends. In fact, there is some evidence that they had been seen together.

Witnesses at Parkland Memorial Hospital saw Jack Ruby at the hospital, immediately after the assassination.

An indication that Jack Ruby was familiar with some Cuban activities occurred the night of Nov. 22, 1963. DA Henry Wade was asked at a Dallas police station press conference about Oswald's being a Communist. According to Wade: I said, "well, now, I don't know about that, but they found some literature, I understand, dealing with Free Cuba movement. Following this—I looked up and Jack Ruby is in the audience, and he said, no, it is the Fair Play for Cuba Committee." HSCA Vol. 9, page 187

A young man in his twenties wearing plaid apparently walked up the grass knoll with what appeared to be a gun case an hour before the assassination, while Jack Ruby waited in a pickup truck. A young man wearing plaid and in his twenty's was seen behind the picket fence atop the grassy knoll at the time of the assassination. After the gunshots a police officer was seen running directly to the spot where the young twenty-year-old had been located and a commotion ensued. It would appear, based upon two eyewitnesses, that there was a young man in his twenties wearing plaid that could have been involved in events that occurred on the grassy knoll. Who that young man was and what happened to him, or where he went, following the assassination are all good questions?

FBI document dated 11/27/63, says: "On November twenty last, the Dallas Police sighted **two** unknown **men sighting in a rifle near scene of where President was later assassinated**. Rifle being sighted in at two silhouette targets.

The House Select Committee on Assassinations believed, "based on the evidence available to it, that President John

F. Kennedy was probably assassinated as a result of a conspiracy. The committee is unable to identify the other gunman or the extent of the conspiracy."

If there was a conspiracy and a great deal of care went into the planning, wouldn't you think that the planners would recognize that the risk they were taking would be greatly reduced and the probability of success would be greatly enhanced with multiple shooters and complementary scapegoats to point at? What if the second patsy, or an actual assassin, or assassins got away? How much more believable would the assassination story have been if there had been a second shooter and a second patsy to point at on the grassy knoll?

## TERRE HAUTE

I have to be honest with you and I hate to have to say this but for a very long time, up until about the late 1960's, Terre Haute had a reputation and a very colorful past. You know how the current TV commercials say, "what happens in Las Vegas, stays in Vegas," and how Vegas is now referred to as "Sin City." Well, Terre Haute was the first to officially hold the title of "Sin City." Terre Haute is roughly three and a half hours south of Chicago and was about thirty years ahead of Vegas. You name it; we had it in Terre Haute.

At one time Terre Haute had at least four major breweries and numerous distilleries.

Terre Haute's industry was so large prior to 1917 that the Terre Haute District of the IRS was consistently one of the top two districts in the nation in tax collection at $1 million or more a month. In one year, more than $22 million was collected. [10]

Not to mention a notoriously large brothel, or red-light district, which was finally eliminated by the community and law enforcement by 1973.

Rumor has it that in the 1920's Al Capone and his gang came down to Terre Haute, from Chicago quite often.

In early September 1933, John Dillinger, the prime mover in the infamous Dillinger Gang, entrusted Pearl Elliot with $27,500 in cash. The purpose of this substantial sum was to facilitate the purchase and outfitting of a secure hideout in Terre Haute. With the funds, Pearl Elliott successfully acquired a house at 2531 Fenwood Avenue.

However, the intended purpose of the hideout was thwarted.

On the morning of November 8, 1933, a raid was conducted involving approximately 150 members from the Indiana National Guard, Terre Haute Police, and Indiana State Police. Their target, 2531 Fenwood Avenue. Unfortunately, the Dillinger Gang was tipped off by someone and the gang left the night before. [11]

The Terre Haute House had a bar room in the hotel called the Marine Room. Yes, this is the very same Terre Haute House that Harry checked into in our story. I was told a story by a local that John Dillinger used to sit in a chair in the Marine Room of the Terre Haute House, right next to a door that led to all of the underground tunnels in Terre Haute. If I had to estimate, the Marine Room of the Terre Haute House was probably no more than two hundred feet from the closet where we found the signature cards from 1963. I hadn't heard this story when I recovered the records from the closet, else I would have tried to find the door to the tunnels as well. We have more fun in Terre Haute!

Dillinger along with Baby Face Nelson had a plan to rob the Dixie Flyer train in Terre Haute. Dillinger would end up being gunned down in Chicago by the FBI. Guy Banister, who ran the detective agency down in New Orleans located at 544 Camp Street and who may have played a role in the Kennedy assassination was with the FBI in Chicago at that time and was there when Dillinger was shot. You will see more on Banister later. [12]

In November 1955, the city of Terre Haute gained infamy when it was labeled "Sin City" by *Stag Magazine*, then *Amazing Detective* magazine echoed the title of "Sin City" some two months later. The negative national attention continued to escalate when, on November 29, 1957, the U.S. Treasury Department conducted a raid that exposed the largest international gambling ring ever uncovered in the United State, with Terre Haute at its core. Leading this illicit operation was Chicago mobster Leo Shaffer, renowned in the industry as "Bookie," who, along with Jules Horwick, also from Chicago, had established the gambling enterprise on the third-floor, address 671 ½ Wabash Avenue.

During the raid, a significant amount of evidence was confiscated, including sports betting cards, walkie-talkies, eight telephones, a ticker tape machine, adding machines, and telephone lists. The bets placed through this operation reached staggering amounts, with wagers as high as $25,000 covering a wide range of sports, particularly horse racing and boxing.

In August 1958, a grand jury was convened in Indianapolis, issuing 175 subpoenas to some of the most prominent gamblers across 43 states, as well as in Cuba and Canada. Among the individuals summoned were notable figures such as H.L. Hunt, an oil baron from Dallas (whose name would later surface in investigations related to the Kennedy assassination), and Zeppo Marx, the renowned comedian from the Marx Brothers, Beldon Kattleman, the owner of a Las Vegas hotel, was another significant name included in the subpoenas.

The subsequent trial, which commenced in June 1959 at the U.S. District Court in Terre Haute, spanned six weeks and presented compelling evidence regarding the syndicate's activities. Over a three-month period, the gambling ring had accepted bets totaling a staggering $3,363,100.[13]

I don't know how many Frank Sinatra movies I have seen where Frank says, "let's go to Terre Haute to party!" I think I know of at least two. And just a couple of weeks ago on TV the old original 1960 film "Ocean's Eleven," was on TV staring the Rat Pack: Frank Sinatra, Dean Martin, Sam Davis Jr., Peter Lawford, Angie Dickenson, Cesar Romero, and Joey Bishop. The character played by Cesar Romero appears to be someone with connections to the Mafia and he has been hired by the Casino owners to get the word on the street as to who might have pulled off this big heist. So, there is this scene where Romero is calling around to his contacts. The first thing out of his mouth is, "get me so-and-so in Terre Haute!"

Incidentally the Mafia don Johnny Rosselli, who plays a big role in this Kennedy assassination story, hung out with the Rat Pack, and was originally involved in bootlegging in Joseph Kennedy's crew and later with Al Capone in Chicago. You will learn more about Johnny Rosselli later in our story.

I am happy to report, that to my knowledge there is currently absolutely no connection that I am aware of, to organized crime in Terre Haute. This all finally withered away by the late sixties. Terre Haute, however, is a major educational center. There are no fewer than four major educational institutions in Terre Haute, which is remarkable for a city the size of Terre Haute. Indiana State University, Rose-Hulman Institute of Technology, Saint Mary of the Woods College, and Ivy Tech Community College of the Wabash Valley.

Indiana State University is an outstanding, high quality, educational institution with a focus on delivering real world experience to its students through its College of Business, Education, Technology, Arts and Sciences, Health and Human Performance, and Nursing school. Training tomorrow's educators, business, technological, engineering, insurance, financial, pre-med, scientific, and nursing leaders, not to mention future authors and criminology majors. As a matter of fact, at one point during this writing, the Deputy Assistant Director of the FBI's Directorate of Intelligence was an ISU graduate in Criminology.

U.S. News and World Reports currently ranks Rose-Hulman Institute of Technology number one in the nation for bachelor's and master's Degree Programs in Engineering, as determined by a survey of deans and senior faculty throughout the nation. Rose-Hulman has held this honor for consecutive years beginning in 1999 and continuing to this day.

Saint Mary of the Woods College attracts students from across the United States and from many foreign countries because of their first-class liberal arts education with more than 50 majors from which to choose, all located in a beautifully picturesque campus setting.

Ivy Tech Community College of the Wabash Valley offers outstanding technical training for today's business and industry.

Perhaps Harry came to Terre Haute to get an exceptionally great education!

I kept asking myself if there is something to all of this, then why Terre Haute?

# TERRE HAUTE AND THE CIA

April 25, 1999, four years into this study I first learned about **William King Harvey and Ray Cline**, from a five-part article in the Terre Haute Tribune-Star, which told about **two native sons of Terre Haute**, who both ended up in the CIA. The articles were by Mike McCormick. Mike McCormick as mentioned above is a local attorney and he wrote an historical column for the Terre Haute Tribune-Star. It turns out that both **Ray Cline and William King Harvey were both major players in the CIA!**

Both went to Wiley High School in Terre Haute. William King Harvey graduated from Wiley in 1931. Ray S. Cline in 1935. The last year of Wiley High School's existence was my sophomore year in high school. I had the privilege of walking the same halls and occupied the same classrooms, which makes this story all the more interesting to me. I can guarantee that the halls and classrooms at Wiley when I went there had not changed from the 1930's, except for the occasional replacement of a pencil sharpener.

When I saw that William King Harvey oversaw working with the Mafia and the anti-Castro Cubans to assassinate Castro, and there is talk that that operation, Operation Mongoose, might have flipped and gotten President Kennedy. Well, let's say it got my attention. Could this have anything to do with the rifle being left in Terre Haute, Indiana?

# WILLIAM KING HARVEY, AMERICA'S JAMES BOND

Bill Harvey was born on September 13, 1915, in Danville, Indiana, a small town about 20 miles west of Indianapolis. His father was a prominent attorney; his grandfather owned the local newspaper. [14]

Attorney Drenan R. Harvey, Bill's father, died from spinal meningitis July 25, 1916, when Bill Harvey was 10 months old. Consequently, little Bill resided with his grandparents, while his mother completed college, earning a degree at Central Normal College in Danville, and later a Ph.D. at Northwestern University with doctoral research at Oxford. [15]

Widow Sara King Harvey brought her son to Terre Haute, Indiana in 1923, when she became an associate professor of English at Indiana State Normal [now Indiana State University]. Sara Harvey was a woman very much ahead of her time. [16]

Bill Harvey was only 13 years old when he enrolled in Wiley High School and 15 when he graduated June 5, 1931. He was an outstanding student, nurturing a photographic memory and a mind that could remember minute details, about which legends later flourished. [17]

Bill earned Eagle Scott in record time. B.F. Small a Terre Haute attorney whose advice and council Bill Harvey cherished throughout his life wrote the following letter to young Bill Harvey back in 1933:

You have been given by nature **what may prove a blessing or a curse** to you, depending upon how you handle it...

a brain far above that of the average human being. At twelve and thirteen, you were registering the intelligence of twenty-one. Now, at your present age, you have a brain ability and a comprehension superior to the average man of thirty to forty... When [this] happen[s] to a man during his development, it leaves him pretty much in the situation of a Model T Ford fitted up with a twenty-four-cylinder Duisenberg engine. He is overpowered, or super-powered. Just as such a powerful engine would tear to pieces a Ford chassis, so will a powerful brain shatter the life career of an individual, unless it is throttled down and managed by the sheer will power of the individual. [18]

How prophetic this letter may have been? You may see.

Bill Harvey attended Indiana State Teacher's College in Terre Haute in 1931, now known as Indiana State University. [19]

Bill Harvey's great, great grandfather, great grandfather, grandfather, and his father graduated from Indiana University's Law School. [20]

Bill Harvey entered Indiana University, in Bloomington, Indiana in 1933, was a member of the Sigma Chi Fraternity, Phi Delta Phi, the Order of the Coif and he was the Associate Editor of the Law Review. He graduated from Indiana University, School of Law, with his Law Degree, LLB with Distinction and six years of credit [in four years] in 1937. [21]

William King Harvey and Elizabeth Howe McIntire were married on April 4, 1934.

Bill joined the ranks of practicing attorneys in Maysville, Kentucky when on February 8, 1938, he passed the Kentucky Bar Exam and became Maysville's Assistant Prosecutor. According to an FBI report dated 9/30/47, William Harvey is said to be intellectually honest and an ethical lawyer. He is intelligent and extremely honest, thoroughly patriotic, and greatly interested in Government service. He is reserved and withholds any information that he believes confidential. _FBI_ 124-90092-10021 FBI 124-90092-10027

Harvey became a member of Rotary International and the National Rifle Association. He also worked with the Boy Scouts of America and the Red Cross. His hobbies were fishing, hunting, and firearms. December 9, 1940, William King Harvey apparently had had enough of the mundane and decided to put his photographic memory and his knowledge of the law to work at the Federal Bureau of Investigation, in Elmhurst, Long Island, New York. FBI 124-90092-10021, FBI 124-90092-10027, FBI 124-90092-10021 _FBI_ 124-90092-10024

In an FBI background check, prior to the FBI hiring Bill Harvey, a local judge is recorded as saying: "Bill is a smart boy, very tactful, and knows his law pretty well, always a gentleman." The report also says of Bill, "He is levelheaded and is very much interested in guns and is quite a good marksman." The Chief of Police said: "one of the most respectable citizens, thoroughly an American boy."

William Sebold a naturalized U.S. citizen visited his native Germany in February 1939 and was coerced into becoming a spy for Germany. Sebold reported this to U.S. authorities and in May 1940, FBI agents, led by a young Bill Harvey, setup a shortwave radio station on Long Island in conjunction with William Sebold for the purpose of supplying disinformation to the Nazis. Radio contact was made with Germany and over the next 16 months over 300 misleading messages were transmitted to Nazi Germany. This operation became known as the TRAMP case, and it resulted in a rollup of a dozen or so German agents in the U.S.

Interestingly, Robert Maheu who will appear later in this story was involved in the CIA/Mafia attempts to assassinate

Castro, was a classmate of Bill Harvey at the FBI's Quantico training facility. Maheu also worked with Bill Harvey on the TRAMP case.

The FBI's Robert Lamphere says of Harvey, "I reported to Bill Harvey. Harvey was odd-looking, with protruding eyes and a pear-shaped body. His voice was like that of a bullfrog; once you'd heard it-and the intellect behind it-you never forgot it. Bill Harvey became the FBI's resident counterintelligence expert." [22]

In Bill's first six months with the FBI, he exposed 37 German agents in the U.S., recruited a German consulate staffer who delivered countless top secret German documents to the FBI and for high drama, the squads Bill oversaw successfully captured German saboteurs as they were dropped off by a German U boats off the east coast.

While on the FBI's German desk Bill worked alongside Mark Felt. Mark Felt later played a major role as "deep throat" in the Watergate affair.

I remember watching a television program, probably on the History Channel, which told how the FBI had worked with the Mafia, during World War II to catch spies in this country. Being as the Mafia at the time exerted great influence with the dockworkers on the east coast, the FBI had worked closely with the Mafia in an effort to try and gather information and catch German spies on American's docks during World War II. As a result, I wondered how far back Bill Harvey's relationship with the Mafia went?

William Harvey was with the FBI during World War II, working a substantial amount of the time in Washington on German intelligence matters; but eventually he moved over to work on the Soviet Desk. *Rockefeller Commission* 178-10002-10324

Even though the Soviets were our allies during World War II they had in place in the United States an extensive spy organization. In 1945 the FBI moved three of its best and brightest in place to confront the growing problem of Soviet spying in this country. Bill Harvey was one of only three agents in the country working to thwart the Soviet menace toward the end of World War II.

Bill Harvey was 30 years old in 1945 and had been with the bureau for five years. **He was the head of Division Five**, which was responsible for investigating communism and communists in the United States. In November of that year, Elizabeth Bentley, a former Soviet courier, came forward to the FBI and admitted being a part of a Soviet spy ring operating in the U.S. Harvey took the lead in working with Bentley to identify some 51 important individuals in the U.S. who were spying for the Soviet Union. A number of important individuals were employed by the Federal Government, including Alger Hiss. [23]

This was a major breakthrough for the FBI's effort to combat Soviet espionage. Harvey's work in this case earned him a reputation as one of the FBI's top counterintelligence experts.

Congressman **Richard Nixon** was named to the House Un-American Activities Committee in 1946 and became nationally known as a result of his participation in the **Alger Hiss** case. As a result, in 1950, Alger Hiss was convicted of perjury.

Surely Bill Harvey played a role in the Alger Hiss case and became acquainted with Richard Nixon early on as a result. Nixon surely would have been in communication with Harvey, as it appears that William Harvey would have been one of the early experts on the matter.

While we are discussing Richard Nixon in this timeframe there is an FBI memo in the national archives dated November 24, 1947, which states: "It is my sworn statement that one Jack Rubenstein of Chicago noted as a potential witness for hearings of the House Committee on Un-American Activities is performing information functions for the staff of Congressman Richard M. Nixon. It is requested Rubenstein not be called for open testimony in those aforementioned hearings." Jack Ruby worked for Richard Nixon in 1947 [as an informant]!

Bill Harvey's FBI efficiency reports contain comments such as: "I am impressed with the amount of both intelligent research and file review and logical thinking and conclusions…a manifestation of real supervision." Another report says of Bill Harvey: "vigorous, forceful and aggressive…definitely outstanding as to intelligence, ability and application…One of the best supervisors at the Seat of Government."

In 1947, President Harry S. Truman determined that it was in the best interest of the United States of America to form an independent civilian intelligence agency, focused on foreign intelligence gathering and analysis, rather than expanding the FBI's mandate or extending the life of the military's wartime intelligence organization the OSS.

The official story was that on July 15, 1947, at 10:00 am, Bill Harvey's wife Libby called the FBI to report that Bill was missing and hadn't come home that night. Turned out that a few FBI agents, including Bill Harvey, had gotten together that night to have a few beers. As told by the FBI agent Robert Lamphere, "Harvey had about two cans of beer." As you will see later in this story two cans of beer was well within Bill Harvey's enormous capacity for alcohol consumption. Being as Libby had gotten the FBI all excited and stirred up with her phone call, Bill had to explain what had happened. According to Bill, because of a tremendous rainstorm his car hit a large mud puddle on his way home that night and the engine flooded. He couldn't get the car to restart, so he ended up falling asleep in the car as he waited. Supposedly by the time he arrived home, it was too late, the damage was already done by Libby's phone call to the FBI.

The official story line continues that J. Edgar Hoover did not tolerate agents who didn't conduct themselves in a certain manner and on July 23, 1947, Hoover issued a memo recommending that his star agent be transferred to Indianapolis. Harvey was reportedly crushed by this decision, and he submitted his resignation to the FBI. In his resignation letter, Harvey was careful not to burn any bridges and he expressed his gratitude for the opportunities that he had been given during his time at the FBI. Bill Harvey then immediately applied and was accepted by the newly created Central Intelligence Group (CIG), which later became the CIA. Bill Harvey's performance reviews with the FBI up to this point were all excellent. [24]

The real story of how Bill Harvey left the FBI and went to work for the CIA: According to William R. Corson, later a counterespionage colleague of Harvey's, the real story was very different. **"Bill Harvey was Hoover's mole in the CIA. He started off as a plant, or a spy for the FBI."** (Footnote in *"The Secret History of the CIA"* from interview with W. Corson on June 4, 1990) Hoover knew that Harvey would not be accepted in the CIA unless he had left the FBI, its rival, under a cloud. [25]

So, Harvey started out as Hoover's eyes and ears in CIG, the future CIA. Bill Harvey was just one of the many J. Edgar Hoover spies that left the FBI and went to work for the CIA.

J. Edgar Hoover was bound and determined not to help

this new competing intelligence organization, the CIA, by providing any of its intelligence information. But Hoover ended up providing the next best thing, or perhaps the best thing, William King Harvey, and his photographic memory, capable of recounting the dates, times, and minutest of details concerning any operation. FBI agent Robert Lamphere is quoted as having said, "That was too bad, because his drive and intelligence were the FBI's loss."

At the time of Bill's departure from the FBI his records show that he had ninety-seven days of unused vacation time. His last review at the FBI states that he had done "a tremendous amount of voluntary overtime." It said Bill had "an excellent knowledge of Russian espionage and Communist activities. His grasp of the details of Russian espionage operations in this country was a revelation... Agents are so enthused... It is hoped that eventually it will be possible to give [Bill's course on Soviet espionage] to every Special FBI Agent who is investigating Communist and Russian matters."

Apparently the newly formed Central Intelligence Group (CIG) was as anxious to get Bill Harvey, as Hoover was to get Bill in the CIG, because we have this CIG document dated 29 August 1947. It shows a listing of seventeen candidates that CIG is considering hiring, upon which they ask the Bureau to perform background checks, prior to hiring. The letter states: "It is requested that the investigation concerning the person whose name is marked "P" above be handled on a priority basis." There is only one name marked with a "P," that was Harvey, William K. *CIG Letter* Dated 29 August 1947.

The FBI apparently checked out applicants from the United States for the (CIG). On an FBI document concerning Bill Harvey there are these instructions: "This case is to be assigned IMMEDIATELY and reports of the complete investigation must be submitted AIRMAIL, SPECIAL

DELIVERY, by September 30, 1947. *FBI* 124-90092-10024

A CIA Personal History report dated 8/25/47 shows that Bill Harvey was considered a specialist in counter-intelligence operations, analysis, and evaluation and his immediate supervisor at the FBI had been none other than the Director himself, J. Edgar Hoover. *FBI* 124-90092-10021

When he transitioned from the FBI to the CIA, he was 31 years old, 6 feet tall, and weighed 185 pounds, had blonde hair, green eyes, and sported a mustache. *FBI* 124-90092-10021

In the FBI report on Bill Harvey dated October 10, 1947, a Mr. Thurston of the then Central Intelligence Group, advised he has been acquainted with William Harvey for the past six years. He stated that he believes the applicant to be a man of good character and habits. The applicant impressed him as being very intelligent and industrious, whom he could recommend most heartily. There is no question about the applicant's loyalty. *FBI* 124-90092-10026

Mr. Galliher, applicant's neighbor, recommended Bill Harvey based upon his intelligence and his apparent zeal for his work. He stated that there was no doubt as to the applicant's loyalty. The only derogatory information he could offer would be that he thought the applicant might be having an affair with a woman [So I guess Mr. Galliher's has no doubt about Bill's loyalty to his country but has some doubts about his loyalty to his wife]. He stated that his reason for believing this was that the applicant had on many occasions, over the past three or four years, told him that he had worked late at night. He stated that while he knew the FBI employed the applicant, he did not believe that he was working the late hours, which he claims to have worked. Mr. Galliher stated that he had presumed from this that the applicant must be involved in some situation, which he did not desire to become known. _FBI_ 124-90092-10026

Bill Harvey departed the tightly regulated environment of the FBI in favor of the more relaxed atmosphere offered by the CIA. Known for his ability to handle copious amounts of alcohol, it was not uncommon and even expected, for Bill Harvey to indulge in three-martini lunches while agents gathered to discuss recent events and operations. Such behavior, which would have been deemed unacceptable in the highly regimented FBI, was embraced in the CIA. This newfound freedom and autonomy resonated well with Harvey. Unlike the era of J. Edgar Hoover's FBI, the CIA fostered an environment that encouraged critical thinking, innovation and imagination-traits the Bill Harvey possessed in abundance.

Harvey, however, soon noticed a profound difference among his CIA colleagues: they hailed from wealthier backgrounds and belonged to a higher strata of society. As he transitioned from a world populated by law enforcement officers and local attorneys, he found himself entering an organization comprised of academics and Wall Street lawyers. [26]

Kim Philby describes the situation this way in his autobiography: "The men of the FBI, with hardly an exception, were proud of having sprung from the grass roots... They were therefore whisky drinkers, with beer for light refreshment. By contrast the CIA men flaunted cosmopolitan postures and served Burgundy above room temperature. It points to a deep social cleavage between the two organizations." [27]

All sources agree, at this time in history, the CIA was run by a group who mostly sprang from privileged families and the self-defined socially elite, more commonly referred to as the "Ivy Leaguers." Bill Harvey referred to this group as the "Fifth Avenue Cowboys." Bill Harvey's father had been a small-town lawyer in Indiana, as had his grandfather and great grandfather. Bill Harvey seemed to detest their elitism. He disliked the Ivy Leaguers in the Agency.

The CIA's Paul Garbler observed that Bill Harvey's behavior changed dramatically when he went to work for the CIA. "He seemed to do everything to accentuate the background differences between himself and other CIA officers."

Faced with the challenge of assimilating into the Ivy League milieu, Harvey opted to distinguish himself rather than conform to the Ivy Leaguers' norms. Proud of his background as a cop, he embraced his law enforcement identity. Driven by a deep sense of confidence in his own abilities and an impatience to make a tangible impact in the fight against communism, his ambition for reaching the top stemmed from a desire to be unencumbered in his mission rather than seeking personal power. He projected an aggressive attitude, driven by an unwavering determination to aggressively safeguard America from the perils of the world.

Harvey's foundation and training as a cop shaped his approach. He was acutely aware of the ruthless, underhanded tactics used by the KGB, seeing himself as the law enforcement agent tasked with apprehending criminals. Art Thurston of the CIA described Bill Harvey as, "the most highly trained, most professional man available for counterintelligence work. Harvey did not go about establishing his presence meekly. Harvey established his presence with unwavering confidence, refusing to be meek or submissive."

There was no doubting the remarkable capabilities of Harvey's mind. He possessed a philosophical outlook admired by his CIA peers, characterized as the "wider view" that was complemented by an extraordinary memory.

During a conversation about the Bentley case, Richard Helms, a rising star within the CIA, was astounded as Harvey effortlessly recounted intricate details without relying on any notes. It was a remarkable tour de force that left Helms pondering why J. Edgar Hoover had allowed Harvey to depart from the FBI. [28]

Bill Harvey's daughter says, "He used to recite poems to me for hours! It was amazing and it wasn't just his memory, it was the way he delivered his poems. His voice, the tone quality, the whole articulation. At times it could be the most booming voice in the whole world, and at other times he was so quiet you could hardly hear him. But it was one that was hypnotizing, is the way I would describe it. [29]

In a TV Documentary entitled "Indiana's James Bond," Bill Corson, an Intelligence Analyst who had worked with Bill responded to these charges that Harvey didn't fit in with the social elite in the CIA saying with a great deal of emotion, "Bill Harvey could hold his own intellectually with anybody. And so, in an attempt [by Harvey's CIA contemporaries] to not feel inferior, because they really where, they had to play like they were socially superior." [30]

Not a social animal or overly diplomatic Bill Harvey tended to tell it like it was. Bill had little patience for bureaucracy. He had an urgency to get things done and the less encumbrance the better.

His personal mannerisms again seemed designed to differentiate himself and to place emphasis on his pride in being a middle class American, a Midwesterner, and a product of the FBI. Harvey was an avid gun collector and a proficient marksman. Bill Harvey, from the beginning, always carried two handguns, one was always tucked into the waistband in the back of his trousers. Harvey was known for clicking the lid of his Zippo lighter, or spinning the chamber on his pistol, paring his nails with a hunting knife, and incorporating very uncouth and colorful language, even in mixed company, while engaged in a conversation. [31]

To many in the CIA, Bill Harvey embodied and personified the appropriate spirit of the CIA; he was determined, inspired and inspiring, persevering, and a sleep-deprived taskmaster. To others, his mannerisms, especially to the OSS veterans who had faced true danger during the war, well they were a little put off by Harvey's leveling one of his .45s at co-worker's foreheads, smiling, and clicking off the safety. [32]

Bill Harvey detested publicity. No one was better at keeping his cards close to his chest, avoiding being photographed and keeping operations off of paper and undocumented. While in the FBI he had identified Soviet Spies in the OSS and various important agencies in the U.S. As a result, he distrusted many in the upper class, many of whom seemed to support communism as trendy, or in their mind thought it socially responsible. Based upon his experience, Harvey was naturally guarded and suspicious of the privileged upper class. [33]

The newly formed CIA immediately put Bill Harvey in charge of the counterintelligence group known as Section C. The choice was obvious, Bill Harvey had been one of only three agents in the FBI, or in the whole country for that matter, who had had any experience going up against Soviet espionage operations.

In his new position, Bill Harvey now had the ability to take the fight to those who wished to rule our world. CIA personnel quickly noticed Bill Harvey's high energy level, enthusiasm, and dedication to his work. It was infectious.

In summary, Bill Harvey's work ethic amazed everyone, late nights, cigarettes, and very long hours were the norm. Words that are used to describe Bill Harvey: never in doubt of his own abilities, a great analytical capacity, worked eighteen-hour days, most highly trained, most professional man we had, not a social animal, inclined to argue points based upon operational effects with less regard to the political fallout and a disdain for bureaucracy or bureaucratic delay, not meek and could be deliberately loud and outspoken, could see the wider vision, was aggressively protective of the United States.

What is interesting about this Ivy League vs. Midwestern Big Ten distinction is that William King Harvey and Ray Cline both have their roots going back to Terre Haute, Indiana and even the same high school. Harvey graduated from Wiley High School in June of 1931 and then attended Indiana University where he earned a law degree. Ray Cline graduated from Wiley in June of 1935, then graduated from Harvard University in 1939, then studied at Oxford and received his PhD in 1949 from Harvard. Mike McCormick told this author that he first told C.G. Harvey, Bill Harvey's second wife, that Bill Harvey and Ray Cline were from the same hometown and had attended the same high school, only at different times. C.G. Harvey told Mike McCormick that, "she knew Ray Cline, but that she was not aware as to whether Bill Harvey ever knew that Ray Cline was from Terre Haute."

If Bill Harvey had known about Cline, perhaps this would have changed Bill's perception as to where some Ivy Leaguers may have come from. I suspect however that Harvey probably made it his business to know everything he could about all his fellow spies and perhaps Harvey just didn't care for an elitist, clubbish, cliché-ish attitude.

Judging from an FBI Memorandum, Bill Harvey was one of the early liaisons between CIA and the FBI, up until Feb. 2, 1951. _National Archives_ 124-90092-10014

Bill Harvey lived in Washington D.C. and Alexandria, Virginia 1947 – 1952. *CIA* 104-10106-10578

# JAMES JESUS ANGLETON

Bill Harvey's first exposure to James Jesus Angleton came when they both were assigned to the CIA's counterintelligence division. And yes "Jesus" was apparently pronounced "Jesus" as in "Jesus Christ."

James Jesus Angleton was born in Boise, Idaho. His family then moved to Dayton, Ohio where his father, Hugh Angleton worked for the National Cash Register Company (NCR). When Jim was age 14 Hugh Angleton moved the family to Milan, Italy where he owned and ran the NCR franchise for all of Italy.

In 1938, Jim Angleton attended Yale. He was a poor student. In his junior and senior year of college he managed to achieve two F's, four D's, and dropped out of a course in his major, which was English. He ended up in the bottom 25% of his class. Angleton joined Skull and Bones at Yale. Angleton then moved on to Harvard Law. While at Harvard he met and married Cicely D'Autremont. Shortly thereafter the Japanese attacked Pearl Harbor and the U.S. entered World War II. James Jesus Angleton was consequently drafted by the Army. [34]

The Office of Strategic Services (OSS) was the United States intelligence agency during World War II. **Allen Dulles**, a future Director of the CIA, served in the OSS during the war and was posted in Bern, Switzerland.

Back in the 1930s, Allen Dulles first met Hugh Angleton, the father of James Angleton, while Dulles was on a business trip to Italy. Hugh Angleton, in addition to running the NCR franchise in Italy, became a longtime business agent for Allen Dulles in Italy. [35]

During the war Hugh Angleton offered his services to the OSS and became the second in command to the OSS commander in Italy.

Jim Angleton always asserted that it was his decision to enlist, during the summer of 1943, in military intelligence during the war. Military Intelligence went under the moniker of the Office of Strategic Services, the OSS. However, an OSS memo in 1943 reveals that Angleton's dad pulled some strings to get Jim out of the regular Army and into the OSS. I suspect that Allen Dulles, longtime friend, and business associate of Hugh Angleton, also helped to get James Jesus Angleton into the OSS. [36]

The OSS dispatched Jim Angleton to London as his initial assignment to acquire knowledge and expertise in the field of counterintelligence. In this endeavor he received instruction from **Harold "Kim" Philby**, a member of the British intelligence service known as MI6. The training of American operatives by their British counterparts was deemed necessary due to the British intelligence's extensive experience and prowess in the realm of counterintelligence, surpassing that of the United States at that time.

Following his training, Angleton was subsequently deployed to Rome, Italy, where he assumed the role of commanding officer for the OSS's counterintelligence operations. Consequently, both father and son ended up serving in the OSS in Italy. [37]

During his time in Italy, Jim Angleton forged remarkable and highly productive alliances with various influential entities. He established an exceptional working rapport with the Italian Mafia, the Roman Catholic Church and the Jewish operation dedicated to facilitating the escape of persecuted Jews seeking refuge in Palestine. Notably, Angleton engaged in intelligence exchanges with the Vatican, fostering a mutually beneficial relationship. Among Angleton's network of agents operating in Italy was Monsignor Giovanni Montini, who would later assume the title of Pope Paul VI. This alone attests to Angleton's extensive connections and influence that he managed to build at this time. [38]

**James Angleton** worked closely with **Allen Dulles** during World War II and both were closely associated with the British spy, **Kim Philby**.

Right from the outset, Jim Angleton harbored a deep-seated suspicion towards everyone. Each morning, his routine involved crawling on his hands and knees throughout his office to meticulously inspect for any potential listening devices or surveillance equipment. Angleton possessed a commanding presence that easily dominated and intimidated those who worked under him. Sitting across from him on a sofa, his desk towered over you, he would peer down through a labyrinth of papers, leaving you with an overwhelming sense of his authority.

Angleton tolerated no rivals, whether they were real or imagined. His mind was often described as brilliant and intricate, constantly delving into deeper meanings. He adamantly refused to concede any weakness in his perception and firmly believed he was always right. Unyielding and uncompromising, he displayed an unwavering confidence in his unorthodox conclusions, leading some to speculate that he must have some information that others didn't.

Despite his soft-spoken voice and reserved demeanor, Angleton had a commanding presence in conversations. He projected an aura of complexity, suspicion, secrecy, confidence, paranoia and conspiratorial thinking. One of his notable achievements was establishing a bond of trust with the newly formed state of Israel, which provided valuable information through emigrants from behind the Iron Curtain.

Insomnia plagued Angleton for most of his life. He would spend hours into the night reading poetry and chain-smoking. During the war and throughout his career, he maintained a slender figure, standing 6 feet 1 inch and weighing a mere 150 pounds. Among his agents, he acquired the nickname "the Poet" or "the Cadaver." Angleton's attire consisted of dark formal suits, and an old-fashioned black homburg hat and thick horn-rimmed glasses. Over time, he developed a stooped and twisted posture, as if shaped by the convolutions and intrigues of his profession. It seemed as if he was perpetually leaned down to either whisper or receive some profound secret. His physical form appeared to mirror his surname, Angleton.

A fellow OSS member said, "I considered [Jim Angleton] extremely brilliant but a little strange. He had a strange genius, full of impossible ideas, colossal ideas." This Ivy League aesthete "struck us right off the bat as weird. The guy was just in another world."

Angleton loved crafting fishing lures and fly-fishing, poetry, and raising rare orchids. Numerous authors, before me, offer up this analogy: Fly-fishing and catching spies are pretty much the same, requiring patience and study, coaxing forth the secret life that lurks beneath the surface.

After the war, Angleton chose to remain in Italy, delaying his return to his wife and young son by two years. In July 1948 he, along with his wife and son, relocated to Washington, D.C., to join the newly established Central Intelligence Agency (CIA). Angleton assumed a senior position at the CIA as the top aide to the director of the Office of Special Operations (OSO), which had responsibility for espionage and counterespionage. Angleton's role involved overseeing special studies across various countries, as his desk served as the clearinghouse for all OSS cables and communications with field operatives throughout the world. [39]

William King Harvey came over to CIG from the FBI at about the same time James Jesus Angleton merged into this new organization from having served in the OSS. Angleton was a natural at counterespionage.

Harvey and Angleton initially clashed, emerging as direct competitors and exact opposites. Their rivalry was intense and engendered a true battle within the CIA. A CIA officer aptly described their dynamic, stating, "Harvey and Angleton were direct competitors, I mean direct competitors-from the word go. We had a real fight going between Harvey and Angleton." The two men presented a stark contrast in terms of physical appearance, cultural backgrounds, intellectual approaches, and professional styles.

Harvey, stocky in build and affectionately nicknamed "the Pear," had a military gait, very stiff backed. On the other hand, Angleton, known as "the Cadaver," "the Poet," and code-named Mother, ambled along in a contemplative manner, often slumped over. Standing side by side, they resembled a mismatch akin to Mutt and Jeff. Harvey hailed from a small midwestern town, while Angleton was the son of an expatriate. Harvey had a background rooted in the Big Ten, while Angleton represented the Ivy League. Harvey's education in espionage was obtained through the highly regimented FBI, while Angleton honed his skills in the more freewheeling atmosphere of the OSS. Harvey had a passion for collecting firearms, while Angleton crafted fishing lures. Harvey embodied the archetype of a cop, while Angleton embraced his role as a spy. These two seasoned individuals converged to become an integral component of the postwar espionage apparatus at the CIA-the Poet and the Pear.

Despite their contrasting traits, Harvey and Angleton eventually developed a fondness for each other. Angleton expressed his admiration for Harvey, stating to author Joseph Trento, "Harvey was full of bravado…but he had an exceptional mind. I think what I most remember about him was his ability to remember details of cases he had worked on. My first months at the CIA were spent listening to Bill Harvey recite relevant cases he had worked on for the FBI… Hoover wouldn't give us anything back in those days…We had Bill, and that was just as good." [40]

From Bill Harvey's point of view, Angleton had amassed a considerable amount of counterespionage experience and organizational and personal connections, while serving in the OSS.

In the beginning Bill Harvey was appointed the head of Staff C, what had been the OSS's counterespionage wing or counterintelligence (CI) and Jim Angleton reported to Bill Harvey.

It was **Angleton's friendship with Kim Philby though that would come to concern Bill Harvey the most**.

During the war in London in 1942, Kim Philby had the opportunity to meet and entertain Allen Dulles and Richard Helms, both of whom were captivated by Philby's charm and influential connections. It was during this period the Philby began imparting his knowledge of counterintelligence to Jim Angleton, forging a deep bond between them. From 1949 to 1951, British intelligence Agent Kim Philby found himself stationed in Washington D.C. as a liaison to the FBI and the CIA. During this time, Philby and Angleton became exceedingly close friends.

CIA security records provide evidence of the frequent

interactions between Philby and Angleton. Philby would visit Angleton's office multiple times a week and the two would have lunch almost every week. As a result, Philby enjoyed access to the CIA's most highly classified information through his association with Angleton. Philby reflected on their relationship, writing, "The driving force in the new organization at the time was Jim Angleton, who has earned my utmost respect. We developed a regular habit of meeting for lunch once a week." [41]

In his book "The FBI-KGB War," Robert Lamphere, recounts a dinner party held at Kim Philby's residence in Washington DC in January 1951. Lamphere describes a gathering of approximately twenty-five to thirty individuals, comprising both FBI and CIA personnel. Among the attendees were Bill and Libby Harvey, as well as James Jesus Angleton. While Lamphere had heard much about Angleton, this occasion marked their first personal encounter. According to Lamphere, Angleton embodied the essence of the CIA, boasting an extensive network of contacts within intelligence services worldwide. Lamphere found Angleton to be tall, slender, sharp-tongued, intelligent, reserved and yet charming.

Lamphere noted that during the party, the FBI and CIA groups tended to engage in separate conversations, mingling within their respective circles. He found the discussions among the CIA personnel to be primarily speculative and detached from reality, focusing on far-reaching ideas that were not grounded in practicality.

Lamphere felt more at ease conversing with Bill Harvey, an old friend from his FBI days who had of course transitioned over to the CIA. Harvey provided insights into Angleton, describing him as highly intelligent, a rising star with a background at Yale University and the OSS. However, Harvey's portrayal of Angleton contained some elements that were less than flattering. Libby Harvey joined their conversation.

After dinner, Guy Burgess, a British embassy employee, living with the Philbys, returned home in an inebriated state. Burgess, known for his flamboyant homosexuality and heavy drinking, approached Libby Harvey and made a remark about recognizing her face from his doodles. At Libby's urging, Burgess proceeded to draw a caricature of her legs spread. Bill Harvey reacted by attempting to physically confront Burgess and had to be restrained. Angleton intervened, taking Bill for a walk around the block to help calm him down. Shortly thereafter, the party came to an end.

This incident had a significant impact. Bill Harvey harbored no affinity for the privileged upper class and the close friendship between Philby and Burgess did not sit well with him. Harvey driven by his determination, delved into Philby's and Burgess's past, uncovering information that indicated Philby's first wife had professed communist beliefs and that Philby had maintained connections with Soviet spies during World War II. These discoveries prompted Harvey to piece together a growing puzzle. [42]

**Harvey's first major known CIA contribution came in 1951 from suspecting and exposing a major Soviet spy named Kim Philby.** Philby was British and worked for British Intelligence. Philby had major access to American and British Intelligence and was well known and was liked by many in the CIA. Harvey was the only one who managed to assemble the pieces of the puzzle in order to finger Kim Philby.

Bill Harvey's encyclopedic memory missed nothing and spared no one. It would be Harvey who risked his career on hints that Philby was unreliable. [43]

The United States Government threw Kim Philby, out of the

country, declaring him persona non grata.

CIA Director Allen Dulles would later say that Kim Philby was "the best spy the Russians ever had."

No one was closer to Philby than Angleton, yet Bill Harvey was the one who nailed Philby, bringing about an ever-increasing competition between Angleton and Harvey.

All CIA personnel who had any exposure to Philby were told to submit a report describing their interactions with Philby. At the bottom of Angleton's report Harvey wrote: "What is the rest of this story? OSOD (Oh Shit Oh Damn)."

Harvey found it hard to believe that Angleton did not know what Philby was up to. In a conversation with a colleague, Harvey voiced his suspicion that there might have been a homosexual relationship between Angleton and Philby. At a certain point, Harvey went as far as accusing Angleton of being a Soviet spy. The deep animosity between the two men eventually erupted into a public confrontation. Harvey directly confronted Angleton, accusing him of protecting Philby. Although a lie-detector test supported Angleton's innocence, Angleton's ego suffered a significant blow. One officer said: "Harvey could take credit, and **I think Angleton held a grudge against Harvey because of it**." [44]

Harvey may have been right about Philby's and Angleton's relationship. Kim Philby would later admit, while being interrogated in May of 1951, that he and Guy Burgess were occasional lovers.

The possibility of Angleton being involved in a homosexual relationship with Philby is serious because many times information like this, especially back then, would be used by the Soviets to blackmail individuals into working for the dark side. Individuals involved in counterintelligence were top priority targets for the Soviets. If there had been a relationship between Philby and Angleton to be exploited you can bet the Soviets would have known about it, via Philby, and the Soviets may well have even encouraged Philby to bring this relationship into being, for the very real purpose of blackmail. Angleton would have been most definitely at risk and open for blackmail by the Soviets.

As it turns out, Angleton had the opportunity to blow the whistle on Philby a full year before Harvey but failed to do so. An Israeli named Teddy Kollek has told the following story: he was at CIA headquarters in September 1950, on his way to Angleton's office, when he spied Kim Philby walking down the hallway. Kollek immediately told Angleton of Philby's associations and numerous communist connections. Angleton never said a word to anyone![45]

So here we have Angleton being told that Kim Philby was a communist spy nearly a year before Bill Harvey pieced it together. I think this raises serious questions about James Jesus Angleton's loyalty.

About his run in with Bill Harvey, Kim Philby said on page 166 in his book *My Silent War*, which wasn't published until years later in 1968: "I may be accused here of introducing a cheap note. Admitted. But [Harvey] played a very cheap trick on me, and **I do not like letting provocation go unpunished**." This statement by Philby: "I do not like letting provocation go unpunished," sounds like a threat, or given the date of the book, perhaps a claim of retaliation. Please keep Philby's threat, that was aimed at Bill Harvey, in mind as we proceed through events.

Kim Philby appears very bitter towards Bill Harvey for plunging him into near financial ruin and for seriously damaging, if not ending, his intelligence career. Philby writes: "The Chief told me that he had received a strong letter from Bedell Smith [then Director of the CIA] the terms of which precluded any possibility of my returning to Washington. I learned later that the letter had been drafted in great part by William King Harvey, whose wife Burgess had bitterly insulted during a convivial party at my house. I had apologized handsomely for his [Burgess's] behavior, and the apology had apparently been accepted. It was therefore difficult to understand Harvey's retrospective exercise in spite. From Harvey, of all people! After this, it was almost a formality when the Chief called me and told me, with obvious distress, that he would have to ask for my resignation." [46]

In suddenly going from being "a major behind the scenes player" on the world's stage to a "washed up has been," Philby experienced bouts of deep depression. Gone was the excitement, the status, and his importance. Judging from Philby's writing, **Philby never forgave Bill Harvey for pointing the finger at him.** Philby would never play a "major behind the scenes" role again, <u>**or would he**</u>?

Over the next eleven years the British and the Americans were never able to prove beyond a reasonable doubt the charges made by Bill Harvey. Kim Philby's intelligence career, however, was severely damaged, relegating him to relatively low-level functionary for British intelligence. In January of 1963 leading up to the assassination of President Kennedy in November of 1963, Philby confirmed that he was a Soviet spy when he left his low-level position for British intelligence in Beirut, only to reappear in Moscow having defected to the Soviet Union.

Harvey should have been a hero at headquarters at the time he exposed Kim Philby, he was not. His dogged efforts to expose Philby, instead of advancing his CIA career, crippled it. The CIA hierarchy was a tight-knit organization based on friendship and the old boy network. **Harvey had gotten a member of the club.** [47]

For the longest time my impression from reading books was that Kim Philby's father Harry St John Bridger Philby (Jack Philby) was simply a British Civil Servant in India. Well, he was initially until he was dismissed for sexual misconduct and then he went to work for the British secret service, MI6. Turns out Harry St. John Bridger Philby, Jack Philby, Kim Philby's dad, was the most influential person in the modern history of the Middle East, the renegade British intelligence agent who plucked an obscure Arab leader out of the desert to make him the king of Saudi Arabia. Ibn Saud was very much Jack Philby's creation.

In 1915, Jack Philby moved to Baghdad and began organizing the Arab Revolt against the Ottoman Turks. Jack Philby and Lawrence of Arabia were contemporaries in the Middle East, both were British, and both were working with the various Arab sects. Philby stole information from British intelligence files and insured military victory for the House of Saud against Arab leaders supported by the British government. Jack Philby engineered Saudi control over the holiest shrines of the Moslem world [and eventual its vast oil reserves].

Jack Philby was a very colorful character. A renegade British intelligence agent, a rebel, an egotist, an adrenaline junkie, a manic depressive, anti-Semitic, a womanizer, a chameleon, a Socialist, an explorer, and like his contemporary and acquaintance T. E. Lawrence (Lawrence of Arabia) they both "went native." Lawrence of Arabia and the British government favored one side of the power struggle being waged in the area, Philby being the renegade that he was decided to favor the other side. Ibn Saud's side won with the help of Jack Philby and the intelligence information that he provided.

Allen Dulles's uncle was Robert Lansing. Robert Lansing had

been the U.S. Secretary of State and he founded the State Department's first intelligence unit. Upon graduation from college, Allen Dulles went to work for the State Department in Europe during the First World War. Following the war in 1921, Allen Dulles worked for approximately five years for the State Department as chief of the Near East Division and was stationed in Istanbul running a spy network for the State Department in the Middle East when he meets the British spy Jack Philby. Philby helped Dulles to jump-start his career by feeding him timely information.

Jack Philby and Ibn Saud betrayed the British Empire and made the American oil companies the economic masters of the region. The man who helped them do it was **Allen Dulles**, an American spy who had befriended Philby while he was coordinating American intelligence gathering in the Middle East in the first half of the 1920s. [48]

Knowing about Jack Philby's and Allen Dulles's longstanding relationship and the power position Jack Philby had in the world, goes a long way in explaining why it has been said that Kim Philby was seen by Allen Dulles and the Ivy Leaguers in the CIA as a member of the club, a member of the old boy network, and explains why when William King Harvey pointed the finger at Kim Philby, Allen Dulles passed word to British intelligence that Kim Philby was okay and that perhaps Bill Harvey was just getting a little carried away. Not only was Bill Harvey's accusation embarrassing to James Jesus Angleton, an extremely close friend of Kim Philby, and perhaps a homosexual lover, it also had to have been very embarrassing to Allen Dulles, given his close friendship with Kim's dad, Jack Philby.

Much later on September 30, 1960, while on a visit to see his son Kim in Beirut, Jack Philby sat up in bed and exclaim to his son at bedside, "God, I'm bored," and then he died.

No wonder Bill Harvey was not popular with the good old boys and the soon to be Director of the CIA, Allen Dulles.

**In fact, to the CIA leadership, Philby was still a member of the club**, whereas Harvey never would be. The CIA's William Corson explains, "They wanted Bill out of headquarters, and he knew it. That's why he took [the assignment in] Berlin." [49]

The other message sent by the Harvey/Philby Affair was that Bill Harvey was not a guy that you would want to mess with. Harvey was one best kept on your good side; else he was capable of tenaciously and doggedly digging and probing until he had something. I think this is a lesson, or message, that Jim Angleton received loud and clear as later in there interactions back in the states, Harvey and Angleton seemed to walk side by side, with mutual respect and shared confidence, in lock step together. I think Angleton might have been practicing, "keep your friends close and your [potential] enemies closer," especially if you are spying for the Soviets.

In a CIA study conducted in 1974, Clare Edward Petty, an officer at the agency, reached the unsettling conclusion, that his superior, James Jesus Angleton, was a Soviet agent. This revelation echoed the suspicions harbored by William King Harvey, who had originally suspected that Kim Philby was a Soviet spy back in 1951. [50]

Bill Harvey demonstrated throughout his career a certain dislike for bureaucracy and politics. He was a straight shooter who did not hesitate to tell it like it was. He was a press forward, get things done kind of a guy, fully capable of making complex decisions quickly. He was renowned for his ability to keep secrets and information close. A post in Germany offered him an opportunity to run his own show. Running his own show was a tendency Bill seemed to demonstrate throughout his career.

Bill Harvey was proud of his Hoosier heartland, Indiana background, and proud of his family and their many achievements. He would bow down to no one. Rather than trying to conform or bend to the ways of the well bread elite of the CIA, Harvey seems determined to play the role of street wise tough guy through the use of colorful language and the open display of his sidearms. Harvey was confident, blunt, and outspoken.

Alex MacMillian is quoted in the book *Flawed Patriot,* as saying: "He [Harvey] wanted to get up there to the top [of the CIA] and fix everybody. I'm sure he had no heroes [in the higher echelons]."

Bill Harvey appears to be driven to climb to the top of the CIA, not based on ego, but simply because there would be less frustration and encumbrances on his abilities to fight and win against the enemy. Bill was a guy who believed in getting things done, even if it meant bending the rules a little bit. Bill Harvey would become a legendary spy.

In the beginning James Jesus Angleton was under Bill Harvey who was the head of Staff C (what had been the OSS's counterespionage wing), but over time Angleton proved to have better connections and was more adept at politics and Bill Harvey's influence with the Ivy Leaguers began to decline. Bill Harvey left for Germany; James Angleton moved up to what had been Bill Harvey's position as the head of Counterintelligence.

Germany was where the action was. Where East met West. Said one intelligence officer: "Germany was the biggest show we had, and Berlin was probably the most important base the Agency had," outside of CIA Headquarters.

Berlin was a turbulent and dynamic setting. After the

conclusion of World War II, the city was divided into four zones under the control of the Americans, British, French and Russians. Within this divided landscape, the Berlin Police Department recorded a staggering 229 confirmed kidnappings and 328 attempted kidnappings between 1945 and 1961. Amidst this atmosphere, Bill Harvey found his niche and excelled. Berlin had become the undeniable hub for espionage, attracting spies from all corners of the globe. [51]

Harvey became the head of the CIA's operation in Berlin; Angleton took over as the head of Counterintelligence. Angleton projected an image of increased paranoia over the years in his supposed hunt for spies suspected of having infiltrated the CIA. Some would argue that Angleton's witch-hunts for Soviet spies where a way of hobbling and demoralizing the effectiveness of the CIA. Intended or not Angleton's paranoia and numerous accusations against others in the CIA did eventually and effectively bring the CIA to its knees. Angleton became the most feared man in the CIA. Once accused by Angleton, your career at the CIA was pretty much over.

If by no other means than Kim Philby, the Soviets knew absolutely everything there was to know about James Jesus Angleton. The heads of Counterintelligence organizations worldwide were high priority targets for the Soviets.

Harvey heeded the call to glory. Angleton followed the path to power. Harvey was heading for the front; Angleton broadened his base in Counterintelligence until he had the most powerful and impregnable fiefdom in the secret realm. If Harvey was the point man for the secret war, Angleton was the paper man, building his counterintelligence staff and its file and capabilities into a more menacing force than Harvey's entire armory of guns. [52]

No one waged the secret war with greater intensity than William King Harvey. For the better part of three decades Bill Harvey confronted the KGB and communism in a daily battle of deception, a battle fought in a maze of agents and double agents, spies and counterspies, intelligence, and counterintelligence. Both William King Harvey and James Jesus Angleton were critical player in this confusing world of intrigue that Angleton called the "wilderness of mirrors." One stood for good, arguably at least to a point in his life, the other stood for pure evil.

# BERLIN

In 1952, Bill Harvey divorced Libby. Bill Harvey was appointed CIA Chief of Station, Berlin, Germany ("Berlin Base") and he moved along with his five-year-old son to Germany. *Rockefeller Commission* 178-10002-10324 & 124-90092-10016

Not long after arriving in Germany, Bill Harvey met and a couple years later married Clara Grace Follick (C.G. for short) on February 3rd, 1954. C.G. was an attractive, strong willed and independent woman who had been in the Women's Army Corp (the WACs) during World War II and who was now serving as a U.S. Foreign Service's officer in Frankfurt, Germany. She was loyal to Bill, just as outspoken, and just as much of a fighter as he was. They were a perfect match. CIA 104-10106-10578

As an officer in the Women's Army Corps, during World War II, C.G. was military liaison for Eleanor Roosevelt and George C. Marshall. After the war she was the top aide to Gen. Lucien K. Truscott, who was the first CIA station chief in Berlin. You see C.G. was CIA all the way. *Andy Alderton/C.G. Harvey Interview*

Here again is where fate enters the story. I was talking to Mark Edwards one day and had told him of my interest in Bill Harvey and Ray Cline. Mark informs me that Andy Alderton had gone over to Indianapolis and had videotaped an interview with C.G. Harvey! Andy Alderton, as you may recall, was the Production Manager at WTWO, whom I called back in 1995, to find out how to get in touch with TV reporter Mark Edwards. Tell me this isn't fate.

The Harveys, as you will later learn, ended up living in

Indianapolis. Andy Alderton's brother, Scott, worked at an assisted living facility over in Indianapolis and had gotten to know this really fascinating 85-year-old women who had been witness to quite a bit of history. Andy, his wife Amy, and his brother Scott sat down with Mrs. Harvey one afternoon with a home video camera.

Here is a little history on C. G. Harvey and some of what she had to say: She had a master's degree in psychology from Ohio State University and at the start of World War II, C.G. was in the first Women Army Officer's Class at Fort Des Moines, Iowa. C.G. was among the first four hundred and forty-four women out of 100,000 applicants to be admitted as an Army Officer. Following that the Army sent her to learn Army Personnel Management at Fort Washington, Maryland. Then they sent her over to the Pentagon. "I was in personnel in the Adjutant General's Office. The Adjutant General is the person that moves everybody around." *Andy Alderton/C.G. Harvey Interview*

C.G. was a character. Andy Alderton told me that C.G. told him that toward the end of the war in Europe she changed, on her own, some paperwork in the Adjutant General's Office and rerouted a large number of troops who were slated to go to Europe and sent them to the Pacific. She said she just changed some numbers here and there. She said, "McArthur needed them more." She seems like a perfect fit for Bill Harvey. Bill also seemed fully capable of moving things around to get things to work at the CIA.

"President Roosevelt was too crippled," says C.G. "to tour the military bases and so he wanted Eleanor to go out and inspect the various training stations and come back and tell him how it was going and how the morale was. So, Eleanor needed a military person to go with her. So, they sent me over to the White House." C.G. would coordinate the visits and she made sure that Mrs. Roosevelt got to see what she needed to see. "[Mrs. Roosevelt] She was so kind. She would make you feel like you were the only person in the world, when she was talking to you, and planning with you. I just worshiped her. I just thought Eleanor Roosevelt was something once again. Mr. Roosevelt was also very nice. I just thought the sun rose and set with those people." _Andy Alderton/C.G. Harvey Interview_

"Scott tells me you knew Jessie Owens," says Andy. "Yes. We were in square dancing class together at Ohio State. He was absolutely fabulous. We were all students together. The thing of course that upset me was that Hitler didn't recognize him, wouldn't award his medals, and then had the news announce that a German had won Jessie's Olympic Event. And I got up, after seeing about the third one of these newsreels at the movie theater, and I said, "that's a lie, Jessie Owens won that! And this Jewish leader that we had with us said to be quiet and sit down you'll be arrested, and we will never hear from you again. Shut up and be quiet." Andy says, "Oh, so you did that in Berlin?" "Oh yeah." Andy, "Did you go to Berlin just to see the Olympics in 36?" "I went to see the Olympics. When I went back in 38, that was to take a group from the University of Michigan, and I was a tour guide for 12 girls." _Andy Alderton/C.G. Harvey Interview_

"We got off the ship and got our bicycles in Amsterdam and we bicycled across Belgium, and Luxemburg, and up into Switzerland, like idiots trying to bicycle the Alps. Going down was the scary part. We put branches between the tires and the fenders, trying to slow down our descent, and then we hung on for dear life on the turns. This all took us six weeks." _Andy Alderton/C.G. Harvey Interview_

"Now there was something about Werner Von Braun," asked Andy? "No, I wasn't with him, but I was with his family. A lot of them. I made 26 black flights back and forth across from Wiesbaden to D.C. carrying the families of the people that put us on the moon. They were all Germans, and the Russians were stealing part of them, and we were stealing part of them. The Russians had told these families that they would never make it to America that they would all be pushed out over the ocean. So, I rode these black flights to pacify them and make sure they got there all right and were all happy. But we flew black because the Russians wanted to shoot us down. So, we flew navigating by the stars." Laughing she said, "and I always made sure I had a good navigator before I got on." (This operation was known as Operation Paperclip.) *Andy Alderton/C.G. Harvey Interview*

"After the war, I got out of the military and went back to Washington D.C. and took the Foreign Services exam and I was admitted as the only women in the Foreign Services Officer's Class, because I had 10 points for being a veteran, so my points were higher than the rest, so they had to take me, otherwise they wouldn't have taken me because they weren't taking in women." *Andy Alderton/C.G. Harvey Interview*

"Bill always believed that one person could make a difference. And he did. He made a difference in Berlin when he built the tunnel. He held Berlin for the west. There were only seventy-five of us up there. I was one of the intelligence officers working for him. I married the boss. It was a time when nobody wanted to go in there and work because we were behind the iron curtain, and it was a very difficult way to live. But those of us who were there, the seventy-five, held Berlin for the west. Knowing that, you and your husband spent your whole life fighting to have the downfall of Communism, so that they couldn't blow us up and rule the world. The only way to be safe is to be strong," said C.G. *Andy Alderton/C.G. Harvey Interview*

Berlin was a wild place. July 8, 1952, shortly before Bill Harvey arrived, a German lawyer named Walter Linse, who was involved in uncovering human rights violations in the

Soviet occupied zone, was bundled into a car and kidnapped by the East German Stasi. The kidnappers were pursued amid a hail of gunfire, escaped capture, and Walter Linse was then handed over to the KGB, he was then later executed. There were 24 kidnappings in Berlin over a two-year period.

Upon his arrival, Bill Harvey found Berlin Base in need of a little reorganization and a clearly defined mission. It was time for the U.S. to take on the Russians and find out just what the hell the Russians were up to!

West Berlin was a city that was surrounded by communist East Berlin and East Germany, making it the perfect location for espionage at the beginning of the Cold War between East and West.

For Bill Harvey, Berlin was an opportunity to start fresh. He was given the freedom to select whomever in the CIA he wanted on his staff, and he was given the freedom to run his own show. Harvey personally interviewed and hand selected each of his staff. He represented the newer tougher breed of CIA. He was one of only a few who had gone up against the Soviets and understood how they operated. He was anxious and ready to go "toe to toe," "man to man," "eyeball to eyeball" with the God-awful communists.

Upon Harvey's arrival he gathered the Berlin staff together and announced, "the Soviets 'are criminals' and we are cops." He lectured them on how the NKVD [future KGB] operated in the United States. He asked them if they "packed heat." When he got confused looks from this uneasy audience, he promptly pulled an ivory-handled pistol out of his pocket and held it up. Bill Harvey's first goal was to replace the café atmosphere at Berlin Base with a sense of urgency. He immediately ordered all CIA agents to start carrying side arms. [53]

The CIA's Bayard Stockton, who worked for Bill Harvey

in Berlin said, "Bill Harvey was a determined, inspired and inspiring, persevering, and a sleep-deprived taskmaster. There were none like him. We vastly underestimated Bill Harvey [upon his arrival in Berlin]. We had no inkling of the surging quality of the man, nor how he would affect our lives, let alone the impact he would have on CIA. Harvey worked twenty-hour days. Over time Berlin gave Harvey stature as an innovative and daring intelligence operator and executive, albeit an unconventional one. Berlin became the place to be."

According to the CIA's Paul Garbler, "It was clear that Harvey's intentions at Berlin Base was to make certain it became known as an outpost for guys with guts...a place where things happened. It was that attitude, spelled out again and again to Harvey's men over three-double-martini lunches." Says the CIA's Bayard Stockton, "Harvey could, if so inclined, be one of the most charming, considerate, and compassionate men in the CIA. On the other hand, he would not hesitate to unapologetically ride roughshod into what had been a gentlemen's club. Harvey proceeded to show us how to evade as many regulations as we needed to break." [54]

Harvey's office was adorned with rows of firearms, accompanied by carefully positioned explosives atop each safe, poised to obliterate the files should a Russian invasion occur. He maintained a constant vigilance, carrying two sidearms throughout the day and keeping two more within reach under his pillow at night. [55]

Allen Dulles once said of Bill Harvey, "That fellow Harvey is a conspiratorial cop. The only trouble is, I can't decide if he is more conspiratorial, or more cop." [56]

It has been written and said that Bill Harvey didn't know German, while stationed in Berlin, however in a CIA Personal History report dated 8/25/47 it shows that Bill Harvey knew some German. It wouldn't surprise me if the whole time he was in Germany he kept this secret to himself while sitting around listening to conversations others thought he didn't understand. People were on a strictly "need to know" basis when it came to Bill Harvey.

During their downtime, the Harveys' splendid villa, boasting a swimming pool, served as the ultimate party hub. According to CIA officer Thomas Parrott, "the Harveys would tirelessly serve martinis until every guest was thoroughly intoxicated. We called it, "trial by firewater." Bill Harvey's penchant for drinking would become the stuff of legends. Numerous books have portrayed him as having a drinking problem, but it's essential to recognize that **Bill Harvey was put in the public record for a reason and portraying him in the best of light was perhaps not the objective**. While it is true that he had a remarkable capacity for consuming alcohol, it should be noted that Harvey's physical appearance underwent some changes. Standing around six feet tall during his time at the FBI, he weighed approximately 180 pounds. However, by the time he arrived in Berlin, his weight had increase to around 200 pounds. Here is what the CIAs John Barron had to say, "I'm aware of the stories about his excessive drinking, of course. In Berlin, it was like a twenty-four-hour-a-day fraternity party, but I never saw Bill intoxicated. I didn't see anything wrong with him later, in Washington. I've known alcoholics. Bill didn't have to have a drink…" Bayard Stockton fondly recalls, "In those days, we had a tendency towards irreverence at the Berlin station. One day, we caught sight of an unforgettable silhouette down the hall. Whispering to one another, 'Oh my god, he looks like a pear!' We all struggled to suppress our laughter as we settled back into our chairs. And so, the nickname 'The Pear' was born. Most people assume it was meant to be derogatory," Stockton explains, "but it wasn't." [57]

Here are the words used by people who served under him in Berlin: He backed his people, recognized, and lauded honesty, hard work, daring and devotion. They referred to themselves as the Berlin Brotherhood, as Harvey's Boys. Harvey developed his team, his boys, through mentoring and tutoring. Harvey was developing a core of officers for their future advancement, grooming them for higher things. Harvey was a workaholic and a tough taskmaster. His intelligence-collecting operations were imaginative. He had a higher intellect – he could quote the German philosophers, like Kant and Hegel. Bill Harvey was a very honest guy, loyal to his friends, and nurtured his people. Never missed a day of work and never showed the strain. He was essentially a trainer of young officers. He told them what to do, and how to do it. He was a "constant all-out effort to serve his country." Could be a disciplinarian with humor. Harvey had a fantastic memory, the ability to marshal facts to support his argument, was goal oriented, and had the ability to work with subordinates. [58]

Banyard Stockton encapsulated it succinctly, stating, "Bill Harvey was a warm and honorable man. We genuinely cared for him. We discovered that his gruff exterior was merely a mask. We emulated him. And yes, I would say we loved him. We, the Harvey Boys, were devoted to him." Harvey faced no difficulty in persuading individuals to relocate to Germany and join his team. The Berlin Base was universally recognized as the CIA's premier operating base, a gateway to advancement within America's intelligence service. Serving there meant standing shoulder to shoulder with the finest, looking the enemy in the eye without faltering. This became the myth and mindset ingrained within the Berlin Base. Assembling the bulk of his team took Harvey a year of concerted effort. John Sherwood, a CIA agent who worked under Bill Harvey at the Berlin Base, shared his perspective,

"Bill Harvey had a group of guys who displayed relentless determination. Among the ordinary ranks, Harvey had attained near-God like status within the intelligence community. For Harvey the chemistry between individuals was the cornerstone of a successful spy organization. That's why he was an exceptional leader and a genuinely decent man." Sherwood added, "Harvey went above and beyond to support those under his command. He was exceptionally generous and free from personal insecurities. He was a peculiar individual…Just think, he must have grown up as this eccentric-looking, highly intelligent kid who likely was smarter than everyone else… That's no easy life… In truth, he was one of the rare truly decent people in the CIA." Bill Harvey proved himself a highly competent spymaster, an extraordinarily skilled case officer. He demonstrated discipline and excelled in meticulous operational planning, leaving no detail unaddressed. Being well acquainted with the temptations of life, he planned accordingly. Harvey possessed street smarts and even enlisted a string of prostitutes, as a part of his network of agents. [59]

Will Potocki, served under Bill, CIA Berlin, "Bill respected the people who worked for him, and they in return respected him. They had a great deal of confidence in Bill. They considered him one of the outstanding intelligence officers in the CIA and they were happy to work for him. People were always attempting to get an assignment in Berlin in order to work for Bill Harvey, during that period." [60]

Mrs. Potocki, "I have seen that man literally work around the clock for two or three days running. And there wasn't a night, that he did not report back to the office." [61]

Tom Huston, Former White House Intelligence Aide said, "Bill Harvey was kind of the George Patton of the secret services. When he was good, he was damn good, when he was ornery, he was real ornery. He didn't fit the role of what one generally identified with agents in the CIA, in that he wasn't one of the Ivy League establishment types predominant after the post World War II period. And I think he was kind of the odd man out." [62]

**Ray Cline [our second CIA guy from Terre Haute]**, former Deputy Director of Intelligence said, "Bill Harvey was a colorful character in the CIA. We tended to have a lot of colorful characters and they tended to fall into two or three different groups. The one that Bill Harvey belonged to was what I call the gang busters." [63]

Art Thurston, CIA Retired, Shelbyville, Indiana, "Bill was the most professional and the most highly trained man that they had. He soon became a leader in the entire group. A pretty tough guy. Blunt, outspoken, and **a man you wouldn't want to fool around with**." [64]

An anonymous high-ranking military officer had this to say about William Harvey: "By patience and example he trained many of the best case officers in the Agency. He disliked bureaucracy and had little time for red tape. He would become impatient with poor performance or laziness. Officers falling, to frequently, into these categories, weren't around long." [65]

Hugh Montgomery, U.N. Ambassador, "I had the great privilege of serving with him in Berlin. It seems to me, that unfortunately, the contribution Bill made to his country has been sorely neglected for far too long. Hopefully by breaking some of this code of silence, that by so doing, perhaps we can convey some of his sense of dedication and patriotism and love of country to another generation, which never knew him, nor was able to share in the many accomplishments, unsung though they may be, which he made for the security of his country by his silent service." [66]

Bill Harvey was a legendary marksman and always armed.

A colleague said, "Bill could handle a 44 magnum like a toy. Seldom using the two-hand grip of most marksmen, he could control it with one hand." [67]

Harry was once asked why he always carried his pearl-handled revolvers. His reply, "When you need 'em you need 'em in a hurry. I know too many secrets." [68] Perhaps Bill had an overactive imagination on this point, perhaps Harvey's concerns were somewhat justified. According to an FBI report, dated 2/25/65 concerning the arrest of Robert Glenn Thompson on conspiracy to commit espionage. Thompson stated, in regard to William K. Harvey, "that STEVEN, his Soviet principal, asked him about this individual [Harvey] and Thompson told Steven whatever he knew about this individual. *FBI* 124-90092-10002

Thompson believed that the Soviets either showed a picture of Bill Harvey or asked him about Harvey. *FBI* 124-90092-10001

According to an unnamed senior military official, "Bill Harvey lived a very dangerous life and was a targeted, vulnerable person. Harvey's intense preoccupation with firearms may have been unnecessary, as there was kind of an unwritten understanding between the CIA and the KGB, not to kill each other's officers. However, if the Russians had decided to make an exception to this rule, Bill Harvey would have been a good place to start." [69]

Meanwhile back in America, on November 21, 1955, Angleton recommended to Richard Helms the number two man in Operations, that U.S. mail to and from Russia be opened and photographed. Opening the mail was expressly illegal, but Angleton believed the Soviets counted on this for a secure method of communications. The mail opening operation was code named HT/LINGUAL. Letters would eventually be opened including letters to congressmen, senators, and a presidential candidate, Richard Nixon. An aide to Angleton said that if the operation were blown, "it should be relatively easy to 'hush up' or at worst, "**it might become necessary...to find a scapegoat to blame** for unauthorized tampering with the mail."

What set the stage for Bill Harvey and his fellow CIA cold warriors? The CIA's Doolittle Report released in 1954, it states: "It is now clear that we are facing an implacable enemy whose avowed objective is world domination by whatever means and at whatever cost. There are no rules in such a game. Hitherto acceptable norms of human conduct do not apply. If the United States is to survive, longstanding concepts of 'fair play' must be reconsidered. We must develop effective espionage and counterespionage services and must learn to subvert, sabotage, and destroy our enemies **by cleverer, more sophisticated, and more effective methods** than those used against us."

Clever, more sophisticated, more effective methods is exactly what Bill Harvey did next. Known as Harvey's Hole, Bill Harvey, after much effort, will and determination, convinced CIA Headquarter to let him construct a tunnel under the Berlin border for the purpose of tapping into the phone lines of the Soviet military. Harvey's Hole allowed the United States and Britain to monitor Soviet communications across Europe.

This communications tap generated an enormous quantity of information concerning everything that was going on behind the iron curtain. It took a whole army of analysts to sift through the volumes of information. Providing Ray Cline's side of the house, "CIA Intelligence," with more intel than they could have ever imagined possible.

On April 21, 1956, approximately eleven months and eleven days after the completion of the tunnel, Soviet and East

German border guards were observed excavating near the far end of the tunnel on the East Berlin side. In response, Bill Harvey swiftly issued orders to remove the advanced electronic equipment from the tunnel. He then proposed the demolition of the tunnel, but his request was denied by Washington. Undeterred, Harvey devised an alternative plan.

Within the tunnel, sandbags, barbed wire, and a formidable .50 caliber machine gun was strategically positioned, complemented by a sign in both German and Russian. The sign boldly proclaimed, "You are now entering the American sector." Positioned behind the formidable machine gun was Bill Harvey, bracing himself as the approaching footsteps of the Soviet and East German guards grew nearer and nearer.

With a resolute grip, Harvey pulled back on the breech of the machine gun, producing a distinct metallic sound that echoed throughout the tunnel. The reverberating noise of the breech caused the advancing footsteps to turn tail and run, retreating in the face of the formidable presence that awaited them. [70]

Upon the revelation of the tunnel's existence, Western intelligence anticipated that the Soviets and East Germans would take immediate measures to conceal the fact that their military phone lines across Europe had been compromised. The situation was undeniably embarrassing for them. However, to the astonishment of the West, the East chose a different path, opting to bring attention to the tunnel rather than conceal it. They went so far as to arrange tours of the tunnel for the press corps, seemingly under the impression that such an act would elicit outrage.

Contrary to the East's expectations, the response from the public and media took an unexpected turn. Instead of condemning the tunnel operation, it was hailed as a remarkable demonstration of technological prowess, engineering excellence and the resourcefulness of the American spirit. The press celebrated the venture as a shining example of Yankee ingenuity, elevating its status to one of admiration and awe. This unforeseen reaction brought delight to the West, who reveled in the positive portrayal of their accomplishment in the public eye. [71]

In 1959, at CIA Headquarters, CIA Director Allen Dulles bestowed upon William King Harvey the Distinguished Intelligence Medal in recognition of his remarkable achievements. During the ceremony, Dulles declared the tunnel, known as "Harvey's Hole," as "one of the most valuable and audacious projects ever undertaken." Reflecting on the operation, Dick Helms would later acknowledge that, in hindsight, the "Tunnel stood as an operational triumph. He credited Bill Harvey, who tenaciously navigated through an untold number of challenges, some of which seemed insurmountable. "Bill Harvey deserves great credit for his achievement." [72]

Bill Harvey at this point had achieved near God-like status in the intelligence community. He not only exposed the greatest penetration that the Soviets had (Kim Philby), but he had created the greatest United States penetration of the Soviet Union (Harvey's Hole).

In February 1956, Nikita Khrushchev delivered a speech at the Twentieth Congress of the Soviet Communist Party where he denounced Stalin's previous approach to communism. The significance of the speech prompted CIA Director Allen Dulles to request that a copy of the speech be obtained, which sparked a competition between the Deputy Director of Intelligence (DDI) and the Deputy Director of Plans (DDP) to see who could obtain the transcript first. Angleton obtained the first copy through an Israeli spy.

This underscores the fact that if Bill Harvey had a rival in the realm of clandestine operations, it was Angleton, who achieved this remarkable feat of acquiring this speech.

To validate the document's authenticity, Wisner called upon Ray Cline, a knowledgeable historian with an intellectual fearlessness, who headed the Chino-Soviet section of the Office of Current Intelligence (notably the second CIA representative from Terre Haute in our story). The DDP's reliance on Cline was a notable shift for them, as there was usually limited interaction between the two groups, given Plans insular nature and intense emphasis on security in tradecraft. While providing textual evidence supporting Khrushchev's authorship of the document, Cline found himself in a debate with both Wisner and Angleton, who preferred to selectively leak fragments of the speech to specific audiences which would, in their minds maximize the impact. Cline stated, "They kept insisting on 'exploiting' the speech rather than allowing it widespread dissemination and simply allowing everyone to read it." [73]

Angleton expressed the view that the utilization of Nikita's speech should be postponed for months, possibly even years, until the operational groups had completed their training in West Germany. He contended that only after these armies of Poles, Hungarians and Romanians had reached a satisfactory level of readiness should selective excerpts from Khrushchev's speech be strategically released to the captive populations. This calculated approach aimed to incite revolutionary fervor and provoke political upheaval, thereby fueling the activities of paramilitary forces. [74]

Shortly after verifying the invaluable document, Cline paid a visit to the Director's office to finalize a speech with Allen Dulles. During their conversation, Dulles requested that Cline elaborate on the rationale behind releasing the Khrushchev speech in its current form. Cline presented his reasons and later recalled that Dulles exclaimed, "By golly, I am going to make a policy decision!" Without delay, Dulles informed Wisner (who received the news graciously), obtained approval from his brother, John Foster Dulles, who headed the State Department and promptly forwarded the unedited text to The New York Times. On June 5, the majority of the speech was published by the newspaper. [75]

**Angleton disparaged Cline's input. "He wasn't a party to the discussions on the clandestine side," Angleton would declare later. Says Cline, "The decision to publish the Khrushchev speech was made by Eisenhower, Allen Dulles, and John Foster Dulles. They decided its significance should take precedence over political action...." [76]**

To hear Angleton tell it, "Ray Cline's achievement had unintended and devastating consequences when, against his objections, Dulles decided to share a copy of the speech with the New York Times. Angleton argued that the ensuing uproar caused by the publication of the speech directly triggered the Hungarian revolt, which was brutally suppressed by Soviet tanks. Angleton claimed that the CIA had been clandestinely training Hungarian exiles at a covert facility in Germany in anticipation of such an uprising. However, the premature release of the speech ignited the revolution before the Agency-trained force was fully prepared." [77]

Clearly Angleton was not happy with Cline having won the argument about what to do about the speech. Angleton might also have had the impression that Cline went over his head, running to Dulles, the Director of the CIA, with his plan. A speech that Angleton had acquired through his Israeli sources and a speech, which he might have felt he should have been allowed to exploit the way he saw fit. **Angleton may have had a simmering resentment toward Ray Cline as a result, much like Angleton's communist**

**friend Kim Philby had against William King Harvey (keep these two important grudges in mind for later).**

"This was one of the few examples of a genuine policy decision that I was involved in directly," said Cline. "It was an event of historic significance, documenting Stalinism as a fantastic political evil, forcing Khrushchev into a milder style of totalitarian control, and beginning the alienation between the Soviet leaders and China's Mao Tse-tung. Getting and publishing the secret speech let the whole world see the momentous cracks in what had been perceived as a Communist monolith," Ray Cline. [78]

Berlin under Bill Harvey produced the people who would go on to dominate the CIA's operations worldwide for years to come.

One major force in the CIA that came up under Harvey was the Blond Ghost, **Ted Shackley**. Shackley worked for Harvey in Berlin, then would end up running JM/WAVE the big anti-Castro Cuban CIA operation out of Miami, Florida, before moving on to Laos and the Southeast Asian war in Vietnam. Harvey treated Shackley like a son. Thus, the nickname, "Son of Pear."

William Harvey was issued the pseudonym "Daniel M. Presland" in 1956 and he used this pseudonym until he retired in 1967. He was also issued the alias William Walker in May 1962 and he continued to use it until June 1963. *CIA* 104-10310-10211

An example of Bill Harvey's tendency to tell it like it is, regardless of whom it might offend, came when the Soviets rolled their tanks into East Berlin to crush unarmed protestors. Harvey fired off a red-hot memo that in effect said that the U.S. through its propaganda had encouraged the uprising and the U.S. should get in there and confront the Russians and stand up to its responsibilities, even if it meant risking a showdown with the Russians. Although William Harvey was probably morally right, this was probably not a smart move politically on Bill Harvey's part, being as Allen Dulles was in charge of the CIA and his brother Foster Dulles was the head of the State Department and between the two they were probably the architects of this flawed strategy.

Some stories about Bill Harvey seemed to exhibit a distrust of headquarters and seemed to have a contempt for authority and rules when it came to Bill Harvey and his operations.

There is this CIA document, which says: "Bill Harvey served in Berlin, Germany from December 1952 to September 1959." <u>CIA 104-10106-10578.</u> However, I have also seen it written that **details of Bill Harvey's career abroad between 1952 and 1959 are being withheld by the CIA. In Bill Harvey's eulogy it listed Japan among the countries that Bill Harvey had served. Oswald of course was posted at Atsugi, Japan 1957-1958**, prior to his defection to the Soviet Union in October 1959. **Could it be that Bill Harvey was working in Japan while Lee Oswald and Richard Case Nagell were stationed there?** All I know is that Harvey's eulogy listed the following places where Bill Harvey apparently had served: America, Germany, Japan and Italy and the period between 1952 and 1959 is the only timeframe available where Bill Harvey was stationed abroad.

## RETURN TO WASHINGTON

It seemed logical at the time, that upon Bill Harvey's return to CIA Headquarters, that he would be placed in charge of the Soviet Russian section. After all Bill Harvey had the greatest history and success in confronting the Soviets compared to anyone else in the CIA at that time. The only problem with this, as explained by the CIA's Robert Crowley was that Allen Dulles and Richard Bissell would have to interact with Bill Harvey on a daily basis and according to Crowley, "They couldn't stand the sight of him. But Berlin Base was the shining jewel in the CIA's crown, so promoting Harvey without having to deal with him was the methodology they followed." So, they made him the chief of Staff D. Staff D monitored the signal intelligence that was generated by the super-secret NSA. [79]

## PRIOR TO THE BAY OF PIGS INVASION

In 1959, Fidel Castro emerged as the leader of a guerilla movement in Cuba, successfully overthrowing the Batista regime and seizing control of the Caribbean Island. Situated merely 90 miles south of Florida, Cuba had long been a playground for the Mafia, with Batista allowing them to operate gambling casinos and other illicit activities. However, Castro's true political leanings became apparent as he revealed himself to be a communist. Shortly after assuming power, Castro initiated a series of nationalizations, taking control of numerous businesses in Cuba, some of which were owned by influential Americans, potentially including the Dulles family, who were rumored to have interests in the Cuban sugar industry. [80] Castro also immediately shut down the Mafia's casinos. Needless to say, these powerful U.S. business interests and the Mafia were not at all pleased about their financial loss that was brought about by Castro.

Most of the Mafioso left Cuba as Castro's forces took over. One who stayed and was detained was Santos Trafficante, the reputed Mafia boss from Tampa, Florida. It was reported that Trafficante was visited, while he was being detained, by a man named Ruby. It is thought that Jack Ruby visited Santos Trafficante and shortly thereafter Trafficante was allowed to leave Cuba. There seems to be evidence that Jack Ruby had been involved in the smuggling of weapons to Castro's forces. This might help to explain how Ruby was allowed to visit Trafficante.

It is believed by many, that a part of the negotiations for

Trafficante's release included a secret agreement between Castro and Trafficante concerning drug trafficking and joint cooperation. This did not bode well for the future CIA assassination operations targeted at Castro, being as the CIA included Trafficante in its assassination planning. The implication is that Trafficante was tipping Castro off, as each operation against him was launched.

Bill Harvey was busy with his new role as the head of Staff D, while others at CIA were busy planning the invasion of Cuba, which came to be known as the Bay of Pigs invasion, or fiasco.

The U.S. President leading up to the Bay of Pigs invasion was President Eisenhower, however Vice President Nixon appears to have been the one approving most of the actions as "the Project Chief," (source E. Howard Hunt's book: *Give Us This Day*). The Director of the CIA at the time was Allen Dulles. Allen's brother John Foster Dulles was the Secretary of State.

In 1954, prior to the problems in Cuba, the CIA has successfully overthrown the democratically elected government of Guatemala, partly because the land reform being sponsored by the Arbenz government was threatening the American owned United Fruit Company, which the Dulles had long been associated with. To plan the 1961 invasion of Cuba, Allen Dulles turned to the same team that had pulled off the successful coup d'état in Guatemala in 1954.

We will call this team **"the Guys from the Guatemalan Coup," or the GFGC.** The guys from the Guatemalan coup primarily **consisted of the CIA's Richard Bissell, Tracy Barnes, E. Howard Hunt, David Atlee Phillips, David Sancez Morales, New Orleans Private Investigator Guy Banister** (Banister worked through his Anti-Communist League of the Caribbean), **Colonel Philip J. Corso, and Mafia don - Johnny**

**Rosselli.** Said E. Howard Hunt in his book *Give Us This Day*, "the nucleus of the project [for the Bay of Pigs], was a cadre of officers I had worked with to overthrow Arbenz in Guatemala." (We will see this cast of characters recur throughout this Kennedy assassination study, or perhaps we could simple refer to this study as just another coup d'état by "the Guys from the Guatemala Coup.")

The United Fruit Company possessed vast land holdings in Guatemala and had some investments in Cuba. John Foster Dulles, a partner in the law firm Sullivan & Cromwell, had been extensively involved in legal matters concerning the United Fruit Company's operations in Guatemala. Additionally, Allen Dulles, who served as the head of the CIA, had also provided legal services to United Fruit, and had previously served on its board of directors. The Guatemalan coup took place while Allen Dulles was leading the CIA and John Foster Dulles was serving as Secretary of State under President Eisenhower. The support for the execution of the Guatemalan coup was orchestrated by the Dulles brothers. This raises concerns about a potential conflict of interest, as the Dulles brothers had maintained a close relationship with United Fruit for nearly four decades. [81]

**David Atlee Phillips** was the CIA's chief of propaganda for the Cuban Bay of Pigs Project. The CIA's **E. Howard Hunt** was the chief of political action for the project. CIA Deputy Director of Plans, **Tracy Barnes** oversaw the Cuban invasion operation as he had done with the Guatemalan Coup.

## PRESIDENT KENNEDY IS ELECTED

John Kennedy ran for President against Vice President Richard Nixon and won. The day after the election – Jack Kennedy announced two reappointments, J. Edgar Hoover, the FBI director, and Allen Dulles, the director of the CIA. Bobby Kennedy, the President's younger brother was appointed to the highest law enforcement office in the nation, that of the Attorney General of the United State.

Bobby Kennedy had promised to deport New Orleans Mafia boss Carlos Marcello following the election of his brother. Bobby made good on his promise, on the afternoon of April 4, 1961, just prior to the Bay of Pigs invasion and 8 years after Marcello had been ordered deported, Mafia don Carlos Marcello was finally ejected from the United States. As Marcello walked into the INS office in New Orleans for his regular appointment to report as an alien, he was arrested and handcuffed. He was then rushed to the airport and flown to Guatemala. The Mafia don was reportedly enraged. HSCA Vol. 9 Page 71

President Kennedy inherited the CIA's Bay of Pigs operation when he became President.

# THE BAY OF PIGS

The Bay of Pigs invasion of Cuba began on April 18, 1961, and was a CIA operation with the intent of overthrowing Cuba's Fidel Castro and it involved the use of CIA trained Cubans exiles. The world's perception was supposed to be that the exiled Cubans had risen up and raised arms against Castro to regain their country, without the help of the United States.

According to a CIA source, Bill Harvey knew all about the Bay of Pigs invasion plan from its inception and "Bill refused to have anything to do with the invasion plan and he had made his doubts known to anyone who would listen." [82]

In conjunction with the invasion of Cuba, Phase One if the assassination attempts on Castro was under the direction of the CIA's Edwards and O'Connell. Phase One was initiated in August 1960 under the Eisenhower administration (speculation is it was authorized by Vice President Nixon). From _1967 CIA Inspector General's Report_

Kennedy took office in January 1961 and the Bay of Pigs invasion took place just three months later in April 1961. Castro defeated the CIA-trained brigade in two days of intense fighting, killing 114 and taking 1,200 prisoners. The prisoners from the Bay of Pigs were later released in December 1962, in exchange for $53 million in medical supplies. One major cause of the defeat was the lack of U.S. military air support, which was withheld by President Kennedy. _HSCA_ VOL. 10 Page 66

# THE BAY OF PIGS AFTERMATH

Although publicly President Kennedy took responsibility for the Bay of Pigs fiasco, privately he blamed the CIA. The CIA and all involved on the other hand blamed President Kennedy for the failure of the Bay of Pigs by not approving the U.S.'s direct involvement by providing air support from the U.S. military.

Privately President Kennedy was furious with the CIA and took the following measures:

On June 28, 1961, the National Security Action Memorandum No. 57 was issued limiting CIA operations to those operations that required no greater firepower than that of a handgun. This memorandum in effect limited the CIA covert operations to that of small skirmishes. It defined the responsibility for future paramilitary operations. It called for future operations to be submitted to a Strategic Resources Group, which first considers each proposal. The group can then pass a proposal on to the President for approval. The memo basically limits future large-scale operations to the U.S. military (it specifically identifies in the memo the Cuban invasion as an example of a future <u>military</u> operation) and the memo relegates the CIA to smaller preapproved operations.

In the fall 1961, President Kennedy created the Defense Intelligence Agency (DIA) specializing in defense and military intelligence, which answered to the Secretary of Defense. The DIA was a part of the Department of Defense (DOD). The Director of DIA was to be either a three-star general, or an admiral. Approximately one-fourth of the President's Daily Brief was now DIA intelligence.

According to statements made by Robert Morrow, a CIA operative, it was alleged that Vice President Lyndon Johnson provided information to the CIA regarding President Kennedy's intentions. The information obtained from Johnson indicated that after the failed Bay of Pigs invasion, President Kennedy expressed his desire to dismantle the CIA and disperse its influence. President Kennedy had said that he would like "to splinter the CIA in a thousand pieces and scatter it to the winds." President Kennedy reportedly discussed this intention with the Chairman of the Senate Appropriations Committee, exploring the possibility of significantly restricting the CIA's unaccounted funds. Furthermore, it was claimed that President Kennedy aimed to redefine the CIA's role by transferring its authority to the newly established Defense Intelligence Agency (DIA), and thereby placing the CIA under the auspices of the newly created DIA. [83]

At this same time Bobby Kennedy wanted to conduct a full-scale investigation of the CIA and its activities and in effect the President had Bobby trying to somewhat oversee and ride herd on the agency. In summary, President Kennedy starting in 1961 limiting and restricting the CIA's power and the CIA was aware of the threat of further actions by the President of the United States.

As a result of the failure of the Bay of Pigs, Jack and Bobby appear determined to win against Castro at all costs. **Ray S. Cline** said, "They were a couple of Irishmen who felt they had muffed it...and, being good fighting Irishmen, they vented their wrath in all ways that they could."

The CIA's Director of Plans at the time was Richard Bissell. Bissell was called on the carpet by the brothers Kennedy shortly after the Bay of Pigs Invasion and chewed out in the Cabinet Room for "sitting on his ass and not doing anything about getting rid of Castro and the Castro regime."

Ray Cline: "Bobby was as emotional as he could be, and he always talked like he was the President, and he really was in a way. He was always bugging the Agency about the Cubans. I don't doubt that talk of assassinating Castro was part of Bobby's discussion with some Agency people."

As a result of the Bay of Pigs disaster, **President Kennedy fired CIA Director Allen Dulles and the Deputy Director for Operations, Charles Cabell**. Allen Dulles would later serve on the Warren Commission in the investigation of the assassination of President Kennedy. Charles Cabell's brother happened to be the Mayor of Dallas on the day President Kennedy was assassinated in Dallas. John McCone was appointed as the new CIA Director following Dulles's dismissal.

Although John McCone was appointed as the new CIA Director, CIA Deputy Director **Richard Helms**, who had managed to keep his distance from the Bay of Pigs operation and its resulting disaster, **emerged as the one calling the shots in the CIA**. Helms from this point forward appears to be the one making all the clandestine decisions and **he and Bill Harvey would go on to withhold information from Director McCone concerning the assassination attempts on Castro. There are numerous examples where Bill Harvey was very good about conferring with and informing Richard Helms as to what he was doing**. Bill Harvey had labels for nearly everyone. He referred to Helms as "the boy diplomat." Richard Helms was the Deputy Director of Plans, the division of the CIA that oversaw all of the clandestine operations and dirty tricks.

An FBI report dated 11/29/61 said this about the CIA's Bill Harvey: "He is currently responsible for clandestine collection of communications intelligence. For several years he oversaw CIA operations in Berlin, Germany. He has acquired a wide knowledge of Soviet intelligence activity. We do not believe he has the necessary capability to be a top-flight administrator. He has never demonstrated a high degree of friendliness to the Bureau. *FBI* 124-90092-10013

No one was better at keeping a secret to himself and off paper than Bill Harvey. Harvey possessed an exceptional ability to safeguard secrets, ensuring that they remained undisclosed and undocumented. According to CIA reports covering 1960 to 1962, the reports were positive, but did make the point that Bill Harvey is, "less than forthcoming with information about operational matters, in which he is engaged." These characteristics made him an ideal choice to lead the highly classified Staff D, a secretive division dedicated to the decryption of codes. Staff D undertook various covert activities, such as stealing codebooks from foreign embassies, breaking into safes, abducting couriers, and opening and resealing cryptographic pads discreetly. The crew assembled by Bill Harvey consisted of some pretty tough customers, who were confident, professional criminals - second story men, adept at criminal activities like burglary and skilled in locksmithing and construction. Despite carrying out numerous missions, they always managed to avoid detection and capture. Harvey's remarkable talent for identifying individuals with such exceptional abilities might have been facilitated by his connections with the FBI, which likely aided in identifying highly skilled criminals within the United States. [84]

During this period Harvey had many occasions to work directly with Mr. Helms and had a close working relationship with him. *SSCI interview with William Harvey, National Archives* 157-100004-10138

From the book, "*Battleground Berlin,*" as an unrelated side note: In March 1961 Henry Kissinger, as the National

Security Council's consultant on Germany, asked the CIA to review possible clandestine action that "could be undertaken in support of the U.S. position on Berlin." The CIA's William Harvey, who had directed clandestine operations in Berlin for seven years in the 1950s, told a meeting at CIA headquarters in Washington that it would be "unrealistic" for America's policymakers to conclude that the agency could be effective in organizing resistance groups inside East Germany. "Our abilities are not equal to this task when balanced against the defensive capability of the East German security services."

## THE PROBLEM WITH CASTRO

As was mentioned earlier, in 1959 Castro overthrew the corrupt Cuban dictator Batista and shortly thereafter it became apparent that Castro had decided to throw in with the Communist side. In so doing, Castro also took over and nationalized American businesses in Cuba and he shut down the Mafia owned casinos in Cuba and kicked the Mafia out of the country.

Communist Cuba was perceived at the time as a very big threat to the Western Hemisphere. We had Communists knocking at our back door wanting to get in.

Initially in August of 1960, Richard Bissell, who was at that moment the CIA's Deputy Director of Plans, asked Colonel Sheffield Edwards, the Director of Security, if Edwards could establish contact with the U.S. gambling syndicate that had been active in Cuba. *HSCA* Vol. 4 Page 135 (The thinking being that the Mafia would still have people in Cuba that might be capable of assassinating Castro.)

Sheffield Edwards then turned to Mr. James P. O'Connell, CIA, who contacted Mr. **Robert Maheu**, asking Mr. Maheu to identify someone within the underworld who would have contacts within the Cuban gambling syndicates. [Robert Maheu was a former FBI Agent.] Maheu was also at times a contract employee for the CIA's Office of Security and had been utilized in various sensitive operations. [Robert Maheu was also Howard Hughes's right-hand man] Robert Maheu in turn introduced Mr. O'Connell to **Johnny Rosselli**, who was believed to be a member of the Las Vegas [Chicago] underworld syndicate. Following this initial contact in September 1960, Johnny Rosselli recruited reputed

Mafia godfathers Sam **Giancana**, of Chicago and Santos **Trafficante**, of Tampa, Florida to assist in the attempts to assassinate Castro. _CIA_ 104-10133-10015

The CIA's official account stated that they sought assistance from the Mafia due to their purported connections with individuals in Cuba that might be capable of assassinating Fidel Castro. To maintain plausible deniability, the CIA engaged Robert Maheu as an intermediary, creating a buffer between the agency and the Mafia. In intelligence circles, such a buffer is commonly referred to as a "cutout." According to the official narrative, Robert Maheu contacted Johnny Rosselli, a figure believed to have been involved in a number of Mafia murders. Rosselli direct report in the Mafia was Chicago's Mafia boss, Sam Giancana. The only problem with this official story is that it might not be the whole story as there is evidence that the **CIA was already familiar with and had worked with the Mafia and Johnny Rosselli back as early as 1954 on the Guatemalan Coup.** [85]

A memorandum of 23 May 1975 by Steve Hunt of the Office of Security wrote in response to a statement in a May 22, 1961, memorandum. The memorandum written in 1961 said that Dulles [the CIA's Director] was unaware [of the assassination plots]. Steve Hunt writes in 1975: The Office of Security files show that Allen Dulles approved the entire operation against Castro. Steve Hunt then states that Dulles would have been aware of plans to approach Robert Maheu and the other underworld figures. _SSCIA_ Memorandum 157-100005-10067, by Andy Postal.

As history bears witness, Edwards, O'Connell, Maheu, Giancana, and Trafficante were not effective in their attempt to eliminate Castro.

As was mentioned earlier, Bobby Kennedy jumped all over the CIA's Richard Bissell, for having not yet taken care of

Fidel Castro down in Cuba. This ugly scene took place in the Cabinet Room in November 1961. **Bissell immediately went to William Harvey and told him to take over the Mafia operation to get Castro.** Harvey had already been placed in charge of ZR/RIFLE, Bissell's "stand-by executive action capability" [assassination teams] naturally it made sense to consolidate the two operations. HSCA Vol. 10 Page 152

Harvey says that Bissell instructed him to take over Edwards' contact with the criminal syndicate and thereafter to run the operation against Castro. **Harvey adds that, as a completely unrelated development, shortly after this discussion with Bissell he was told by Helms that he was to be placed in charge of the Agency's Cuba task force.** HSCA Vol. 4 Page 142

Bissell asked Harvey in the fall to turn the ZR/RIFLE approach to Castro and pick up the Rosselli operation. Bill Harvey might have spoken to Bissell a short time before the Kennedy inauguration (which would have meant that Bissell was more likely to have been referring to the Eisenhower/Nixon White House as having pressured Bissell to set up an executive action capability). On the other hand, he [William Harvey] had the strong impression that the second time he was told by Bissell, i.e., in the fall, Bissell again implied that the renewed pressures had been recent, thereby strongly suggesting that, at least at that point, it was the Kennedy White House, which was involved. SSCI 157-100004-10138

**Harvey** states that after the decision was made to go ahead with the creation of an Executive Action Capability, and while he was still discussing its development with Bissell, he **briefed Mr. Helms fully** on the general concept but without mention of the then ongoing plan to assassinate Castro. HSCA Vol. 4 Page 141

Harvey's notes show that he and O'Connell went to New York

City to meet Rosselli on the 8th and 9th of April 1962. Harvey says that only he and O'Connell met with Rosselli; O'Connell says that Maheu was also present at the meeting. *1967 CIA Inspector General's Report*

Harvey is certain he would have remembered if Maheu were present. **Bill Harvey and Maheu were in the same FBI training class at Quantico in 1940 and had worked on the FBI's Tramp case together.** Harvey does not remember having seen Maheu since he, Harvey, came with the Agency in 1947, although he acknowledges that he may have seen him once or twice socially. Harvey is sure he has not seen Maheu since 1952 when he was assigned to Berlin. *1967 CIA Inspector General's Report*

O'Connell describes a series of events that reassure him of the accuracy of his memory. The four of them traveled separately to New York. They met at the Savoy Plaza Hotel (Savoy Hilton?) where all four stayed. After discussions, Maheu suggested dinner at the Elk Room, a fashionable restaurant in a nearby hotel. O'Connell says that Maheu picked up the tab. They finished dinner about 9:30 or 10:00 p.m. Rosselli wanted to buy the group a nightcap, but since it was Sunday night nearly all the bars were closed. They walked around the neighborhood looking for an open bar and finally wound up at the Copacabana. They were refused admittance to the bar because of a rule restricting admission to couples, so they sat at a table where they could watch the floor show. Rosselli found himself facing a table at "ringside" at which Phyllis McGuire was sitting with Dorothy Kilgallen and Liberace for the opening night of singer Rosemary Clooney. To avoid Phyllis McGuire's seeing him, Rosselli got his companions to change their seating arrangement so that his back was turned to Miss McGuire. (Robert Maheu and Rosselli were parties to a wiretap gone bad that concerned Phyllis McGuire.) Maheu was an integral part of the wiretap.

## *1967 CIA Inspector General's Report*

Harvey is legendary for his ability to remember every little detail. I asked myself why didn't Harvey want it known that Maheu was involved and that the two had been in contact? The answer may come from a CIA Inspector General's Report that says, "The significance, ...is whether Maheu did or did not know that the operation continued under Harvey." The reason why Harvey and CIA didn't want it known that Maheu was apparently still involved in this activity, is because Harvey and the CIA have claimed all along that when Harvey took over, he cut out Giancana, Trafficante, and Maheu from the assassination planning and it was supposedly only Harvey and Rosselli that knew about and were involved in the plots from that point on. For some reason the CIA did not want Maheu to appear to be involved. I would assume the reason would be that Maheu would then act as a bridge or connection to others or other activities. Who might that be? Well, he used to be associated with the FBI and at the time he was working for Howard Hughes. Or it could be surmised that if Maheu had not been cut out of the operation, then perhaps Giancana and Trafficante weren't either.

In a meeting on January 19, 1962, Bobby Kennedy told Richard Helms "A solution to the Cuban problem today carried top priority in the U.S. Government. No time, money, effort—or manpower is to be spared. Yesterday...the President had indicated to him that the final chapter had not been written—it's got to be done and it will be done." **[What was Helm's immediate response to this? He did the same thing that Richard Bissell did. He went running to William King Harvey, the CIA's big gun, and placed Harvey in charge of the Cuba task force.** Helms must have reasoned that this would show the White House that the CIA was serious. Not only that, but this was a smart political move on Helms part. The act of putting Harvey in created a buffer for Helms and put some distance between Helms and the incessant pressure of the White House to fix the Cuban problem.] SSCI 157-100004-10138

Shortly thereafter, Mr. Helms (who was clearly slated to take over as Deputy Director of Plans DDP, even while Mr. Bissell was still its nominal head) asked Harvey to set up Task Force W, to be the new working group that was to handle all the Cuban matters for the CIA. It was no secret that Harvey wanted to head up the CIA Soviet Division, but Helms apparently convinced Harvey of the priority and importance that the White House was putting on Cuba. Cuba was where the action was going to be. SSCI 157-100004-10138

Harvey told Helms that he would take on the responsibility of the Cuban operation and Task Force W, on the condition that **he could put in totally fresh people and not take anyone from the old Latin American division, <u>which did not please them</u>**. SSCIA 157-10004-10136

The reference to the old Latin American division with respect to Cuban operations has to be referring to "the Guys from Guatemala." Bill Harvey is shunning them and cutting them out of the picture and here we learn in an SSCIA report that "the Guys from the Guatemala Coup," the once proud CIA guys, who plan the coup d'états, were not at all pleased about this slight.

Richard Helms told Larry Houston, "My God, these Kennedys keep the pressure on about Castro." [86]

In 1961, Bill Harvey's immediate supervisor was Richard Helms. CIA 104-10106-10578

Helms immediately sent out a notice to all CIA stations stating that Bill Harvey was now in charge of the Cuban operation, "Task Force W," the CIA's portion of "OPERATION MONGOOSE."

By announcing this to all CIA stations the word surely got back to the Russians. They knew very well that putting Big Bill Harvey in meant that the CIA meant business and that Cuba had become a top priority. It may have provoked the Soviet to ramp up their own efforts to the point of eventually moving nuclear missiles into Cuba.

In a SSCIA interview, Harvey emphasized that the destruction of Castro was the top priority item for the Kennedy administration in foreign affairs at the time. They wanted him overthrown at all costs, but on the other hand, insisted that it be done by clandestine means. Harvey said he told his superiors that he could produce a provisional government for a few days on the island which could ask for help, but that was really all that he could guarantee and that then the U.S. would have to send in assistance—which the Kennedys were unwilling to do. As a result, he says, there was a great sense of frustration and an effort to try to comply with the Kennedy's wishes to topple the regime clandestinely. He says that Bissell reiterated at that time the statement that he was being prodded by the White House to explore the questions of executive action (meaning assassination). SSCIA 157-10004-10136

The intense pressure, which Bobby Kennedy brought to bear on Richard Helms and the people at the CIA, is legendary. Bobby Kennedy's intensely competitive nature is also legendary. It appears that the Kennedy brothers and especially Bobby Kennedy became obsessed with the idea that Castro had beaten the Kennedys. I am sure Robert Kennedy found this thought to be abhorrent.

As a result of this no-win situation that Richard Helms found himself, he demonstrates how politically astute he was by thrusting William King Harvey forward as the sacrificial lamb. Here is our best and our brightest. Our can-do guy.

The guy we go to in the clutch. Hero of the Berlin Tunnel, catcher of spies. Gun toting, hard charging, blindly patriotic, never says a bad word about anybody, you can't make me talk, Bill Harvey. Richard Helms must have thought Bill Harvey would surely demonstrate to the Kennedy brothers how truly serious the CIA was concerning the Castro problem.

Certain individuals had received discreet indications from Helms that joining the Cuba group within the CIA would not be a good career move. Tom Polgar, a European operative, found himself in a similar situation in which he was offered a prominent position within the Cuban group. Seeking guidance, Polgar approached Helms and inquired, "What are your thoughts?" In response, Helms said, "Tom, remember, I have always been a friend to you. I did not extend that job offer to you." Polgar interpreted Helms' response as a warning and subsequently declined the job offer. It is evident that Bill Harvey did not receive this same level of consideration in this matter. [87]

Isn't this amazing. In a very short time Bill Harvey was given responsibility for the Cuban problem and called upon to do the dirty work of assassinations. Both politically explosive. Both can end your career in a heartbeat, or even land you in jail. It really makes one sick to see what is happening here. Here you have a man who by all accounts is intellectually superior, who really cares deeply about his country and its ideals, who is the definition of the word patriot up to this point in his life, who at one point worked with the Boy Scouts for God's sake, who is out there trying to fight back the very real threat of communism. Who seems to be the only one really doing anything? And then you have these smug, pipe smoking, don't expect me to get dirty [ ] holes, who cower behind him for protection, while pushing him forward into the fray.

Early in the Kennedy administration, Bissell called Harvey

in to discuss what Harvey referred to as an Executive Action Capability, i.e., a general stand-by capability to carry out assassinations when required. Harvey's notes quote Bissell as saying, "The White House has twice urged me to create such a capability." _HSCA_ Vol. 4, Page 140 (It is not clear if it was the Eisenhower/Nixon White House, or the John and Bobby Kennedy White House, or both, which had encouraged Bissell to develop this new capability.)

Bill Harvey said, "At no time did I or anyone else connected with the Castro assassination operation [Helms, Edwards, and O'Connell] ever have the slightest doubt that this was fully authorized. But my sense of the existence of this authorization came solely from my conversations with Richard Bissell. My initial discussion with Richard Bissell about establishing an Executive Action capability was the first-time assassination was ever raised with me in any context other than as a subject of general philosophical discussion." _SSCIA_ 157-10011-10124

Many years later, Sam Halpern, the executive officer of Task Force W and trusted colleague of Bill Harvey confided to author Seymour Hersh that "After the election, Kennedy asked Bissell to create a capacity for political assassination. That's why Harvey set up ZR/RIFLE." [88]

There wasn't any doubt in the CIA concerning the authorization to dispose of Castro. Said the CIA's Jim Critchfield when asked to take over the operation prior to Bill Harvey being asked; "I had no desire to get involved in **Bobby Kennedy's operation to dispose of Castro**." [89]

# ZR/RIFLE

Originally, ZR/RIFLE's role was to develop talent capable of cracking safes and kidnapping couriers. *HSCA* Vol. 4 Page 142

There seems to be very little written documentation of activities left behind by William King Harvey. There is however this one very interesting handwritten document on lined notebook paper entitled Project ZR/RIFLE. In it Harvey sketches out the purpose of Project ZR/RIFLE as the spotting, developing, and the use of agent assets for Division D operations. The objective of this project is the procurement of code and cipher materials and information concerning such materials in accordance with requirements levied on the clandestine services, primarily by the National Security Agency (NSA). Division D will conduct the project with assistance from area divisions and stations as needed. *HSCA* Vol. 4 Page 197-203

Background: In response to the increasing requirements for the operational procurement of foreign codes and cipher materials, Division D in 1960 began the spotting of agent assets as a developmental activity. During the same period requirements from NSA became more refined and, in many respects, more sensitive. It was determined that Division D, which was in close touch with the NSA on procurement requirements [procuring an adversary's code books], would be the best place to conduct such activity. *HSCA* Vol. 4 Page 197-203

Harvey went on to write that the agents must be professional, proven operationally competent, ruthless, stable, (CE) counterespionage officers (few available) - [Bill

Harvey of course was one], able to conduct a patient search and with guts be able to pull back if instinct, or knowledge tells him he should, with a high regard for operational security. Everything is to be conducted by "word of mouth," strictly person-to-person, singleton ops, no projects on paper. Assessments are all important. Maximum security and non-attributable. <u>HSCA</u> Vol. 4 Page 197-203

But then in this same document it is written: "Possible use of defectors for these actions." As we all know, Lee Harvey Oswald was a defector to the Soviet Union from the United States. It is interesting and perhaps significant that Harvey's group was thinking about using defectors in order to shift blame and in the same document it speaks of "blaming Sovs [Soviets] or Czechs [we might add Cuba] in case of blow [blowback]." The document then goes on to suggest another technique very similar to what appears may have happened with the CIA's files on Oswald, the tampering with or falsifying CIA 201 files is also mentioned: "forged and backdated. Should look like a CE [Counterespionage] file. <u>HSCA</u> Vol. 4 Page 197-203

Angleton later recalled, "Bill came to me for help in obtaining phony backdated counterintelligence files to 'prove' that assassins had connections to the KGB, not the CIA, if their deeds ever became public. This material would be released to friendly newspaper reporters when necessary." [90]

I would point out however the source of Bill's alleged tampering with the files. Once again, we have Jim Angleton hanging Bill Harvey out in the public record. As you will soon see, most all the information concerning Lee Harvey Oswald in the CIA appears to be under the control of James Jesus Angleton and his closely held SIG counterintelligence operation.

We do have this rumor to keep in mind however, from

*YouTube*: William Harvey was one of only three people involved in a covert program to send false defectors into the Soviet Union and was undoubtedly aware of Oswald's defection. In a document Harvey outlined a profile of the ideal assassin as a person with communist credentials that could be used if the cover was blown.

One must stop and wonder. Bill Harvey started out as an Eagle Scout from the conservative Midwest and a student of law. Assassinating someone would surely raise some questions in Bill's mind.

A note in Bill Harvey's handwriting, managed to survive at the CIA, dated January 25th and 26th, 1961 and it contains the words "last resort beyond last resorts and a confession of weakness," "the magic button," and "never mention the word assassination." Bill Harvey later testified in 1975 before the "Church Committee" that on January 25 and 26, 1961, immediately after receiving his instructions from Richard Bissell, he met with Joseph Scheider (Sidney Gottlieb) aka "Dr. Death," the Chief of the Technical Services Division (TSD) concerning available methods for (in my words, basically killing people) using Bill's euphemistic words "to discuss available capabilities for 'Executive Action.'" January 25th and 26th are respectively the fifth and sixth day following the inauguration of President Kennedy.

Harvey speculated that the word "bankruptcy" in his cryptic notes referred to [his opinion]—that there was a bankruptcy of policy on the part of the CIA, or USA, if there had to be a resort to assassination. Harvey called it "the last resort beyond last resort and a confession of weakness." *SSCI* 157-100004-10138

Harvey could not recall what he meant in his notes when using the phrase "the magic button" but said that he assumed this was a euphemism either he or Gottlieb used for whatever mechanism was eventually chosen. SSCI 157-100004-10138

Harvey said he had also discussed with the Office of Medical Services and TSD, medical and other scientific aspects of interrogation techniques (e.g., truth serum) **and control techniques (e.g., post-hypnotic suggestion for controlling agents).** SSCI 157-100004-10138

There is compelling evidence of Oswald's being hypnotized, Jack Ruby also. [91]

According to the book, *"Final Judgment,"* **ZR/RIFLE in fact, was one of Angleton's pet in-house CIA projects, which he ran in conjunction with his CIA colleague, William Harvey.** [92]

The following comes from Dick Russell's book *On The Trail of the JFK Assassins:* In 1999, the CIA released a memorandum concerning Project ZR/ALERT. A Study of the Use of Psychological Programming for Intelligence Purposes." Concerns: "exploration and experimentation **by the CI Staff** of the use of hypnotism in certain operational situations." CI referred to Counterintelligence, the Agency branch run by **James Angleton**. The memo went on to say: "Special handling of the documents from Mexico City is called for, I believe... The events described in these documents took place in the summer of 1963, a period in the life of the Mexico City Station, which was of intense interest to the House Select Committee on Assassinations. (The author Dick Russell points out that Mexico City Psychological Programming activities comes into play at the same time as Angleton's CI branch was increasingly becoming the Agency's primary repository for everything regarding Lee Harvey Oswald's activities.)

Under Dulles, MK/ULTRA was created. MK/ULTRA's goal was the mind control of individuals.

Ira Feldman (Ike) from 1953 to 1969 was undercover for CIA, officially FBI Narcotics. Feldman was the right-hand man to George White. George White worked with the CIA's ultra-secret MK/ULTRA program, which experimented with the effects that drugs and hypnotism had on individuals. George White started out as a newspaper reporter. OSS sent him to the Far East. After the war he worked for the FBI. White, like Bill Harvey, always carried a gun.

On occasion, according to Feldman, "CIA officials from other branches would come around, expressing keen interest in what the MK/ULTRA program was revealing. One of these was **James Angleton**, the Agency's chief of counterintelligence. He came to San Francisco to see me and made me a proposition."

Another was **William Harvey**, who at the time oversaw the CIA's Cuban desk. Feldman: "Harvey reminded me of a salesman selling ladies shoes. Harvey was directly involved with us, yes. Bill Harvey was White's compatriot. I met Bill Harvey through White, who must have told him what we were involved in. Harvey was very much interested in it. I went to White and said, 'He wants to know more and more and more.'"

Feldman: "There was one meeting I was at about assassinating Castro, with **Dulles**, White, and Harry Anslinger from the Bureau of Narcotics. It never went ahead."

Feldman: "White knew more people as stool pigeons than we got hair on our head."

Feldman: "Johnny Rosselli (Mafioso worked with Bill Harvey on assassinating Castro) also served as one of White's informants. More than once, White sent me to the airport to pick up Rosselli and bring him into the office. Their ties went back to Chicago, where Rosselli hailed from originally and where White was the FBI's District Supervisor between 1945 and 1947."

"Following a big opium smuggling bust in 1947, Jack Ruby was picked up and hauled in for interrogation, then let off the hook by none other than George White. Federal Bureau of Narcotics files indicate Jack Ruby was yet another of White's legion of stool pigeons." (Feldman himself had admittedly been tight with L.A. gangster Mickey Cohen, utilizing some of Cohen's "girls" in the CIA's Operation Midnight Climax, where unsuspecting male clients were lured by prostitutes to a CIA safe house and given cocktails laced with heavy doses of LSD.)

Feldman goes into how the story was that both Oswald and Ruby had been hypnotized. [93]

The door to Bill Harvey's office was barred, twenty-four hours a day, by a Marine guard. There were three combination safes in Harvey's office, but that was not secure enough for Harvey, so he brought in a one-ton safe of his own. [94]

**Bill Harvey had an asset, code named QJ/WIN**, who apparently had the knack for spotting or identifying people with specialized talents. People capable of obtaining documents, or packages, from couriers. Bill Harvey said, "QJ/WIN's instructions for asset spotting did not change at all after Project ZR/RIFLE was established as far as I know." [Apparently QJ/WIN's instruction from the very beginning was to list all of the skills possessed by people whom he spotted.] Additionally Bill Harvey added: "[     ] continued to be the intermediary between myself and QJ/WIN. I never met QJ/WIN." *SSCIA* 157-10011-10124

Essentially, said Harvey, QJ/WIN canvassed the technological, human asset, and organizational potentials in being, for that which might be organized under the clandestine services. The Bureau of Narcotics files reflect an excellent performance by QJ/WIN. *HSCA* Vol. 4 Page 197-203 & *SSCI* 157-100004-10138

The Executive Action program [or the assassination program] cover name ZR/RIFLE's principal asset was an agent, QJ/WIN, who had been recruited earlier for use in a special operation in the Congo. *HSCA* Vol. 4 Page 141 and *SSCIA* 157-10011-10124

In a CIA memo dated February 1962 Richard Helms, Deputy Director [Plans] approved ZR/RIFLE and the employment of QJ/WIN.

Further evidence that Bill Harvey always got approval from Richard Helms and always reported what he was doing: January 11, 1961, a CIA cable from William K. Harvey to the Directorate of Plans, Richard Helms, noted: "QJ/WIN was sent on this trip for a specific, highly sensitive operational purpose which has been completed."

Years later, the Senate Intelligence Committee determined that QJ/WIN was a foreign citizen with a criminal background recruited out of Europe. Richard Helms has testified, "If you needed somebody to carry out murder, I guess you had [this] man who might be prepared to carry it out."

Ted Shackley was a thirty-four-year-old protégé of Harvey's, beginning in Berlin. When Bill Harvey took over the Cuban operation, he put Ted Shackley in charge of JM/WAVE, the CIA's Miami station. JM/WAVE grew to some 650 agents utilizing fleets of cars, boats, and mansions on the water, serving as a base of operations against Castro. Hundreds of millions of dollars were spent on the JM/WAVE operation alone. The Miami station grew to six hundred case officers and became the largest CIA base in the world. Case officers interrogated the 2,800 Cuban refugees arriving in Florida every day.

Following the failure of the initial attempts, which had been primarily handled by the Office of Security, Rosselli was turned over to Mr. William K. Harvey, a senior DDO officer, who continued to utilize Rosselli's underworld contacts in various unsuccessful attempts to assassinate Castro. Mr. Harvey's operations involving Rosselli began in early 1962. *CIA* 104-10133-10015

From late 1961 to early 1962, Bill Harvey was very busy with a number of projects. Said Harvey, "During this period, I had to set up Task Force W, including recruiting its members. I also had to continue the ongoing Cuban operations and write frequent memos to Lansdale and Robert Kennedy on these subjects. When I was requested to take over the Rosselli operation, I assessed it and determined that the operation should be terminated because it had little chance of success. But, because of the tremendous repercussion potential, I delayed the termination. I subsequently terminated the Rosselli operation as soon as feasible after the missile crisis, which occurred October 1962. It would have been terminated earlier except that during the crisis I could not cut off any potential assets. Had I been given the original assignment of removing Castro, **this is not the way I would have done it**." *SSCIA* 157-10011-10124

Will Potocki, who worked with Bill in Berlin, said this about Bill Harvey: "It was like he had a computerized mind. He was able to put things in the proper perspective and come up with a series of possibilities to solve the problem. He was brilliant in that respect." [95]

Harvey was the quintessential intelligence officer, a man with a fertile operational mind and prodigious memory, who always saw the pitfalls of any scheme and who could suggest five better ways of running an operation. [96]

Bill Harvey's daughter has said: "When you had a problem and you went to him, he would say okay, well let's lay it all out, and he would do his A, B, and Cs. He would always do his A, B, and C." [97]

"He made me a person who could see both sides of things," said his daughter. "There are two sides to every issue, and two sides to every person." [98]

Perhaps it is of little wonder that they picked William King Harvey. According to Bill Corson, Intelligence Analyst and Author, "He was top drawer, an exceptional intelligence officer." [99]

## BILL HARVEY'S & JIM ANGLETON'S RELATIONSHIP 1961

As we have seen, early on in their initial relationship Harvey and Angleton had had a contentious relationship, but over time their relationship changed. Bill Harvey and Jim Angleton became seemingly very close friends.

Here is a good illustration of Harvey and Angleton's relationship, it comes from the Book: *Spy Catcher*, written by British intelligence agent Peter Wright:

Bill Harvey and Jim Angleton meet with Peter Wright for lunch in 1961 to discuss what to do about Castro. Angleton asked, "How would you handle Castro?"

Bill Harvey asked: "Would you hit him?" Peter's response: "We're not in it anymore, Bill."

"We're developing a new capability in the Company to handle these kinds of problems," explained Harvey, "and we're in the market for the requisite expertise."

"Whenever Harvey became serious," said Wright, "his voice dropped to a low monotone, and his vocabulary lapsed into the kind of strangled bureaucratic syntax beloved by Washington officials. He explained ponderously that they needed deniable personnel, and improved technical facilities —in Harvey jargon, 'delivery mechanisms.'"

"The French!" Peter Wright said brightly. "Have you tried them? It's more their type of thing, you know, Algiers, and so on. Use non-Americans, like French Corsican hit men, not Sicilians, work through the CIA in South Korea."

Angleton scribbled in his notebook.

"What about technically—did you have any special equipment?" asked Harvey. Wright describes how a poison dart fired from a cigarette killed a sheep. Then he said, "after witnessing this tragic scene, I knew that assassination was no policy for peacetime."

"Beyond that," said Wright, "there was little help I could offer Harvey and Angleton. The sight of Angleton's notebook was beginning to unnerve me. They seemed so determined, so convinced that this was the way to handle Castro, and slightly put out that I could not help them more."

You are not holding out on us over this, are you?" Said Harvey suddenly. The shape of his pistol was visible again under his jacket.

Wright replied, "I've told you, Bill. We're out of that game. We're the junior partner in the alliance, remember? It's your responsibility now."

"Harvey was not the kind of man to laugh at a joke. Come to that, neither was Angleton," observed Wright. [100]

# OPERATION MONGOOSE

Harvey found the Mafia's Johnny Rosselli more honest than most of the people in Washington.

Rosselli confirmed that he directed six assassination attempts against Castro over the period September 1960 to February 1963. <u>CIA</u> 104-10122-10366

The CIA devised some unconventional methods to eliminate Castro, some of which were pretty extravagant and off the wall. Harvey believed, I am sure, in the effectiveness and reliability of a rifle, to simply get the job done.

Harvey has said: that he "went through the entire analysis of the plan" [to assassinate Castro using the Mafia and] he called it among other things a "damn fool idea to start with" ... he thought it had been handled in an incredibly amateurish fashion. Harvey also thought we were dealing with what he referred to as a huge hand grenade, that he could not afford to have go off, so far as outside knowledge of it was concerned. <u>Rockefeller Commission</u> 178-10002-10324

Harvey: "It was not just a question of my not being able to afford that it go off, but in the aftermath of the Bay of Pigs failure, it was not the kind of an explosion that the Government, the Agency, or anybody else could well afford." One of Harvey's concerns was that so many people seemed to know about the plan. <u>Rockefeller Commission</u> 178-10002-10324

Bill Harvey would later testify: "This was an ongoing matter which I was injected into **on explicit orders from Helms**." Harvey said of the Mafia – CIA Operation to get Castro, it was a "damned dicey operation" that carried the "very pregnant possibility of this government being blackmailed either by Cubans for political purposes, or by figures in organized crime for their own self-protection, or aggrandizement." HSCA Vol. 10 Page 179

The CIA/Mafia operation to assassinate Castro under William King Harvey's direction has been identified by the CIA as Phase II. Here is an example of the CIA's and William King Harvey's official position concerning Phase II:

One of the first things Bill Harvey did was to cut Giancana and Trafficante out of the operation and he decided to deal with Rosselli directly. Sam Giancana and Santos Trafficante were two Mafia "dons" who Attorney General Robert Kennedy had targeted in his war on organized crime. Giancana was the Chicago chieftain of the Cosa Nostra and successor to Al Capone, and Trafficante [located in Tampa, Florida] had been the Cosa Nostra boss of Cuban operations." NARA-FORD 178-10002-10297

James Angleton said that "William Harvey had made one mistake with Rosselli. You never become involved, at his level, with the operators. You put people between you." [101]

Again, we find William King Harvey front and center when it came to the important, dirty, and difficult work. Harvey appears to be a roll up your sleeves, get in there and get the job done, kind of a guy. From what I gather he was also one you could rely on to keep his mouth shut and to not put things on paper. He would tell only those things that you needed to know, for you to get your job done and no more.

May 11, 1962, William King Harvey was age 47, 6' tall, 225 lbs., had green eyes and blond hair. His cover name was William Walker. CIA 104-10106-10559

Operation Mongoose was a combination of propaganda, economic sabotage, and the infiltration of small teams of exile aimed at creating an internal revolt in Cuba.

The paramilitary operators of the CIA, "the PMs," or the "cowboys," worked in the field, training and helping to organize the raids on Cuba by the exiled anti-Castro Cubans. The CIA's **Ray S. Cline** once said, "You've got to have cowboys- the only thing you don't let them do is make policy. You keep them in the ranch house when you don't have a specific project for them."

General Edward **Lansdale** had been with CIA from 1952 to 1955, while he was in the Philippines and Vietnam, then he reverted to the Air Force and became Assistant to the Secretary of Defense Robert McNamara until about 1964 or 1965, then he returned to Vietnam where he was an assistant to the Ambassador. *NARA-Ford* 178-10004-10112

Lansdale and Bobby Kennedy oversaw the Special Group (Augmented), which oversaw operation Mongoose. Operation MONGOOSE was an interdepartmental affair and was under the operational control of the Defense Department. (Senate Committee, McCone, 6/6/75, p39.) Bill Harvey's CIA Task Force W was a part of Operation Mongoose and was the CIA's action arm of Operation Mongoose. Operation Mongoose was a covert action program whose objective was to overthrow the Cuban government. Task Force W operated out of CIA headquarters and through its massive operation in Miami known as the JM/WAVE station. **Bill Harvey reported directly to the CIA's Deputy Director of Plans, Richard Helms**.

Opposite Edward Lansdale in this project was Bill Harvey. Lansdale reported that President Kennedy once playfully teased him, comparing him to James Bond. Lansdale modestly suggested that the true American James Bond, counterpart to 007 was none other than Bill Harvey, who had recently been assigned to the Cuban case by Helms.

Intrigued by this notion, President Kennedy expressed an interest in meeting the man referred to as **"America's James Bond."** Consequently, Harvey and Lansdale found themselves seated outside the Oval Office, awaiting their audience with the president. During their wait, Lansdale turned to Harvey and casually inquired, "You're not carrying your gun, are you?" Without hesitation, Harvey replied, "Of course" and he proceeded to reach for a revolver in his pants pocket. Recognizing the potential danger, if Bill were to pull out his weapon in the presence of the Secret Service, Lansdale told Harvey to "keep the damn thing in his pants until he could explain to the agents that Bill would like to check his gun. Which they then proceeded to do. However, just as they were about to enter the Oval Office, Harvey suddenly remembered something. Harvey reached around and pulled out his .38 Detective Special from a holster in the small of his back and handed it to the startled Secret Service Agent.

President Kennedy extended his congratulations to Harvey upon his appointment as the head of the Cuban Task Force W. In a lighthearted exchange, the president playfully inquired whether Harvey, shared James Bond's success with women? Harvey later confided to Angleton that he liked the president but could not stand Bobby Kennedy. [102]

And what did President Kennedy think of William Harvey? Given Harvey's unique pear shape, said Lansdale, "He thought I was pulling his leg. He told me later, 'Ahhhhh, that wasn't James Bond.'"

According to Lansdale, his relationship with Harvey was marked by mutual distrust. Harvey was known for playing his cards very close to his chest, even with his superiors, (I would add, except for Helms. This study illustrates that Bill Harvey seemed always very careful about clearing everything with Richard Helms.) Lansdale said, "At times I'd go in and talk about things with Harvey's bosses and just draw blanks." As for the then CIA Director John McCone, "he didn't know enough about what was going on in the agency in order to have an opinion. He just didn't have that much say in things, frankly." Regarding Harvey's and Lansdale's relationship, it wasn't necessarily Harvey's fault; Lansdale was always coming up with off the wall ideas that weren't workable. To Harvey, Lansdale was worse than a security risk, he was wacky [103]

Bill Harvey was always cautious and calculating. He recognized the seriousness and the danger involved in his work. He knew the importance to his mission and that people's lives hung in the balance. He knew to not broadcast to everyone what was taking place under the surface. On the other hand, Bobby Kennedy appeared in public and was in open direct contact with anti-Castro Cubans and Edward Lansdale actually put words like "assassination" in government memos. Neither appeared to appreciate the gravity of the situation and the importance of secrecy.

The President and his brother made an effort to try and control the CIA by running proposed operations through the Special Group (Augmented). It was through the Special Group (Augmented), that Bobby Kennedy and Bill Harvey would come together in an effort to do something about Castro. It didn't take Harvey long to conclude that Bobby Kennedy was now micromanaging the agency.

Bobby Kennedy soon became fascinated with the power that came from knowing so many secrets. Bobby Kennedy began to believe he was running the whole world and as Ray Cline has commented, "in many ways he was…."

In 1962, Bill Harvey confided to Ted Shackley, who oversaw the CIA's JM/Wave operation in Miami, that the driving force behind U.S. Cuban policy stemmed from a personal vendetta.

According to Harvey, President Kennedy and his brother Robert felt deeply humiliated by the unsuccessful outcome of the Bay of Pigs invasion and they were determined to do something about Castro, be it palace revolt, military coup, popular uprising, or assassination. [104]

The CIA's Sam Halpern said, "The Kennedys were on our back constantly to do more damage to Cuba, to cause an uprising, to get rid of Castro." [105]

"You don't know what pressure is until you get those two sons of bitches laying it on you," said Halpern. "We felt we were doing things in Cuba because of a family vendetta and not because it was for the good of the United States." Things were being done "for personal reasons – because the family name was besmirched by the Bay of Pigs. It wasn't national security. Their father always said: 'Don't get mad; get even.'" [106]

Walter Elder of the CIA said, "We had the impression that Bobby was simply Jack's ruffian. Jack could sit above it. Bobby was the one who wanted action. There was an intense dislike in the CIA for Bobby." Thomas Parrott, a CIA official said, "Bobby, in my view, was an unprincipled sinister little bastard." [107]

As told by those in the CIA at the time, Bobby Kennedy became both feared and despised.

A senior officer in the Kennedy State Department recently said, "Bobby was an action man who wanted to take action on things he knew nothing about." While seasoned professionals watched in amazement at their unprofessional maneuvers, the brothers believed their intellect and fierce determination would carry the day [108]

A major frustration for Bill Harvey was the exercise of getting the approval of the Special Group (Augmented). The

Special Group (Augmented) consisted of Bobby Kennedy and an interagency team that was pulled together to orchestrate the ouster of Castro. The Special Group, like most committees was very slow moving and tended to analyze everything to death. There were approximately forty meetings in a year's time that Bill Harvey was required to attend. This had to be excruciating to meet nearly every week and explain what was going on. Perhaps if Bill hadn't had to spend so much time in meetings, he could have gotten more done. Bill Harvey was an action guy, used to calling his own shots. Bill Harvey complained to the Director of the CIA, McCone, about the Special Group (Augmented), but to no avail.

Over Bill Harvey's career he demonstrated little patience when it came to politics. He seems to have pushed forward on a number of initiatives, either because he believed it was right, and/or logical. Any concern for appearance seems always to be addressed by the CIA through indirect associations, obfuscation, plausible deniability, and confusion. In Bill's defense I would add however that **Bill Harvey always seemed to be very good about checking with Richard Helms and with James Jesus Angleton**.

Bobby Kennedy was a force to be reckoned with, he was willing to bully anyone. According to Thomas Parrott, the Special Groups Secretary, "Bobby Kennedy was very difficult to deal with. He was arrogant, he knew it all, he knew the answer to everything. He sat there; tie down, chewing gum, his feet up on the desk. "Bobby Kennedy would invariably arrive late at highly classified meetings and put his feet up on the conference table, so that others had to look at the soles of his shoes," reports Parrott. His threats were transparent. It was, 'If you don't do it, I'll tell my big brother on you.'" Bobby Kennedy browbeat and bullied Harvey and his aides so relentlessly that after one session General Maxwell Taylor turned to Bobby and said, "You could sack a town and enjoy it." [109]

Witnesses tell how Bill Harvey tended to sometimes speak too long in a meeting, while Bobby Kennedy would sit impatiently drumming his fingers on the table.

The Attorney General Robert Kennedy would call CIA headquarters from time to time to bark out some orders and then hang up, leaving the CIA man wondering whether he had just talked to the President's brother or a prankster. The Attorney General frequently dealt directly with some of the Cuban exiles, which were supposed to be Harvey's agents. [110]

To Harvey, it was so much amateurish meddling. Soon he started referring to Kennedy in private as "that fucker" and began suggesting that some of the Attorney General's actions bordered on the traitorous. Bill Harvey hated Bobby Kennedy's guts with a purple passion. [111]

Bobby Kennedy would later say in a taped interview, "The people the CIA had originally, were not very good .... I was trying to do things, mostly trying to get them to come up with some ideas about things to be done."

On top of everything else Bill Harvey and Ed Lansdale couldn't stand one another.

Rumors began to circulate about confrontations that were occurring between Bill Harvey and Robert Kennedy. In one encounter, an impatient Kennedy supposedly demanded to know why Shackley had not yet infiltrated a team into Cuba. Harvey responded by explaining that the team members had to be trained. "I'll take them out to my estate and train them," Kennedy said. Replied Harvey, "What will you teach them, sir?" "Babysitting?" [112]

Andy Alderton said to Mrs. Harvey, "I understand that you knew the Kennedys as well." She goes "Oh," and looks up at the ceiling and pauses, showing some distress at having to answer. "Well, you know **Bobby Kennedy and my husband were absolutely enemies. I mean just pure enemies.** He [Bobby] did not have a very good philosophy. And he had no confidence in himself because his brother put him in a job, he wasn't really capable of handling. It made a lot of stress for the people who were working in law enforcement." _Andy Alderton/C.G. Harvey Interview_

Rosselli brought to the CIA information about Trafficante knowing of a man high up in the Cuban exile movement who might do the job. He identified him as Tony Varona head of the Democratic Revolutionary Front. Trafficante approached Varona. _1967 CIA Inspector General's Report_

Harvey arrived in Miami on 21 April 1962 and found Rosselli already in touch with Tony Varona. Harvey described the manner in which the lethal material was to be introduced into Castro's food, involving an asset of Varona's who had access to someone in a restaurant frequented by Castro. _1967 CIA Inspector General's Report_

After his Miami trip Harvey decided to deal directly with Johnny Rosselli as he felt that Maheu and Giancana were "untrustworthy" and "surplus" and cut them out of the operation.

The four poison pills, fabricated by the Technical Services Division, were given to Rosselli by Harvey who said that they "would work anywhere, at any time, with anything." Rosselli passed the pills on to Tony Varona for the hit squad. _1967 CIA Inspector General's Report_

There were changes in the original cast of hoodlum players. Harvey specified that Giancana was not to be brought in on the operation, and he believes that Rosselli honored the request. Rosselli once reported to Harvey that Giancana had asked if anything was going on, and when Rosselli said that nothing was happening, Giancana said, "Too bad." Additionally, Santos Trafficante was [supposedly] no longer involved. Rosselli now had a man known to Harvey as Maceo, who also used the names Garcia-Gomez and Godoy. Harvey is unable to identify Maceo; he describes him as "a Cuban who spoke Italian." *1967 CIA Inspector General's Report*

Rosselli remained a prominent figure in the operation, but worked directly with the Cuban exile community and directly on behalf of CIA. Rosselli needed Giancana and Trafficante in the first phase as a means of establishing contacts inside Cuba. He did not need them in the second phase, because he had Varona. However, it would be naïve to assume that Rosselli did not take the precaution of informing higher-ups in the syndicate that he was working in a territory considered to be the private domain of someone else in the syndicate. *1967 CIA Inspector General's Report*

When the pills were given to Varona through Rosselli, Varona requested arms and equipment for the support of his end of the operation. Rosselli passed the request to Harvey. Harvey, with the help of Ted Shackley, the chief of the JM/WAVE Station, procured explosives, detonators, twenty .30 caliber rifles, twenty .45 caliber handguns, two radios, and one boat radar. Harvey says that the "shopping list" included some items that could be obtained only from the U.S. Government. Harvey omitted those items, because Rosselli, posing as a representative of private business interests, would not have had access to such equipment. *1967 CIA Inspector General's Report*

Harvey and Shackley rented a U-Haul truck under an assumed name, loaded it with the arms and equipment, and parked it in the parking lot of a drive-in restaurant. The keys were then given to Rosselli for delivery either to Maceo, to Varona, or to Varona's son-in-law. Evidently Harvey and Rosselli had not yet come to trust each other. Perhaps fearing a double-cross, each set about independently to assure himself that the equipment reached the proper hands. After parking the truck, Harvey and Shackley kept the parking lot under surveillance until the pass was completed. Rosselli, accompanied by O'Connell, did the same. Neither supposedly knew that the other was watching. Eventually the truck was picked up and driven away. It was returned later, empty, and with the keys under the seat as prearranged. Harvey returned it to the rental agency. Harvey says that Shackley never knew to whom delivery was made nor for what purpose. *1967 CIA Inspector General's Report*

May 1962, Harvey and Rosselli arranged a system of telephone communications by which Harvey was kept posted on any developments. Harvey, using a pay phone could call Rosselli at the Friars Club in Los Angeles at 1600 hours, Los Angeles time. Rosselli could phone Harvey at Harvey's home in the evening. Rosselli reported that the pills were in Cuba and at the restaurant used regularly by Castro. *1967 CIA Inspector General's Report*

June 1962, Rosselli reported to Harvey on 21 June that **Varona** had **dispatched a team of three men to Cuba**. Just what they were supposed to do is pretty vague. Harvey said that they appeared to have no specific plan for killing Castro. They were to recruit others who might be used in such a scheme. If an opportunity to kill Castro presented itself, they, or the persons they recruited were to make the attempt —perhaps using pills. Harvey never learned their names or anything else about them. From the sequence of the reports, the pills were sent in ahead of the three-man team, but this is not now ascertainable. *1967 CIA Inspector General's Report*

Richard Helms has said that Bill Harvey "pretty much kept the operation in his back pocket," and never told the Special Group (Augmented) about the ongoing operation to assassinate Castro. This of course would also be consistent with Bill Harvey's concern about the potential that the United States might be subject to blackmail. Bill Harvey also recognized the deadly seriousness of his work and the need for secrecy; something Bobby Kennedy unfortunately may have learned the hard way on November 22, 1963.

In May 1962 Bobby Kennedy got wind of the first attempts to assassinate Castro made by Edwards, O'Connell, and Maheu, using the Mafia's Rosselli, Giancana, and Trafficante and a bungled wire-tapping attempt on Giancana's girlfriend Phyllis McGuire. As a result, Edwards and CIA Legal Counsel Houston were called upon to brief Bobby Kennedy about the operation. *HSCA* Vol. 10 Page 188

Houston later testified: "If you have ever seen Mr. [Bobby] Kennedy's eyes get steely and his jaw set and his voice get low and precise, you get a definite feeling of unhappiness." Houston testified that Bobby Kennedy had stated, "I trust that if you ever try to do business with organized crime again —with gangsters—you will let the Attorney General know before you do it." (They didn't tell the Attorney General that although they had terminated their operation, Harvey's operation with Rosselli was ongoing.) *HSCA* Vol. 10 Page 188

It is interesting to note that Bobby Kennedy reportedly did not object to the thought of assassinating Castro, he only objected to using the Mafia.

Harvey later said that he recalled Edwards later briefing him on this conversation with Bobby Kennedy, but he does not remember what Edwards said, or whether Edwards said that Kennedy had been upset regarding the use of Mafia without his knowledge, or the assassination effort without his knowledge. **Harvey does remember Kennedy was angry**. Harvey also did not recall whether Edwards indicated they had told RFK it was a finished operation or not. *SSCIA* 157-10004-10136

I find this incredible for one who is renowned for having an incredible memory and capacity for recall. Harvey admits knowing that Bobby was mad. Well, either Bobby is mad because of the assassination attempt, or he is mad because the Mafia is involved. Either way, I would interpret this to mean that Harvey should have stopped immediately his operation with Rosselli and the Mafia, but instead Harvey pushes on. Actions speak louder than words. All the documentation portrays Harvey as opposed to the use of assassination, but this action seems to suggest otherwise.

This might explain why Bill Harvey did not recall Edwards informing him on this point: In the CIA Inspector General's Report it says, Edwards informed us that he has no specific recollection of having told Harvey of Kennedy's warning that the Attorney General should be told in advance of any future CIA use of gangsters. (Edward's admitted this, years later, to the Inspector General. This contradicts what his memo said he told Harvey.) *1967 CIA Inspector General's Report* (But the point remains, Bill Harvey understood that Bobby Kennedy was mad.)

Edwards told Bobby Kennedy that the assassination project had been terminated, which was not true, being as Harvey had given the poison pills to Rosselli only two weeks before. To protect himself, Edwards wrote a memorandum stating, "On this date Mr. Harvey called me and indicated that he was dropping any plans for the use of Subject [Rosselli] for the future." Harvey found out about the memo when questioned by the Senate Intelligence Committee in 1975, and he was furious. He declared that it "was not true, and Colonel Edwards knew it was not true"; the falsification was intended to show that Edwards was "no longer chargeable" should the operation backfire. *1967 CIA Inspector General's Report*

**Harvey** states that on 14 May he **briefed Mr. Helms** on the meeting with the Attorney General, as told to him by Edwards. Harvey advised against briefing John McCone the CIA Director at the time and General Carter and states that Helms concurred in this.

The first opportunity Harvey had for killing off the assassination attempts came when he and Richard Helms discussed whether to tell CIA Director, McCone, about the assassination operations. Harvey admits that he might have urged on Helms (for a number of reasons) that McCone not be briefed. In any event, says Harvey, "it was definitely Helms' decision." SSCIA 157-10004-10136

The second opportunity Harvey had for killing off the assassination attempts came in August 1962. Harvey witnessed in a meeting, Defense Secretary McNamara proposing "assassinating Castro" and he learned as a result how CIA Director McCone was violently opposed to this kind of action.

The CIA Inspector General's Report dated April 25, 1967, says, "We cannot overemphasize the extent to which responsible Agency officers felt themselves subject to the Kennedy administration's severe pressures to do something about Castro and his regime. The fruitless and, in retrospect, often unrealistic plotting should be viewed in that light. HSCA Vol. 4 Page 130

Lansdale was a brainstormer. However, his ideas often lacked realism and ventured into the realm of absurdity. They were downright wacky. One such concept, his plan called "Elimination by Illumination," which aimed to deceive the Cuban people into believing that the Second Coming of Christ was taking place. According to Lansdale, the plan involved spreading the message in Cuba that Christ was imminent, and that Castro was the anti-Christ. Additionally, a U.S. submarine would be stationed just beyond the horizon, which would launch starshells, creating the illusion of the Second Coming and leading to the overthrow of Castro. The CIA's Thomas Parrott explained that other ludicrous ideas were proposed by Lansdale including using exploding seashells in areas where Castro went scuba diving and another idea: employing a chemical agent to make Castro's beard fall out. This is the kind of stupid stuff Bill Harvey had to deal with. [113]

Following the August 10th meeting of the Special Group (Augmented), Lansdale addressed a memorandum on August 13th to William Harvey (CIA). The memorandum assigned responsibility for drafting papers on various subjects related to the Cuban operation. Harvey's assignment included: "Intelligence, Political (splitting the regime, [portion excised from the CIA file copy, which was an assignment for Bill Harvey concerning the 'elimination of leaders'])." *1967 CIA Inspector General's Report*

On 14 August, **Harvey submitted a memorandum to the DD/P (Helms) reporting the Lansdale communication and what Harvey had done about it**. Harvey's memorandum to the DD/P states that the excised portion had consisted of the phrase: "including elimination of leaders". Harvey wrote that he had phoned Lansdale's office and had spoken with Frank Hand in Lansdale's absence. Harvey said he had protested the use of the phrase and had proposed that steps be taken to have it excised from all copies. This was agreed to. Harvey deleted the phrase from his own copy and assumes that instructions were given to other recipients to do the same. Harvey told us that Lansdale repeatedly tried to raise the matter of assassination of Castro with him over the next several weeks. Harvey says that he always avoided such discussions. Harvey estimates that five persons in Lansdale's office were generally aware of the sensitive details of Project MONGOOSE and of Lansdale's interest in assassination as an aspect of it. *1967 CIA Inspector General's Report*

In 1976, a Senate Select Committee report says, "I don't know how strongly Harvey will testify along these lines. He is generally very hesitant to poormouth anyone. Harvey said that he knew of no basis for Lansdale to have originally put the reference to liquidating leaders as a study item in the memorandum, which upset Harvey so. He said that whenever Lansdale thereafter tried to raise the subject with him, he simply turned off the discussion. *SSCIA* 157-10004-10136

General Lansdale was not a standup guy. Whenever Robert Kennedy complained about the progress, General Lansdale blamed Bill Harvey.

Bobby Kennedy was impatient. He had meet many of the exiled anti-Castro Cubans and he began actively going over Bill Harvey's head and communicating directly with many of the Cuban commandos and agents who were serving under Bill Harvey. Many times, Bobby would tell the agents not to tell anyone in the CIA of their conversation. When Bill Harvey found out about this, he was furious. Not only did this not reflect well on Harvey in the eyes of his troops, but being the brother of the President, it was a very dangerous thing to do because Castro was bound to find out. Castro would know that the Kennedys were personally out to get him. [114]

Operation Mongoose would eventually have 60 to 70 agents infiltrated into Cuba, but Castro's agents were everywhere in Miami and in the U.S. in general. Bill Harvey would turn to J. Edgar Hoover and the FBI for help in identifying Cuban agents in the United States.

April 21, 1962, Bill Harvey met with Johnny Rosselli in Miami.

Robert Morrow, a CIA contract agent heard tell that Harvey was a real wild man. Morrow met William King Harvey twice. Morrow reports, "**William Harvey met regularly with John Rosselli, Santos Trafficante, Sam Giancana, Robert Maheu, and Eladio del Valle, through whom I originally met Harvey."** [115]

Morrow's information is very important and interesting concerning Bill Harvey's having met regularly with Maheu, Trafficante, and Giancana. I was under the impression from all of Bill Harvey's testimony that he had immediately cut Trafficante, Giancana, and Maheu out of the assassination operation. I don't think that Morrow put this out in his book as disinformation, but rather as a casual matter of fact side comment of no particular relevance to him and here is why I say that. His statement saying, "Harvey would meet regularly with John Rosselli, Santos Trafficante, Sam Giancana, Robert Maheu, and Eladio del Valle, through whom I originally met him," is not even a part of the story being told by Morrow, but rather it is in his endnotes for chapter eight and is simply for the purpose of explaining how he came to know who William King Harvey was.

One more point that I would make, however, concerning Bill Harvey's claim of having cut out Maheu, Trafficante, and Giancana. Bill Harvey may have lied to minimize the damage to the CIA, but for whatever reason, Bill Harvey's credibility is critical and here it appears he lied. Couple that with his recommendation to Helms that they not tell the CIA director McCone about the assassination plots which was a little less than honest. If he lied here, what other things might he have lied about?

Bill Harvey and Johnny Rosselli became very good friends. C.G. Harvey told Mike McCormick that she and her husband took vacations together with Johnny and they stayed at each other's homes. *My Interview with Mike McCormick*

In fact, here is what C.G. told Andy Alderton: I loved Rosselli. My husband always said that if he had to ride shotgun, Rosselli, that's the guy I would take with me. Rosselli was the kind of guy who if he gave you his friendship, well, he was going to stick by you. He definitely was Mafia, and he definitely was a crook, and he had definitely pulled off all kinds of stunts with the Mafia, but he was a patriot. He believed in the United States. And he knew that my husband was a patriot. And that's what drew him to Bill. *Andy Alderton/C.G. Harvey Interview*

By April 1962 Bobby, disappointed with the speed at which things were progressing regarding Castro, decided to run his own operation. The CIA assigned to Bobby Kennedy, Charles Ford, an experienced CIA agent. **At Bobby Kennedy's direction** and while continuing to work for Bill Harvey, Ford spent the next 18 months, up until President Kennedy's assassination, traveling around the country meeting with various Mafia figures in an attempt to get rid of Castro. "It was possible," Halpern said, "that **Bobby Kennedy's primary purpose in dealing with Charles Ford was to do what Bill Harvey was not doing—find someone to assassinate Fidel Castro.**" [116]

I believe there is evidence to suggest that the CIA set Bobby Kennedy up with Lee Harvey Oswald as a part of an operation that Bobby Kennedy was running. More on this later.

Andy Alderton asked C.G. Harvey, **"Tell me about operation Mongoose the whole plot to assassinate Castro? C.G. responded:** "From what I understand Bobby Kennedy gave an order and the whole Rosselli thing." Later in the conversation she said: "And he [Rosselli] had been recruited by another guy from the FBI for assassination purposes on Kennedy, or um on Castro by Bobby. **Bobby was running this** other guy..."

**C.G. Harvey also said to Andy Alderton, "I am sick and tired of having them say that Bill Harvey tried to assassinate Castro when the guy who was doing it was Robert Kennedy!"** Andy Alderton/C.G. Harvey Interview

It wasn't until 1997 that the CIA's Richard Helms finally said, "There isn't any doubt as to who was running that effort. It was Bobby Kennedy on behalf of his brother. It wasn't anybody else!" [117]

A CIA Agent who worked closely with Harvey and who insisted on anonymity said in 1995, **"Bill Harvey 'sandbagged' the whole operation. Bill gave the attempts only a half-hearted effort at first, but soon decided against going through with them for a variety of reasons. First, it went against his Hoosier upbringing. I remember Bill pacing the office saying, 'Bobby's plan to kill Castro is the worst thing I've seen in my career. How on earth can I convince that idiot that this is so wrong?'** Bill used to say that Bobby couldn't grasp the meaning of 'unattributable' operations ... [He felt that] the Kennedys thought of it as a game. Bill knew that this was no game. It was serious business. **I know that Bill personally stopped the plots in their tracks. Any effort that continued had nothing to do with Bill Harvey and everything to do with Bobby Kennedy."** [118]

Perhaps Bill Harvey meant what he wrote in one of the few handwritten documents, which managed to survive at the CIA, dated January 25th and 26th, 1961 it said concerning assassinations that is the "last resort beyond last resorts and a confession of weakness."

Cuba Project officer Sam Halpern described the following: "I happened to be in Harvey's office one day when he got a telephone call from Bobby Kennedy. And he started to bawl Harvey out and pointed out that he, Kennedy, thought that when we did things secretly, how come it ended up in the press. And Harvey had to explain in words of one syllable that when you blow something up, it's going to make headlines somewhere. And it was the Kennedy brothers who were demanding the 'boom and bang' all over the island." [119]

The CIA's head of JM/WAVE in Miami, Ted Shackley explained the situation this way, "Bobby was being besieged by Cubans. Everyone had access to him ...they were always whispering in his ear and influencing him. Eventually, Bobby was running stuff parallel to the Agency. Every Cuban in Miami had ideas about killing Castro. Two or three of them together and you had a plot...and Bobby would listen to them." [120]

Bill Harvey was gravely concerned about Bobby Kennedy's personal relationships with the Cuban exiles and the safety and security risks it represented. CIA analyst Dino Brugioni wrote, "Harvey argued unsuccessfully that someone of Bobby's stature and position should not be known to the covert operatives, much less be seen with them." Cuba spies were as thick as fleas in the U.S.

Harvey once complained to fellow officer Sam Halpern that "Bobby was carving a path in the operations so wide that a Mack truck could drive through." Sam Halpern was Bill Harvey's executive assistant before, during, and after the October 1962 crisis.

According to one witness, during a visit to the CIA's station in Miami, Bobby Kennedy began "barking orders at everyone like he knew what the hell was going on." Later, Kennedy tore some communications from a Teletype machine and started to walk out the door with the classified information in hand. Harvey yelled, "Hey! Where are you going with that?" Harvey then walked up to the Attorney General and ripped the paper from his hand. This confrontation most likely sealed Harvey's fate. [121]

Bobby Kennedy's personal relationship with the exile fighters may have backfired in a major way. After a Cuban exile agent meet with attorney general Robert Kennedy in Washington the Cuban agent ended up being infiltrated into Cuba, he was captured by Cuban security and reportedly tortured. Ted Shackley and the principals of JM/WAVE feared that he would confess that he had conferred with the president's brother. The agent was tried by Cuban authorities and was executed. [122]

August 20, 1962, President Kennedy was told by General Maxwell Taylor that the Special Group (Augmented) did not feel that it was possible to overthrow Castro, without using the U.S. military.

August 23, 1962, Bill Harvey was ordered by the Special Group to compile a list of possible sabotage targets relevant to an invasion of Cuba. At the same time the Pentagon began planning a paratroop assault on Cuba.

Bill Harvey flew down and met with Johnny Rosselli in Miami on the 7th and on the 11th of September. Varona was said to be ready to send in another team of three men. They were supposedly militiamen whose assignment was to penetrate Castro's bodyguard. During this period the "medicine" was reportedly still in place and the three men of the first team still safe. *1967 CIA Inspector General's Report*

September 1962 – although Harvey received several reports that the militiamen were poised to take off, presumably from somewhere in the Florida Keys, they did not actually leave. First, "conditions inside" were given as the reason for delay; then the October missile crisis threw plans awry. *1967 CIA Inspector General's Report*

Bill Harvey finally concluded that Varona was stalling and

cut him loose. Harvey and Rosselli then decided to use snipers from Point Mary in the Florida Keys. The book by Bradley Ayers called *"The War That Never Was,"* tells of a Colonel Rosselli at Point Mary. It also tells about Bobby Kennedy's visits to this operation.

The information that Bill Harvey was receiving was second and third hand. He testified that he wasn't sure that anything was really being done in the field. By September of 1962 Harvey had doubts about the assassination of Castro. He had planned to cut the operation off sooner, but then the Cuba missile crisis came along, and he felt that he should keep all of his options open.

Sam Halpern is quoted as saying, "Bill Harvey was a rough and tough SOB, but when push came to shove, he couldn't deliver. He had no more expertise than you and I in eliminating anybody. We never killed anyone, but not for lack of trying." [123]

A memo dated back on February 20, 1962, and signed by the Chief of Operations Brigadier General Edward G. Lansdale-- specified late October 1962 as the target date for Castro's ouster and suggested that American military force might be required to accomplish that objective.

October 1, 1962, Defense Secretary McNamara meets with the Joint Chiefs of Staff and a decision is made to intensify Cuban contingency planning. Admiral Robert Dennison, is directed "to be prepared to institute a blockade against Cuba." The U.S. Navy and Air Force are directed to preposition military equipment and weapons needed to execute an airstrike. [124]

October 6, 1962, Admiral Dennison of CINCLANT directs increased readiness for a possible invasion of Cuba with readiness to execute Oplan 312 an airstrike against Cuba. Troops, aircraft, ships, equipment, and supplies begin moving based upon the contingency of an invasion based on Oplan 314 and Oplan 316. [125]

CINCLANT OPLAN 316-62: the Invasion of Cuba as formulated during the Cuban Missile Crisis called for an initial massive airstrike against identified sites such as missile sites, and radar installations, followed by a warship bombardment, then the 101st Airborne paratroopers would capture airports and bridges, followed by an amphibious assault and the injection of the 1st Infantry Division. Estimated length of the engagement 8 to 18 days.

Defense Secretary Robert McNamara later insisted that despite the American covert activities against Castro, and despite the preparation of military contingencies in October 1962, the Kennedy administration did not intend to invade Cuba; that is, no political decision to invade Cuba had been taken, and no serious discussions to consider such an operation had taken place among senior policymakers.

The following was reported by Tom Cochrun, Channel 13, Indianapolis, in a local TV documentary in 1986, entitled *Indiana's James Bond*: "Tonight for the first time we can report, secret Presidential orders for the invasion of Cuba. The 82nd Airborne Division and the Green Berets, with full naval and air support were ready. But problems coordinating intelligence between the commands arose. Bill Harvey was called to get operations back on course. The commanding Generals offered Bill Harvey the full VIP treatment, the suite last used by the President himself. But true to Harvey's style and character he insisted on being with his men on the night before the invasion." [126]

An anonymous high-ranking military officer appears on the screen and says: "We were all suited up ready to jump into Cuba. For Harvey and his men, it was time to put the plan into action. The only caveat we were given was to not fire on, or involve, Russian troops." [127]

"As commanders sat in aircraft waiting for take-off, the invasion of Cuba was suddenly aborted. The command decision was made at the highest level, by an individual for whom Bill did not have the highest respect. This was a big blow to him. The order came from Robert Kennedy! It outweighed Harvey's intelligence estimates. It would have been over in 48 hours. And the Russians wouldn't have offered any defense, whatsoever. They even had a government setup; I think in Miami." [128]

## THE CUBAN MISSILE CRISIS

At some point President Kennedy and his brother Bobby Kennedy decided to establish what is known as a "backchannel" or direct communications between themselves and the Soviet Union's leader Nikita Khrushchev.

In July of 1962, Khrushchev suggested through the backchannel that relations with the Soviet Union would improve if the U.S. would stop aerial surveillance of Soviet ships. While President Kennedy was concerned about the potential of Berlin being a flash point between the Soviets and the United States. So, the President proposed to stop the surveillance of Soviet ships, in exchange for the Soviets agreeing to "put Berlin on ice." President Kennedy received word through the backchannel that Khrushchev agreed with this proposal and was "satisfied with the president's order to curtail U.S. plane inspections of Soviet ships at sea." The Kennedys had no idea that the reason that the Soviets wanted the surveillance curtailed was because the Soviets were afraid that the surveillance of their ships would tip off the U.S. to the fact that the Soviets were shipping nuclear missiles into Cuba. [129]

Gaeton Fonzi was on the staff of the House Select Committee On Assassinations (HSCA) and reports that Ted Shackley said; "JM/WAVE had been passing along reports and knew that there were missiles going in Cuba long before the policymakers would accept that reality."

The *National Intelligence Estimate* (NIE), September 1962, bearing the signature of Sherman Kent, refuted reports from agents and refugees from Cuba about the presence of Soviet ballistic missiles on the island. Quite simply, reports of eyewitnesses were overcome by beliefs about what the Soviets would and would not do, based exclusively on what the CIA analysts knew they themselves would or would not do. But intelligence officers are paid to look outward, not inward. In this case they were watching something happen and saying, "This can't be happening, because I wouldn't do it." For Kent and **Ray Cline**, the name of the game was not to second-guess Khrushchev, but to figure out what he was doing. The analysts simply played the wrong game. [130]

As of September 20, 1962, CIA interrogators of Cuban refugees had been hearing for more than a year that Soviet missiles were in Cuba. [131]

Per the CIA's JMWAVE intelligence chief, Warren Frank, "In a two-month period, Bill Harvey's operation JM/WAVE reported some 200 possible missile sightings. Shackley, head of JM/WAVE said that he read the reports and believed that there were hints about offensive missiles going into Cuba, but nothing conclusive." [132]

All the missile sighting reports from the various agents stationed in Cuba, as well and the reports of missiles collected from the newly arrived Cuban refugees, were being funneled to Ray Cline in the Intelligence wing of the CIA for analysis.

C.G. Harvey talked to Mike McCormick and Andy Alderton about Bill Harvey's concern that word was not getting passed on by Bobby Kennedy to the President concerning a possible missile buildup in Cuba.

By early October 1962, William King Harvey concluded that Attorney General Robert Kennedy was not treating seriously intelligence reports about a massive Soviet missile buildup in Cuba, although they were undetected by early U-2 over-flights. (The U-2 was a high-altitude U.S. spy plane.) Bill's wife C.G. said that, "Bill kept giving Bobby Kennedy information about the missile buildup, but that Bill didn't think that Bobby was passing the information on to the President." *Andy Alderton/C.G. Harvey Interview and Terre Haute Tribune-Star, Mike McCormick, May 23, 1999*

The evidence is clear. Beginning, at the very least, in the summer of 1962 various organs of the U.S. government were receiving reports that were coming in through Bill Harvey's Task Force W concerning missile sightings in Cuba. Bobby Kennedy was receiving information and appears to not be passing this information on to the President. At the same time the Soviet's Nikita Khrushchev was reassuring the President, through the backchannel, to the effect that the Soviet's would not do anything to make things difficult for the President's administration prior to the upcoming congressional elections.

On September 12, 1962, an accountant in Cuba sat in his office and watched as a very large missile was towed down his street.

On September 15, 1962, one of Bill Harvey's agents in Cuba reported that Soviet soldiers were guarding an area in San Cristobal and that there was construction work being done related to missiles.

On September 20, 1962, the same Cuban accountant was being interviewed at the CIA's Opa-Locka, Florida refugee center, after having left Cuba to start a new life in the United States. He was shown some pictures of missiles and he was able to identify a Soviet medium-range ballistic missile as the one that he had witnessed being towed down his street in Cuba. The Opa-Locka refugee center was a part of Bill Harvey's JM/WAVE operation.

On September 27, 1962, a second Cuban refugee at Opa-Locka confirmed seeing the same type of missile in Cuba as the Cuban accountant had seen.

To verify his agents' reports, **Harvey went to McCone and requested coverage of Cuba by the U-2 reconnaissance plane**. [133] Based upon the reports that had come in, the San Cristobal area in the western region of Cuba was targeted for a U-2 spy-plane photographic reconnaissance mission.

Monday, October 15th, the U-2 captured photographic evidence showing that in fact the Soviets and the Cubans were building missile sites in Cuba for Soviet SS-4 nuclear missiles.

At 8:30 P.M. on Monday, October 15, 1962, Ray Cline called the White House's McGeorge Bundy. Cline says to Bundy, "Those things we've been worrying about in Cuba are there." The U-2 spy plane originally requested by Bill Harvey had just returned with photographic evidence of a Soviet nuclear missile sites in Cuba.

Ray Cline wrote: The first notice, that the crisis was on, went to Bundy at the NSC via a phone call from me on the evening of October 15. Simultaneously I insured that General Carter, Acting Director of Central Intelligence on that day in John McCone's absence, would alert all the intelligence and policy chiefs in the Pentagon. The next day, October 16, I went with a few staff officers to show the photographs to McGeorge Bundy, Robert Kennedy, and a few other senior officials, and Bundy then took them to the President. [134]

One of the most thrilling moments of his life, said Ray Cline, was reporting this fact and delivering that picture at the White House early in the morning of October 16, 1962. It may have been the high point of American intelligence performance in the entire period down to that day. [135]

The agent and refugee reports and the U-2 fly over of Cuba all played a very important role, but that is not the whole story. There was more that went into the United States discovery and reaction to the missiles in Cuba: Harvey's team obtained the first evidence of Soviet missiles in Cuba. The evidence, a war plan, pirated from Castro's desk. Their targets, cities from New York to Lima, Peru. [136]

On Oct. 20, 1962, the Wiley High School alumnus, William King Harvey, felt compelled to bypass the attorney general and go directly to the president. While President John F. Kennedy was making Midwest campaign appearances -- the 1931 Terre Haute Wiley graduate concluded the threat required instant attention. *Andy Alderton/C.G. Harvey Interview and Terre Haute Tribune-Star, Mike McCormick, May 16, 1999*

Bill Harvey flew to Chicago, toting alarming unidentified documents surreptitiously procured from Fidel Castro's safe in Havana. FBI agent Paul Cotter, a member of the president's security team, respected "America's Secret Agent 007" and promptly ushered him into Kennedy's hotel suite. What occurred there is unrecorded. However, the President suddenly contracted "an upper respiratory infection," canceled all appearances and returned to Washington. *Andy Alderton/C.G. Harvey Interview and Terre Haute Tribune-Star, Mike McCormick, May 23, 1999 (source CG Harvey)*

C.G. Harvey told Mike McCormick that, "two days later, President Kennedy told the nation about the Cuban Missile Crisis."

C.G. Harvey said Bill lost 9 agents stealing a contract between Khrushchev and Castro, out of Castro's desk. And then Bobby Kennedy would not allow Bill to show it to Jack. And Bobby said, Bobby was so naive and such a dumb jackass, he said treat them like gentleman and they will treat you like gentleman. I mean that's impossible for communists, I mean, their world is so different from our world." *Andy Alderton/C.G. Harvey Interview*

"My husband was the one man who went out to the airport," said C.G., "bought a ticket, flew to Chicago, had a good friend [Paul Cotter] who was in the outfit that was guarding President Kennedy. Because they had both worked together in the CIA, Bill showed him the contract that Castro and Khrushchev had to blow us all up. He took Bill right in to see Jack Kennedy. Jack Kennedy knew Bill; they had dealt with each other, and Jack said what should I do Bill? And Bill said, face them eyeball-to-eyeball, they'll withdraw. And well of course that is exactly what they did. He did just what Bill said. And Bill saved us because they were within 18 hours of hooking it up to blow us up. And Bill got that to him, and Kennedy immediately left Chicago and went back to Washington." Andy Alderton says, "He took sick, didn't he?" "Yeah, that's the cover story they gave to get him back, so the Russians wouldn't know that we had discovered what they were doing. And after that who gets all the credit, Bobby Kennedy! Nobody ever mentioned that the CIA alerted Jack. Nobody gave Bill one drop of credit for what he had done. He even paid his own way to get on the plane to get out there to talk to Jack. He always believed that one person could make a difference. And he did. He made a difference in Berlin when he built the tunnel. He held Berlin for the west. There were only seventy-five of us up there. I was one of the intelligence officers working for him. I married the boss. It was a time when nobody wanted to go in there and work because we were behind the iron curtain, and it was a very difficult way to live. But those of us who were there, the seventy-five, held Berlin for the west. After knowing that you, and your husband, spent your whole life fighting to have the downfall of Communism, so that they couldn't blow us up and rule the world. The only way to be safe is to be strong." <u>Andy Alderton/C.G. Harvey Interview</u>

On the Travel Channel, August 30, 2004, it said the U.S.

obtained the manuals for the missiles in Cuba before the U-2 flights confirmed their presence. Perhaps this is the document C.G. Harvey spoke about. Either way, it was probably obtained by William King Harvey's network of spies.

Bill Harvey had little respect for the younger Kennedy's ability to analyze intelligence reports and even less confidence that report of vital importance were being passed on to the President. <u>Andy Alderton/C.G. Harvey Interview and Terre Haute Tribune-Star, Mike McCormick, May 16, 1999</u>

Bill Harvey's operation and agents were sending numerous reports to Washington, warning of missiles going into Cuba in the fall of 1962, but official Washington seemed to be ignoring the warning signs. Finally, the Republicans in Congress got wind of what was happening and began to raise questions publicly on October 10, 1962. Four days later October 14, 1963, a United States U-2 spy plane confirmed that the missiles were indeed there.

The two CIA guys from Terre Haute, Indiana were the first to alert the White House about the missiles going into Cuba. William Harvey's agents and operation first got wind of the missiles and Bill Harvey requested the U-2 flyovers. Ray Cline received the photographic evidence from the U-2 and rushed to inform the President. Bill Harvey boarded an airplane for Chicago and personally showed President Kennedy some important documents that his agents had managed to steal from Cuba. President Kennedy immediately returned to Washington and two days later announce the "Cuban Missile Crisis" to the world.

Bill Harvey's operation and agents discovered the missiles going into Cuba. Once again, Bill Harvey should have been recognized as a hero. He wasn't.

October 22nd, President Kennedy addressed the American

people on television and announced a naval blockade of Cuba in an attempt to stem the flow of missile shipments into Cuba.

October 23rd, in meetings recorded at the White House Robert Kennedy expressed irritation about the failure of US intelligence to discover the missiles earlier. [137]

October 24th, President Kennedy derides Khrushchev's backchannel "horseshit about the elections," presumably referring to earlier assurances by the Soviets that there would be no political complications before the November elections. [5:03] [Source: JFK Library release notes prepared by Sheldon M. Stern]

All the military war games, the hit and run Cuban exile sabotage conducted out of Florida, the numerous assassination attempts, the abortive Bay of Pigs invasion, military exercise CINCLANT OPLAN, and probably the placement of William King Harvey in a role of prominence in the Cuban operation had all been noted by the Soviets and Castro resulting in the military and missile deployments in Cuba. All this threatening activity served only to drive the Cubans further and further into the arms of the Soviets.

In his speech on October 22, 1962, President Kennedy alerted the nation concerning the nuclear missile threat that we were suddenly facing in Cuba, but he failed to mention what the Soviets and the Cubans already knew, that it was in part due to his administration's policies, posturing and actions which precipitated the crisis in the first place.

By October 1962, tensions between Bill Harvey and Bobby Kennedy had reached a boiling point, as an angry and ongoing confrontation developed between these two. Their mutual dislike for one another had been festering for months. Harvey grew increasingly weary of Bobby Kennedy's incessant pressure and meddling to get Castro and his interference in various matters, including Bobby's involvement with Harvey's anti-Castro Cubans. On the other hand, Bobby Kennedy was frustrated and disappointed by the perceived lack of progress in ousting Castro.

According to a CIA official, Bobby Kennedy found Bill uncooperative, while Harvey continually confronted Bobby with what he thought Kennedy was doing that was misguided, dangerous and wrong. In a meeting just weeks before the onset of the missile crisis, Harvey fell asleep in a meeting, providing Bobby Kennedy the opportunity to vent all his pent-up frustration, as he proceeded to rip Bill Harvey up one side and down the other. Bobby's verbal attack on Harvey went on for eight to ten minutes. Later testifying before the Church Committee, General Charles Johnson III, who was in the meeting said it was the "damnedest tirade" he had ever witnessed, "it was embarrassing." [138]

At the height of the Cuban missile crisis, Bill Harvey, in coordination with the Military's Joint Chiefs of Staff sent a submarine to Cuba with sixty of Bill Harvey's anti-Castro Cuban agents. Their mission was to help guide and support a possible U.S. invasion.

Upon learning about the deployment of these anti-Castro Cuban teams, Bobby Kennedy was furious. Under who's authority was this action taken? The Kennedys harbored genuine concerns, recognizing the potential that a provocation like this could potentially escalate into a nuclear exchange and World War III. Bobby Kennedy demanded to know from Bill Harvey why he had taken this action? Bobby Kennedy said to Harvey, "You have two minutes to explain."

In response, Harvey said, "The military wanted it and that it had been supported by Lansdale." Bobby Kennedy shot back that he had already talked to Lansdale who had denied involvement. It was at this point that Bill Harvey shocked the entire room as he shot back at Bobby, what everyone had been saying for a while, but just not to the face of a Kennedy. He said, "Well if you guys hadn't screwed up in the first place [referring to the Bay of Pigs and perhaps the CINCLANT OPLAN operation] we wouldn't be in this mess." Everyone in the room was aghast. You don't say that kind of thing to their face! Bill Harvey continued talking as Bobby Kennedy got up and stormed out of the room. [139]

CIA Director John McCone was furious with Bill Harvey. You don't say that kind of thing about the President of the United States. That evening when McCone returned to CIA headquarters, he told **Ray Cline**, his Deputy Director for Intelligence, "Harvey has destroyed himself today. His usefulness has ended." At Bobby Kennedy's insistence, Bill Harvey was out and Desmond FitzGerald was in as the head of the Cuban operation. "Des Fitz" came from a wealthy Boston family, not unlike the Kennedy family. **Richard Helms and Jim Angleton would find a place for Bill Harvey as the CIA's station chief in Rome, Italy.** [140]

Harvey's assistant Sam Halpern would later point out, "The CIA doesn't have submarines! Where the hell do you think Bill Harvey got the submarine? Bill Harvey was working with the Joint Chiefs of Staff. Lansdale was also involved in this effort and Richard Helms also knew all about it." [141]

CIA Director McCone was furious and mad as hell at both Bill Harvey and Sherman Kent. Sherman Kent, who led the intelligence analysis department, stubbornly had refused to accept the mounting evidence indicating that the Soviets were indeed installing missiles in Cuba. He simply couldn't imagine that the Soviets would dare to do such a thing. McCone summoned Bill Harvey and Sherman Kent to his office. Afterwards Kent said, "I've just been made a charter member of the bleeding asshole society, but Bill Harvey, well Bill he's the president." [142]

Ted Shackley said, "This dismissal was a fatal blow to Harvey's psyche. In my view, he never recovered from it. In effect, this incident ended the brilliant career of an old curmudgeon. Harvey was not an adept practitioner of the fine art of Washington public relations." [143]

Years later in testimony before the Senate Intelligence Committee, Bill Harvey would say, "there was a 'confrontation' during which the Attorney General took a great deal of exception."

October 28, 1962, Khrushchev announced on Radio Moscow, that the Soviets were dismantling and removing their missiles from Cuba. The naval blockade appeared to have worked, everyone, in the U.S. anyway, was left with the impression that the Soviets had backed down.

The truth is, to resolve the missile crisis Bobby Kennedy met secretly with Soviet ambassador, Dobrynin at the Soviet Embassy, October 23, 1962. The Kennedys agreed to remove U.S. missiles from Turkey in exchange for the removal of the Soviet missiles in Cuba, and President Kennedy pledged that the United States would not invade Cuba. The Russians agreed not to public disclose the U.S. concessions concern the removal of missiles from Turkey and the Kennedys never told the American people that they had agreed to removal the missiles from Turkey.

Khrushchev and Kennedy also agreed to keep the backchannel open.

The Kennedy's personal vendetta and unrelenting harassment of Cuba helped to bring the world to the edge of nuclear annihilation and at what price? Well, perhaps at whatever price the Soviets could have demanded in the future, to keep their secret deal, secret. Which is not a very advantageous place to be, at least not for our side.

Having met, as Bobby Kennedy and Dobrynin did in the Soviet Embassy, would have made it easy for the Soviets to record the conversations, discussions, and the secret agreement between Dobrynin and Bobby Kennedy. It seems to me that here we have a future opportunity to blackmail the President of the United States. It is probably not a wise thing to have to trust an adversary with information that would be politically fatal. Especially if that information revealed that you weren't quite straight with the American people about the resolution of the missile crisis.

On December 8, 1962, Bill Harvey sent a CIA Memorandum, to the Director of CIA, via the Deputy Director of Plans, and he copied the Deputy Director of Counterintelligence (Jim Angleton). The subject: "A Possible Plot to Assassinate President Kennedy." *National Archives* 104-10506-10016

The memo stated: On 7 December 1962 at 2235 hours this Division received a cable from our Station in Miami, Florida, reporting information on a possible plot to assassinate President Kennedy. In brief, a letter was mailed from Havana, Cuba, to an individual in Miami, Florida. The individual was not known at the address and the letter was turned over to our Miami Station. The letter contained information on a possible plot to assassinate President Kennedy. [Information turned over to Secret Service and FBI] *National Archives* 104-10506-10016

It was around this time that Peter Karlow was experiencing problems with Angleton. Karlow reports, "Bill was a lovely person, but he didn't take any shit from anyone… When I was having trouble with Angleton… and many of the CIA guys were trying to freeze me out… Bill Harvey went over to the FBI and talked to some of his old friends, then he came back and said to me. 'They've cleared you over there!' When others turned and walked away, Bill Harvey stuck by his friends." [144]

Also, in December of 1962 the Kennedys arranged for millions of dollars in medicine to be exchanged for the captured anti-Castro Cubans from the Bay of Pigs. On December 27th in Miami's Orange Bowl Stadium, President Kennedy addressed the Cuban brigade and told them how sorry he was. The brigade presented President Kennedy with their flag from the Bay of Pigs, and President Kennedy promised to return it to them in a free Cuba.

Operation Mongoose was shut down, however, the CIA arm, **Task Force W,** continued its existence as the **Special Affairs Staff (SAS)**, located at the CIA's Miami station. Sabotage operations and assassination attempts against Cuba continued even though President Kennedy ordered a halt to all Cuban operations.

## FINISHING HARVEY

Although Bill had his run in with Bobby Kennedy in October 1962 during the missile crisis Bill remained the head of Task Force W until approximately February 1963. During Bill's remaining time as head of Task Force W, Bill is reported by the CIA as having been in Miami between December 22, 1962, and January 6, 1963. He saw both Rosselli and Maceo several times during that period. He made a payment of $2,700 to Rosselli for Varona for the expenses of the three militiamen. Harvey and Rosselli had telephone discussions about the operation between 11 and 16 January. Harvey says that Rosselli wasn't kidding himself. He agreed with Harvey that nothing was happening and that there was not much chance that anything would happen in the future. As far as Harvey knows, the three militiamen never did leave for Cuba. He knows nothing of what may have happened to the three [previous militia men] reported to have been previously sent to Cuba. *1967 CIA Inspector General's Report*

Desmond Fitzgerald (whom Harvey did not regard very highly) took over Task Force W in February 1963 and Task Force W was renamed the Special Affairs Staff (SAS).

FitzGerald's initial impression of attorney general Bobby Kennedy was that "he was a young punk." FitzGerald found Bobby Kennedy a little reckless. Bobby was willing to bully anyone and was very difficult to deal with. FitzGerald confided to his daughter that he "was scared of Bobby's power. That he felt threatened by him. That Bobby was only there because he was the president's brother. He thought he was an amateur, and he didn't really like him." [145]

February 1963, Bill Harvey is officially removed as the head of Task Force W. I find it interesting that at this same time, February 2, 1963, the **CIA started the Domestic Operations Division headed by Tracy Barnes and at the direction of Desmond FitzGerald, David Atlee Phillips moved to Mexico City** to run the Cuban operation there. Tracy Barnes had been the CIA's chief of the psychological and paramilitary staff during the Bay of Pigs. **E. Howard Hunt also moves to the newly created Domestic Operations Division**. So, in other words "the Boys from the Guatemala Coup" and the Bay of Pigs fiasco are back!

Although Bill Harvey was no longer in charge of the Cuban operation it is interesting to note below how Bill Harvey continued to meet with Johnny Rosselli during the period February 1963 through June 1963. June of 1963 would have been just prior to Bill's departure for Rome.

February 1963, Harvey was in Miami 11-14 February. He had no contacts with any of the principals, but he left word for Maceo that there was nothing new and that it now looked as if it were all over. <u>1967 CIA Inspector General's Report</u>

Harvey left Miami on 15 February to meet with Rosselli in Los Angeles. They agreed at the Los Angeles meeting that the operation would be closed off, but that it would be unwise to attempt to precipitate a break between Rosselli and Varona. Rosselli agreed that he would continue to see Varona, gradually reducing the frequency of contact until there was none. <u>1967 CIA Inspector General's Report</u>

April 13 to 21, 1963, Bill Harvey is staying at the Plantation Yacht Harbor motel/marina on the Bay side, room 22 in Plantation Key, Florida. John A. Ralston, also known as Johnny Rosselli, is shown as registered in room 21, right next door. [146]

Then on April 20, 1963, an unusual thing happened. The CIA by way of Bill Harvey's expense account paid for the hotel room and airplane ticket for Rosselli to fly from Miami, Florida to Chicago. What is unusual about this is that Rosselli had always paid his own way, never taking a dime from the CIA. It leads me to suspect that this may have been intentional on Bill Harvey and Rosselli's part as a method of tying or associating the CIA with Rosselli in the public record. Governmental Agencies seem to have a history of covering up information, if that information might lead to the public's speculating about their appearing to be associated or involved with some kind of disreputable character or activity and this action created a record binding the CIA to Rosselli. This association would also afford Rosselli a certain amount of protection in the future should he do something that could potentially embarrass the CIA, if their association were to be known. Also entered in Bill Harvey's expense log on this day and just prior to the airline ticket for Rosselli is an entry that reads: "Termination payment ZR Rifle/MI-no receipt, $1,000.00." Presumably the payment was to terminate Rosselli's services to ZR Rifle, or someone.

In April 1963 Johnny Rosselli called Bill Harvey. Also, in April the Mafia begins funding and arming the Cuban exiles and organized then under a Dr. Paulino Sierra Martinez, a Cuban attorney out of Chicago.

A duly sworn, handwritten note by Joseph H. Langosch, CIA, located in the National Archives says: "I became C/SAS/CI [Special Affairs Staff/Counterintelligence] about time Dec. 7, I took over helm of SAS (June 1963). Didn't travel w/ Harvey as his asst – but did know of his travels. **Harvey trip to Fla Keys – April 1963** vaguely recall it – **went to see Ted Shackley** – COS/WAVE doesn't know what Harvey did then." HSCA 180-10143-10159, *CIA, Agency* #28-16-03

April 24, 1963, Lee Harvey Oswald moved to New Orleans from Dallas.

April-May 1963, Harvey says that he received two telephone calls from Rosselli during this period. Harvey decided that it would be best to have one last meeting with Rosselli before he left for his assignment in Italy. **He states that he reported this decision to Mr. Helms who gave his approval. (Here again is evidence of Harvey religiously reporting to and getting approval from Richard Helms.)** *1967 CIA Inspector General's Report*

**June 27, 1963, Harvey recommended terminating QJ/WIN**, but also recommended consideration of using him in Europe, namely Germany, or Austria, if the CIA stations there were interested. The CIA did not terminate QJ/WIN until February 14, 1964.

June 1963, Rosselli flew to Washington to meet with Harvey around the middle of June. Harvey met Rosselli at Dulles airport. Harvey had by then closed on his own home in preparation for leaving the country and was living in the house of a neighbor who was out of town. Rosselli stayed with Harvey as a houseguest in the neighbor's home. That evening Johnny Rosselli, Bill Harvey, and Mrs. Harvey went out for dinner. The conversation apparently turned to their shared dislike for Bobby Kennedy, Rosselli due to Bobby Kennedy's (admirable and) relentless pursuit of the Mafia and Bill Harvey for many reasons, one being Bobby Kennedy's meddling with Harvey's precious tradecraft. (Apparently, we are to assume that the FBI was tailing Rosselli). The report goes on to say that the FBI agents claimed to not know who Bill Harvey was, yet they called Sam Papich who was the CIA liaison for the FBI and who just happened to be himself dining with of all people Jim Angleton. From the description over the phone, we are told that, they were able to identify Bill Harvey. (Boy what luck? They knew where Papich was having dinner; they were able to contact him. They guessed Papich would know who Bill

Harvey was and Angleton just happened to be right there to help and not only that they managed to hear what was being discussed.) The report goes on to say, while dining, Harvey received a phone call from the FBI's Sam Papich who wanted to know if Harvey knew the identity of his dinner guest. Harvey said that he did. *1967 CIA Inspector General's Report*

The CIA report continues, it subsequently developed that the FBI had Rosselli under intense surveillance at that time, and Harvey speculates that he was picked up as he left the airport parking lot and was identified through his auto license number. The FBI agents watched with shock and amazement as America's James Bond met with a notoriously known Mafioso. (Or so we are supposed to believe.)

My opinion, they wanted this relationship documented in the public record for future implication. The documentation of this meeting between William King Harvey and Johnny Rosselli was not happenstance. This was intentionally documented in the public record for future use, establishing links to follow for culpability, or in the case of the FBI in this instance, to try and demonstrate a lack of culpability. In this instance a link between the Mafia and the CIA is being documented and a link between Bill Harvey and Johnny Rosselli is being documented, also documented, their common dislike for Robert Kennedy. The FBI is also portrayed in this account as disapproving. Associations and the appearance of culpability can prove useful in motivating an individual or organization to assist in a future cover up of certain things, or in general, may be used as leverage to get individuals or organizations to do certain thing.

Harvey met with the FBI's Sam Papich for breakfast the next morning and explained that he was terminating an operational association with Rosselli. Papich reminded Harvey of the FBI rule requiring FBI personnel to report any known contacts between former FBI employees and criminal elements. Papich said that he would have to report to J. Edgar Hoover that Harvey had been seen with Rosselli. Harvey said he understood Papich's situation and did not object to such a report being made. Harvey said that he asked Papich to inform him in advance if it appeared that Hoover might call Mr. McCone—Harvey's point being that he felt that McCone should be briefed before receiving a call from Hoover. Papich agreed to do so. **Harvey said that he then told Mr. Helms** of the incident and that **Helms agreed that there was no need to brief McCone unless a call from Hoover was to be expected**. *1967 CIA Inspector General's Report* (Here is just another example of how Bill Harvey is very good about reporting everything that he is doing to Helms and how Helms and Harvey are very good about not informing their boss the Director of the CIA.)

This was (supposedly) Harvey's last face-to-face meeting with Rosselli, although he has heard from him since then, according to a 1967 CIA Inspector General's Report.

Harvey and Rosselli genuinely liked each other. "Rosselli was a patriot," so says Mrs. Harvey. That certainly is the term most used to describe William King Harvey. Behind Bill's desk hung a poster that read, "The Tree of Liberty is Watered by the Blood of Patriots." Rosselli was never paid for his efforts except for one hotel room and airplane flight. Of course, we also need to keep in mind that working with the CIA was probably, in Johnny Rosselli's mind, and in reality, his "get out of jail free card."

One of Bill Harvey's last acts as the head of the Cuban operations was to write a memo to CIA Director McCone pointing out that the administration's continued push for further use of "commando and sabotage operations, except in rare instances, will serve little purpose" as the intervention of any U.S. military support in any internal revolt was no longer possible, given the Kennedys' pledge not to invade Cuba.

"He lost his self-confidence for the first time in his life," Angleton said of Harvey. Angleton attempted to lift Harvey's spirits by personally handcrafting a custom leather holster for Harvey's .38 Detective Special.

The task force organized a farewell party for him before his departure to Italy. "It was a tearful kind of thing," one participant said. "Everyone felt that Harvey had been treated unjustly. Instead of being relieved of his command, they believed he deserved recognition for assembling the global intelligence network that had successfully uncovered the missiles going into Cuba just in time. The members of the task force made a concerted effort to uplift Harvey's spirits, fully aware of his bitterness and profound sense of hurt. [147]

"Bill Harvey's usefulness was over," or so said Director McCone.

**Bill Harvey was a giant of a man who appears to have looked out for his country more than he looked out for himself.**

Harvey went to Rome in June 1963 remained until 1966. He came back to the Agency in Washington in 1966, and he retired from the Agency December 31, 1967. Rockefeller Commission 178-10002-10324

## THE BIG FAT QUESTION IS

The Kennedys and in particular Bobby Kennedy ruined Bill Harvey's career and he was busted down to being the Station Chief in Italy.

The big fat question is: Did William King Harvey plan and carry out the assassination of President Kennedy? Some suggest that he did.

Or did the "Guys from the Guatemalan Coup" the GFGC and James Jesus Angleton set Bill Harvey up to appear to have planned the assassination and to take the fall?

# ROME, ITALY

There are various reported activities, and the physical and psychological condition of Bill Harvey during his time in Rome. It is important to try and separate the reports into the period leading up to the assassination and thereafter. It appears that in the period leading up to assassination his fitness report was excellent, and he was drinking tea. Following the assassination, he went on his downhill slide.

Bill Harvey's CIA fitness report in October 1962, some eight months prior to his move to Rome, says: "It is difficult to prepare a fitness report on this outstanding officer, largely because forms do not lend themselves to measuring his many unique characteristics, professional knowledge… toughness of mind and firmness of attitude." Bill Harvey is "one of the few distinctly outstanding officers."

"When he first came to Rome, Bill tried to be very careful about his drinking," said a staff member. "At cocktail parties he would drink iced tea." [148]

"He was wonderful. Couldn't have been nicer," said Mark Wyatt, Harvey's deputy in Italy. Harvey even helped the Wyatts find a home. [149]

For most CIA agents, Italy was a nice, civilized, cosmopolitan assignment. Mostly it had involved sharing information with the Italians over lunch. That is until Bill Harvey arrived on the scene. The staff had to work a hell of a lot harder following Bill Harvey's arrival.

What was Bill Harvey doing in the four months leading up to the Kennedy assassination when he was in Rome, or supposedly in Rome?

"What was really upsetting," said C.G. Harvey, "was when Jack [Kennedy] was in Rome visiting the embassy, my husband being the head of the CIA there had to assign two men, along with his group of service men protecting him, and these two men were required to get Italian prostitutes into Jack's bed, two at a time. And it was a sorry thing. They were working for my husband and my husband told me, so I think it is true. Then while he was doing that in Rome, she [Mrs. Kennedy] took off for Greece and was on the ship with Onassis." "Huh? While they were married?" asked Andy. "Yeah, she was carrying it on with Onassis on the ship, while he was carrying it on with the prostitutes. I mean they were a lousy group of people. I mean they were really scum." <u>Andy Alderton/C.G. Harvey Interview</u>

Concerning Bill Harvey's apparent absence from his post in Italy. Mark Wyatt a CIA Officer under Bill Harvey said: "I was actually running the office **most of the time, while he [Bill Harvey] was off** in Elba or **some place**, drying out." [150]

Author Anthony Summers writes in his book *Conspiracy*, "I have learned that Bill Harvey visited anti-Castro camps in Florida, at a time when he was theoretically already in Rome." [151]

The most damning clue of all came from C.G. Harvey herself when she complained about her experiences while living in Italy, she said, **"Bill was in Washington. He left me to deal with the rats and the Communists."** [152]

# FAIR PLAY FOR CUBA COMMITTEE

August 5, 1963, Oswald approached, Carlos Bringuier, who was a principal with the DRE in New Orleans, a CIA supported anti-Castro Cuban group, and Oswald offered to help them in their struggle against Castro. Four days later, on August 9th Bringuier would have a confrontation with Oswald on the street concerning Oswald's handing out of the Fair Play for Cuba Committee (FPCC) pro-Castro literature. Some are under the impression that this confrontation and later publicity was staged to put Oswald in the public record as being pro-Castro and pro-communist. Lee Oswald then traveled to Mexico City and arrived there on September 27, 1963. While in Mexico City he supposedly visits the Cuban and Russian Embassies and on October 2, 1963, Lee Oswald left Mexico City, returning to Dallas, Texas. October 15, 1963, Lee was hired at the Texas School Book Depository. November 22, 1963, President Kennedy was assassinated just outside of the Texas School Book Depository.

Anthony Summers points out in his book *Conspiracy;* that Lee Oswald wrote in his August 4th letter to the Fair Play for Cuba Committee (FPCC) about the altercation between himself and anti-Castro Cubans while he was handing out FPCC literature in New Orleans. The only problem with this is that this altercation did not occur until five days later August 9th, which indicates that either Lee Oswald was psychic, or the event was planned and staged. Judyth Vary Baker, girlfriend of Lee Oswald in New Orleans writes in her book *Me & Lee,* Lee deliberately wrote to the FPCC, to link the FPCC with his arrest, as all of Lee's mail was regularly opened by the FBI. This information was to be used against the FPCC. Lee wanted to be officially connected to the FPCC so that his actions would ultimately discredit them.

As far back as 1961, the **CIA's David Atlee Phillips** was running a domestic destabilization operation against the FPCC, with the aid of future Watergate conspirator, James McCord.

Orestes Peña, proprietor of the Habana Bar in New Orleans is on record as reporting that FBI agents were taking pictures while Oswald was handing out his Fair Play for Cuba broachers, which means that the FBI must have had advanced notice. Orest Peña also told attorney and author Mark Lane that Lee Oswald, while in New Orleans, was working closely with **FBI special agent Warren DeBrueys**.

From Church Committee Vol. V: According to the FBI documents, on September 16, 1963, the CIA advised the FBI that the "Agency is giving some consideration to countering the activities of the Fair Play for Cuba Committee (FPCC) in foreign countries." (The Special Affairs Staff SAS, which was concerned with anti-Cuban operations, was discussing with the FBI an operation to discredit the Fair Play for Cuba Committee in a foreign country around the time of Oswald's visit to Mexico City).

# PHILBY!

Bill Harvey called Kim Philby to everyone's attention in 1951. By the late 1950s, Philby found work as a reporter and would routinely meet with CIA officers and other high-ranking CIA executives. He met with Angleton several times during this period and used those opportunities to reassure his American friend of his innocence. Philby and Angleton are even known to have meet as recently as 1960.

British intelligence eventually decided to put Philby back to work. Philby was prevented from being hired as a staff officer, but this did not prevent the Secret Intelligence Service (MI6) from hiring him as a freelance agent. By July 1956, Philby was back in the spy game, this time as an agent in Beirut working undercover as a journalist.

Philby finally confirmed that he was a Soviet Spy by ducking behind the iron curtain in January of 1963 leading up to the assassination in November of that year.

In an FBI memo it says: Philby is a former British Intelligence Service officer and an admitted Soviet agent who was in the U.S. from October 1949 to June 1951. In January 1963, Philby fled from Lebanon to Russia and the Soviets publicly acknowledged his presence there in July 1963. FBI 124-10073-10055

Jack Martin and David Lewis were private investigators who worked for Guy Banister's detective agency down in New Orleans in the years leading up to the assassination. The reason we even know about the operation at 544 Camp Street is because in the evening on the day of the assassination Jack Martin and David Lewis accused Banister in his office of being involved in the assassination and they threatened to tell. Banister knocked both in the head with his pistol, warning them that they and their families would be in danger. Their reply was that they would most likely remain silent regarding him, but not about David Ferrie "under any conditions." Jack Martin required medical treatment and ended up talking to the New Orleans District Attorney Jim Garrison concerning some of things that had been going on at 544 Camp Street.

Martin and Lewis wrote a couple of affidavits for New Orleans District Attorney Jim Garrison that resulted in the following FBI Memorandum, dated 4/12/68, the FBI Memorandum states the following:

> [Jack]J. S. Martin and David F. Lewis, Jr., two new Orleans men who have been described as [         ] have given New Orleans District Attorney Jim Garrison two affidavits analyzing the assassination. The affidavits are irrational and nonsensical. **Essentially, they indicate that Kim Philby and Robert F. Kennedy were responsible for the assassination.**
>
> Martin and Lewis allege that Kim Philby, assisted by influence [which] he exercised over Robert F. Kennedy, and through international intrigue involving Cuba, Guatemala, and France, was responsible for the assassination of President Kennedy. <u>FBI</u> 124-10073-10055
>
> The FBI memo continues saying: They [Martin & Lewis] **mention in the affidavit, New Orleans FBI Special Agent Regis Kennedy, as a contact of Banister** and indicate Regis Kennedy was reporting directly to "Assistant FBI Director Mohr...by-passing [President] Kennedy's own local SAC." **They indicate in the affidavit that Regis Kennedy's FBI reports went to Philby and Robert F. Kennedy.** <u>FBI</u> 124-10073-10055
>
> The affidavits are written in a completely nonsensical and insane style from the beginning paragraphs to the very end.

<u>HSCA 180-10023-10382</u> *(So said the FBI.)*

Beware the easy brush off. Remember, Harry and the rifle in Terre Haute were easily brushed off, so were potential missiles going into Cuba. You and I have an advantage over the Select Committee on Assassinations and the FBI, being as we know about the Terre Haute connection. Meaning the connection of the rifle to Terre Haute and Terre Haute to William King Harvey, and William King Harvey's exposure and ruination of the Soviet spy, Kim Philby.

The Terre Haute information combined with Martin and Lewis's claim about Philby working with Bobby Kennedy on some projects takes on new significance as to why the rifle may have made its appearance in Terre Haute, Indiana! If Philby was pulling some strings, supposedly helping Bobby Kennedy to get rid of Castro (or so Bobby Kennedy thought), as added icing on the cake, **would Philby have not found it delightful to setup Bill Harvey to take a very hard fall?** Philby's casting aspersions at the very least might lead to the end of Bill Harvey's career at his beloved CIA, much as Philby's spy career was seriously damaged by Bill Harvey some eleven years earlier.

Could it be that the rifle was left in a Terre Haute Hotel as an attempt by Philby to try and get even with Bill Harvey, by trying to make Bill Harvey look guilty, or by trying to call attention to Bill Harvey's guilt and or involvement in the Kennedy assassination? A rifle is discovered in Terre Haute, Indiana. Why Terre Haute, Indiana? Well, who is from Terre Haute, Indiana? Oh yeah. Wouldn't it be logical, that if Philby was involved, that he would find the idea delightfully intriguing to hang this one on America's James Bond, Bill Harvey?

Kim Philby said in his book entitled *My Silent War*: "I may be accused here of introducing a cheap note. Admitted.

But [Harvey] played a very cheap trick on me, and **I do not like letting provocation go unpunished**." (Is this a threat, or given the date of the book 1968, five years after the assassination, a claim of retaliation, or retribution?)

Let's look at the mysterious Jack Martin. Jack Martin ended up playing a very large role in this story, five foot nine, in his forties, with a small mustache. He dressed perpetually in a gray suit and a black porkpie hat, his tie pulled down. Jack bore the pallor of an alcoholic and looked out at you through weak blue eyes ("a skinny, messy little guy," Garrison's secretary thought). Jack Martin chain-smoked and subsisted on bad coffee. He seemed a broken-down, harmless individual, a hanger-on who worked for Guy Banister as a sometimes-private eye.

Jim Garrison said of Jack Martin, "Almost always, unless he intended it otherwise, what Jack Martin told you checked out."

According to the book *A Farewell to Justice: Jim Garrison, JFK's Assassination, and the Case That Should Have Changed History* by Joan Mellen: Jack Martin had served in military intelligence and was associated with CIA. Says Mellen, one CIA routing sheet concerning Jack Martin flowed though Angleton's Counterintelligence Research & Analysis section.

CIA or not, Jack Martin was a fly on the wall who soaked up and noticed everything, and he acted like he had no allegiance to anyone as he went about distributing information to various entities from Jim Garrison to the FBI. I suspect however, Jack Martin was given the job of calling attention to what was going on at 544 Camp Street and Bobby Kennedy's and the FBI's involvement in it.

To illustrate the mysterious connections of Jack Martin we have this story: One day Jack Martin had Joe Newbrough meet him at a coffee shop at nine a.m. Lo and behold outside the coffee shop Carlos Marcello was handcuffed and hustled off. It was the day Marcello was deported, and Jack Martin had foreknowledge of the kidnapping of the Mafia don engineered by Robert Kennedy. How did Martin know this was going to happen?

Visitors to Banister's office included **General Edwin Walker and Nazi George Lincoln Rockwell, who was introduced to Banister at that time by Jack Martin.** Rockwell's name and address was later found in Lee Harvey Oswald's address book. [153]

The question remains, how the hell would Jack Martin and David Lewis, two private eyes have known about, or even come up with the name Kim Philby in 1963, unless there is something to this? Philby's profile, position, and visibility had been pretty much taken down to near nothing as a result of Bill Harvey's accusations way back in 1951.

# THE MARTIN AND LEWIS AFFDAVIT
# (SUPPLEMENTED & EDITED)

So, what about this charge that **Kim Philby and Robert F. Kennedy were responsible for the assassination?**

Here are excerpts from the Jack Martin and David Lewis affidavit that was given to the New Orleans District Attorney Jim Garrison: *Martin & Lewis, HSCA 180-10023-10376*

This FRD [anti-Castro] group, through Banister was additionally serviced by an **FBI Special Agent, Regis Kennedy, who we often met during this period at Banister's office.** Sometimes, we would run into him several times a day. Banister once told [another of his investigators, Joseph] Newbrough and we that **[Regis] Kennedy's** daily **reports** on these activities were forwarded straight to one Assistant FBI Director Mohr, subservient only **to John Edgar Hoover** in Washington, always by-passing Kennedy's own local Special Agent in Charge (resident agent) for numerous top-security reasons. **From here, they were viewed by none other than Philby and RFK**, the story goes. *Martin & Lewis, HSCA 180-10023-10376*

(Note: **If true, this indicates a direct link between J. Edgar Hoover and Banister's office at 544 Camp Street in New Orleans. Also, if true, it indicates that Robert Kennedy might have been working with a Soviet spy, Kim Philby. Remember Banister used to be in charge of the FBI office up in Chicago**, so it is not too much of a stretch for Banister to be associated with FBI Director Hoover.)

Inasmuch as we were for many years associated with Banister, we had upon occasion engaged (independently) in some of these activities, cooperating with FRD and Dalzell operations. From time to time, our code names had been "El Gringo" and "Jauquin" during these periods. *Martin & Lewis, HSCA 180-10023-10376* (William Wayne Dalzell would describe himself as having "founded ... [the] Free Voice of Latin America and a group known as Friends of Democratic Cuba." The "Friends of Democratic Cuba? They were the ones looking to buy ten trucks from Bolton Ford in January 1961 using Lee Harvey Oswald's name, while Lee was in Russia. (NOTP; November 3, 1967; Section 1, p1))

Returning to the subject, RFK allegedly tendered several documents in the form of **"Letters-Marques"** giving "carte-blanche" status to any and all of those about to participate in this pending pseudo-legal hijacking. These were directed to all concerned to "seize munitions or arms, the property of a foreign government, that are illegally located within the US, which might otherwise be used against nations friendly to the US, using any and all means to do so." They, of course, supposedly **bore the signature of none other than RFK himself**, because they were issued on Justice Department Attorney General's letterhead stationery. *Martin & Lewis, HSCA 180-10023-10376*

Needless to say, as we recall it, everyone was overjoyed by this prospective arms hijacking. Furthermore, someone had said that either **the FBI, or CIA, were to supply the keys** to pull this "job" (robbery), so no locks would be broken. *Martin & Lewis, HSCA 180-10023-10376*

Later, on that following afternoon, we heard Banister talking over the telephone to who we were told was a Mr. M.E. Loy, the South-Eastern Manager of Schlumberger in New Orleans. (Loy at this writing is the President of all Schlumberger incorporations here in the US, whose home office is in Houston, Texas.) This conversation was in regard to the pending Schlumberger operation. Banister seemed to be setting the time and date, like H hour and D date. In short, they of **the Schlumberger Company knew that we were coming in the fake bakery truck**. .... *Martin & Lewis, HSCA 180-10023-10376*

Note: **David Ferrie** was involved with **Sergio Aracha Smith**, adventurer **Gordon Novel** and **Layton Martens** in a raid on a munitions dump in Houma, La. *HSCA* VOL. 10, Page 109 Novel told friends and a polygrapher that he was a CIA operative and that this was **"no munitions burglary, but it was a materials pickup made at the direction of his CIA contact."** He said, "It was the most patriotic burglary in history. The keys to the bunker were provided." They delivered the munitions to Ferrie's home, Novel's office, and Guy Banister's office. My notes from Jim Garrison, New Orleans Library microfilm)

**That evening, FBI Agent Kennedy made his daily appearance at Banister's office** as usual. It was about this time that the Letters-Marquee and the keys showed up. No one ever said that Agent Kennedy brought them, but they did come to light shortly after he had left. *Martin & Lewis, HSCA 180-10023-10376*

Anyway, the story goes that it was in the dark of night that the very "chosen people" hijacked those munitions at the Houma Schlumberger bunker, transported, and stored them in their designated location, the storage area adjoining Banister's office. The following day, everyone in the "know," came to look and gloat. Boy, ol' Castro should sure catch hell now! .... *Martin & Lewis, HSCA 180-10023-10376*

The House Select Committee substantiates this saying, "Both Ferrie and Banister were implicated in a raid in late 1961 against a munitions depot in Houma, La., in which various weapons, grenades, and ammunition were stolen." *HSCA* Vol. 10 Page 127

Jack Martin was separately recorded saying on the phone: "You see, here's the deal. I don't want to talk about the CIA. I don't want to talk about the ammunition or any of that bullshit. I was in on that stuff; I saw that stuff. I know all about it. There's nothing about it, goddamn it, that I don't know." *National Archives* transcribed 6/5/67

"The ammunition from Schlumburger. All that stuff, that was back in 1961. Those arms were in the United States illegally. They were going to be used against Martinique and Guadalupe. The stuff [ended up] in Guatemala. *National Archives* transcribed 6/5/67

Schlumburger is a French-owned company, home office Paris, France. **They were anti-Gaulists**. This is an anti-Gaulist pocket [New Orleans]. You know what went on here? And that was a very serious thing. Hell, they cashiered four French generals and hung one of them; disbanded the Foreign Legion. These were French munitions in here, man. *National Archives* transcribed 6/5/67

How did Bannister get involved in this?

To help the Cubans originally. He had been working with some people at O.N.I. [Office of Naval Intelligence] and then somebody gave him a connection with CIA. I know how that happened – It happened through a blind post office box in New York. I know exactly how it all happened. *National Archives* transcribed 6/5/67

That was back in '61. You remember when all of a sudden, he [Banister] got a lot of confidence behind him? He started carrying his gun again, and this and that. He had a "letter of marque" signed by Robert Kennedy, dad. Ferrie had a letter of marque. *National Archives* transcribed 6/5/67

You saw them?

Absolutely. In fact, everybody that was working with Bannister and had anything to do with this had a photostat of the letter of marque. So, I mean we had "carte blanche" on everything from grand theft to murder. *National Archives* transcribed 6/5/67

Did anybody commit grand theft?

Well in service of your government to seize arms that were illegally within this nation that might be used against an otherwise friendly nation or nations. And dispose of same as directed. It didn't say how. *National Archives* transcribed 6/5/67

Who signed that?

Robert Kennedy: The Attorney General of the United States. It was **delivered to Martens** and by courier. In hand. All these letters were delivered in hand. *National Archives* transcribed 6/5/67

Well, at any rate, it appears that after the Houma bunker haul, **Philby and company may have progressed in activity**. We say this because later the next evening, apparently some other band of thieves filched those promised arms and munitions from the safety of their hiding place at Banister's office. *Martin & Lewis, HSCA 180-10023-10376*

Some bastard, about this time, circulated the rumor. We understand that it was believed by all, or most of the Cubans, that Dr Arcacha had either sold, or had given away these arms and munitions to the pro-Castro. With this, the Cubans really believed that they'd been crossed, and Sergio Arcacha Smith left town immediately in fear of his life. .... Arcacha did return to New Orleans on the sneak from-time-to-time. *Martin & Lewis, HSCA 180-10023-10376*

Now, what happened, and where did they [the stolen

arms] go? It seems that there were some others, a bunch of discontented people, who just wanted to take over Guatemala using these weapons far more than we needed them to give the "works" to Castro. Thus, **via Philby and company**, General Ydigoras went out of office, and Guatemala had a completely new political administration. Somebody fulfilled the vendetta for the Carlos Marcello caper in spades! JFK had gotten his revenge one way or another. (After Bobby Kennedy had Marcello kidnapped and deported to Guatemala. Guatemala treated Marcello well while he was there and Marcello was also able to leave Guatemala and return to the U.S.. David Ferre is said to have flown down to Guatemala, collected up Marcello and flew Marcello back to the states.) *Martin & Lewis, HSCA 180-10023-10376*

Note: President Kennedy did supposedly encourage a military coup in 1963 against the U.S.'s own favorite, *right-wing* president, Miguel Ydigoras Fuentes. It almost sounds like Philby may have played a role in this operation to restructure Guatemala.

[With Arcacha leaving town,] this left Dr Cardona's Frente under the total command of Arcacha's former assistant, Carlos Quiroga. He claims to be an avid anti-Communist. We believe he protests far too much upon this subject. Hence, we did some checking. Quiroga, ... may well be as Philby, a double agent. *Martin & Lewis, HSCA 180-10023-10376*

The affidavit continues: Super-clandestine, Machiavellian Communist counterspy, Kim Philby. Who, by well laid plans pulled the strings of political intrigue expediently throughout the world, including right here in New Orleans. *Martin & Lewis, HSCA 180-10023-10376*

Who is Kim Philby? This subject's true name and identity is, Harold Adrian Russell Philby. He was born in India 56 years ago, the son of a minor British government official. (Not correct, Jack Philby, Kim's dad was the righthand man to the House of Saud in Saudi Arabia and a friend of Allen Dulles.) Philby went to the right schools, Cambridge; worked for the right newspaper, The London Times; and he traveled with the right social set. During WWII he was employed by none other than MI-5, British Intelligence. *Martin & Lewis, HSCA 180-10023-10376*

Philby was Chief of a special branch department operating against the U.S.S.R. and the international communistic functions of the M.V.D. (Russian Secret Police). Because of his successful victories he was knighted, awarded the O.B.E. *Martin & Lewis, HSCA 180-10023-10376*

From 1949 through 1951 Philby headed a special British Intelligence Mission in Washington (D.C.). This was at the same time that Billy B. Little-Horse, alias William W. **Dalzell**, a former partner of ours, was serving as **a Defense Department Intelligence Agent and who was well acquainted with Philby**. *Martin & Lewis, HSCA 180-10023-10376*

Philby's function at this time was organizer of the most secret of all the anti-communist operations. However, a cloak of silence hovers over his position, presence, and general whereabouts from 1951 (when Bill Harvey spotlighted Philby) until 1963. Why? There were more than enough powerful people to assist secrecy and maintain a complete blackout over it. Of course, **Philby's most intimate "friends" were, Allen Dulles, L.B.J., J.F.K., R.F.K., Frank Wisner (CIA)**, and a host of others. Although, this fails to include Banister, and Walter Sheridan who it is understood served Philby as "hatchet-men" from time-to-time. *Martin & Lewis, HSCA 180-10023-10376*

It was early November 1963, that Philby left his known haunts (Beirut) and slipped behind the Iron-Curtain. The record indicates that shortly afterwards he gave all of our Top-Secrets, and those of the British as well, to his "fellow" Russians. *Martin & Lewis, HSCA 180-10023-10376*

In December 1967, Philby "surfaced" behind the Iron-Curtain. The Moscow newspaper *Izvestia* published a long interview with him. He was elated over the fact that, "Control had decided to summon me back to the Soviet Union with the aim of guaranteeing my safety." In fact, Philby reported with pride that he had been a Soviet Agent the entire time that he had served as a "career" British Intelligence Agent, a German-Nazi Intelligence Officer, as well as during his tenure with the American Central Intelligence Agency. *Martin & Lewis, HSCA 180-10023-10376*

Philby boasted proudly of his systematic destruction of every anti-Communist agency or operation instituted by the combined efforts of our CIA and British Intelligence. Saying, "Moreover, amongst the Western Country's Intelligence Services, I know far more than anyone else. I have devoted my entire life to this struggle... That is, to see our Communism rule over all." *Martin & Lewis, HSCA 180-10023-10376*

Records indicate that while Philby served with the German-Nazis, he may have well done so, serving as a double-agent. Files of the British Intelligence show that many of their own people suffered by Philby's presence at the time. Moreover, in so-doing **Philby** became **a triple-agent**, [British/Nazi/Soviet] since he also served the Russians too. *Martin & Lewis, HSCA 180-10023-10376*

Accordingly, R.F.K. had exceptionally fine political and family intelligence. He should have examined all of his police powers and spy connections. Remember, R.F.K. commanded the whole Justice Department, and was ex-officio Chief of all Federal Law Enforcement during this period of time. Moreover, records indicate that he continued such a power-grabbing, mad-cap trend, and mingled with numerous CIA operations functions throughout his entire tenure of office. In short, **R.F.K.** had more than a natural, or at least a terrific influence over the President, and **coupled with Philby's friendship, he had convinced himself that he ran the whole show!** *Martin & Lewis, HSCA 180-10023-10376*

To Philby, R.F.K. as the President's little brother, fulfilled a purpose. Above all, it was good politics, especially in the spy business. *Martin & Lewis, HSCA 180-10023-10376*

Philby's tactics were employed at every turn, as were Banister's methods! Thus all concerned became victims of either their own stupidity in most cases: Although, in others, it was naught but pure gluttony and natural immaturity, as in the instance of R.F.K. and associates. Of course in all, **there must have been some degree of mental illness…that depth which compels people to plot and then to execute an act of murder**, or criminal-insanity. *Martin & Lewis, HSCA 180-10023-10376*

(Martin and Lewis illustrated how according to them Philby was able to manipulate Bobby Kennedy and the Schlumburger incident in order to screw things up for the United States in respect to our relations with numerous other countries.) They explain, "About this time a split in France's political structure arose. The rank and staff of all French government were divided at this time. There were DeGaulle and anti-Gaullest factions, all secretly backstabbing each other, fighting over the political and territorial severances from the whole-government of Metropolitan France proper." *Martin & Lewis, HSCA 180-10023-10376*

The French political pot was brewing, especially in the

Gulf-Caribbean area. For at that moment, it was in the planning stage to execute a military coup to take over the isles of Guadeloupe and Martinique. These insurgent units were anti-Gaullest militants desiring to institute separate insurgent governments on the two French islands. *Martin & Lewis, HSCA 180-10023-10376*

Martin and Lewis allege that the late Brigadier-General (Chep) Morrison, U.S. Ambassador said that he would use whatever influence he might have to secure the necessary recognition for the French-Insurgent-Governments.

The Schlumberger Company had locations, the world over [also apparently had a location in] the Dutch Antilles, became involved in this political tangle and insurgent activity. This happened through an operation of the anti-Gaullest faction of the D.G.S.S. (the Direction General Service Specialiux, a French counterpart of our CIA). Philby and company jumped on this one. *Martin & Lewis, HSCA 180-10023-10376*

The removal of the munitions from the Schlumberger bunker and their apparent subsequent use in the overthrow of the Guatemalan government, according to Martin and Lewis, resulted in the following reactions:

Wow! What an ensuing state of affairs [this Schlumberger incident became]. This Guatemala business [the demise of that government] "turned-on" most of the otherwise friendly Latin-American element. The anti-Castro Cubans were raising hell that they'd been "had," [because someone stole, their stolen munitions]. The anti-Gaullest factions were very "hot" too, to say nothing of ol' De Gaulle himself, over Chep Morrison and other general events. And of course the Communist-Castroites were "playing-it-up," by "beating-the-drum," in full propaganda treatment, just to make matters a little worse. So, R.F.K.'s friend Philby was jumping around in diabolical glee, 'cause the people in the Kremlin were happy too, we hear! For now the U.S. had nearly everyone on its neck. *Martin & Lewis, HSCA 180-10023-10376*

Banister himself joined the memberships and participated in several political groups. These he used in numerous ways as a front for personal stature, purposes of infiltration, and/or association in ulterior motive. In short, it was a combination of discordant elements and personalities from many levels of perhaps these and other sources, but not the actual organizations proper, nor by their knowledge. For these issues concerned only those individuals themselves, not necessarily their groups. Coupled…together with the apparent Philby puppet-sophistry and organizational ability…we witnessed in effect the birth of 'Philby-and-company," as it were. *Martin & Lewis, HSCA 180-10023-10376*

Along came the Cuban Missile Crisis, and the Berlin clash with the Communists, this is to say nothing of what was going on right here at home in our own backyard in industry, and of course the civil-rights matter. *Martin & Lewis, HSCA 180-10023-10376*

It was around this time that we witnessed **an extreme-right-wing conservative group, which was rather close to Banister** at one time. Baumler had worked for Banister undercover, as a student-agent, had known Morris Brownlee for years, had been in-and-out of Banister's office during that period, and had known Ferrie, but never mentions it, nor will comment about it. Baumler has **bragged** to Barbara Reid, Brownlee, and others **about** he, Davis, and others being **Neo-Nazis**…About their **big takeover**, et cetera, **to come** within the future. And this was at the time these groups were very active. This was also the same Davis who asked us to join he and **General Edwin Walker in Oxford, Mississippi**, at one time. *Martin & Lewis, HSCA 180-10023-10376*

Things had just about come to a head. **There were many unhappy citizens** and other people at hand. **Philby knew it and organized these into tight little silent groups.** Philby and company were convinced that they'd neatly engineered our Country into a state where it was on the brink of near revolution. Philby and company figured that they could set the wheels in motion and did. **Philby made the necessary plans before dropping behind the Iron-Curtain.** *Martin & Lewis, HSCA 180-10023-10376*

Surprisingly enough, **proof of this lies in a document** shown us by none other than Guy P. Johnson, Banister's old liaison officer and legal adviser. We call it the "Homme Report," inasmuch as it involves one H.G. Homme assistant legal counsel of the U.S. Senate's Committee of the Judiciary, transcript of which we last saw in the hands of Johnson a few weeks ago. This was the "little-gem" which was to light the Philby "fuse." **For it exposes the fact that the "genius" R.F.K. put out his own personal "contract"** (order to murder) **on Cuba's Fidel Castro.** *Martin & Lewis, HSCA 180-10023-10376*

**The gears had meshed smoothly, the wheels silently moved, and the trap had sprung! In short, the President was "hit"** (murdered), **before the "hit" on Castro could be completed...Philby's little groups had struck within, before those of R.F.K., could strike without.** But their job was yet unfinished, there was more to come, so the little groups stood by. *Martin & Lewis, HSCA* 180-10023-10376

**The final stroke, the grand finale of it all was now in the making, while an entire Nation was stunned and confused. For evidence of this last move lies within the files of our Country itself. And can be found in most any public library.** *Martin & Lewis, HSCA 180-10023-10376*

We refer to the "National Emergency Reorganization Plan," found in Volume 27, Number 35, subheaded Title 3, of 20th February 1962, which is listed in the Federal Register, National Archives, **under Presidential Documents, Executive Orders #10995, through #11005 ff, and #11051, and Part One, Section 101-d; the brain-child sired by Philby and company,** its father originally. **A piece of existing standby legislation already written into and passed in Federal Statute, whereby they could invoke an immediate and instantaneous dictatorship over the United States at the stroke of a pen on any given, or so-called emergency.** *Martin & Lewis, HSCA* 180-10023-10376

**Yes, as it had been sired by Philby, this is an existing law given birth under the Kennedy administration at their guidance and sponsorship. A law which would exchange our current way of life for one of Martial Law and a direct Socialistic Rule by single party system, instituting Dictatorship under a lone American Neo-Nazi, or American Neo-Communistic Party authority.** *Martin & Lewis, HSCA* 180-10023-10376

**This legislation parallels the German-Nazi law under which Hitler seized power. So, if Hitler could have done it, why couldn't Philby. After all, he had the help of R.F.K. and others!** *Martin & Lewis, HSCA* 180-10023-10376

Philby thought his "master-plan" couldn't fail once it entered the operational stage. However, **it was really ol' "L.B.J.-who-saved-the-day."** Yep, the great opportunist grabbed the rains, pulled back hard, and leveled things out, bringin' ol' Nellie to a screeching halt right there in the middle of Main street...For-the-Texas Cowboy, on that dark day of American history, with one masterful hand, clamped the lid down tight upon the "commode of top-security to maintain silence, and pulled hard the "chain" of expediency, flushing that entire mess down the political "sewer"...Known as the Warren-Commission. To accomplish the same purpose as the Pearl-Harbor-

Commission of yesteryear, i.e., to side-track, confuse, muddle, and eventually suppress the whole "stinking" matter! **Thus, saving the genius R.F.K., who blinded by his own foolish stupidity and naive asininity, accompanied by a host of "friends," all murdered his own brother! Of course, they had to cover up some other blundering facts in addition to this one, but the "bird has flown."** .... <u>Martin & Lewis, HSCA 180-10023-10376</u>

There is nothing new in our report. We've attempted to give enough material to various leading law enforcement agencies from time to time, so they could acquire the same results. However, they failed to take heed or accept what we had to say and let things ride. But by so doing, we fulfilled our obligation of citizenship, regardless of whether they acted upon it or not. For this conduct they must answer. .... <u>Martin & Lewis, HSCA 180-10023-10376</u>

I don't know about you, but I enjoyed Jack Martin and David Lewis's colorful prose and exceptional insight, although their commentary is more than a little disconcerting.

# IN THE PERIOD PRIOR TO THE ASSASSINATION

## *544 Camp Street*

Given that Guy Banister was helping with the logistics of getting weapons to the anti-Castro Cubans prior to the Bay of Pigs invasion, we know that leading up to and during the Bay of Pigs operation, Banister had to be working with, or helping the CIA Guys from the Guatemalan Coup/Bay of Pigs fiasco. It is less clear after the Bay of Pigs operation, as Banister seems to be more connected to the FBI and to Attorney General Robert Kennedy.

An FBI memo dated March 22, 1967, says, "Immediately following the assassination of President John F. Kennedy, this Bureau received allegations Ferrie was acquainted with Lee Harvey Oswald and was involved in the conspiracy to assassinate the President. Allegations emanated from Jack Martin (true name Edward S. Suggs), a self-described private investigator." DOJ 179-20003-10183

Based on a CIA routing sheet concerning Jack Martin, that passed though Angleton's Counterintelligence Research & Analysis section, it would appear that Jack Martin was a CIA asset.

We know about 544 Camp Street initially because of Jack Martin and the information he meted out to the FBI and to New Orleans District Attorney Jim Garrison immediately following the assassination in 1963. Then in 1967 when the Mafia's Johnny Rosselli started talking, Jim Garrison started his investigation, which produced the story, as told by Perry Russo an insurance salesman, of a party in which David Ferrie, Clay Shaw, and a Leon Oswald talked about assassinating President Kennedy by a triangulated crossfire using rifles.

At this point we must ask ourselves why do we know so much about 544 Camp Street? I think the answer is Jack Martin and others were instrumental in exposing this operation for some reason. The reason had to be to expose, or put in the public record, who or what was associated with 544 Camp Street and the activities that were taking place there. Who seems to be most associated with 544 Camp Street? The answer appears to be the Attorney General Bobby Kennedy and the FBI.

Guy Banister was a former FBI agent who had a private detective agency located at 544 Camp Street, New Orleans. Banister originally got involved in helping the anti-Castro Cubans. Guy Johnson, Guy Banister's attorney said, "Banister had been working with some people at O.N.I. (Office of Naval Intelligence) and then somebody gave him a connection with CIA. **Banister went to Washington, and saw** a high official in the Justice Department. **Presumably** it was **RFK**." [154]

When did Bobby Kennedy get connected to 544 Camp Street? The Garrison investigation established that the Schlumberger munitions heist occurred August 22, 1961, and we have been told from numerous sources that Bobby Kennedy supplied what are called Letters of Marque for that operation. Letters of Marque are in effect a government license authorizing, in this case, the seizure of munitions. The Letters of Marque were originally used to authorize the actions of privateers in attacking and capturing enemy vessels. Therefore, we know that Bobby Kennedy was tied into 544 Camp Street as early as August 22, 1961, just four months after the Bay of Pig disaster. We also know that at this time the "Guys from the Guatemalan Coup' (the GFGC) were running the Cuban show until Bill Harvey took over Cuban operations in late January 1962. We also know that

Kim Philby was also apparently involved in pulling some strings behind the scenes in this little munitions caper, because Jack Martin tells us this in the affidavit for DA Jim Garrison. Therefore, if Philby was involved behind the scenes in this theft of munitions from the Schlumberger Company's bunker and Bobby Kennedy was involved in this, as evidenced by the Letters of Marque, then we might conclude that Bobby Kennedy and Kim Philby were working together, behind the scenes, as early as August 1961. *HSCA* VOL. 10 Page 109 and *Martin & Lewis, HSCA 180-10023-10376*

Therefore, Bobby Kennedy was tied in with 544 Camp Street from the very beginning of the Kennedy administration and prior to William King Harvey's taking over Cuban operations in late January 1962. We know that Banister was helping to supply the anti-Castro Cubans during the Bay of Pigs run up, so at that point Banister was helping the GFGC's invasion operation.

Who was involved in extracting the munitions from the Schlumberger bunker: Gordon Novel, Sergio Arcacha Smith, Jack Martin and David Ferrie.

In early 1962, both Guy Banister's investigative service and Sergio Arcacha Smith's anti-Castro organization, the CRC's, moved their offices to the Newman Building at 544 Camp Street. *HSCA* VOL. 10 Page 110 (The CIA's E. Howard Hunt was the person who was responsible for setting up and organizing the CRC prior to the Bay of Pigs operation. In fact, the CIA's E. Howard Hunt, member of the GFGC, had an office located at 544 Camp Street at in the time leading up to the Bay of Pigs invasion.)

Layton Martens told author Guss Russo, "544 Camp Street became a center not only for arms procurement for Bobby Kennedy's sabotage program, but for intelligence gathering from what remained of the Cuban underground back on the island. This office became a White House priority because of the information we were getting. **We had the FBI at our disposal. We reported what we heard to [FBI Agents] Regis Kennedy and Warren DeBrueys. They set us up with a direct link to the White House and Bobby Kennedy."** [155]

Layton Martens knew David Ferrie originally from the same place Lee Oswald knew David Ferrie, from being a member, as a teenager, of the New Orleans Civil Air Patrol (CAP). Layton Martens was staying at David Ferrie's at the time of the assassination. In August 1993, Layton Martens said, **David Ferrie had "...been working under the Attorney General."** [156] Just more evidence that Bobby Kennedy was working with 544 Camp Street: David Ferrie, Layton Martens, Jack Martin and Arcacha Smith all participated in the Schlumberger arms transfer, all approved by Bobby Kennedy including letter of marque signed by Bobby Kennedy. [157] <u>HSCA</u> VOL. 10 Page 109

Bill Harvey then took over the Cuban operations in late January 1962 and it is not clear that Bill inherited 544 Camp Street as a part of the Cuban operation, as I haven't seen any reference to Bill Harvey having traveled to or having been seen at 544 Camp Street or having any involvement with 544 Camp Street. Bill Harvey took over the Cuban operations and immediately terminated the continued use of the "Guys from the Guatemala/Bay of Pigs Operations," in his operation. He told Helms that he would take on the responsibility of the Cuban operation and Task Force W, on the condition that he could put in totally fresh people.

David Ferrie went to work for Banister at 544 Camp Street, February 1962, **just a month after Bill Harvey took over**. According to CIA contract agent and author Robert Morrow, the **CIA's Tracy Barnes knew David Ferrie**, because Barnes briefed both Ferrie and Morrow prior to their flying into

Cuba at the time of the Bay of Pigs operation, April 16, 1961. Therefore, **David Ferrie has a history of working with the CIA's Tracy Barnes.**

August 1963, **Tracy Barnes** apparently felt the need to **send William Case Nagell**, our *Man Who Knew Too Much*, to 544 Camp Street to "infiltrate the Guy Banister-David Ferrie group." Why did Tracy Barnes "infiltrate the Guy Banister-David Ferrie group" with Nagell and perhaps with Ferrie? All indications at that time are that the information and communications from 544 Camp Street is flowing from Banister through the FBI and to Bobby Kennedy and allegedly Kim Philby as told to us by three people: Jack Martin, David Lewis, and Layton Martens. 544 Camp Street and Banister might have been primarily an FBI operation.

FBI Director, J. Edgar Hoover's phone records show that he was in communication with Banister in the summer of 1963. These phone records were made available in 1992 as a result of the JFK Assassination Records Act. [158]

Victor Marchetti, a former CIA Executive Assistant to Richard Helms, confirmed that "**David Ferrie was a contract agent for the CIA** in the early sixties and had been involved in anti-Castro Cuban activities." [159] In 1979, Richard Helms testified in a trial, saying **Clay Shaw** "was one of the part-time contacts of the **Domestic Contact [Operations] Division**, which was the CIA operation **run by Tracy Barnes**. It was David Ferrie and Clay Shaw, both CIA assets, and a Leon Oswald that gave us the impression that 544 Camp Street might have been involved in the assassination, as we were told about this party that took place in New Orleans. And then Jack Martin, an alleged CIA asset, reinforced this notion of 544 Camp Street being involved in the assassination when he reported that he had accused Banister of being involved in the assassination and according to Jack Martin he received a blow to the head from

Banister. As a result of Ferrie, Shaw (both CIA Tracy Barnes's assets), and Jack Martin, we all jumped to the conclusion that Banister and 544 Camp Street was involved in the Kennedy assassination. **Could the CIA's Tracy Barnes have taken these steps to make it look like the FBI was involved in the assassination and to draw attention to Bobby Kennedy's involvement in trying to get rid of Castro?** There have been allegations that Lee Harvey Oswald was also working with the FBI. According to Richard Nagell, Barnes also wanted him to determine if Oswald was acting as an informant for the FBI (or at least this is what Barnes wanted Nagell to plant in the public record about Oswald, that he might have been working for the FBI). [160]

Concerning the triangulation of crossfire party participant Leon Oswald. You will see later in this book that Leon Oswald is reportedly William Seymour, masquerading as Lee Harvey Oswald. William Seymour was a longtime employee of the CIA's front company Double-Chek. The CIA's Double-Chek was reportedly taken over by the FBI's Division Five leading up to the assassination. Seymour was also a part of the CIA financed group called Interpen, where Seymour was originally involved in training anti-Castro Cubans snipers in Florida and New Orleans.

How does 544 Camp Street end up appearing as if it was involved in the assassination? Notice how Guy Banister was not at the party that discussed triangulation of rifle fire and the assassination of President Kennedy. The triangulation discussion was solely conducted and participated in by CIA assets, David Ferrie, Clay Shaw and Leon Oswald (CIA, real name William Seymour). 544 Camp Street, an apparent FBI, Attorney General Bobby Kennedy operation, gets established in the public record by Perry Russo's triangulated rifle party report. Consequently, it is assumed that 544 Camp Street was involved in the assassination, even though Banister wasn't at the party and the party consisted of all CIA assets. Add to this the visibility supplied by Jack Martin (apparent CIA) and statements put in the public record by Nagell, another apparent CIA asset of Tracy Barnes and I would say that the CIA intentionally attempted to establish, in the public record, 544 Camp Street and its connection to the FBI and Bobby Kennedy. But the nexus, that of tying the 544 Camp Street operation into the possible participation in the assassination was all created by CIA assets: David Ferrie, Clay Shaw, Leon Oswald (William Seymour), Richard Case Nagell and Jack Martin.

And when did this information about the discussion of assassinating the President by triangulated crossfire come to light? It came to light when the Garrison investigation started. And when did the Garrison investigation start? It started almost immediately following when the Mafia's Johnny Rosselli started talking in 1967. Garrison seemed to suspect and accuse almost everyone of being involved in the assassination, except the Mafia. Was Garrison attempting to raise the profile of the CIA, FBI and Attorney General Bobby Kennedy, in an attempt to keep the Mafia from being left hanging out in the wind all by itself? I don't know.

Oswald shot at General Walker April 10, 1963, and moved to New Orleans April 25, 1963, where he was associated with 544 Camp Street. The question is: Was Oswald's move to New Orleans in April during the time that Bill Harvey oversaw the CIA's Cuban operation? The answer is no, Bill Harvey was officially removed from the Cuban operation in February 1963 when Desmond FitzGerald took over the Cuban Operation and Richard Helms setup the CIA's Domestic Operations Division headed by Tracy Barnes who reportedly had run the defector program and thus Oswald, back when Lee Oswald defected to the Soviet Union. Conclusion, it appears that the CIA's Tracy Barnes may have directed Oswald's move to New Orleans and Oswald's incorporation into 544 Camp Street.

[Jack] Martin told the House Select Committee on Assassinations, the HSCA, that he saw Lee Harvey Oswald with David Ferrie in Guy Banister's office in 1963. *HSCA* VOL. 10 Page 130

To quote Judyth Vary Baker, Oswald's New Orleans girlfriend, "No question Ruby, Ferrie, Oswald, Marcello, Clay Shaw, all knew each other." [161]

Writes Joan Mellen in *A Farewell To Justice*, David Ferrie and Clay Shaw knew each other; Clay Shaw even cosigned a four hundred dollar loan, so that Ferrie could purchase an airplane. [162]

Delphine Roberts, Banister's long-time friend and secretary, stated to the committee that Banister had become extremely angry over Oswald's use of the 544 Camp Street address on his handbills [his pro-Castro handbills]. *HSCA* Vol. 10 Page 128 (I am guessing that Tracy Barnes probably directed Oswald to place the address of 544 Camp Street on the handbills as another method of tying Oswald to Camp Street in the public record.)

During another interview, Delphine Roberts told the committee that Oswald came into the office seeking employment and sometime later brought Marina in with him. She stated she saw Oswald come into Banister's office on several occasions. Judyth Vary Baker states in her book that it was she, and not Marina Oswald, who had accompanied Lee Oswald on his visit to Banister's office, which Delphine Roberts is reporting above.

**David Phillips was seen with Oswald a month before the assassination and was placed in Guy Banister's office, along with Sergio Arcacha Smith, by Gordon Novel.** [163]

Judyth Vary Baker, girlfriend of Lee Oswald in New Orleans writes in her book *Me & Lee,* "When I first told investigators that Bobby Kennedy was privy to Banister's doings and was involved in some of them, in 1999, they were stunned. I gave leads to researchers, and since 2000, evidence has kept emerging helping to verify my statements." [164]

**Individuals associated with 544 Camp Street**, New Orleans, Guy Banisters Private Detective Agency, a hot bed of anti-Castro activity:

• Guy Banister – former FBI, was the-special-agent-in-charge of the FBI office in Chicago from January 4, 1954, to December 11, 1954, when he retired to become the Police Chief of New Orleans for a short time beginning January 1955. Local newspapers reported that Banister served as a munitions supplier for the 1961 Bay of Pigs Invasion.

• David Ferrie - was a contract agent for the CIA, a pilot, was Lee Harvey Oswald's Civil Air Patrol leader when Oswald was a young boy. Reported as having been seen with Lee Harvey Oswald and Jack Ruby. Associated with the Mafia's Carlos Marcello.

• Clay Shaw - In 1967, Clay Shaw of New Orleans was charged, by District Attorney Jim Garrison, for being a part of a CIA plot to assassinate President Kennedy. The CIA's Richard Helms confirmed Shaw's association with the CIA when in 1979 Helms testified in a trial, saying Clay Shaw "was one of the part-time contacts of the Domestic Contact [Operations] Division, which was the CIA operation run by Tracy Barnes."

• Lee Harvey Oswald – no question, Lee was seen at 544

Camp by numerous people and stamped the 544 Camp Street address on some of the Fair Play for Cuba literature (Was this deliberately done to call attention to 544 Camp Street or was this an oops? I think, no oops, it was intentional.)

- E. Howard Hunt – CIA, GFGC member, had an office at 544 Camp. E. Howard Hunt's job for the Bay of Pigs was to form the political umbrella for the invasion. The Cuban Revolutionary Council (CRC) was organized by E. Howard Hunt. Sergio Arcacha Smith – anti-Castro Cuban, was the head of Cuban Revolutionary Council (CRC) in New Orleans, had direct communications with Bobby Kennedy, and Arcacha is reported to be the handler for Lee Oswald and David Ferrie. The CRC chapter had its offices at 544 Camp Street from October 12, 1961-1962.

- Attorney General Bobby Kennedy

- David Athlee Phillips is reported as having been seen in the offices of 544 Camp Street.

- Jack Martin – reported the activity at 544 Camp Street to the FBI and to the New Orleans District Attorney Jim Garrison, claiming that David Ferrie was involved with Oswald and with the assassination.

- Banister's Secretary Delphine Roberts reports seeing both Johnny Rosselli and Robert Maheu in the offices of 544 Camp Street.

- Carlos Marcello was the reputed head of the Mafia in New Orleans and was associated with Ferrie and Banister.

# CIA ACTIVITY

February 1963, Bill Harvey officially leaves Task Force W, which is renamed the Special Affairs Staff (SAS) under **Desmond FitzGerald**. At approximately the same time the CIA created the Domestic Operation Division under **Tracy Barnes**, where he is joined by **E. Howard Hunt**.

Six months prior to the assassination in June of 1963 **Rosselli** stopped reporting to Bill Harvey and began reporting to **David Morales** at JM/WAVE in Miami. [169] According to the FBI, during his trip to Miami in early October 1963 Ruby met twice at different hotels with Johnny Rosselli. [170] **David Morales** is now working closely with **David Atlee Phillips** who is now posted in Mexico City. According to Cuban intelligence, **Dave Phillips** took over ZR/RIFLE, the CIA assassination operation. **Everyone ultimately reports to Richard Helms the Director of Plans in the CIA.** June 27, 1963, Harvey recommended terminating QJ/WIN, but also recommended that the CIA consider using QJ/WIN in Europe, however the CIA's Richard Helms kept QJ/WIN on the payroll, whose job it was to recruit assassins and those with other talents. In October 1963, Rosselli met twice in Miami with **Jack Ruby**. [171]

Bill Harvey left Cuban operations February 1963. So, who oversaw the Cuban operations (or SAS) in April 1963 when Oswald went to New Orleans? Answer: **Desmond Fitzgerald**? And who oversaw the CIA's Domestic Operations at that time? Answer: **Tracy Barnes**.

So, who were our CIA Guys from the Guatemalan Coup (GFGC), our CIA Guys from the Bay of Pigs fiasco, our CIA personnel in the field leading up to President Kennedy's assassination?

- Tracy Barnes
- E. Howard Hunt
- David Athlee Phillips
- David Morales
- Johnny Rosselli
- Philip J. Corso
- Richard Bissell (fired by President Kennedy following the Bay of Pigs fiasco)
- Guy Banister

## *Tracy Barnes*

- During World War II, Tracy Barnes was stationed in Switzerland with Allen Dulles and Richard Helms.

- Richard Case Nagell said, "Tracy Barnes was familiar with Oswald, as Barnes had utilized Oswald before in the Soviet Union."

- Tracy Barnes oversaw the Bay of Pigs planning.

- The "guys from the Guatemalan Coup/Bay of Pigs Planning" were working with the "guys at 544 Camp Street" leading up to and during the Bay of Pigs invasion.

- April 15, 1961, Robert Morrow and David Ferrie flew into Cuba in a multi-engine airplane. They were briefed on their mission and directed by the CIA's Tracy Barnes and General Cabell. Therefore, back in 1961 we know that David Ferrie was a part of a Tracy Barnes operation.

- February 1963, when Bill Harvey stepped down from overseeing Cuban operations, a new CIA division was created called the Domestic Operation Division, headed by Tracy Barnes.

- On a return trip back from Greece, Robert Morrow was given a large manila envelope to transport back to Tracy Barnes in the U.S. The envelope was from a CIA agent named William Harvey and it contained information concerning Centro Mandiale Commerciale. Clay Shaw was a member of its Board of Directors.

- August 1963, Tracy Barnes sent Nagell to New Orleans to make contact with and to observe Lee Harvey Oswald and the Banister-Ferrie group.

- Robert Morrow says in his book First Hand Knowledge, "I bought the three Mannlicher rifles that [unbeknownst to me] would be used to shoot Kennedy and I supplied Kennedy's three hit squads with communications devices,"[upon the request of Tracy Barnes, and with instructions from del Valle that they be turned over to David Ferrie]. The Mob, the leaders of our nation, and our government's intelligence agencies conspired together to assassinate very important people [perhaps the CIA's Ray Cline?], including the President. Said Morrow, "I realize how impossible and illogical it sounds to assert that the CIA would orchestrate the assassination of the President of the United States. To comprehend why the CIA found it necessary to commit the seemingly treasonous act of murdering the Commander-in-Chief, one must understand the circumstances that led up to the assassination." (Notice how Morrow indicated that there would be more than just President Kennedy who would be assassinated when he said: "conspired together to assassinate very important people," people - as in more than one important person and conspired meaning a conspiracy. On November 10, 1963, Robert Morrow reported to attorney Marshall Diggs, that he had been told that President Kennedy was going to be assassinated in Dallas. Diggs said that he would relay this information to Tracy Barnes. Therefore,

Tracy Barnes should have been in a position to prevent the assassination.

• The CIA's Tosh Plumlee flew a group, which included Johnny Rosselli, into Dallas on the morning of the assassination. Tosh Plumlee says among others which included Bill Harvey, he says that he was "a contract operative for the CIA, associated with Tracy Barnes…"

• The FBI's Domestic Intelligence Deputy Director, William Sullivan, issued the directive, which removed Lee Harvey Oswald from any security risk lists [the FBI's Security Index]. According to Robert Morrow, Sullivan issued this directive to delete Oswald's name at the insistence of the CIA's Tracy Barnes.

• In 1979, Richard Helms testified in a trial, saying Clay Shaw "was one of the part-time contacts of the Domestic Contact [Operations] Division, which was the CIA operation run by Tracy Barnes.

• Tracy Barnes reportedly told Morrow to tell the anti-Castro Cuban Mario Kohly that Mary Meyer, CIA Cord Meyer's ex-wife, needed to be eliminated because she knew too much.

• The CIA's Robert Crowley said that Tracy Barnes was one of Richard Helms's top men.

• Tracy Barnes reported to Richard Helms.

## David Athlee Phillips

• Anti-Castro Cuban Antonio Veciana confirmed in 2013 that he witnessed David Atlee Phillips meeting with Lee Harvey Oswald in Dallas in September 1963.

- Dave Phillips took over ZR/RIFLE.

- Just before his death, David Athlee Phillips told Kevin Walsh, an investigator with the House Select Committee on Assassinations: "My final take on the assassination is there was a conspiracy, likely including American intelligence officers."

- Lee Oswald said to Judyth Vary Baker, "Know how we wondered who my handler was? Well, he's from Fort Worth, so it must be Phillips. He is the traitor. Phillips is behind this. I need you to remember that name," Lee said, repeating it with cold anger. "David Atlee Phillips." Phillips was coordinating the JFK assassination plot in the field.

- David Athlee Phillips was reportedly in Banister's office at 544 Camp Street after Bill Harvey had departed for Rome and prior to the assassination of President Kennedy. David Phillips was seen with Oswald a month before the assassination and was placed in Guy Banister's office, along with Sergio Arcacha Smith, by Gordon Novel.

- During his testimony before the HSCA (House Select Committee on Assassinations), Phillips claimed that no CIA photographs of Lee Harvey Oswald in Mexico City in September 1963 had been taken because the CIA surveillance cameras were not working at that time. However, subsequent findings revealed that this statement was not true, the cameras were working.

- In his final days, while struggling with lung cancer, David Atlee Phillips confided over the phone to his estranged brother James Atlee Phillips that he was indeed present in Dealey Plaza, November 22, 1963. James Phillips hung up on him.

## E. Howard Hunt

- E. Howard Hunt is a part of the Domestic Operation Division under Tracy Barnes.

- E. Howard Hunt was the CIA's liaison to Arcacha's CRC and Arcacha had a direct line to Bobby Kennedy and Oswald is reporting to Arcacha.

- E. Howard Hunt is the case officer for Bobby Kennedy intimate anti-Castro Cuban Harry Williams. Harry Williams connected Bobby Kennedy up with the Commander of Cuba's army, Juan Almeida, thus setting the stage for the Kennedy/Almeida coup.

- E. Howard Hunt was the CIAs liaison to the OAS. Jean Souetre was the OAS's liaison to the CIA and the CIA's E. Howard Hunt. Souetre is suspected as having been the French/Corsican assassin involved in President Kennedy's assassination. Jean Rene Souetre was present in Dallas on November 22, 1963. Souetre was associated with Otto Skorzeny (QJ/WIN?). Souetre maintained an informal OAS office at Guy Banister's 544 Camp Street. Additionally, Souetre maintained ties with the Mafia's Meyer Lansky's associates in the Corsican Mafia and with General Walker. There were extremely close ties that existed between the anti-Castroites in Florida and Souetre's group of French right extremists. In March-April 1963 Souetre met E. Howard Hunt in Madrid Spain.

- Frank Sturgis was an Anti-Castro activist who worked for the CIA on the Bay of Pigs and in the Congo. Frank Sturgis was a close associate of E. Howard Hunt. Everyone from Bill Harvey to the Mafia has indicated that Sturgis was involved in the assassination.

- Marita Lorenz testified that in November 1963 she worked for the CIA, and she worked with Frank Sturgis. Marita testified that she had witnessed E. Howard Hunt, code named Eduardo, making payments to Frank Sturgis. On November 21st, the day before the assassination in their hotel room she witnessed E. Howard Hunt delivering a large amount of money to Sturgis. Frank Sturgis pulled the money out of the envelope and counted it. About an hour after E. Howard Hunt left a second fellow came to the hotel room. Marita testified; it was Jack Ruby.

- The Sunday News Journal, August 20, 1978, by Joe Trento and Jacquie Powers, reported seeing a 1966 CIA memo that placed E. Howard Hunt in Dallas Nov. 22, 1963. The memo was initialed by Richard M. Helms, former CIA director, and James J. Angleton, former counterintelligence chief. As evidenced by the memo, three years after the assassination (1966) apparently Helms and Angleton felt it necessary to discuss covering up the fact that Hunt had been in Dallas. Helms and Angleton felt that a cover story, giving Hunt an alibi for being elsewhere the day of the assassination, "ought to be considered." E. Howard Hunt was in Dallas the day of the assassination.

## George Joannides

- In late 1962 – 1963, George E. Joannides was the deputy director for psychological warfare at the C.I.A.'s Miami station (JM/WAVE) and became the DRE's case officer around the time of the Cuban missile crisis. When Joannides took over responsibility for the DRE, it was on direct orders from Dick Helms, who told the Cubans that Joannides would report out of channels directly to himself.

- Later in 1978, George Joannides was the CIA's liaison to

the House Select Committee on Assassinations, however the Committee was not informed of Mr. Joannides's role with the DRE at the time of the assassination.

### Robert Maheu

- In August 1963 Robert Maheu is reported as the field coordinator for the assassinations. Maheu was originally a part of Bissell's "Executive Action" operation, which morphed into Bill Harvey's ZRRIFLE. ZRRIFLE at the time of the Kennedy assassination appeared to be run by David Phillips.

The Cuban State Security Department upon reviewing their own and the U.S. investigations concluded that Richard Helms, David Phillips, and Santos Trafficante, planned the Kennedy assassination, participants where: Sam Giancana, John Rosselli, General Charles Cabell, Frank Sturgis, Robert Maheu, Gerry Hemming, and E. Howard Hunt. [182] (Note: Cuban Intelligence does not include William King Harvey on their list.)

# PRESIDENT JOHN KENNEDY'S ASSASSINATION

President Kennedy was assassinated November 22, 1963, in Dallas, Texas.

Writes Tosh Plumlee: Approximately 1962 through 1963, I was assigned to Task Force W Section-C-7-tab B and D known as the Cuban Project (also known as Operation Mongoose) which operated at the time from the JM/WAVE station attached to Miami, Florida's 'Cuba Desk' of the Central Intelligence Agency (CIA). I operated as a contract, "undercover pilot" and, at times, I was assigned to specialized Cuban operations of the CIA's "Covert Action Group" (CAG) I was engaged in many secret operations throughout the early sixties.

Tosh Plumlee also writes, "My case officers were associated with William 'Wild Bill' Harvey, Tracy Barnes, and Rip Robertson," consequently, "I was a contract operative for the CIA, associated with Tracy Barnes, Wild Bill Harvey, Frank Bender, and John Martino." [183]

Tosh Plumlee was the co-pilot on a top-secret Military Intelligence flight that was supported by the CIA. The flight began in Palm Beach, Florida on November 21st, flew to Tampa, Florida where Johnny Rosselli and a couple of others got on board, stopped in New Orleans where two people got off and three others got on, flew on to Houston, and then on into Dallas, Texas the morning of the assassination, November 22nd, 1963.

In an interview on June 4, 1992, Tosh Plumlee said, "The impression I was under at that time was that we were flying a team into Dallas to abort the assassination [of President

Kennedy] and John Rosselli was on board that flight as well as a couple of Cubans and people that were connected with organized crime in New Orleans. November 22, 1963, I was observing the attempt on Kennedy's life. I was at Dealey Plaza on the South Knoll." [184]

Plumlee was accompanied in Dealey Plaza by a person he referred to as Sergio. Johnny Rosselli had departed the airplane at the Dallas, Garland Airport. When weather permitted, Plumlee then flew the airplane over to Dallas's Redbird Airport. The Garland Airport was the last Plumlee saw of Rosselli that day.

Plumlee reports hearing four or five shots, while in Dealey Plaza, with one being fired from over his left from atop the south end of the overpass. He speculates, and I thought the same thing when I visited Dealey Plaza, that the "Triple Overpass" has on each end a concrete railing that is pillared, and which is angled at thirty degrees to the east on each side of the overpass. People standing on the overpass (40 feet north of this position) and focused on the arrival of the President, would not have been able to see a person if they were to have come from the south parking lot and they could have hidden behind this angled railing with concrete slats while in a shooting position. "Sergio and I," says Plumlee, "did not notice this possible hiding place until many years after the event." This author noticed the same thing and I would also add that I noticed that there is a metal drain grate located in the overpass's pavement just below and up next to this slotted railing.

"When leaving via the south side of the underpass near the train tracks, Sergio and I smelled gunpowder," writes Plumlee.

One report states: November 22, 1963, Bill Harvey, and his deputy Mark Wyatt were at a CIA base of operations in Sardinia, Italy when a telex arrived reporting the assassination of President Kennedy. Bill Harvey was awakened from an afternoon nap following one too many drinks. When told of the assassination by his deputy, Bill Harvey reportedly said, "This was bound to happen and it's probably good that it did." Once back in Rome, Harvey discovered that his deputy Mark Wyatt was spending time receiving condolences from local officials, Harvey declared, "I haven't got time for this crap." [185]

This is not exactly how C.G. Harvey remembers it! On November 22, 1963, C.G. Harvey's recollection, two and a half decades later: "Bill was in Sicily, talking to the Mafia about drug smuggling to the United States." [186]

Mark Wyatt, Bill Harvey's deputy in Rome, the same person who two paragraphs above stated he woke Bill Harvey up from a nap, years later says to a French investigative journalist, "You know, I always wondered what Bill Harvey was doing in Dallas in November of 1963." Wyatt is reported by his children to have been deeply suspicious of Bill Harvey, concerning the Kennedy assassination. [187]

Back on May 13, 1963, after Bill Harvey had already left the Cuban operation, anti-Castro Cuban **Harry Williams** relayed to Bobby Kennedy that the Commander of Cuba's army, Juan Almeida was willing to stage a military coup in Cuba. There appears to be no question, Bobby Kennedy ran this Kennedy/Almeida operation. The operation was kept secret and was finally declassified in 2005, in part to protect Commander Almeida and I suspect in part to protect Bobby Kennedy's persona.

The plan was for Almeida and the Cuban military to overthrow Castro, the United States would immediately recognize the new government, put in place a naval blockade, warn the Soviets not to intervene, blame a patsy in order to mask Almeida's participation thus keeping Almeida in the good graces of the Cuban people.

According to Harry Williams the CIA's role was "to have a person who would 'take the fall' for killing Fidel Castro and that person would be a 'Russian' or a 'Russian sympathizer.'" CIA code name for this operation: "AMWORLD."

What was Oswald supposedly trying to do just prior to the period leading up to President Kennedy's assassination? He was trying to get into Cuba via Cuba's Consulate in Mexico City. According to a recently declassified memo, the CIA's role leading up to the Almeida coup was "the introduction by CIA, as soon as practicable, of assets into Cuba..." In my opinion, this activity by Oswald and its timing, in and of itself, is nearly proof enough that Oswald was working at the direction of the CIA and was a part of Bobby Kennedy's Almeida coup. Harry Power as well, for all I know.

The time for moving the CIA assets into Cuba, late September 1963, and the last week of November 1963 (Lee Oswald visited the Cuban Consulate on September 27, 1963). **All four of the known young men who tried to get into Cuba before the coup were in their early twenties** (At the time Oswald was 24, Harry Power was 20 years old).

Had President Kennedy not been assassinated, a mere eight day later the JFK/RFK/Almeida coup was supposed to have occurred, it was scheduled for December 1, 1963!

Sources told columnist Jack Anderson that "The CIA Director John McCone rushed to Bobby Kennedy's home following the assassination. McCone anguished with Bobby over the terrible possibility that **the assassination plots sanctioned by the president's own brother may have backfired**." [188] (The JFK/RFK/Almeida coup is probably what they were talking most about. I haven't seen any evidence that Bobby Kennedy knew anything about the asinine CIA's AM/LASH operation, and I don't know what Bobby Kennedy may have had going with CIA operative Charles Ford.)

In the afternoon of the assassination Bobby Kennedy called Harry Williams. Harry Williams was an anti-Castro Cuban who was very close to Bobby Kennedy. Harry Williams is the one that put Bobby together with Cuban Commander Almeida for the coup attempt on Castro that was to take place in just eight more days. Robert Kennedy was reportedly utterly in control of his emotions and sounded almost studiously brisk as **he said in his phone call to anti-Castro Cuban Harry Williams, "One of your guys did it."** [189]

This confirms in my mind that Lee Oswald, and possibly Harry Power, were a part of the Bobby Kennedy/Almeida coup whose mission was to get into Cuba, perhaps knowing, or not knowing that they were to be a patsy for the murder of Fidel Castro. Bobby Kennedy said, "One of your guys did it." How many guys are believed to have been involved in the assassination? So, whom must Bobby Kennedy be referring to? He must be referring to Oswald, the only person officially recognized to have been involved in the assassination, even to this day. It seems that Bobby Kennedy must have known something about Oswald in order to say, "one of your guys did it." Guys is also plural implying that there might be more than one individual involved in some operation.

According to Harry Williams, "Bobby called the shots in the Cuba Project. Bobby ran the CIA. Bobby's anti-Castro campaign continued right up until the assassination." [190]

This seems to confirm that Oswald may very well have been working on Bobby Kennedy's Almeida Coup. Adrian Alba, worked in the parking garage next door to the Reily Coffee Co. in New Orleans and became acquainted with Oswald, who used to spend some time looking at Alba's gun magazines at the garage. Alba reports he once saw Oswald take a large envelope from an FBI "agent from Washington." But more surprising was what Alba learned from a Secret Service agent after the assassination.

According to author Gus Russo, "Oswald's friend Adrian Alba…told Frontline investigator Scott Malone that RFK's network in New Orleans had considered recruiting Oswald for the Castro assassination plot [the Almeida coup?]."

Adrian Alba said that "Oswald was one of ten dossiers given to RFK for the purpose of assassinating Castro." Alba's source for this information included John Rice of the Secret Service (who parked his car in Alba's garage). [191]

Seven days after the assassination, on November 29, 1963, the German newspaper in Munich, Deutsche National Zietung," said, "The murderer of Kennedy [Oswald] made an attempt on U.S. General Walker's life early in the summer when General Walker was sitting in his study. The bullet missed Walker's head by inches. Oswald was seized, but the investigation, as it was reported to us—was stopped by U.S. Attorney General, Robert Kennedy. If Oswald had been investigated, he would have been in prison, so he would not have been able to commit the murder of John F. Kennedy." FBI 124-10022-10486

Two things are interesting about this article, first the allegation that Bobby Kennedy stopped an investigation of Oswald in the General Walker shooting and second the fact that authorities in the United States did not find out from Marina Oswald until December $3^{rd}$ that her husband had attempted to kill General Walker. Now, how did the German paper know 4 days before US authorities knew? As it turned out this article was partially correct, Oswald apparently did shoot at General Walker. If that is correct, then the question is: Might it also not be correct that Bobby Kennedy intervened with the Dallas Police to get Oswald off in the General Walker shooting attempt? (The date that information was made available to U.S. authorities comes from HSCA 180-10100-10289)

In the microfilm that I purchased from the New Orleans Library, which contains snippets of information from District Attorney Garrison's investigation, I found that it said: "In a Marksmanship article (story not confirmed) it says Oswald was arrested for shooting at General Walker, but Robert Kennedy intervened." (So, there are at least two published sources that made this allegation, plus I have seen an article from back then where the National Enquirer was saying the same thing.)

Also remember, the Terre Haute Police had the impression that Harry L. Power was investigated for shooting at General Walker and The Assassinations Committee speculated, **"That if it could be shown that Oswald had associates in the attempt on General Walker, they would be likely candidates as the grassy knoll gunman."** The *Man Who Knew Too Much* said that Harry L. Power was associated with Oswald and they had been seen together on numerous occasions in Texas.

All the evidence seems to indicate that Lee Oswald was known to Bobby Kennedy and further Oswald could have had a part in the JFK/RFK/Ameida coup that Bobby Kennedy was running to get Castro. When **Bobby Kennedy** heard the name Lee Harvey Oswald in conjunction with the assassination of his brother, he might have immediately **recognized the fact that any serious investigation of the assassination of his brother's assassination could lead to the discovery of his own questionable activity against Castro.** Knowledge of Lee Harvey Oswald might also explain how the attorney general was able to pick up the phone and say to someone, "One of your guys did it." Bobby Kennedy must have been referring to Lee Harvey Oswald and must have known things concerning Oswald in order for him to say: "one of your guys did it." There are no other individuals in the official assassination story.

Author, Seymour Hersh wrote in his book *The Dark Side of Camelot, page 286,* based on a conversation with the CIA's Sam Halpern, right hand man to Bill Harvey: There was further humiliation for the men of Task Force W. Bobby Kennedy, increasingly impatient with the lack of progress in Cuba, decided in the early spring of 1962 to run his own operation. On Bobby Kennedy's orders an experienced clandestine CIA operative named Charles Ford was assigned as the attorney general's personal agent. Ford spent the next eighteen months, until the assassination of President Kennedy, making secret trips, at Bobby Kennedy's direction, to Mafia chieftains, while continuing to serve with Harvey and Halpern on Task Force W. "It was possible," Halpern said, "that Bobby Kennedy's primary purpose in dealing with Charles Ford was to do what Bill Harvey was not doing—find someone to assassinate Fidel Castro."

The CIA was in a position to set Bobby Kennedy up by injecting, introducing, or connecting Oswald to Bobby Kennedy and or any of Bobby Kennedy's initiatives.

Sergio Arcacha Smith was the head of the New Orleans portion of the anti-Castro, Cuban Revolutionary Council (CRC). **Sergio Arcacha Smith had a powerful ally, the Attorney General of the United States, Robert Kennedy. Says Arcacha, "Whenever we needed anything in New Orleans, I'd call Bobby Kennedy."** HSCA, Volume 10, P. 127

In an interview in 1997 with author Gus Russo, **Sergio Arcacha Smith said: "Whenever we needed a plane, for example to send arms to the camps in Nicaragua, I'd call Bobby. We used to call Mr. Bobby Kennedy whenever we had anything to report, or to ask advice. He knew what we** were doing all the time." [192]

Richard Davis leader of the anti-Castro (MDC) or Christian Democratic Movement told author Harold Weisberg that **Arcacha handled David Ferrie and Oswald.** <u>My notes from Jim Garrison investigation, New Orleans Library Microfilm, conversation between Richard Davis and author investigator, Harold Weisberg Jan. 24, 1968</u>

Orestes Peña, proprietor of the Habana Bar is on record as reporting that Gaudet was a "CIA-FBI agent" and Gaudet's office was housed in Clay Shaw's International Trade Mart. William Gaudet is on record as saying, "I suppose you are looking into **Ferrie**. He was with **Oswald**. Another vital person is **Sergio Arcacha Smith. I know he knew Oswald** and knows more about the Kennedy affair than he ever admitted." [193] (It is a documented fact that William Gaudet stood in line right next to Oswald, when both Oswald and Gaudet received their Mexican tourist cards, before Oswald left for Mexico City.)

**Jack Martin also told Jim Garrison that "Oswald knew Sergio Arcacha Smith**, who was close to Bobby Kennedy and his special group training to assassinate Fidel Castro." [194]

Here we have Gerry Hemming, a singleton for Angleton, an asset of James Angleton the CIA's Chief of Counterintelligence putting Bill Harvey in the public record when he said, he believed that **it was "'one or more of Bobby's boys gone bad' who had killed Bobby's brother, as Bobby shared operatives with the CIA's William Harvey, tool of the DDP, Richard Helms."** (Here Hemming is saying what I am theorizing. My theory, Bobby Kennedy was setup with Oswald by the CIA as a part of Bobby's operations and Oswald must be one of Bobby's boys gone bad who killed the President, because the only person in the assassination story is Oswald. Hemming is saying that Bobby shared, or used, some of Bill Harvey's operatives, perhaps meaning Lee Harvey Oswald.) However, keep in mind Hemming's close affiliation with Angleton was a persistent theme found in the Garrison interviews, writes Joan Mellen in *A Farewell To Justice*. This public record entry might have been an attempt by Angleton's Gerry Hemming to link Bill Harvey in through guilt by association, through the use of one of Bill Harvey's past operatives?

In the months preceding the assassination Oswald had become well known to Bobby Kennedy and his closest colleagues in the anti-Castro movement. Gerald Patrick Hemming tells of Bobby helicoptering from Palm Beach to a training facility near Homestead Air Force base. Bobby met with some Cubans and according to Hemming, among the Cubans stood Lee Harvey Oswald. [195]

In 2005, Angelo Murgado sat down for an interview with author Joan Mellen. Writes Mellen, "by 1963 Bobby Kennedy had gathered together many trusted Cubans, one was Angelo Murgado. The groups mission was to help Bobby Kennedy plan the assassination of Fidel Castro and to protect the President from hotheaded Cubans who blamed President Kennedy for the failure of the Bay of Pigs." Angelo reports, "The group was aware of Lee Harvey Oswald and whom he was associated with." In one meeting Bobby Kennedy was even shown a picture of Lee Harvey Oswald. At some point says Angelo Murgado, Bobby learned that Oswald was working for the FBI. **The group contacted Sergio Arcacha Smith to learn more about Oswald, as they knew Arcacha knew and was connected with Oswald."**

Angelo Mugado then says the same thing that CIA connected Gordon Novel has said, that "there were additional Oswalds waiting in the wings, other Oswalds who had been prepared and were ready to go." Being as this is the Bobby Kennedy group's perspective, we can draw the conclusion that Lee

Oswald was perceived as being prepared for a role in a Fidel Castro assassination attempt as well as the numerous other Oswald look-a-likes in the public record, (like perhaps one Harry L. Power). Murgado's impression was also that "Oswald's IQ was not much greater than his age."

But then, Angelo Murgado, a part of Bobby Kennedy's operation, goes on to reveal that "it was he (Angelo) and Bernardo de Torres (Leopoldo) and Lee Harvey Oswald (Leon Oswald) who visited Sylvia Odio at her home." Of course, as the story goes, it was not until the next day that Leopoldo called Sylvia Odio on the phone, out of earshot and unbeknownst to Leopoldo and to Lee Oswald. Leopoldo told Odio over the phone that, "Leon Oswald had said that some Cubans should kill President Kennedy."

The purpose of this meeting with Sylvia Odio was probably two-fold. To try and establish in the public record that Oswald was advocating the assassination of President Kennedy and to try and establish in the public record a link between Lee Harvey Oswald and Angelo, a member of Bobby Kennedy's operation. [196]

In Jim Garrison's files there is a memorandum detailing a conversation with Richard Case Nagell in 1969. Nagell said that **both Angel [Angelo] and Leopoldo had worked in the past with "an outfit called Movement to Free Cuba, headed by the CIA's Tracy Barnes."** That same memo reported Nagell saying: "[David] Ferrie also knew both [Angel (Angelo) and Leopoldo]." [197]

Andy Alderton asked C.G. Harvey, "Tell me about operation Mongoose the whole plot to assassinate Castro? C.G. responded: "From what I understand Bobby Kennedy gave an order and the whole Rosselli thing." Later in the conversation she said: "And he [Rosselli] had been recruited by another guy from the FBI [Maheu?] for assassination purposes on Kennedy, or um on Castro by Bobby. **Bobby was running this other guy..."**

**In other words: when Andy Alderton asked C.G. Harvey about the operation that some think may have flipped and gotten President Kennedy. C.G. Harvey's response was in effect, no it was Bobby Kennedy's operation, "Bobby was running this other guy..."**

**C.G. Harvey also said to Andy Alderton, "I am sick and tired of having them say that Bill Harvey tried to assassinate Castro when the guy who was doing it was Robert Kennedy!"** Andy Alderton/C.G. Harvey Interview

If you were going to commit a crime like the assassination of a U.S. President and you wanted to get away with it, wouldn't it be useful to tie the top law enforcement officer, the Attorney General, in with the crime?

In my opinion the surest way for Oswald to provide protection for the plotters would be if an investigation of Oswald would have led to an association of Oswald with those who would have been the investigators and the prosecutors of the crime. That would be the best protection of all. Who was the nation's top prosecutor? The answer: Attorney General, Bobby Kennedy. And who was over the FBI, the Justice Department, and to a large extent the CIA? The answer is the normally combative and aggressive Bobby Kennedy.

I think that the CIA, perhaps in conjunction with Bill Harvey, may have set Bobby Kennedy up by incorporating Lee Harvey Oswald into the operation Bobby Kennedy was running to assassinate Castro. I would add that perhaps Johnny Rosselli, who was known to Bobby, might also have been involved in this project for the very same reasons. I say that based upon C.G.'s comment, "From what I understand Bobby Kennedy gave an order and the whole Rosselli thing." We learned above that the CIA's Charles Ford (alias, real name withheld by CIA) was assigned to the attorney general whose primary purpose may have been to find someone to assassinate Fidel Castro. We are told above that Charles Ford is continuing to report to Bill Harvey. Bill Harvey and the CIA may have intentionally set Bobby Kennedy up with Oswald and Johnny Rosselli via Charles Ford. It is important to remember that Johnny Rosselli is not unfamiliar to the Kennedys as Rosselli first worked in bootlegging for Joseph Kennedy, father of President Kennedy and Bobby Kennedy, prior to Rosselli's move to Al Capone's gang in Chicago.

Harry L. Power told me that his dad was in the bootlegging business out of Chicago and knew Al Capone and those guys. Above we learned that Johnny Rosselli was in the bootlegging business with Joseph Kennedy, before moving to Al Capone's gang in Chicago. As a result, perhaps Harry Power's dad knew Johnny Rosselli and Jack Ruby, who was also originally a part of the Chicago Mafia? Perhaps as a consequence, Harry Power, as a young boy may also have been acquainted with Johnny Rosselli and Jack Ruby for that matter? Perhaps Harry knew Jack Ruby and Johnny Rosselli from an early age?

Rosselli in effect told columnist Jack Anderson that the same crowd working on assassinating Castro arranged the Kennedy's assassination.

The logic, as presented to Robert Kennedy by the CIA for using someone like Oswald in his operation to get Castro, or for using someone like Harry Power for that matter, perhaps would have gone something like this: In order to get some guys in place in Cuba, we will need to use our guys who have established their credibility with Cuban Intelligence, based upon their pro Castro, pro-communist posturing, which we have built up in the public record over the last couple of years.

As you have seen, Harry Power may have had "Cuban intelligence connections," via Louisa Calderon. Lee Oswald probably established his bone fides in defecting to the Soviet Union and perhaps giving up the U-2.

If Harry Power had been investigated for and possibly involved in the shooting at General Walker, as the Terre Haute Police had been led to believe, and Bobby Kennedy is alleged to have intervened with the Dallas Police concerning this incident to get Oswald out from under investigation, then perhaps Harry was also a part of Bobby Kennedy's machinations.

I would add that the FBI shut down the anti-Castro Cuban training operation on Lake Pontchartrain near New Orleans within days of Oswald's alleged visit to the site. The FBI reported directly to the Attorney General Bobby Kennedy. Perhaps Pontchartrain was shut down as a result of something reported by Oswald. According to Texas Attorney General Waggoner Carr, Lee Harvey Oswald was assigned an FBI ID number of S-179.

Bobby Kennedy, by all accounts was very combative and competitive. What did Bobby Kennedy do when his brother was shot? Did he come out swinging? No, he went the exact opposite direction. Here you have the Attorney General of the United States, the top law enforcement official with the FBI reporting to him. Wouldn't you think that Bobby Kennedy would have used the FBI to turn over every rock trying to find out who killed his brother? I think the CIA and/or Bill Harvey may have set Bobby Kennedy up with Lee Harvey Oswald as a part of Bobby Kennedy's operation to assassinate Castro. Therefore, Bobby Kennedy knew that any serious investigation of President Kennedy's assassination would have led to his attempts to kill Castro.

On the microfilm from New Orleans, on 11/1/67, Jim

Garrison, District Attorney, New Orleans claimed, "Robert Kennedy, does not want the truth to be brought out. Robert Kennedy is obstructing justice."

In return for all of Bill Harvey's hard work over the years, the Kennedys in effect ruined Bill Harvey's career during the Cuban Missile Crisis in November 1962. April 24, 1963, Lee Harvey Oswald moved to New Orleans from Dallas. Bill Harvey's meeting and phone activity with the Mafia's Johnny Rosselli appears to have picked up in February, March, and April of 1963. Bill Harvey officially stepped down from running the Cuban operations in the spring of 1963. Charles Ford had been reporting to William King Harvey. What isn't clear is who Charles Ford was reporting to on April 24, 1963 when Oswald appears to have been put into play in New Orleans.

## WE HAVE RECOVERED 3 BULLETS

Concerning the assassination itself we have this: Life Magazine, December 6, 1963, (published two weeks after the assassination), article entitled: "*End to Nagging Rumors: The Six Critical Seconds*" reported among other things: "Three shots were fired. Two struck the President, one Governor Connally. **All three bullets have been recovered-one deformed from the floor of the limousine; one from the stretcher that carried the President; one that entered the President's body.**"

Or to quote the Director of the FBI's memo dated November 29, 1963, at 1:39 PM: "**three shots were fired at the President, and we have them**." "The President was hit by the first and the third bullet and the second hit the Governor."

Approximately 10 months after the "Life Magazine" article and J. Edgar Hoover's memo, the Warren Report said on page 111 "three shots were fired, it follows that one shot probably missed the car and its occupants."

If Life magazine and the Director of the FBI reported that authorities had three bullets, then apparently over the ten-month period prior to the Warren Report the authorities lost one of the bullets, or three bullets plus one miss equals four shots, which means more than one shooter. More than one shooter, because one bolt action rifle cannot fire fast enough to fit four shots in the time frame allowed, this would indicate more than one assassin and perhaps more than one patsy. Perhaps an assassin and a patsy for everyone to point at on the grassy knoll?

We don't need to look any farther than this to establish that the Warren Commission was wrong and something's fishy!

# PARKLAND HOSPITAL, NURSE PHYLLIS HALL

I turned on the local TV news in 2013, around the 50th anniversary of the assassination, and Nurse Phyllis Hall appeared on my screen. Turns out she currently lives in Illinois, not far from Terre Haute, but on the day of the assassination she ended up in the Trauma Room 1, Parkland Hospital, cradling the President's head.

Nurse Hall was 28 at the time and although she had previously worked the Trauma Room, she had only come down to visit when suddenly the Presidential motorcade swept into Parkland Hospital, and she was called on to help.

Says Hall, "While cradling the President's head I could see a bullet lodged between the President's ear and his shoulder. **It was pointed at its tip** and showed no signs of damage. There was no blunting of the bullet or scarring around the shell from where it had been fired. I'd had a great deal of experience working with gunshot wounds, but I had never seen anything like this before. It was about one-and-a-half inches long – nothing like the bullets that were later produced. It was taken away but never have I seen it presented in evidence or heard what happened to it. It remains a mystery." [198]

From Wikipedia, 7.65x53mm Argentine

## ALEK JAMES HIDELL ANAGRAM: JAILED LEAK HELMS

Robert Clayton Buick was an American bullfighter down in Mexico City whose name was written on one of the pages I received from the Lyndon Johnson Library concerning Harry L. Power. At the bottom of one of the pages someone had written "For Report on Robert Clayton Buick, see individual file on Buick." Buick happened to be frequenting a bar at the Hotel Luma in Mexico City at the same time as Lee Oswald, and he was followed and recruited in the field by a couple of U.S. intelligence operatives. The reason for the recruitment: Oswald and Richard Case Nagell were meeting at the Hotel Luma in Mexico City in 1963 and some people wanted to know what was being said.

Robert Clayton Buick has written a book entitled, *Reflection-Behind the Rain*. On page 185 Buick reveals that the two intelligence agents he was working with in the field were David Atlee Phillips, known to him at the time as "Bishop," and Frank Sturgis, known to him as "Jack Hamilton."

While in the bar someone apparently told Lee Oswald that Robert Clayton Buick was a bullfighter and the two ended up having a drink together. During the conversation, according to Buick, Oswald indicated that "a hit was on to assassinate the President of the United States." And he said, "It's all set, the machinery is already in gear." Obviously, this is important information, but what I want to focus in on was at the beginning of the conversation. Oswald introduced himself as "Alek Hidell." Buick writes that he said, "Alright Alex"... Buick then writes, Oswald quickly corrected me, "Its Alek", putting careful emphasis on the "k".

When Buick reported back to Phillips and Sturgis, who were waiting outside in a car, Buick referred to Oswald as "that weasel-faced psycho, Hidell." Bishop questioned, "You said his name was Hidell?" "Yeah, Alek Hidell." Sturgis inquired, "He did say his name was Alek?" "Yes", I answered, "as a matter of fact he corrected me when I referred to his name as Alex with an 'x'. He adamantly said his name was Alek with a 'k'." Again, Phillips and Sturgis glared at one another.

Now why is the point about the spelling of Alek and Alex so important? And why was the use of Alek, instead of Alex, so disconcerting to Phillips and Sturgis?

On the day of the assassination Lee Harvey Oswald carried in his wallet a selective service card and a certificate of service - U.S. Marine Corps. Both cards displayed the name Alek James Hidell. Discovered by this author in late 2008: on the Internet there is a service where you can run words through to determine all of the anagrams that might be available for a series of letters. I ran "Alek James Hidell" through. With so many letters there are hundreds of possibilities. The one anagram of interest: **"Alek James Hidell," with letters rearranged, comes out "Jailed Leak Helms."** This might be your proverbial "get out of jail free card." In other words, Oswald might have been saying to those who might find the cards significant or curious, "you put me in jail and I'm going to leak that Richard Helms, Director of Plans, CIA, is behind the assassination." Oswald was obviously being put in jail when this information came to light. The act of being put in jail thus gives meaning to a portion of the message. So, if it is true that he is being "jailed," might not the remaining portion of the message also be true? This threat alone, or sign of intent, "Jailed Leak Helms," is probably enough to get your ass shot; enter Jack Ruby.

This possible perception of the anagram by those who are

accustomed to passing coded messages and looking for such things, would have been significant to Richard Helms, the CIA, and their arch nemesis the FBI. Naturally, one of the very first questions when Oswald arrived at Dallas Police Headquarters was about the card, Oswald replied: "You're the cop. You figure it out."

During one of Oswald's interrogations, he was again asked about the cards showing the name Alek James Hidell, Oswald showed a rare moment of anger, replying: "Now I have told you all I am going to tell you about the card in my billfold. You have the card yourself, and you know as much about it as I do." Perhaps Oswald himself hadn't a clue about the message the cards were sending, or of the name's significance. The name A.J. Hidell is how authorities were able to tie Oswald to the alleged assassination rifle. Thus, making the cards and the name on the cards absolutely critical and indispensable to the case against Oswald. The die was cast the minute Oswald was arrested. Authorities could absolutely not ignore, destroy, or accidentally lose this one critical piece of indispensable evidence that absolutely had to be made a part of the public record. Oswald had allegedly ordered his rifle by mail order, and it was delivered to a Post Office box that was registered to Lee Oswald, Marina Oswald, and A. J. Hidell.

"...you know as much about the card as I do..." declared Oswald. Oswald truly may have been ignorant of the name's significance. He's on a need-to-know basis. **Those who had been asked, or ordered to plan the assassination may have taken measures to protect themselves by planting a little evidence as to who had approved the assassination.**

On the other hand, Oswald may be today speaking to us from beyond the grave by leaving a clue as to who authorized the assassination and proclaiming, "...you figure it out."

Any evidence that Lee Oswald might be familiar with rearranging letters as anagrams? Judyth Vary Baker claims to have been romantically involved with Lee Oswald and appears to have been seeing Lee Harvey Oswald when Lee was in New Orleans. Judyth mentions leaving Lee Oswald in New Orleans by a sign that read "BINGO TONITE," while she went to get her typewriter from her apartment. Upon her return to that location there stood Lee by the sign, writes Judyth, "I noticed Lee had changed the Bingo sign to read, 'I BINGE NOT.'" (Oswald may be guilty of theft, as one of the "Os" is missing.)

Concerning this possible thread "Jailed Leak Helms" and Richard Helms possible authorization to assassinate the President of the United States: Author Bayard Stockton who wrote the book *Flawed Patriot* had an opportunity to view the file that was kept at home by William and C.G. Harvey. Says Stockton, "I got the impression that only a couple of documents were kept in this file. Apparently one of the most important documents of Harvey's career was **a memo signed by Richard Helms**, Deputy Director (Plans) dated February 1962, which **authorized Bill Harvey to retain the services of Principal Agent QJ/WIN**. This single piece of paper seems to be significant especially when compared to the depth and breadth of Bill Harvey's total career, experience, and achievement. Why did Bill Harvey feel that it was necessary to keep this one particular piece of paper? It seems apparent that it was important to Bill Harvey that he have proof that his actions were known and authorized by Richard Helms."

Richard Nagell, our *Man Who Knew Too Much*, said that Richard Helms is the person of authority in the CIA who gave the order for John F. Kennedy's murder, a view shared by Colonel William Bishop, a Nagell CIA associate. Bishop told author Gary Shaw, "Richard Helms gave the order for the assassination." Gerry Patrick Hemming concurs, "Helms is behind the entire operation to kill JFK." (Oswald's ID card in his wallet may have been telling us the same thing in anagram fashion, "Alek James Hidell" becomes: "Jailed Leak Helms.")

Intelligence officer John Patrick Quirk worked and traveled with David Atlee Phillips. Quirk said that "Phillips, along with Allen Dulles and Richard Bissell hated John F. Kennedy." According to Quirk, "Lyndon Johnson met with Phillips two days after the presidents' murder, and yes, the CIA's David Atlee Phillips was Maurice Bishop." [199]

It is interesting that two documents remained in CG Harvey's possession, the second document is not explicit as to which type of operation is being discussed. Harvey of course oversaw stealing enemy crypto codes and he was also in charge of the assassination attempts. The second document appears to be references to **assassinations by these two groups - the KGB and by the Nazis**, with no reference to the theft of crypto codes. **Was this a clue left by Bill Harvey?**

One of those Bill Harvey/CIA documents, concerning operational capability says: "Within Kubark [CIA], one focal point for control, search, training, case officering, etc. **DDP authority in this focal point mandatory**. (The DDP - Deputy Director of Plans at the time was Richard Helms and his okay for these types of operations is mandatory.) **DCI officially advised?** (The DCI – Director Central Intelligence was John McCone. Notice the "?" Harvey's group was unsure if the Director would be informed of this kind of operation.) [200]

# NORTH BY NORTHWEST

North by Northwest was a 1959 movie that was a spy thriller produced by Alfred Hitchcock, staring Cary Grant, Eva Marie Saint and James Mason.

Cary Grant's character, Roger Thornhill is mistaken by, Soviet agents, for a guy named Kaplan who is supposedly a U.S. Government intelligence agent.  Cary Grant ends up being pursued by the Soviet agents.  Cary Grant ends up at one point in the movie on a dirt road in Indiana and is buzzed by a crop-dusting airplane, before Grant eventually makes his way in the movie to Mount Rushmore. At Mount Rushmore's visitors center the U.S. Intelligence Agency coordinates with Cary Grant and fakes his death as he is shot by their undercover agent played, by Eva Marie Saint who plays Eve Kendall.  Eva, or Eve, uses blank cartridges in her gun, as she proceeds to shoot Cary Grant. The Soviet agents assume that Cary Grant had been shot and is dead. A station wagon style ambulance arrives on the scene and Cary Grant is loaded into the ambulance and is driven away. No blood, or fake blood, is shown when Cary Grant was shot, perhaps this is because the movies were not so graphic back in 1959?

The movie North by Northwest just strikes me as similar to when Oswald was shot by Jack Ruby in the basement of the Dallas Police Station. Oswald might have been mistaken for a U.S. Government intelligence agent (not really, not at the time anyway).  A U.S. Intelligence Agency stages his apparent shooting. Oswald is loaded into a station wagon style ambulance and driven away. No blood or fake blood is seen, perhaps this is because things were not so graphic back in 1963?

Not unlike the Twilight episode referenced earlier, might this be "life imitating art?" I know that Oswald was offered his choice of either a red or a black sweater, before he walked out before the cameras in the basement of the Dallas Police Station. He first said red, then he changed his mind and went with the black sweater. Just speculation, red or black might be the two best colors to not show blood, if anyone were to question blood not having been so readily visible?

Robert H. "Bob" Jackson is the photographer who took the Pulitzer Prize winning photograph of Lee Harvey Oswald, right as Jack Ruby shot Oswald in the basement of the Dallas Police Headquarters. In an interview with Bob Jackson many years after this event, he commented on the fact that he had noticed after the shooting that he never saw any blood! Not one drop. Even though he remained there for a period of time. Obviously, he found this a little strange, but didn't mention it until many years later.

## THE BACKCHANNEL

Is it possible that Kim Philby and the Soviets were working with Bobby Kennedy to oust Castro as a part of the Almeida coup and that operation flipped and got President Kennedy?

On February 19, 1962, U.S. News & World Report came out with the following article entitled: *Bobby Kennedy: Is He the 'Assistant President'?* For nearly two years Robert Kennedy was engaged in **backchannel communications** and negotiations with the Soviets. In an interview in 1964 Bobby Kennedy said, "Most of the major matters dealing with the Soviet Union and the United States were discussed and arrangement were made.... We used to meet maybe once every two weeks." Bobby said in a taped interview, "I didn't write many of the things down. I just delivered the messages verbally to my brother, and he'd act on them. I think sometimes he'd tell the State Department- and sometimes he didn't." The President's usual sources of expertise and advice, the State Department, CIA and the Defense Department were all aware of the existence of the backchannel but had limited knowledge about what was being discussed and agreed to. They were largely excluded from the decision-making process. This deliberate exclusion of the experts and their advice was seen by the State Department as an unwise and risky decision by the Kennedys, as it was felt that the Kennedys knowledge regarding international affairs and their trust of the communists and the agreements, they would make was misguided and a mistake. [201]

# THE ALLEGED KHRUSHCHEV - KENNEDY AGREEMENT

Below you will see in an FBI report how Dr. Penabaz, General Walker, and Carlos Bringuier were at the same conference following the Kennedy assassination, explaining what happened in the Kennedy assassination. Dr. Penabaz you may recall is the Cuban who reported to the FBI that Jack Ruby was a member of the Young Communist League. General Walker you may recall was shot at by Lee Oswald and Harry Power was suspected as having been a part of the shooting at General Walker, or at least the Terre Haute Police had gotten that impression. Carlos Bringuier was a member of the anti-Castro Cuban group, the DRE in New Orleans and Bringuier is the individual who got in a scuffle with Oswald when Oswald was handing out Fair Play for Cuba leaflets down in New Orleans.

They talked about **an agreement between President Kennedy and Soviet Premier Khrushchev for the elimination of Fidel Castro**. They said that Castro reportedly learned of this agreement. They said that Lee Oswald and Jack Ruby were two of six members of a Communist Cell, which was active in Dallas, Texas.

The Martin and Lewis affidavit claimed that Robert Kennedy was working with the Soviet spy Kim Philby.

Here is an allegation that the Kennedy's drive to get Castro may have included working with Soviet Premier Khrushchev in an operation, perhaps the Ameida coup, which ended up backfiring, flipping, or transforming into an operation against President Kennedy:

In an FBI report dated 3/3/64, the Reverend Fowler of Duluth, Minnesota reports that he attended an anti-Communist meeting in Shreveport, Louisiana from February 17-21, 1964, sponsored by the Christian Crusade, directed by the Reverend Billie James Hargis. Representatives from twenty-five states attended, among them, **General Edwin Walker**, Billy James Hargis, and Dr. Fernando **Penabaz**, who was a reporter for the *"Fort Lauderdale News."* HSCA 1802003510333

Reverend Fowler stated that during the four-day meeting he had been told by Dr. Penabaz that the assassination of President Kennedy arose from **an agreement between President Kennedy and Premier Khrushchev for the elimination of Fidel Castro** with the provision that Cuba would remain Communistic. Castro reportedly learned of this agreement and then made his own plans for the elimination of President Kennedy. HSCA 1802003510333

Fowler indicates that there was an agreement between President Kennedy (Bobby was the intermediary) and Premier Khrushchev for the elimination of Castro. Martin and Lewis said the same basic thing in their affidavit: "…fact that the "genius" R.F.K. put out his own personal "contract" on Cuba's Fidel Castro. The above says, Castro learned of this agreement and made his own plans. Martin and Lewis said: "In short, the President was "hit" (murdered), before the "hit" on Castro could be completed…Philby's little groups had struck within, before those of R.F.K., could strike without." (Perhaps referencing the JFK/RFK/Almeida coup, where President Kennedy was assassinated just eight days before the coup was to take place. In Cuba.) Castro struck within, before RFK could strike without.

## ANY EVIDENCE OF PAST CIA KGB COOPERATION?

Anthony Summers wrote in his book: Conspiracy, "As far back as 1959, William King Harvey was one of only three officers privy to plans to send false defectors into the Soviet Union. 1959 was the year of Oswald's defection. Genuine defection or not, William Harvey almost certainly knew about it in detail. " [202]

Jim Jesus Angleton definitely knew about Oswald. As early as 1959, Gerry Hemming called Jim Angleton to report that Lee Harvey Oswald had been at the Cuban Consulate in Los Angeles and Oswald had offered to help the Cubans. [203] Immediately upon this report Angleton's Counterintelligence group should have opened a CIA 201 file on Oswald, they did not. Oswald then defected to the Soviet Union, just a month after Hemming's report and still Angleton's group did not create a 201 file. It wasn't until a year later that they managed to finally open a 201 file on Oswald. Kind of make you wonder if Angleton didn't already know what was going on with Oswald, which might explain the lack of urgency.

Inside Angleton's counterintelligence empire was a small handful of Angleton's most trusted and closemouthed associates called the Counterintelligence Special Investigations Group (CI/SIG). CI/SIG held most of the CIA documents on Oswald up to the very day of the assassination. **Oswald's 201 file opening was something that "we worked very closely with Angleton and his staff. It would have all gone through Angleton,"** said Robert L. Bannerman of the CIA Office of Security. [204]

Robert D. Morrow was a CIA operative, or contract employee from 1959 to 1964. **Tracy Barnes** was Morrow's CIA case officer. Tracy Barnes told Robert Morrow that Lee Harvey Oswald, while in the Marines was trained as a radar operator and cryptographer. (A cryptographer writes and solves secret codes, which fits with what Bill Harvey's Division D was into.) Oswald served at our [CIA] base in Atsugi, Japan. Oswald learned Russian while at Atsugi. Atsugi is the base that launched the **covert U-2** high-altitude spy plane for over-flights of China and the U.S.S.R. Oswald served a covert stint in the Philippines with his MAAG group and in September of 1959 at our [CIA's] request, Oswald applied for a hardship discharge. We [CIA] sent him to Russia posing as a defector, [upon which] his discharge [from the Marines] was changed to a dishonorable discharge. Oswald was reimbursed $2,000 dollars from our local New Orleans office located across the street from 544 Camp Street, in the federal building. Oswald had a **top-secret clearance**, as well as a **crypto clearance**, and was on a sensitive mission.

Morrow says, "**Oswald's assignment** was to get into Russia, state that he was revoking his citizenship, and **defect to the other side with our top-secret codes, radar data, frequencies** and whatever else he had memorized. **He would be used for an internal security operation in Russia**. Hence the establishment of his anti-American, pro-Commie identification. His job was to contact a girl in Moscow who was the niece of a KGB colonel, the colonel's only blood relation, and get her out of Russia, so the uncle could defect.

The CIA's Tracy Barnes told CIA contract agent Robert Morrow, "As instructed **Oswald gave the detailed radar, intelligence frequencies and codes to the Russians** and he eventually met up with, fell in love with, and married Marina, the KGB colonel's niece. We [CIA] pulled Oswald and Marina out based on a prearranged plan where he would ask our Embassy to provide him with $400.00 to pay for their transport. On the night of his arrival back in the U.S. our [CIA] people debriefed him and immediately sent him down south. He hooked up with Jack Ruby in Dallas, and we [CIA] think the FBI is also using him." [205]

Notice how the information from Morrow about radio frequency, crypto clearance, radar, and code information matches up with Bill Harvey's Division D and its function of SIGINT (radio signal intelligence) services, cryptographic procurement, and covert intercepts. The normal function of Division D, one would think, is to get the other sides information, not to give them information. The U-2 was an outstanding technological advantage that we enjoyed over the Russians. At the time Oswald defected to the Russians, the Russians were absolutely unable to shoot down the U-2 flying over their own country. Here we are led to believe that Oswald was giving away information that was the most valuable of any information just to establish what the intelligence community calls his bone fides, in other word to make him seem to be sincerely coming over to the other side and to enable him to get Marina out. I don't think so, and I question whether the other side doesn't smell this kind of thing a mile away.

After Oswald defected and while he was in the Soviet Union, the Soviets were supposedly able to shoot down Gary Powers in a U-2. Although there is evidence that the U-2 experienced mechanical difficulties with the flow of fuel. Gary Powers ends up being put on trial in the Soviet Union. I have read and saw where there might have been a picture showing someone who looked like Oswald in the courtroom gallery, while Powers was being tried. I have also read that Oswald indicated to his brother in a letter that he had met Gary Powers in Russia. After the Russians released Powers and upon his return to the United States, Gary Powers went on record blaming Oswald for his being brought down.

There is speculation that the information on the U-2 was given to the Russians because President Eisenhower and Russia's Khrushchev were moving toward détente (better relations). Some have speculated that the information was given to the Russians via Oswald, so that the U-2 could be shot down, just in time to ruin the talks between Eisenhower and Khrushchev, which it did. It may also be that spy-satellites were just coming of age and thus the U-2 would be of less importance going forward. One of James Jesus Angleton's last statements prior to his leaving the CIA in 1974, was to rail against détente with the Soviet Union.

Gary Powers himself noticed that the plane had a mechanical issue which prevented its feeding all of its fuel.

According to Colonel L. Fletcher Prouty, "Powers came down because his aircraft was deliberately sabotaged. "Prouty expressed concern over the intentional fuel shortage that caused Powers' flight to fail. He also noted that the flight deviated from standard procedures, as Powers was carrying extensive identification, including a Department of Defense ID card. Moreover, the removal of Powers' top-secret camera indicates that someone had prior knowledge that the plane might be brought down and fall into the hands of the Soviets. This incident had significant consequences, as it completely undermined the Eisenhower-Khrushchev summit that was to commence just fifteen day later on May 16th. [206]

I also read somewhere in the past, speculation that there were those on both sides of the Cold War who didn't want tensions to subside, for fear that the importance of their intelligence empires would be diminished. It may have been that the "secret services/military industrial complex" on both sides had a vested interest in keeping the cold war pot boiling. Admittedly this is a stretch, but what if Lee Harvey

Oswald was a clandestine, jointly coordinated operation between the two sides to scuttle détente, orchestrated by the CIA and the KGB. Angleton and Philby could have easily facilitated such an operation.

This is a little disturbing: Jim Angleton met with Kim Philby in Italy in 1960. [207] (This would indicate an ongoing relationship and communications between Angleton and Philby. When was Frances Gary Powers shot down? The answer: May 1, 1960. This speculative Oswald/U-2 operation could have been coordinated between the two sides by these two. These two could also have been pulling strings behind the scenes on the Kennedy assassination.)

The U.S. and Russia both gave uncharacteristically quick permission for both Lee and Marina to leave the Soviet Union for their return to the United States. If it is conceivable that one side might scheme to scuttle détente, then it is conceivable that both sides might coordinate together to undermine it.

Per Judyth Vary Baker, "Lee mentioned several actions that he took in the USSR for the U.S. government: For one, he was instrumental in getting information about the U-2 spy plane into Russian hands. This was allowed to happen because the Corolla satellite system had been put into place, replacing the U-2, and the CIA questioned whether Eisenhower's health and mental acuity might not be bested by the Russian Premiere Nikita Khrushchev. Downing the U-2 stopped the summit." [208]

James Jesus Angleton said, "I believe Oswald provided all the information the Soviets needed to knock down the U-2." [209] (I think Angleton "Jesus" Angleton probably would know, being as Oswald told Judyth Vary Baker that he had been sent to the Soviet Union by "Jesus.")

I will inject one further speculation regarding the downing

of the U-2. While reading the book Crime and Cover-Up, page 31, it says, "With the development of spy-satellite technology in the late 1950s, CIA contracts had grown to surpass those of the Air Force: "These huge contracts made Hughes Aircraft a captive company of the CIA," asserts one former Pentagon official. "Their interests are completely merged." (Suddenly the U-2 became vulnerable, the biggest beneficiary, Howard Hughes's spy-satellites.)

Additionally, Oswald may have been a singleton for Angleton in an effort to turn up a mole in the Soviet Division of the CIA. Nagell thought so, he thought that Oswald was a part of turning up a mole this would have been Angleton's supposed area of interest.

## A JOINT CIA – KGB OPERATION

Now what about this House Select Committee document quoting Reverend Fowler concerning President Kennedy and Premier Khrushchev having an agreement to eliminate Castro? I suppose, if it represents reality, the agreement was to help President Kennedy get re-elected and to redeem himself with the anti-Castro Cubans. Being as the Soviet's also still had a ton of military still in Cuba, partnering with Khrushchev would have helped to prevent getting tangled up with them during the Almeida coup. I had obtained this document years ago from the National Archives alleging that the Kennedys had an agreement with Khrushchev to eliminate Castro, read it and discounted it, thinking there was no way the Soviets would agree to this. But when you combine this with the allegation by Martin and Lewis, who worked in Banister's office, that Bobby Kennedy was working with the Soviet Spy Kim Philby to assassinate Castro and then add what Martin and Lewis also said, "the 'genius' R.F.K. put out his own personal 'contract' (order to murder) on Cuba's Fidel Castro and the pieces of the puzzle seem to fit together. The underlying theme being, that the Kennedys were working with Khrushchev to try and dispose of Castro, arrangements via the backchannel and Philby. Then when we consider that Rosselli charged that an operation approved by Bobby Kennedy to get Castro may have backfired, flipped, or transformed into an operation against President Kennedy and we may have additional confirmation that these pieces fit.

I am wondering if Khrushchev really did have this understanding with the Kennedys to do away with a Soviet ally. This kind of loyalty would not reflect well upon a country. Perhaps this explains why Khrushchev got booted out of power so quickly, some eleven months after the Kennedy assassination.

Following the resolution of the Cuban missile crisis Khrushchev finds himself under tremendous pressure inside the Soviet Union after having given the world the impression that Russia had blinked and backed down during the missile crisis, appearing to have unilaterally agreed to pull their missiles out of Cuba. In reality, Khrushchev pledged to remove the missiles from inside Cuba in exchange for President Kennedy's pledge to remove U.S. missiles from Turkey and Kennedy's promise to not invade Cuba in the future, provided Castro would allow inspections for missiles. Castro refused to allow inspections, so theoretically the door was still open to a U.S. invasion of Cuba. Khrushchev was left with very little to boast about to the world let alone to the communist party, being as he had promised to keep this missile trade a secret as well as Kennedy's pledge not to invade Cuba. I am assuming this vow of silence on Khrushchev's part was done at the insistence of the Kennedys, in order to save themselves the political embarrassment of having made such concessions.

Although the missiles were removed from both Turkey and Cuba, the only thing that Khrushchev was left with was President Kennedy's promise not to invade Cuba and in reality, that might only be good for as long as President Kennedy stayed in office. Obviously, Khrushchev's star was now tied to Kennedy remaining in office. What might have helped re-elect President Kennedy and kept him in power? It would have been helpful if Castro was no longer an issue for President Kennedy come the next election. Perhaps, Khrushchev's' assistance in this regard would have been helpful?

How did Khrushchev really feel about Castro? Well, we know

that Khrushchev once roared, "under no circumstances would the Soviet Union sign a military agreement with such an irresponsible man."

Khrushchev began to identify his own political future with that of Kennedy. Few understand that Khrushchev needed Kennedy. Almost exactly a year prior to the assassination, Khrushchev felt it necessary to point out to his Soviet critics that President Kennedy's pledge not to invade Cuba was good because, in Khrushchev's opinion, Kennedy would likely be president until 1968. [210]

Writes Joseph Trento, who presumably got this idea from Jim Angleton: By resolving the missile crisis, Kennedy made Khrushchev into a statesman. **Leonid Brezhnev, Khrushchev's rival within the Soviet Union, realized that if Khrushchev lost his relationship with Kennedy, Khrushchev would lose his support for remaining in power.**

Therefore, we have Khrushchev hoping to see Kennedy stay in office and Brezhnev, Khrushchev's ever developing rival, viewing President Kennedy as perhaps the last stumbling block to his own path to power.

The plan to remove Castro is probably the JFK/RFK/Almeida coup that Bobby Kennedy was running. Is it possible that Kim Philby was involved? Philby dropped behind the iron curtain, or you might say he disappeared and reappeared in the Soviet Union, in the summer of 1963 leading up to the assassination in November. Philby is said by Martin and Lewis to be working with Bobby Kennedy. Philby could also be in contact with Jim Angleton. Angleton and Philby are documented in the public record as having met as recently as 1960, long after Bill Harvey labeled Philby a spy. Khrushchev might be supporting this coup, this removal of Castro, to help keep President Kennedy in office, provided that Cuba still remained under communist control, as suggested in Reverend Fowler understanding of the alleged agreement. All being done to ensure that the U.S. would not invade Cuba in the future, which is now critical for Khrushchev to be able to hold onto his own power. Philby would definitely have been in contact with the KGB. The KGB was controlled, or greatly influenced by Brezhnev, not Khrushchev, so said Angleton via author Joseph Trento. Brezhnev/KGB tells Castro about the Khrushchev/Kennedy plot against him, and the KGB coordinates with Castro and with Jim Angleton via Philby. The result, the same people involved in the JFK/RFK/Almeida coup are manipulated and are at the very least made to appear to have been involved in the assassination of President Kennedy.

Joseph Trento once asked me why I thought that Angleton would have been involved in President Kennedy's assassination, "Angleton was a friend of the Kennedys," explained Trento. In my opinion, by 1963, everyone had so much shit on Angleton and Allen Dulles that they were wide open for blackmail from here to Sunday. You see Allen Dulles and Angleton had a very close association with a great many former Nazis, and ongoing unrepentant Nazis whom Dulles had done business with prior to, during and after World War II. Dulles and Angleton had also assisted in the escape of many Nazis through the European ratlines (the escape routes) following World War II. Their history, in many instances, would not bode well for Allen Dulles or Jim Angleton if the truth were known. Angleton himself explained it saying, "Do you know how I got to be in charge of counterintelligence? I agreed not to polygraph or require detailed background checks on Allen Dulles and 60 of his closest friends. **They were afraid that their own business dealings with Hitler's pals would come out. They were too arrogant to believe that the Russians wouldn't discover it all.**"

Angleton explained to Trento, and I quote: "The idea was to link Oswald to Castro and not to the Soviet Union." He also said: "**Brezhnev, not Khrushchev, was in control of the KGB.**" Writes Trento: "For Brezhnev, the elements had finally come together. Kennedy's assassination was to be conducted by Cuban intelligence as a matter of simple retribution."

Brezhnev understood the humiliation Fidel Castro felt when Khrushchev agreed to pull out the missiles without even consulting Castro. (Not to mention how Castro probably felt after Brezhnev and the KGB told him that Khrushchev had agreed with President Kennedy to do away with him. Add to this any confirmation Castro may have received from Trafficante with reinforcement from Almeida, who I believe was also working for Castro. Castro had to have been left with the definite impression that the Kennedys definitely wanted him dead.)

Concerning Almeida, he never received any retribution for his alleged coup planning with the Kennedys and we know Trafficante had to have told Castro about this operation. Almeida held his position of power until his death in 2009 and in fact was awarded special honors and the title "Hero of the Republic of Cuba" by Castro in 1998.

Angleton told author Joseph Trento, "**I have become convinced that Philby was taken over by a group led by Leonid Brezhnev.**"

Angleton further told Trento "**I believe that Oswald's role was solely to convince Castro that the murder of President Kennedy was a joint KGB/DGI wet operation.**" [211] (A "wet operation" is another way of saying assassinating someone. The KGB of course is the Soviet's intelligence organization and the DGI is Cuba's intelligence organization. Think about what Angleton just said, Castro was to be convinced [by the KGB] that Oswald is working for the KGB. If Angleton, who should have been in a position to know, finds this believable, that Castro would believe that Oswald was a KGB asset, and that Oswald could serve in a joint KGB/DGI wet operation. Then based upon all the evidence we have seen; Castro might have perceived Oswald as a triple agent and a joint KGB/DGI/CIA wet operation. To reinforce this theory, simply add the earlier speculation that **Oswald and the downed U-2 was a jointly coordinated operation between the KGB and the CIA to scuttle détente between Eisenhower and Khrushchev** and the possibility of Castro believing that Oswald is a joint KGB/CIA asset is enhanced. Angleton and Philby were in a position to communicate and coordinate with one another. Oh, what a tangled web we weave. When first we practice to deceive: the Kennedys and Khrushchev may very well have had this agreement to remove Castro from power, and Philby is reportedly working with Bobby Kennedy and quite possibly Angleton, and Philby are also working with and communicating with the KGB, the KGB is working with Brezhnev, Khrushchev's rival, and they in turn are communicating with Castro. With Brezhnev in control of the KGB, and Brezhnev's path to power blocked by Khrushchev's power position with President Kennedy, and given that Brezhnev and the KGB are in a position to enlighten Castro about Khrushchev's agreement with Kennedy to remove him from power and is further able to inform Castro that Oswald, the jointly shared asset between the KGB and the CIA, might be amenable to playing the big shot in a joint KGB/DGI/CIA wet operation, well this does seem to fit with Jim Angleton's original belief and with other parts of this puzzle. An operation conducted by the Soviet KGB, the United States CIA, and in partnership with Castro would certainly appear to be less risky and reassuring to Castro. Castro would surely feel that he had all his bases covered, thinking that he was teaming up not just with the KGB (as Angleton suggested), but also with the CIA. Was Oswald a CIA operative? To answer this question let's ask: Was Oswald being moved around by the CIA? Well at the time leading up to the assassination, the CIA and the FBI reportedly were trying to discredit the "Fair Play for Cuba Committee" at the very same time Oswald was working to engage with the Fair Play for Cuba Committee. Then add to this the fact that the CIA's responsibility in the JFK/RFK/Almeida coup was to try and get young twenty-year-olds into Cuba, who looked like Soviet or communist sympathizers, right at the very time that Oswald was trying to get into Cuba through the Cuban Embassy in Mexico City. Finally, add the impression, based on the filing of CIA records and we find that Oswald appears to be a singleton for Angleton's CI/SIG. As Richard Case Nagell once said, "Mr. Oswald...was the indispensable tool in the conspiracy..."). And if that is not enough, add the allegation from multiple sources that Lee Harvey Oswald is associated in some way with the FBI.

CIA Director McCone was convinced that the Cubans were behind the assassination and told Bobby Kennedy as much on the afternoon of the assassination. The theory is that the United State government covered up this fact over concerns that the American people would demand retribution, had they thought that Castro did it, leading to a possible nuclear confrontation between the Soviet Union and the U.S. Think of how much more likely the perception of a nuclear confrontation between the Soviets and the U.S. would have been to those in Congress had they been led to believe that the Soviets as well as Castro were involved in the assassination. The possibility of all-out war between the Soviets and the United States would be far more believable had the Soviets been perceived as having been involved, so that the true plotters could make the case for covering up everything and limiting the official story to the supposed lone nut assassin Lee Harvey Oswald. Everybody, and I mean everybody had to be, or were meant to look like they were tied into this thing.

Is it believable that the CIA, the Soviet's KGB, and Cuba's DGI would conspire in the assassination of the President of the United States? Well perhaps it can be explained this way: "A big lie" is a Nazi propaganda technique. Adolf Hitler coined the phrase "a big lie" in his book *Mein Kampf*. Meaning, the bigger the lie, the more unbelievable, because most people would not believe that anyone would possibly be so audacious as to do such a thing. Surely no one would take such bold risks and think that they could get away with it. It is inconceivable that such a thing could happen.

# AM/LASH

As far back as 1961 the CIA had recruited **Rolando Cubela**, when he left the Castro regime to finish his medical studies. Lansdale had strongly suggested that Bill Harvey use the former Castro crony for the assassination of Castro. **Harvey refused to use him insisting that Cubela was a double agent.**

Desmond FitzGerald, who had been the head of the CIA's Far Eastern Division, was appointed as Bill Harvey's' replacement as the head of the CIA's Cuban operation. Task Force W was renamed the Special Affairs Staff (SAS).

Ted Shackley, chief of JM/WAVE in Miami recommended that FitzGerald use Rolando Cubela in an assassination attempt on Castro. The CIA code name for this operation: AM/LASH.

The chief of SAS counterintelligence warned FitzGerald that Cubela might be a double agent sent by Castro as witnessed by this CIA affidavit, which states: **Desmond Fitzgerald and the senior level of the CIA were warned that Castro probably knew about the assassination attempts being made against his life** (and of course the AM/LASH operation probably gave Castro confirmation that the President and Bobby Kennedy were behind it) **and this warning was given to Fitzgerald and the senior level CIA, before the assassination of President Kennedy.** _HSCA_ Vol. 4 Page 195

I find it interesting that Ted Shackley suggested that AM/LASH be put in play after Bill Harvey's career had been ruined by the Kennedys. With all the warnings, surely Shackley and Fitzgerald suspected that Cubela was an agent loyal to Castro Therefore, I suspect that the use of Cubela was to confirm for Castro that the Kennedys were out to get him and to provoke Castro into taking some kind of action against the Kennedys, so that the U.S. could justify invading Cuba. Or to make it appear as though Castro knew about the Kennedy backed assassination attempts against him, leading people to believe that Castro might have been provoked into assassinating President Kennedy, again so that we could justify invading Cuba. Either way the CIA sure made it obvious to a Cuban named Cubela, and probably to Castro, as to who supposedly was driving the assassination attempts on Castro. And the decision to do this was made by whom? By Richard Helms, Des Fitzgerald, and Ted Shackley. By guys in the clandestine "Plans" side of the CIA.

According the *CIA Inspector General's Report*, on October 11, 1963, [          ] cabled that **Cubela [Code Name AM/LASH] was insistent upon meeting with a senior U.S. official, preferably Robert F. Kennedy**, for assurances of U.S. moral support for any activity Cubela was to under take in Cuba. *1967 CIA Inspector General's Report* (This seems like a ploy to me, an effort by Castro, or someone, to establish proof of Kennedy involvement in attempts on Castro's life, or as an attempt to provoke Castro into taking action.)

29 October 1963, Desmond FitzGerald, then Chief, SAS arranged to meet with Cubela to give him the assurances he sought. **FitzGerald will represent himself as the personal representative of Robert F. Kennedy**, giving him assurances of full U.S. support, if there were to be a change of the present government in Cuba. *1967 CIA Inspector General's Report*

According to **FitzGerald**, he **discussed** the planned meeting **with the DDP (Helms) who decided it was not necessary to seek approval from Robert Kennedy for FitzGerald to speak in his name.** *1967 CIA Inspector General's Report* (Again we see everything being cleared through Richard Helms and being withheld from his superiors.)

Bobby Kennedy was working directly with the CIA's

Desmond FitzGerald, who was running the AM/LASH operation and the AM/LASH operation's sole objective appears to be the assassination of Fidel Castro. Therefore, and in addition to everything else that we have seen it is not unreasonable to draw the conclusion that Bobby Kennedy not only knew about the attempts to assassinate Castro, but was involved in the process, as C.G. Harvey indicated.

The CIA written record states: A meeting was held on 29 October 1963. FitzGerald informed Cubela that the United States is prepared to render all necessary assistance to any anti-communist Cuban group, which succeeds in neutralizing the present Cuban leadership and assumes sufficient control to invite the United States to render the assistance it is prepared to give. [Those involved, later would recall the purpose of the meeting as being something quite different from that which appears in the written record. FitzGerald recalls that Cubela spoke repeatedly of the need for an assassination weapon. In particular, he wanted a high-powered rifle with telescopic sights or some other weapon that could be used to kill Castro from a distance.]

19 November 1963 **FitzGerald approved telling Cubela he would be given** a cache [of weapons] inside Cuba. The cache could, if he requested it, included...**high power rifles w/ scopes**... *1967 CIA Inspector General's Report*

22 November 1963 [    ] arrived in Paris on the morning of 22 November and met with Cubela late that afternoon. He is not sure, but he believes that Cubela accepted the device but said that he would not take it to Cuba with him. Cubela didn't think much of the device [a syringe to be used with the poison Black Leaf 40]. Cubela was expected to supply his own poison... Cubela asked for the following items to be included in the cache inside Cuba: 20 hand grenades, two high-powered rifles with telescopic sights, 20 pounds of C-4 explosive... **As they were coming out of the meeting,**

[      ] and Cubela were informed that President Kennedy had been assassinated. Cubela asked, "Why do such things happen to good people?" **It is likely that at the very moment President Kennedy was shot a CIA officer was meeting with a Cuban agent in Paris and giving him an assassination device for use against Castro.**  <u>1967 CIA Inspector General's Report</u>

A CIA officer passed an assassination weapon, [intended for use on Castro, to Rolando Cubela, a high-ranking Cuban military officer, code named AM/LASH] at a meeting in Paris on 22 November 1963. The evidence indicates that the meeting was under way at the very moment President Kennedy was shot. <u>HSCA</u> Vol. 4 Page 132 and 145

It seems obvious that someone was trying to make the point perfectly clear: the assassination attempts against Castro are "supposed to be" related to the assassination of President Kennedy. I am not saying that this is the real reason that President Kennedy was assassinated. I am just saying that this is the point that someone in a position to time this thing wanted you to conclude was the reason for the assassination. Because the timing couldn't have been any better, the minute AM/LASH was handed an assassination device was approximately the same time that President Kennedy was assassinated. The symbolism is unmistakable. Who was in a position to time destiny so perfectly?

Jose Aleman was a fairly well to do exiled Cuban who at one time owned Miami stadium. Aleman testified before the House Select Committee on Assassinations that "Trafficante was in some way trying to get Cubela from Cuba." This would indicate a close relationship between Trafficante and Cubela (or AM/LASH). Aleman also said, "**I was talking about Castro maybe being involved with Cubela…in a lot of things**." <u>HSCA</u> Vol. 5 Page 315 In fact a CIA Inspector General Report says, "Trafficante recruited the Cuban official [AM/

LASH]." Trafficante and Cubela (or AM/LASH) had a close relationship.

Here is a list of people, who in addition to everything else they were doing, worked for Mafia boss Santos Trafficante: Bernard Barker (CIA and right-hand man to E. Howard Hunt, Manuel Artime and Tony Varona - both were anti-Castro Cubans and working with CIA) and Frank Sturgis (associated with CIA and Mafia). [212]

Trafficante [reputed head of organized crime in Tampa, Florida] had to know all about the AM/LASH plot and the Almeida coup and with Trafficante as a double agent, working with the CIA but actually supplying information to Castro [as has been alleged by FBI and DEA memos], then another scenario emerges. It is then logical to assume that Castro knew of the AM/LASH and the Almeida coup, and CIA-organized crime [assassination plots] from their inception. Trafficante may have received sanctuary and assistance [from Castro] in smuggling contraband [most likely drugs] in return for such information. (Paraphrased) <u>HSCA</u> Vol. 10 Page 184 – 185

Any triple agents to ensure that everyone has some skin in the game? Here it is, planted in the public record, suggesting that the Soviet KGB and Cuban Intelligence were working together. Concerning Cubela (AM/LASH): **CIA and Army's phone intercepts** captured Pavel Yotskov and Valary Kositkov, [a KGB assassination expert] in Mexico City, **in communications with Cubela. Cubela was clearly reporting everything to Moscow**. [213] (According to the CIA, Cubela is working with them as AM/LASH and at the same time Cubela is reporting everything to the KGB, then this makes him at the very least a double agent. Bill Harvey and Angleton both thought that Cubela was working for Castro. It is not too much of a stretch to think that Cubela, a former high-ranking Cuban military officer of Fidel Castro, would also be reporting everything to Castro as well. Therefore, this makes Cubela a triple agent, Cuba/CIA/KGB.)

Cubela aka the AM/LASH operation served two purposes in my opinion. First it is the evidence for public consumption suggesting that Castro surely knew the Kennedys were after him and thus making it more believable that Castro would do unto Kennedy what Kennedy was about to do unto him. Second purpose served: by showing that Cubela was in communications with a KGB assassination expert Kostikov the nexus being a presumed participation on the part of the Soviets in the assassination of President Kennedy, given that Kositkov is an assassin expert, and he is KGB. Oswald, as you shall soon see is also presented in the public record as having contacted Kostikov by telephone. Tying everything up in an easy-to-follow package, Cubela links to Kostikov, Oswald links to Kostikov, or three countries all linked together: Cuba/Soviet Union/United States. Result: we can't tell the American people that it appears that the Soviet and the Cubans were involved in the assassination of an American president. It would have led to all out war. It must be covered up.

Speaking of triple agents working for the KGB, CIA, and DGI. There was considerable speculation in the book *The Man Who Knew Too Much*, that Richard Case Nagell was a triple agent and at one time you will remember he was meeting with assassination conspirators in Mexico City. Five years after the assassination, in the summer of 1968, Nagell says "I was briefed on a mission by CIA prior to his boarding a train to East Germany." Said Nagell, "I should have known I was being set up when the train stopped, and the East German Police marched right back to where I was sitting." They arrested Nagell, took him off the train and sent him to Russia for interrogation. When Nagell finally got back to the United States the FBI suggested to him that his arrest had been "arranged" so that he could be "debriefed" by a foreign power without suspicion. Nagell himself hinted at CIA-KGB collusion regarding his East Berlin voyage. [214]

Oswald looks like he could have been a joint operation between the Soviets and the United States; given how quickly both sides approved Oswald's return to the U.S. following his alleged defection. Couple this with the rumors that Oswald may have actually traveled to Cuba and meet with Castro, and we now have three (KGB/DGI/CIA) with skin in the game, or three who have an association with Oswald. Add to this the allegation that Lee Oswald was an informant for the FBI and maybe tied into an assassination operation that Bobby Kennedy is running and now everyone is neatly tied in to insure everyone's safety, silence, and future investigative obstruction.

Angleton was convinced that Philby was behind the propaganda campaign in which the KGB leaked stories that the CIA was behind the Kennedy murder. **Angleton believed, that after Philby served his purpose, he probably was perceived as being very dangerous to them.** [215] (Why? What have we seen that Philby might possibly have been involved with that would be very dangerous to the Soviets? The only thing that I can think of would be Philby's knowledge of the role that he and the Soviets may have played in the Kennedy assassination.)

In October 1964, eleven months after the Kennedy assassination, Nikita Khrushchev was removed from power in the Soviet Union; the coup was orchestrated by Leonid Brezhnev.

So, is it possible that Oswald may have been a coordinated operation of the KGB, Cuban Intelligence, and the CIA?

Frank Sturgis was associated with the CIA and the Mafia. Nearly everyone from William King Harvey to the Mafia, pointed their finger at Sturgis indicating their belief that Sturgis was involved in President Kennedy's assassination. In an interview conducted by Gaeton Fonzi and published in the book, *The Last Investigation,* Sturgis said "he thought the Kennedy assassination was definitely a conspiracy, that Oswald was a patsy and that the Government agencies—the FBI, Secret Service and CIA—were all involved in a cover-up." He said "he once refused to join the CIA, even though it gave him an application, because he thought it was infiltrated at its highest ranks with double agents— possibly the same people who conspired to kill Kennedy." (He might be right given that James Angleton, among others, ended up being suspected as an agent for the Soviets.) He [Sturgis] said "**his theory was that the assassination itself involved groups of agents in Russia's KGB, Cuban intelligence and the CIA**."

Sturgis further related to author Gaeton Fonzi that "he recalled an inside informant telling him about a meeting in Havana that occurred just about two months before the Kennedy assassination. The meeting included Castro, his brother Raul, Ramiro Valdez, the chief of Cuban intelligence, Che Guevara and his secretary, Tanya, another Cuban officer, an American known as 'El Mexicano'" and—oh, yeah—"Jack Ruby." The meeting dealt with plotting the assassination of John F. Kennedy. [216]

On October 18, 1963, CIA did advise the FBI that Oswald had met with Kostikov—but failed to mention their belief that **Kostikov was an assassinations specialist for the KGB**. (Remember Cubela - AM/LASH has now also been shown to be in touch with Kostikov.) Not only did the CIA withhold the true identity of Kostikov, but they also made it clear that the information they were willing to mete out was 'of the highest confidentiality,' and should go no further... Thus the one FBI agent, Hosty, responsible for maintaining surveillance on Oswald was kept in the dark." Hosty later said, "I first heard of the Oswald meeting with Kostikov a full month before the assassination—but somebody forgot to tell me exactly how dangerous Kostikov was." Had the FBI in Dallas known they would have taken all necessary steps to neutralize Oswald—perhaps by interviewing him on November 22? [217]

The CIA knew all about Kostikov being an assassination expert from the get-go. The CIA's Ann Egerter recalled the station cable [about Oswald being in contact with Kostikov] "caused a lot of excitement" because of "the contact with Kostikov." Contrary to Ann Egerter's impression that Kostikov was known to be important the moment this information arrived at CIA headquarters, the CIA denied that they figured out Kostikov's connection to Department 13—which handled assassinations for the KGB—until after Kennedy's murder. The Agency ended up claiming that they knew from the very start that Kostikov was KGB, but not that he was an assassination expert. [218]

So, we have seen clearly why Castro might have been motivated through self-preservation or self-defense. We have seen why Brezhnev and the Soviet KGB might have been motivated to remove Khrushchev for having made the Soviets look weak, by appearing to have backed down during the missile crisis and for potentially cutting future backchannel deals with the Kennedys that continued to make the Soviets look bad. We know about the possibility of communications and coordination flowing between Robert Kennedy, Angleton, and Philby.

## LANSDALE INVOLVED OR SET UP?

There is this picture of three tramps that were arrested in the railroad yard immediately after the assassination:

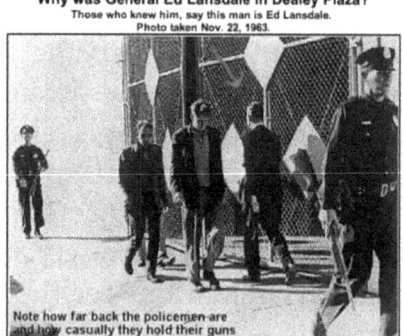

Why was General Ed Lansdale in Dealey Plaza? Those who knew him, say this man is Ed Lansdale. Photo taken Nov. 22, 1963.

Note how far back the policemen are and how casually they hold their guns

In the photo of the three tramps there is a man walking in the opposite direction of the tramps. L. Flether Prouty, U.S. Military Intelligence, identified this individual with his unique walk as being **General Edward Lansdale**. Says Prouty, "I sat in the same office with Lansdale, (OSO of OSD) for years. The first time I saw that picture, I saw the man I knew, and I realized why he was there. Lansdale was a master writer and planner. He was a great "scenario" guy. I am certain that he was behind the elaborate plan and mostly the intricate enduring cover-up. L. Fletcher Prouty served as Chief of Special Operations for the Joint Chiefs of Staff under President Kennedy. In a letter written to New Orleans, DA, Jim Garrison, Prouty indicates his belief that Edward Lansdale planned the assassination of President Kennedy. Says Prouty: "I am positive that he got collateral orders to manage the Dallas event under the guise of 'getting' Castro."

Just days before the Kennedy assassination, Colonel Fletcher Prouty bumped into General Lansdale in the hallway and is informed by Lansdale that he is being dispatched to the South Pole. On November 10, 1963, Prouty, one of President Kennedy's strongest supporters in the military, was on his way to the South Pole. [219]

Lansdale and Bobby Kennedy oversaw the Special Group (Augmented), which oversaw Operation Mongoose. Operation MONGOOSE was the interdepartmental affair and was under the operational control of the Defense Department. Bill Harvey oversaw Task Force W, the CIA portion of Mongoose.

In particular opposition to Lansdale was the CIA's Cuban affairs chief, ex-FBI man William Harvey. Said Lansdale, "Harvey, he was of a type I didn't ever quite trust, and I think it was mutual."

Harvey and Lansdale could not stand one another. Lansdale is the one who introduced Bill Harvey to President Kennedy as "America's James Bond."

Whenever Robert Kennedy complained that nothing was getting done, General Lansdale blamed Bill Harvey.

Lansdale strongly suggested that Bill Harvey use a former Castro crony, Rolando Cubela Secades (AMLASH), for the assassination of Castro. Harvey refused to use him. Bill Harvey was convinced that Cubela was as extreme and unstable as any other member of Castro's revolution.

During the Cuban Missile Crisis, Bill Harvey sent into Cuba 60 agents, after consulting with General Lansdale. Lansdale and Harvey concluded that the President's order restricting the movement of military personnel did not include pre-invasion operations. Harvey would later try and explain to Bobby Kennedy that Lansdale had asked for the agents, but Kennedy responded that he had checked, and Lansdale had done no such thing. Lansdale lied to Kennedy, who believed him.

So, if Lansdale did plan the assassination and he didn't trust Bill Harvey and he was partly responsible for undermining Bill Harvey and his career, then I would think that he would not have included Bill Harvey in any coup attempt. Especially when Bill Harvey surely blamed Lansdale for helping to ruining his career, resulting in Harvey's cooling his heels in Italy.

I was once told by a suspected intelligence operative: "things appear in the press for a reason." Using this same line of reasoning makes me think that this picture was no accident. This picture is almost too perfect. It shows General Edward Lansdale in Dallas, Texas on the day of the assassination passing by three suspects who were pulled out of the railroad yard immediately after the assassination. If you really wanted to even a score with someone and pin the tail on the donkey, wouldn't this be the perfect picture to have? Who would have wanted to do this?

Perhaps Bill Harvey, or the upper echelon planners, arranged for Lansdale to be in Dallas and captured the moment in the picture above, kind of a picture "frame," so to speak. Pin the tail on Lansdale, score one.

Desmond FitzGerald replaced William King Harvey. During the Korean War, Desmond FitzGerald, oversaw the CIA's covert operations run out of Taiwan. He was then the station chief in the Philippines and Japan. From 1957 to 1962 he was the CIA's Far East Division head where he worked closely with Colonel Edward Lansdale. Remember: Oswald was posted at Atsugi, Japan around 1957-1958, prior to his defection. Military Intelligence Agent, Richard Case Nagell and Oswald knew each other in Japan.

## JM/WAVE'S HISTORY

In November 1961, upon his appointment as head of the Cuban task force, Bill Harvey arranged for his trusted associate Theodore "Ted" Shackley's immediate transfer from Berlin to JM/WAVE as the new station chief. Shackley's nicknames "the Ice Man" and "the Blond Ghost."

David Morales began working with Ted Shackley in Berlin back in the 1950s. David Sanchez Morales was Shackley's right hand man in Berlin and at JM/WAVE. Morales was totally dedicated to Shackley.

Back on November 13, 1961, Bill Harvey was the one who cabled the Mexico City CIA station and instructed them to send David S. Morales to JM/WAVE (the CIA's base in south Florida) for permanent posting. (Cable 5816, CIA Station (Scott), 19 Nov. 1961 to Base, confirming receipt of Harvey's cable.)

Bradley Ayers was a Captain in the Army who was attached to the CIA to train the anti-Castro Cubans in the Florida Keys and the Caribbean. In his book *The Zenith Secret*, Ayers reports "David Ferrie being present at JM/WAVE in Miami."[220]

The following comes mostly from Gaeton Fonzi's interview with Ruben Carbajal: **David Sanchez Morales** was a hit man for the CIA. He was a killer. He said it himself. He told his friend Ruben Carbajal he had killed people for the CIA in Vietnam, in Venezuela, in Uruguay and other places.

Morales's lifelong friend Ruben Carbajal said, Morales wasn't in the Army long, maybe six to eight months before he began working for the Agency. In 1954, Morales is listed as a "political officer" with the State Department in Caracas. **Morales was involved with David Phillips in the CIA's planning of the coup in Guatemala** not unlike Antonio Veciana who would later work with Maurice Bishop (David Phillips) in Caracas to plan the assassination attempt on Castro in Chile. **From 1958 to 1960, Morales worked out of the American Embassy in Havana while Phillips worked undercover in his public relations business in Cuba.** From there, **Morales moved with Phillips to take part in the Bay of Pigs operation and, immediately afterwards, to coordinating operations with him at the JM/WAVE station** in Miami. Morales popped up in Laos and Vietnam with **Ted Shackley**; from there he could be found in most of the CIA's hot spots in Latin America when Phillips headed that division. Morales was the can-do kind of guy Phillips needed.

Morales's friend, Ruben Carbajal and Bob Walton spent an evening with Dave Morales in Washington. Walton said, "Their evening with Morales was especially memorable. The drinking got heavy, and Morales began telling his war stories. Of killing in Vietnam and Laos, about being involved in the capture of Che Guevara in Bolivia, of hits in Paraguay and Uruguay and Venezuela."

Walton mentioned the name Kennedy in the conversation and Morales literally almost hit the ceiling. "He flew off the bed on that one," says Walton. "I remember he was lying down, and he jumped up screaming, 'that no good son of a bitch motherfucker!' He started yelling about what a wimp Kennedy was and talking about how he had worked on the Bay of Pigs and how he had to watch all the men he had recruited and trained get wiped out because of Kennedy."

Morales's tirade about Kennedy went on for minutes while he stomped around the room. Suddenly he stopped, sat back down on the bed, and remained silent for a moment. Then, as if saying it only to himself, he added: **"Well, we took care**

**of that son of a bitch, didn't we?"** Carbajal looked at author Gaeton Fonzi and nodded his head. Yes, he was there, it was true. [221]

It has been reported that William Harvey introduced Rosselli to David Morales in November 1961, however Rosselli and Morales probably knew each other from the Guatemalan Coup of 1954.

After Rosselli received Helms's "tacit approval," he was given the rank of colonel, and David Morales, JM/WAVE's hotheaded chief of operations, was formally seconded to the assassination mission. Toward the end of May, the CIA built a small base for Rosselli's unit on Point Mary, Key Largo. The purpose of the base was to train snipers. [222]

Ruben Carbajal said that "he had the impression that, in those last years, a festering disillusionment and resentment towards the Agency was growing in Morales." Dave Morales officially retired to Arizona in 1974; however, he continued to travel frequently. He told his friend Carbajal that "These people never let go of you."

Carbajal remembers all too well the last trip Morales made home from Washington, early in May of 1978. Carbajal said to Morales "Man, you don't look up-to-date." Morales said "I don't know what's wrong with me. Ever since I left Washington, I haven't been feeling very comfortable." That night Morales had what Carbajal calls "a supposed heart attack." David Sanchez Morales died on May 8, 1978. He was 52. [223] This was just before Morales was to testify before one of the Kennedy Assassination investigations in Washington.

# OTTO SKORZENY, QJ/WIN

During World War II, September 1943, German commando, Captain Otto Skorzeny orchestrated and lead the rescue of the imprisoned, or detained, fascist Italian dictator Benito Mussolini during World War II in a daring raid inside of Italy, thus permanently cementing his reputation for daring operations from that point forward.

We have the following information on Skorzeny because Major Ralph P. Ganis purchased all of Otto Skorzeny's personal notes, papers and journals sometime after Otto Skorzeny had passed away and Major Ganis wrote the book: *The Skorzeny Papers: Evidence for the Plot to Kill JFK.*

After the war, future Warren Commission members Allen Dulles and John J. McCloy were instrumental in establishing Otto Skorzeny's secret network.

William Harvey, when he oversaw the CIA Station in Berlin, was in contact with and utilized Otto Skorzeny for certain operations directed against the Soviets.

It is possible that QJ/WIN was one of Skorzeny's operatives within his network. William Harvey's Staff D had direct or indirect access to Skorzeny's assassination capabilities, all monitored by Angleton.

Otto Skorzeny was involved in ZR/RIFLE, the CIA code name for assassinating Fidel Castro.

According to Major Ralph P. Ganis, who has reviewed Otto Skorzeny's journals, "There is evidence indicating that Skorzeny, from his base in Madrid, served as leader of the Agency's QJ/WIN assassination program. The Skorzeny paramilitary assassination group was fully active in Dallas

November 22, 1963," says Ganis. Otto Skorzeny was associated with Staff D's QJ/WIN program. The evidence would seem to indicate Skorzeny organized, planned and carried out the Dallas assassination." [224]

Perhaps this is very telling: June 27, 1963, prior to President Kennedy's assassination in November 1963, Bill Harvey recommended terminating QJ/WIN, but also recommended that the CIA consider using QJ/WIN in Europe, namely Germany, or Austria, if the CIA stations there were interested. Did Bill Harvey foresee, or know what was coming, and feel that it was important to give himself some cover, some protection by documenting in a CIA memorandum that it was his recommendation that the CIA's association with QJ/WIN be terminated. The CIA did not terminate QJ/WIN until February 14, 1964, roughly two and a half months after the Kennedy assassination.

It is important to note that Desmond FitzGerald took over Staff D and replaced William King Harvey, when Harvey moved to being in-charge of the CIA Station in Italy. Bill moved to this new position around June 1963, prior to President Kennedy's assassination in November 1963.

QJ/WIN, the CIA cryptonym for executive action, or foreign leader assassination was used to describe both a program and an individual. Otto Skorzeny's biographical profile and timeline align to an amazing degree with the known facts concerning the mysterious QJ/WIN.

Jean Rene Souetre was present in Dallas on November 22, 1963. Souetre was associated with Otto Skorzeny and his organization. The actual sniper, or team of snipers, may have been directed by Jean Rene Souetre, the former OAS officer wanted by French security services for an attempt on the life of French President Charles de Gaulle in 1962. [225] SSCIA 157-10011-10124, HSCA Vol. 4 Page 197-203 & SSCI

157-100004-10138, and <u>SSCIA</u> 157-10011-10124

I hasten to remind you of this paragraph that was presented earlier that read: Author Bayard Stockton who wrote the book Flawed Patriot had an opportunity to view the file that was kept at home by William and C.G. Harvey. Stockton writes: "I got the impression that only a couple of documents were kept in this file. Apparently one of the most important documents of Harvey's career was a **memo signed by Richard Helms**, Deputy Director (Plans) dated February 1962, which **authorized Bill Harvey to retain the services of Principal Agent QJ/WIN**. This single piece of paper seems to be significant especially when compared to the depth and breadth of Bill Harvey's total career, experience, and achievement." So, I ask why did Bill Harvey feel that it was necessary to keep this one particular piece of paper? It seems apparent that it was important to Bill Harvey that he have proof that his actions were known and authorized by Richard Helms. **My opinion, this is telling. Bill Harvey is telling us that this whole mess was known, approved and probably at the direction of Richard Helms in CIA Plans, and it has come to be my opinion, at the behest of Allen Dulles and with help from Angleton.**

# A GLIMPSE OF CIA HEADQUARTERS ACTIVITY

The day after the assassination, Richard **Helms** (not Director McCone) **assigned** the initial CIA investigation of the assassination to John Whitten who was the head of the Mexico City Headquarters desk of the CIA's **Special Affairs Staff (SAS)**. SAS had been Task Force W under Bill Harvey, which contained the Agencies largest concentration of Cuban experts. This hints at where the CIA felt the investigation was going: the Cuban Operation – Mexico City.

For Angleton, the paranoia heightened with the death of the president.

Immediately following the assassination, Angleton began espousing the notion that the Soviets were somehow involved. He leaned on his friend Allen Dulles, begging him to get the Warren Commission to leave the door open to the notion that one could not rule out a Soviet conspiracy. Angleton's agenda clashed early on with John Whitten's agenda. Whitten had been asked by Helms to conduct an investigation and to write a report, based on existing CIA records. But Whitten found that his investigation, experienced immediate opposition from James Angleton. [226]

Said John Whitten, "Angleton immediately went into action to do all of the investigating. And Helms called a meeting in which Angleton and a lot of others were present and Helms told everybody that I was in charge and that everybody should report everything to me. And that no one should have any conversations with anyone about the Kennedy case without my being present, which was violated from the word go by Angleton, who dealt with the FBI and the Warren Commission and John Foster [probably means Allen] Dulles." [227]

"...Helms refused to make him stop doing this," said Whitten. "Angleton would not invite me to these meetings. I called this to Mr. Helms' attention." [228]

Whitten, unaware of Angleton's agenda, wrote an argument against the notion that Oswald was a Soviet agent.

Whitten's report said, "All of the five consular officers in the Soviet Embassy are known or suspected intelligence officers. Certainly, if Oswald had been a Soviet agent in training for an assassination assignment, or even for sabotage work, the Soviets would have stopped him from making open visits and phone calls to the Soviet Embassy in Mexico after a couple of times. Our experience...indicates that they do make some mistakes, but that they do not persist in such glaring errors." [229]

No wonder Angleton sought to take over the investigation from Whitten! Whitten was blowing the very cover story on Oswald that could effectively guarantee a quiet cover-up.

Late in December 1963, Angleton put on a performance in a meeting criticizing Whitten's report. Richard Helms turned the CIA's investigation over to Angleton and his Counterintelligence Division. Angleton was given control over all agency communications relating to the assassination. Once Angleton had full control of the internal CIA investigation, he quickly obtained the liaison position to the Warren Commission. Angleton assigned Rocca to interface directly with the Warren Commission members.

Angleton testified he was often in contact with [Allen] Dulles after the latter had left the Agency. Angleton testified that Dulles consulted with him before agreeing to President

Johnson's request that he be on the Commission and that he was in frequent contact with Dulles. Warren Commission, GPO edition, P. 169, 175, 652.

## MORE ON THE TERRE HAUTE HOUSE RECORDS

As you may recall, I speculated that there might have been a meeting going on in the Terre Haute House from the 25th through the 27th of November 1963.

In addition to Lt. Col. Leon Corcos from DSAPSO, Columbus, Ohio, we may have some additional registrants in the hotel that might be of interest.

We have one, Salvatore Corso, from Palermo, Italia, who was registered at the Terre Haute House, November 23rd through the 24th. So, Salvatore missed our window for the possible meeting from the 25th through the 27th, but I thought I would be negligent if I didn't at least touch on Colonel Philip J. Corso, who seemed to have signaled over time that he knew a lot about the Kennedy assassination and he said he was going to write a book about it, but must have thought better of it and instead wrote the book: *The Day After Roswell.* Could this Salvatore Corso from Italia be Colonel Philip J. Corso who served during the war in Italy? Colonel Corso was the chief of U.S. Counterintelligence in Rome, Italy and worked with James Jesus Angleton in Rome, Italy during World War II. Just like Angleton, Corso helped many Jewish refugees escape to Palestine and many Nazis escape via the "Nazi Rat Lines" that Allen Dulles and James Jesus Angleton setup. Corso, like Angleton, is reported as the personal emissary to Giovanni Battista Montini at the Vatican, later to be known as Pope Paul VI. Corso was also a member of the CIA team that conducted the Guatemalan Coup. I do not know if Salvatore Corso from Palarmo, Italia is Colonel Philip J. Corso, perhaps a signature expert could examine the signature on the registration card in my e-book: *Documentation Supplement America's Crossroads?*

Next, we have W.T. Radcliffe registered in the Terre Haute House the 25$^{th}$ to the 26$^{th}$. I do not know if this is the same W. Radcliffe, but I found a Wayne Radcliffe in an internet search who was taken to U.S. District Court, Eastern District of Pennsylvania, November 21, 2000, many years after having possibly registered in the Terre Haute House in 1963. Radcliffe was in court for routing missiles to Italy from South Africa and illegally shipping various military and commercial components to South Africa. In the court documentation Radcliffe seemed to be trying to tie the CIA into his activities via a Freedom of Information Request.

November 25$^{th}$ through the 27$^{th}$, we have someone registered in the Terre Haute House with a Chicago Merchandise Mart address. Funny how the "Marts" comes up in the Kennedy assassination story. Clay Shaw's International Trade "Mart," President Kennedy was on his way to speak at the Dallas Trade "Mart," but didn't make it due to his assassination. Clay Shaw is the character that District Attorney Garrison, in New Orleans, accused of being involved in the Kennedy assassination, as depicted in the movie, "*JFK*," and Clay Shaw was the director of the International Trade "Mart" in New Orleans.

Terre Haute House, November 23$^{rd}$ to 24$^{th}$, J.E. Martin, Box 900, Dallas, Texas. I only mention this one because we seem to have a lot of Martins running around in this story and because the address given was Dallas, Texas and the P.O. Box belonged to some oil company enterprise. I believe P.O. Box 900 belonged, back in 1963, to an oil company. The oil company name has changed a few times over the years, but Box 900 still appears to be oil business related.

# FBI DIVISION FIVE

How did the FBI's Division Five enter into this story? For many years I recognized that the entries in the Terre Haute House records had a Lt. Col. Leon Corcos from DSAPSO, Columbus, Ohio. And I had the impression that DSAPSO supplied war material and logistics, as a part of the U.S. Military. It was not until the last few days of finishing up this book that I searched the internet in relation to the location in Columbus, Ohio. Up pops the startling information that the FBI's Division Five is apparently located within this military complex at this same address in Columbus, Ohio!

Additionally, this inadvertent internet search, as fate would have it, brought up references to a book written by a William Torbitt, aka apparent real name David Copeland, a long-time attorney in Texas, the book, or manuscript is called, *The Torbitt Document: NASA, Nazis, and the JFK Assassination.* In an interview by Jim Marrs with David Copeland/William Torbitt, Copeland said that his sources were two government agents, one from the Secret Service and one from the FBI, but he declined to name them. Additional information for the *Torbitt* Document appears to have come from New Orleans, District Attorney Jim Garrison's investigation and from the Warren Commission.

In the book, *The Torbitt Document* it says, that President Kennedy was assassinated by a "fascist cabal." According to the book, the FBI's Division Five planned and supervised the assassination and acted dually with the Defense Intelligence Agency (DIA), which acts on behalf of the Joint Chiefs of Staff in the Pentagon. Found, or located, directly under Division Five and the DIA is the highly secret Defense Industrial Security Command (DISC). *Torbit* argues that the Swiss

Corporation: Permindex engineered the assassination and involved the Defense Industrial Security Command (DISC, Columbus Ohio). The Defense Industrial Security Command was originally created by J. Edgar Hoover as a police force for the **Tennessee Valley Authority, later adding the Atomic Energy Commission,** thus tying it into the Army Intelligence Service. At the time of the assassination the FBI's William Sullivan administered DISC. William Sullivan issued the directive leading up to the assassination, which removed Lee Harvey Oswald's name from any security risk lists [the FBI's Security Index]. According to *Torbit*, **DISC agents included Clay Shaw, Guy Banister, David Ferrie, Lee Harvey Oswald, Jack Ruby and Louis M. Bloomfield of Montreal, Canada.**

Concerning the Tennessee Valley Authority. I have read, I believe it was in an FBI report, where someone recognized Lee Harvey Oswald when he appeared on television, as a result of the assassination, and they reported to the FBI that they had seen Lee Harvey Oswald, sometime prior to the assassination, touring either a Tennessee Valley Authority Museum, or a Tennessee Valley Authority facility, I can't remember which.

The Defense Industrial Security Command (DISC) is a top-secret police force whose duties include espionage and counter-espionage and is concerned with the supply of arms, equipment, ammunition, munitions and DISC vets the manufacturing companies and their employees who have contracts with NASA, the Atomic Energy Commission, the U.S. Information Agency and/or the Pentagon.

The underlying structure for the assassination allegedly consisted of five front organizations: the Solidarists, the American Council of Christian Churches, the Free Cuba Committee, the Mafia and the Security Division of NASA. The Solidarists (were White Russians who wanted their Russian homeland back from the communists – think **George de**

**Mohrenschildt**), the American Council of Christian Churches led by **H. L. Hunt** (big oil man Texas) and the Free Cuba Committee headed by Carlos Prio Socarras (past President of Cuba 1948 until Castro kicked him out in 1952, here we have Cubans who wanted their homeland back from the communists). President Kennedy and Khrushchev seemed headed in the wrong direction for these groups, as well as for the old Nazis who wanted their homeland back in one piece and not permanently divided. President Kennedy and Soviet Premier Khrushchev appeared to be headed for détente and better relations between the U.S. and the Soviet Union, including possible agreements on what to do about Cuba and possibly the flashpoint that was Berlin.

The Mafia is also said to be a part of this underlying structure, headed by a Clifford Jones, **Bobby Baker** (who Bobby Kennedy's Justice Department had in court on the day of the assassination, Baker revelations would have been more than embarrassing for V.P. Lyndon Johnson), George Smathers, Roy Cohn, Fred Black and **Lewis McWillie** (Mafia and friend of Jack Ruby).

Concerning the Mafia, *Torbitt* says, Joseph Bonanno, Mafia, had a business interest in the munitions manufacturing company, Lionel. Bonanno, Marcello (Mafia New Orleans), and the Mafia were all working directly under the Defense Industrial Security Command through their ownership and controlling interests in a large number of companies engaged in manufacturing munitions, hardware and supplies for the Pentagon, Space Agency, AEC and USIA (source *The Grim Reapers,* Ed Reid via *Torbitt*).

Marcello and Bonanno trace their membership in the international Mafia to a Swiss corporation, Permindex and the Rome based Centro Mondiale.

The Bonanno family and Giancana Mafia family of Chicago

are the only entities in this whole Kennedy assassination story who have been honest and admitted their participation in the assassination:

The Bonanno family in the movie: "*Bonanno, a Godfathers Story,*" based on the book "*A Man of Honor: The Autobiography of Joseph Bonanno*" by Joseph Bonanno and "*Bound by Honor,*" by Bill Bonanno. The dialog in the movie goes like this: "So who did the shooting? Giancana and Trafficante organized the shooters. Johnny Rosselli in the storm drain."

As for the Giancana Mafia family, Sam and Chuck Giancana came out with the book: *Double Cross*, in which they say: Sam Mooney Giancana said that the entire conspiracy went, "**right up to the top of the CIA.**" He claimed that **some of its former leaders** [Allen Dulles & Cabell?] **and present leaders** [Helms, Angleton, and the Guys from the Guatemalan Coup?] **were involved**, as well as a "half dozen fanatical **right-wing Texans, Vice President Lyndon Johnson, and** the Bay of Pigs Action Officer under Eisenhower, **Richard Nixon**. Nixon has the power and the backing of the big money, like Howard Hughes and the guys in California and the oilmen in Texas." In the Giancana's very detailed account, I would point out that they had nothing to say specifically about William King Harvey being involved.

Also included in this little caper, per *Torbitt*: former Nazi, Wernher von Braun head of NASA's Security Division, **Vice President Lyndon Johnson**, Walter Jenkins, Fred Korth, **John Connally**, **William Seymour** (aka Leon Oswald, 544 Camp Street), **Robert McKeown** (worked with Ruby running guns to Cuba), **Sergio Arcacha Smith** (544 Camp Street, Arcacha had a direct line to Bobby Kennedy and Oswald is reporting to Arcacha), **Lee Harvey Oswald**, **Ruth Paine**, **Michael Paine**, **Gordon Novel** (544 Camp Street, neo-Nazi, possible CIA connections-known to have met with Angleton once, participated in the Schlumberger munitions burglary in New

Orleans, a Double-Chek agent) and **Clint Murchison** (big oil guy, apparently threw a party for J. Edgar Hoover the night before the assassination, as told in the book *Texas in the Morning*, by Madline Brown, LBJ's girlfriend. At the party, LBJ, Nixon, J. Edgar Hoover and John J. McCloy (McCloy ended up on the Warren Commission)).

**Double-Chek**, a Florida corporation organized and operated as a front for the CIA as the American counterpart to Permindex and Centro Mondiale Commerciale, was **taken over by Division Five** of the FBI prior to the assassination and was used as one of the principal funding agencies for President Kennedy's death planners, so says the *Torbitt* document.

**Gordon Novel**, a Double-Chek employee and Banister agent, upon being called before a New Orleans Grand Jury in 1967, Novel wrote to Seymour Weiss. Novel told Weiss, who was with the **FBI's Division Five**, that Garrison was on to Double-Chek's involvement, warning Division Five to not kill Garrison, but suggested that the DIA be used to subdue Garrison.

**Gordon Novel**'s letter to Seymour Weiss of the FBI's Division Five triggered, former DIA liaison for Bobby Kennedy, Walter Sheridan who gathering up Novel for a lie detector test. Sheridan then put out a press release stating that Jim Garrison's investigation in New Orleans was a fraud. (Remember Garrison said that "Bobby Kennedy was obstructing justice." Sheridan is one of Bobby's boys in the Justice Department and Sheridan ran around doing everything that he could do to undermine Garrison's investigation.)

Later Novel fled from Garrison's investigation to Ohio. When New Orleans District Attorney Jim Garrison attempted to have **Gordon Novel** extradited from the State of Ohio,

Gordon Novel obtained aid from the Defense Industrial Security Command in Columbus, Ohio, in order to avoid extradition, so says *Torbitt*.

Gordon Novel's wife testified to Jim Garrison that Novel resembled Oswald and was in Dallas, Mexico and Forth Worth impersonating and incriminating Oswald prior to the assassination.

Per Volume XXIV, page 642, **Albert Osborne and Gordon Novel** were reported as having been in Tryall, Jamaica on a number of occasions. Tryall is located in Montego Bay, in Northern Jamaica. Tryall is an exclusive club where John Connally owns a Palatial retreat within the tightly guarded compound. L.M. Bloomfield met with John Connally at Tryall on numerous occasions (per IX, 3 and 4; New Orleans District Attorney Records).

**Albert Osborne (John Howard Bowen)** of the American Council of Christian Churches, is the one who trained and had available a team of professional assassins down in Mexico, all housed on Clint Murchison's huge ranch. These are the assassins reportedly used in the assassination of President Kennedy, per *Torbitt*. Per an FBI report Warren Commission Exhibit No. 2195: Bowen worked for the Tennessee Valley Authority back around 1929 to about 1934 and perhaps after 1934 per: *In Silence I Speak,* author: George N. Shuster, Cudahy Publishing Co.

The professional assassins project in Mexico began under the supervision of Albert Osborne in 1943, but this operation was J. Edgar Hoover's brainchild and Hoover maintained close supervision of the 25 to 30 expert riflemen (Buddy Floyd case file).

Albert Osborne was in Clay Shaw's office at 124 Camp Street, New Orleans on October 10, 1963. Later that same day he was in the office of Maurice Brooks Gatlin, an FBI transporter and later still he was meeting at 544 Camp Street with Guy Banister, the FBI Division Five Southern Manager.

Six witnesses identified Osborne and Lee Oswald, as having traveled together on a bus trip to Mexico City in September 1963.

November 22$^{nd}$, **Osborne** and ten of his riflemen were staying at 3126 Harlendale in the Oak Cliff section of Dallas. **Leon Oswald, aka William Seymour,** had been at this Oak Cliff address for about four weeks.

**Guy Banister, FBI Division Five's Southern Director**, employed a long-time employee of Double-Chek named **William Seymour**. Seymour was the same size and weight as Lee Harvey Oswald and resembled Oswald. Seymour was given the name Leon Oswald and fake identification papers with the name Lee Harvey Oswald (XXVI, 834 et seq; New Orleans District Attorney Records).

David Lewis, New Orleans private investigator, was employed by Guy Banister in 1962 and 1963. Lewis first met Leon Oswald in Manchuso's Restaurant, while drinking coffee with Banister's secretary. Carlos Quirega, an anti-Castro Cuban, came into the restaurant and introduced them to Leon Oswald, a person who resembled Lee Harvey Oswald. About a week later Lewis was leaving Banister's office when he saw Leon Oswald, alias William Seymour, Quirega and David Ferrie in the hallway on their way to Banister's office.

Ten days later, Lewis witnessed a meeting taking place in Banister's office between **Banister, Quirega, David Ferrie, Leon Oswald and Robert Ray McKeown** (a gun running partner of Jack Ruby's). Sergio Arcacha Smith left for Houston with McKeown after the meeting.

*Torbitt* says that the Leon Oswald that Perry Russo reported as discussing the assassination of President Kennedy by triangulated rifle fire was William Seymour, because Russo testified that Leon Oswald was the roommate of David Ferrie. Lee Oswald was living with his wife and daughter on Magazine Street at this time and was not a roommate of Ferrie's, so this wasn't Lee Oswald, but Seymour. Also, *Torbitt* says that Leon Oswald, aka William Seymour was the Oswald stand in during the visit reported with Sylvia Odio, which also makes sense because Oswald was said to be in Mexico City at this time and could not have been in two places at the same time.

According to the *Torbit* document, on November 22$^{nd}$, **William Seymour** fired a rifle from the sixth floor of the School Book Depository striking President Kennedy in the back. Seymour was seen running from the School Book Depository Building and was picked up by someone driving a Nash Rambler. The driver dropped Seymore off two blocks from the Abundant Life Temple. The Temple was affiliated with the American Council of Christian Churches. Seymour was stopped by Dallas Police Officer J.D. Tippet, whereupon Seymour shot and killed officer Tippet, before proceeding to the Abundant Life Temple where he remained until it was safe to leave town.

**William Seymour and Gordan Novel** were seen with Jack Ruby in the Carousel Club and other places in Dallas in October and November by such a large number of witnesses, the investigators could not locate and list them all. However, a large number testified to seeing them together and a Dallas attorney overheard them discussing Seymour's planned assassination of someone.

**Seymour** impersonated Oswald in an attempt to connect Oswald to a rifle by using his name at a gun shop in Irving, Texas (enter: Dial Rider). He tried to show Oswald was expecting a large sum of money, by saying that he was expecting a large sum of money, while looking at a car at a Dallas auto dealership. He appeared at a grocery store as Oswald and at a barber shop where he made leftist remarks. During the barber shop, furniture store (enter: Mrs. Edith Whitworth and Mrs. Gertrude Hunter) and a grocery store appearance in Irving, Texas, Seymour was accompanied by Marina, or a woman impersonating her. Seymour gave the name Oswald and attempted to cash a large check at a grocery store.

**Seymour** went to rifle range practice in Dallas quite often posing as Oswald. Several witnesses to Seymour's practice sessions reported that a "**Sporterized Mauser**" was used by Seymour in many of the target practice appearances.

DA Jim Garrison questioned one of Osborne's professionals, Emilion Santana who was the assassin firing from the Dal-Tex Building across Houston Street and behind the President's car. Santana admitted he was a close acquaintance with **Jack Ruby, Clay Shaw, Gordon Novel and William Seymour**. Santana said that Jack Ruby and Clay Shaw had a close relationship. Santana admitted that while he was an employee of Double-Chek, he was an agent for the Central Intelligence Agency.

According to the *Torbitt Document*: Osborne sniper, Manuel Gonzales was the gunmen who fired from the stockade fence atop the grassy knoll in Dealey Plaza.

Following the assassination, according to the *Torbit* Document, the Dallas Police arrested a **Permindex agent, James Powell**, Army Intelligence on assignment from the DIA to the **Defense Industrial Security Command of Columbus, Ohio**. Additionally, the Dallas Police hauled **Jim Braden** of Los Angeles in from the Dal-Tex Building. Braden was also an agent of the **Defense Industrial Security Command of Columbus, Ohio**. Dallas Police Captain Will Fritz released Powell (National Archives, Commission

Document #364 [or 334 or 354 – Xerox copy unclear]; New Orleans District Attorney Records).

In Warren Commission testimony April 6, 1964, Adrian Alba, who worked at the parking garage in New Orleans next to the Reily Coffee Company, where Lee Oswald worked, said that Lee Harvey Oswald told him some weeks before the assassination that he was leaving the Reily Coffee Company and was going to work for **NASA**. In the book *Conspiracy* by Anthony Summers it says, "four of Oswald's colleagues at Reily went to work for NASA within weeks of Oswald's departure." Summers goes on to point out that William Reily, Oswald's ultimate boss at the Reily Coffee Company "was a wealthy American backer of the '**Free Cuba Committee.**'"

Adrian Alba had a contract to look after a number of unmarked cars belonging to the Secret Service and the FBI. "One day in early summer 1963," says Alba, "a man who he thought was an FBI agent visiting New Orleans from Washington, came into the garage. He showed credentials and was given a green Studebaker from the carpool." A day later Alba observed, from his garage, the same green Studebaker as it drove past and stopped out-front of Oswald's place of work – just thirty yards away. As it did, "Lee Oswald went across the street. He bent down as if to look in the window and was handed what appeared to be a good-sized white envelope. Oswald turned and bent over, as if to hold the envelope close to his abdomen, I think he put it under his shirt. Oswald then went back into the Reily Coffee Company building and the car drove off." According to Alba, "Oswald met the same car again a couple of days later and talked briefly with the driver. A few days later the agent from Washington returned the car to the garage."

Adrian Alba says that he was surprised when there was nothing in the Warren Commission about a relationship between Oswald and the FBI.

Orest Pena, a New Orleans bar owner, alleged publicly in 1975 that he had seen Oswald with FBI agent deBueys on numerous occasions and Pena said that deBrueys had threatened him physically before his Warren Commission appearance, warning him to keep quiet about what he had observed. [230]

Harry told me back on August 24, 2006, that he had an "L" clearance. So, I did an internet search. What in the world is an "L clearance?" Well, the Department of Energy has an "L" Clearance and I quote:

"L" allows individual access to:

- Confidential Restricted Data
- Confidential Formerly Restricted Data
- Special Nuclear Material (Category III)
- Confidential National Security Information
- Unescorted Access to Limited and Protected Area
- Secret Formerly Restricted Data
- Secret National Security Information

The Atomic Energy Commission, which you may remember from the above text, fell under the highly secretive FBI Division Five's purview for vetting, which included espionage and counter-espionage activities. As I understand it, the Atomic Energy Commission was folded into the Department of Energy in 1977.

So, my question is, how does a person get an L clearance from the Atomic Energy Commission/Department of Energy who was AWOL from the military and according to an FBI report, was showing a Young Communist League card, whose FBI reports indicate that he has been classified by the FBI as a Security Matter – C, "C" as in Communist, was investigated for the assassination of President Kennedy, and yet now years later Harry has government security clearance? But then again, Harry may not be guilty of anything. Or maybe Harry is on the right side. I am leaving it to you to decide right from wrong, or right from left in this story.

I am now on about the last day of working on this book, which I wrote over a period of many years. I of course have just finished this section on the FBI's Division Five and I am rereading all that I have written over the years and then I read page 81. It says, as you may remember: "Bill Harvey was 30 years old in 1945 and had been with the FBI for five years. **He was the head of Division Five**, which was responsible for investigating communism and communists in the United States." Bill Harvey would probably write on this document, right here: "OSOD" Oh Shit, Oh Damn!

Intended, or not, thank you Harry L. Power for drawing our attention to the possibility that something else might have been going on in the Terre Haute House, which led us to Columbus, Ohio and the FBI's Division Five.

## WHO WOULD HAVE BEEN IMPORTANT ENOUGH TO SHOOT IN TERRE HAUTE?

Who would have been in Terre Haute, important enough to shoot, three days after the Kennedy assassination? I didn't think there would be anyone. Everyone important would have been in Washington at the funeral.

According to Butts and Schoffstall, the Terre Haute Police always believed that the rifle had come to Terre Haute to shoot someone important. There is some indication that authorities in Indiana might have sensed that something was going on because on November 26, 1963, the day after Harry arrived at the Terre Haute House and the day before the rifle was discovered there was this article in the newspaper. It said, "Indiana Governor Mathew Welsh returned from Washington early today after attending funeral ceremonies for President Kennedy and found new security measures in effect concerning his own personal safety but indicated he was following the advice of the State Police."

I decided that it was important to check to see if there was anyone in Terre Haute important enough to shoot. So, I went to the Vigo County Public Library, which ironically now stands exactly where Wiley High School used to stand. Wiley High School of course was the high school that both William King Harvey and Ray Cline had attended. I searched the Terre Haute Tribune microfilm, beginning a month before the assassination and running to the end of November 1963. I found one individual of national significance that came to Terre Haute during this time, "at the Terre Haute House,

Wednesday, Nov. 29, 1963, at 6:30 PM, Dr. Ray S. Cline, Deputy Director for Intelligence, CIA to speak at Wiley High School's Centennial banquet. Ray Cline, Wiley High School graduate June 1935."

I immediately recognized the name Ray Cline, having already read Mike McCormick's five-part series in the Tribune-Star about Terre Haute's two major CIA guys.

Ray Cline, CIA Deputy Director for Intelligence was at the Terre Haute House making a speech to his and William King Harvey's high school alma mater, just a day and a half after the rifle had been discovered in the same hotel, the Terre Haute House.

As you know, I have the registration books from the Terre Haute House for 1963. Harry L. Power originally indicated that he would be staying at the hotel until the 29th, the day of Ray Cline's speech. Obviously, the plan, or Harry's plans, changed and Harry left early, leaving behind the rifle.

Two and a half years after the assassination, Terre Haute's Ray Cline was on the short list of three names that were going to be recommended to Lyndon Johnson for appointment as CIA Director when Johnson appointed fellow Texan, Vice Admiral William Raborn as the new Director of the CIA, replacing McCone in 1965.

After my discovery that Ray Cline was in the Terre Haute House, my theory was that the original plan was to shoot Ray Cline in the Terre Haute House. This part of my theory, however, is not a stretch, as you know Harry came right out and said to me once, "I was sent to Terre Haute to knock off this CIA guy," as first shown in the second paragraph of this book. In Harry's defense he might have meant that it appeared that he was sent to knock off this CIA guy. Either way, theory continues: And to have it appear like he had been shot by a pro-Castro, communist sympathizer, who supposedly had displayed a real(?), or a fake, Young Communist League Membership Card. The act of shooting Ray Cline would have reinforced the notion, first introduced by Oswald (Fair Play for Cuba Committee and alleged commie card carrier) that Castro, and or the communists, were brazen enough to come into our house and attack our leaders. The expected outcome, the American people would rise up and demand that the United States attack Cuba. A scheme very similar to the Joint Chiefs of Staff's plan known as Operation Northwoods, where outrageous acts of terrorism would be performed by the U.S., in the U.S., yet made to look like Cuba did it. The goal being to inspire the American people to demand the elimination of Castro. But for some reason, apparently the plan to assassinate Ray Cline was changed and the rifle was left behind instead.

Two questions occur to me: If this was the plan. Why leave the rifle and why shoot Ray Cline of all people?

Three reasons for leaving the rifle occur to me. The first reason: to create a public record for possible future use. Given the proximity in time to the assassination, given that the rifle was the same make and model as a possible rifle used in the assassination, and given that the stranger indicated he was from Texas, all of this would surely result in just what happened, notification of the local police and the FBI. The FBI Office at the time was conveniently located in the Federal Building directly across the street from the Terre Haute House. Notifying the FBI creates reports, which creates a written record. This written record, this paper trail, I am convinced was originally created to be followed just as I have done here. This written record would be handy if down the road the planners of the assassination needed to come up with another patsy, or another potential assassin, or perhaps to reinforce the idea that Castro was behind all of this. If the rifle had not been left, the trail of clues would not have been created. Additionally, just as it was important to try to tie Lee Harvey Oswald to a rifle through a written mail order receipt, the act of Harry leaving the rifle in a hotel room registered in his name had the same effect, it created a written record tying Harry to this particular rifle. Which leads me to wonder if the rifle, or Harry, or both are significant to the mystery of who shot President Kennedy. At the very least this event drew our attention to William King Harvey and Ray Cline.

The second reason for leaving the rifle: it can call attention to seemingly incriminating things. In this case it could call attention to Harry and what he **may appear to have been involved in**, or whom he may appear to have been associated with. It could call attention to people or activities related to Terre Haute, or activities occurring within the Terre Haute House. For example, it called my attention to William King Harvey. Especially when I learned that Bill Harvey oversaw the Mafia and the Cubans to get Castro. Couple this with the fact that the Kennedy brothers ruined Bill Harvey's cherished career and that Bill Harvey is in the public record as having "absolutely hated Bobby Kennedy with a purple passion." **The rifle and Harry might have been a calling card from Bill Harvey to Bobby Kennedy.** Bobby Kennedy might be expected to ask the same question I am asking here. What is the significance of this rifle being left in this location? Well, who is associated with Terre Haute? Oh, Bill Harvey. Isn't he the fellow who lived for his career and didn't we ruin his career? Naw, can't be. Bobby Kennedy said, "The people the CIA had originally were not very good..." On the other hand, this little incident might have been designed to call attention to Harry and the rifle as a part of the operation that C.G. Harvey claimed Bobby Kennedy was running. Then again, Kim Philby and the CIA's Counterintelligence Chief, James Jesus Angleton, appeared to maintain their relationship long after Bill Harvey trashed

Soviet spy Philby's life and career eleven years earlier. It is documented that Jim Angleton met with Kim Philby in Italy as recently as 1960. Could Philby and Angleton, or for that matter "the Guys from the Guatemalan Coup" have arranged to have Harry and the rifle appear in Terre Haute in order to call attention to Bill Harvey's latest activities, or as an attempt to pin the assassination on Bill Harvey, guilty or not. Another suggestion, perhaps there was a meeting going on at the Terre Haute House that someone wanted to call attention to. Perhaps a meeting to arrange for arms and ammunition for the Second Naval Guerrilla Operation, a.k.a. the CIA's AMWORLD, a.k.a. the U.S. military's OPLAN 380-63, and another attempted invasion of Cuba. An invasion the American people were expected to call for upon learning the supposed facts regarding Castro's involvement in President Kennedy's assassination.

I am sure that Harry had his reasons for leaving the rifle, I am just not sure that even Harry knew, or knows, all the reasons for leaving the rifle. Being on a need to know, you know.

The rifle could have been left as a warning to Ray Cline the CIA's Deputy Director of Intelligence and his direct report, the Director of the CIA, John McCone.

The more dominant divisions of the CIA, at least in this story: Intelligence (Ray Cline's area) - which gathered, analyzed, and interpreted data (which was the original and sole intent of the CIA), Plans (Richard Helms's area) - which is the clandestine, covert, spies in the field, paramilitary, propaganda, dirty tricks, and then there was Counterintelligence (Jim Angleton's area) - designed to thwart spying by foreign powers.

Ray Cline was a major player in the intelligence community, but nobody in this country, outside of Washington DC, probably ever heard of Ray Cline. What would be the point of shooting someone almost no one had ever heard of, besides my earlier point that it was meant to look like the pro Castro communists did it?

Ray Cline reported directly to the Director of CIA. If Ray Cline had been shot, it most assuredly would have been interpreted as being meant to send some kind of a message, or warning, to the Director of the CIA. The first message that might have been received, you had better be careful where you step and what you stick your nose into. The message is, you are vulnerable, and we can reach out and touch you if we want to. The significance of Harry Power and/or the rifle would add further clues as to the message being sent and hints to those receiving the message as to who might be sending the message.

Who planned and carried out the assassination of President Kennedy? In my opinion, the Plans side of the CIA, which included the Guys from the Guatemalan and Bay of Pigs operations, possibly William King Harvey and definitely James Jesus Angleton head of Counterintelligence all at the behest of Allen Dulles. So why shoot Ray Cline? To the general public the death of a CIA agent connected to the President's assassination and linked to an alleged Castro plot would be proof enough that the CIA was not involved in this whole mess. Who would believe that the CIA would shoot one of their own guys? It would have reinforced the notion that Castro was running around the country shooting people, given Harry Power's assumed Cuban Intelligence connections, given what appears to have been built up in the public record about him.

Back to the question: "Who would believe that the CIA would shoot one of their own guys?" "It is an old [Nazi] Gestapo trick. Shoot one of your own people to show that you are not one of them," quote from the movie North by Northwest. In other words, "Shoot one of your own to prove that you played no part in events, as they are perceived."

The CIA much like the State Department, seemed to have had various factions or cliques. They didn't all seem to be marching in the same directions all the time.

Ray Cline had an agreement with CIA Director McCone that the guys in Plans were to tell him everything they were doing, so that he would have a complete picture of what was going on in the world. I don't think the guys in Plans liked this too much. It put Ray Cline in a position of power, almost in a position of approving or disapproving Plans actions. It would surely have seemed to them like they were having to check in with mom all the time.

Cline had also been the one who had crossed Angleton and the men in Plans concerning the releasing of Nikita Khrushchev's speech. They might have gotten the impression that Cline went over their heads to then Director Dulles to win the argument. Angleton was reported to still be mad about this, years later. These guys seemed to hold grudges for long periods of time, the Kennedys with Castro, Angleton with Cline, William King Harvey with the Kennedy brothers, Bill Harvey with Lansdale's betrayal, Kim Philby and Angleton with William King Harvey.

We know from the 1963 hotel register from the Terre Haute House, that Harry originally intended to stay until the 29$^{th}$ of November, but for whatever reason Harry left a day and a half early, leaving behind the rifle.

Whatever was originally planned for Terre Haute, if there was a plan at all, it could have been notorious. Leaving the rifle behind, in close proximity to Ray Cline could be construed as a warning directed at someone, perhaps directed at Ray Cline and his boss the Director of the CIA, John McCone, or it could have been meant to draw attention to certain things, or it could have built a paper trail of evidence in the public record, which it did.

## TERRE HAUTE'S RAY CLINE

Ray Steiner Cline was a leader among peers. In 1934-35, Ray's senior year at Wiley High School, he was class president and captain of the Red Streaks' football team. Terre Haute Tribune-Star, Mike McCormick, April 25, 1999

In 1939, Ray Cline graduated from Harvard University, a Phi Beta Kappa, and studied at Oxford University in England before getting a master's degree and being elected to the Harvard Society of Fellows. In 1949 he earned his Ph.D. [231]

Pearl Harbor, December 1941, marked the beginning of Ray Cline's career in intelligence working at breaking Japanese codes.

Ray Cline's recollection of the war years: "I recall vividly the sense of challenge, of danger, of exultant dedication, and of fascination with the realities of international power." [232]

Cline eventually moved from breaking codes for the Navy to the OSS. In 1943, Cline found himself standing in front of sliding map panels in the OSS war room, briefing General "Wild Bill" Donovan on the tide of battle in places in Russia and the Pacific he had never heard of until the Germans and the Japanese attacked them.

In 1944, Ray Cline, became Chief of Current Intelligence, a job he held until the end of the war and the end of the OSS, October 1, 1945. Immersed in intelligence about foreign affairs, the work he says was inherently addictive.

"Our most important task," said Cline, "was putting in clear language with adequate analysis in many reports from Allen Dulles, the OSS Chief in Switzerland, who had good access to secret agents inside the German government and who managed to arrange in the spring of 1945 the early surrender of all German forces in Italy." [233]

Ray moved to the CIA in early summer, 1949. Ray Cline: "Scholars did have something to contribute in the way of evaluating the secrets discovered by spies." [234]

The highest-level analytical and estimative body in the CIA was the Office of National Estimates (ONE). The staff would review evidence and then write a summary of critical findings on a very broad strategic plane. In 1950 at the age of 32, Ray Cline became the Chief of the National Estimates Board. [235]

"The Berlin Tunnel project [Harvey's Hole] was a great undertaking of the mid-1950s," wrote Cline, "costing the CIA millions of dollars and providing reams of factual information on the USSR. It illustrates the way in which different intelligence functions overlap and supplement one another. Until the tunnel was uncovered in April 1956, most of the communication between East Berlin and the USSR had been recorded for many months and sent back to CIA Headquarters for processing and analysis. The take was voluminous and very useful for Soviet analysts in the economic, scientific, military, and current intelligence research staffs in the CIA." [236]

"This windfall came to us because a clandestine service unit in West Berlin had dreamed up the notion of tunneling under the border dividing the Soviet-controlled east sector of the city from the rest of Berlin. The task of translating and analyzing the messages was monumental. The combination of the talents of the DDP spies, the communications technicians, and the DDI scholars provided one of the best examples of what modern centralized intelligence in the CIA could accomplish," Ray Cline. [237]

Says Cline; "The National Security Act of 1947 which created the CIA said nothing about psychological warfare, covert action, or any secret operations. But there was an elastic, catch-all clause included: "such other functions and duties related to intelligence affecting the national security as the National Security Council may from time to time direct." The responsibility appeared to belong to CIA for meeting the Soviet challenge in those secret 'back alley' battles." [238]

"In mid-1954, the legend of the CIA's invincibility was confirmed in the minds of many by a covert action project in Guatemala that inched one step further toward paramilitary intervention. President Arbenz Guzman had expropriated the holdings of the powerful U.S.-owned United Fruit Company and was about to receive a boatload of Czechoslovakian arms, which was publicized by the State Department (headed by Foster Dulles). This touched off a six-week crisis in which political opponent Castillo Armas launched a desultory invasion of Guatemala supported by three P-47 fighter planes of World War II vintage flying from friendly Nicaraguan territory. The aircraft were provided by the CIA (headed by Allen Dulles) and flown by soldier-of-fortune pilots recruited by the CIA. With not much fighting, support for Arbenz Guzman and his government crumbled," Ray Cline. [239] (Foster Dulles and brother Allen Dulles had financial interest in United Fruit, which screams conflict of interest.)

The stories about the CIA's prowess in toppling regimes increased in volume. "In truth," said Cline, "only two political actions resulted in a change of regime undertaken in the Dulles era: Teheran, Iran and Guatemala City. The tragedy is that the concept of what the CIA was intended to be eventually became gravely distorted by the image projected as a result of the Iranian and Guatemalan capers. The romantic misconceptions were disastrous." [240]

"Having good intelligence is a source of great power," Ray

Cline. [241]

In the latter part of 1954, Eisenhower asked Dulles to prepare an estimate on the probable outcome of a war between the USSR and the United States. Dulles delegated General Bull, Bull chose Ray Cline to go to the Pentagon and actually write the paper. "I was detailed to the Pentagon to assist in preparing a Net Estimate on the USSR in 1954," said Cline. Ray Cline argued that the Pentagon's computer and war-gaming staff be used to create a computerized war-game, for the first time, as part of what would then be the most ambitious Net Estimate yet written. "We made some interesting discoveries," said Cline, "among them, that it was a pretty desperate move for the USSR to attack us with their substantially inferior long-range Air Force, and given the extensive U.S. radar tactical warning systems, it would have been impossible for the Soviets to have launched a surprise attack. Additionally, having discovered that with defensive radar, it is much more profitable to attack at lower levels, allowed the U.S. to ready our aircraft design for the future, well in advance of its time." Ray Cline wrote every word of that year's Net Estimate and Admiral Robbins presented it at the White House. Eisenhower insisted that all top officials of the Defense Department attend this special briefing. This all helped reduce the Soviet military threat in the minds of the U.S. war-planning staff. U.S. policy became based on strategic deterrence and politico-economic alliance-building as a way of containment. "The ideas are familiar now, but they once were new and hard to sell," says Cline. [242]

Cline's ties with the clandestine services became closer than ever before, especially with Dick Helms, the career leader of the intelligence collectors. "Dick and I began to exchange information and views on a regular basis. He handled several agents whose identity was very sensitive. We developed a personal relationship of mutual respect and confidence that lasted throughout the years. I valued this link with the clandestine services environment because it enriched my understanding of agent reporting and enabled me to suggest priorities for collection," said Ray Cline. [243]

Ray Cline was the head of the CIA's Office of Current Intelligence in the late 1950s when they were the first to identify that there was a serious split and tensions between the Soviets and the Chinese. Up to that point the communist movement was perceived by the west as one big monolithic force. This insight and change in thinking made an enormous difference and opened the door to an eventual normalization in relations and a variety of new diplomatic choices for the United States. [244]

It was the dawn of the missile age. Ray Cline had prepared a rather technical item on the Soviet's new "earth satellite vehicle" with guided missile. Dulles thought the President would not understand it and settled on a topic describing Khrushchev's reorganization of the Soviet bureaucracy. Cline rode over to the White House in Dulles's limousine. "You really think that missile test business is important, don't you?" I only had time to nod, reports Cline. Cline says he sat in a chair along the wall next to the door to the hall, ready to place visual charts on an easel and to answer questions if they got too technical for the DCI. On this occasion in 1957 Cline was transfixed, when Dulles ended his briefing with the statement that, "some disturbing new evidence about Soviet weapons was available, which he would like Dr. Cline to present." Cline sprang to his feet and explained. Later after Sputnik went up, Dulles told Cline he was exceedingly grateful that they had slipped that current intelligence item in when they did. [245]

Ray Cline began to formulate in his mind the notion of broadening his intelligence experience with a tour in the field. "The rarefied atmosphere of clandestine work intrigued me," he said. The DDI element of the CIA was comparable to that of the faculty of a university, the DDP spirit was more an action-oriented one. To be a station chief in the intelligence business is to feel yourself in command of troops at the front, sizing up opportunities and dangers on the spot, taking risks as necessary to achieve the results Headquarters wants." [246]

In 1957, Ray Cline was offered a post as chief of station in Taiwan. He supervised the CIA intelligence work there for almost five years, from early 1958 until June 1962. [247]

The CIA Taiwan station was the nerve center of CIA anti-China and other Asian operations in the 1950s and early 1960s. Cline became famous for his drunken binges with Chiang Ching-kuo, who became president of Taiwan. [248]

"The Bay of Pigs was the first great disaster to befall the CIA," says Ray Cline. "Happily," he says, "he was in the Far East at the time and was not involved with it. Cline went on to say, "**Vice President Nixon** was a strong proponent of an active program to topple the Castro regime. The project was the exclusive property of the DDP. **Dick Bissell**, the DDP, and his covert action chief assistant **Tracy Barnes**, managed the project in Washington and issued detailed orders to the field. Bissell and longtime Chief of Security Sheffield Edwards thought that they had been authorized to plan Castro's assassination. This was an unprecedented act for the CIA, it was not illogical to try to do it through the Mafia, since its former Havana gambling empire gave them some contacts to work with and since a gangland killing would be unlikely to be attributed to the U.S. Government," Ray Cline. [249] (This statement of course ignores the possibility of blackmail by the Mafia. This statement also ignores that the CIA and U.S. military had worked with the Mafia during World War II and the 1954 Guatemalan Coup.)

According to Ray Cline, "In January 1961, when preparations for the invasion were at their peak, Bissell ordered William Harvey, a veteran station chief, to set up a "standby capability" for what was called euphemistically "Executive Action," a capability for assassinating foreign leaders as a "last resort." Harvey was a colorful figure, a former FBI man who always carried a pistol when posted abroad, something unique among the CIA officers. I am sure he believed that it was patriotic, even moral, to kill a foreign ruler <u>when ordered to do so</u> by his superiors for reasons of U.S. security. Many of the romantic so-called "cowboy" types of covert action officers would have accepted this proposition, and in 1960-1961, many officials outside the CIA would have subscribed to it as well. In any event, the responsible officers in the CIA, Harvey, and Bissell, were convinced at the time that the White House had orally urged the creation of an assassination planning capability as a contingency precaution." [250]

In March of 1962, McCone called Ray Cline to Washington from Taiwan and offered him the position of Deputy Director of Intelligence (DDI). Here it is in Ray Cline's own words: Cline says in his book *The CIA Reality vs. Myth*: **"One compact I made with McCone was that he would consult me on Deputy Director of Plans (DDP) projects where an analytical DDI opinion might be helpful.** As far as I know he observed this understanding with scrupulous care. The only important thing the DDP became involved in during that period that I did not know of was the continued planning of the assassination of Castro. It is hard for me to understand how this could have happened without McCone's being told, as he clearly was not until August 1963." [251]

I know I have made this point before. I think that Richard Helms, the Deputy Director of Plans, the DDP, might not have appreciated the requirement of running everything that they were doing past Ray Cline, in a sense, almost requiring his blessing. This really puts Cline in the same position of power as the CIA Director himself. Given the incident with Plans and Angleton and Khrushchev's stolen speech, where Cline may have been perceived as going over his peer's heads to the Director to win his point, might not have scored too many points with Angleton and the guys in Plans.

On May 16, 1962, at age forty-four, President Kennedy appointed Ray Cline the Deputy Director of Intelligence.

The CIA's Ray Cline coined the terms "war hawks" and "Picasso doves." These labels were later passed along to the columnists Stewart Alsop and Charles Bartlett, who popularized them. [252] Thus, today's we have the saying: "hawks and doves" which originated with our Ray Cline.

In my research I kept running into people who were referring to "The Invisible Government." And I finally detected that there was a book by that same name that was copyrighted in 1964, the year following the assassination of President Kennedy.

In the book The Invisible Government we are told: The CIA is the biggest, most important, and most influential branch of the Invisible Government. The agency is organized into four divisions: Intelligence, Plans, Research, and Support, each headed by a deputy director.

The Plans Division oversaw the CIA's cloak-and-dagger activities, and it collects all the agency's covert intelligence through spies and informers. Allen Dulles was the first deputy director for plans. He was succeeded by Frank Wisner, who was replaced in 1958 by Bissell, who in turn was succeeded in 1962 by his deputy Richard Helms.

Cline and his subordinates prided themselves on their independence and detachment from operational problems.

They maintain that they evaluate information flowing in from the CIA Plans Division on an equal basis with intelligence coming in from elsewhere in the government. They contend that they do not have any ax to grind or any vested interest or operation to protect and, therefore, they produce the most objective reports of any branch of the government.

In other words, it sounds like Ray Cline's group has set themselves up in judgment of other's initiatives. Something the roll up your sleeves, do the dirty work, gung-ho, get the job done, can do guys in Plans might resent.

Here is where I first learned of Ray Cline's enormous power: The power of the CIA deputy director for intelligence was enlarged following the Bay of Pigs fiasco. Ray Cline was the first DDI to be informed about the secret operations of the Plans Division. Prior to Director McCone's rule, this was not the practice. (Please note how Ray Cline has set himself up with the CIA Director to render opinions about what the Plans side of the house, the DDP or Richard Helms, is doing. This puts Ray Cline in a real position of power. I can't imagine the DDP, Richard Helms, cared much for this arrangement.)

Cline's predecessor as DDI was never told in advance about the Bay of Pigs operation. And there was a feeling that President Kennedy might have abandoned the operation if all his intelligence advisers had not been sponsors and, therefore, devout advocates of the plan. Soon after McCone took office, he decided to change the system.

Perhaps the most important change decided upon by McCone was his instruction to the Plans Division to keep the Intelligence Division continuously posted on all its activities. Thereafter, the Intelligence Division received "sanitized" reports (names of agents removed) on all current operations. The intelligence analysts were thus in a position for the first time to contest the special pleading of the men who were running the operations. Based on the large pool of information available to them from all branches of the Invisible Government, they could recommend changes in or the complete cancellation of doubtful schemes. (I don't think this went over well with Plans.)

Although there is some interchange of personnel, a natural suspicion exists between the Plans Division, which tends to attract activists and risk-takers, and the Intelligence Division, which tends to attract academic and contemplative types.

In its political complexion, the CIA splits roughly along the lines of its major functional responsibilities. "The Intelligence side, the DDI" one veteran CIA official explained, "tends to be liberal. The other side of the house, the Plans side, the DDP has many ex-FBI types [like William King Harvey]. It tends to get more conservative people." [253]

On October 22, 1962, Ray Cline helped draft the President's speech opening up the situation to public knowledge [concerning the Cuban Missile Crisis]. In these years McGeorge Bundy felt free to show the closely held Khrushchev-Kennedy correspondence to Ray Cline as Deputy Director (Intelligence) at the CIA, for vetting, to garner any light it shed on Soviet policies and intentions. "It made it possible for me to guide intelligence output into matters directly germane to policy insights into Khrushchev's attitudes that my intelligence analysts needed to know. I cannot imagine a more intimate linking of intelligence in all functional categories with the highest-level policy decision-making. From that time on until Kennedy's death, McCone and I felt that we were on the first team at the White House." [254]

Ray Cline said, "I myself went to the United Nations in

New York shortly after Kennedy's speech to show the photographic evidence to friendly delegates and to assist in the drafting of Adlai Stevenson's speech of accusation delivered in the Security Council—the one with the dramatic offer to wait till hell freezes over for an honest answer from the Soviet delegate about missiles in Cuba." [255]

"I confess," said Cline, "I was not always pleased when President Kennedy called me up; he was usually angry about something he had read—more often than not in the newspaper rather than in our publications—and he always wanted categorical reassurance on some matter that sometimes was hard to give off the top of my head. I always felt in touch with White House concerns, however, and I nearly always accompanied McCone to National Security Council NSC meetings, often giving briefings on McCone's behalf." [256]

One night late in 1962 [after the missile crisis and the pledge by the Soviets to withdraw the missiles from Cuba] President Kennedy called Ray Cline to ask about the possibility that Soviet missiles were being hidden in caves in Cuba, I checked with the ORR geographers and economists who had formed a task force on Cuba and found that some conscientious soul had prepared a card index on every known cave in Cuba, with indications of size of entrance and suitability for storage of weapons—which they were sometimes used for. When we plunked that file down on the conference table in the Cabinet Room at the White House the next morning and said only a very few missiles could possibly fit into, or get through the entrances of these caves, the problem died right then. [257]

McCone and I talked a lot about the U.S. involvement in Vietnam, and we both agreed in advising that intervention there would pay only if the United States was prepared to engage in a long, difficult process of nation-building in South Vietnam to create the political and economic strength to resist a guerrilla war. The CIA's estimates and analytical papers in the entire Kennedy-Johnson era were soberer and less optimistic that those of the Defense Department, particularly those of McNamara, who in September 1963 predicted victory by the end of 1965. Desmond FitzGerald and I both tried to warn that an Asian guerrilla war was not to be easily won by conventional military forces and weapons, but the message did not get across very well. [258]

"The Kennedy team made a fateful mistake when they let **Averell Harriman**, Roger Hilsman (then Assistant Secretary for the Far East), and Ambassador Henry Cabot Lodge in Saigon encourage the Vietnamese armed forces to overthrow the strongest ruler Vietnam had found, President Ngo Dinh Diem. This State Department-supported coup resulted in the armed forces' murder of Diem on November 1, 1963, only a few weeks before Kennedy's own assassination. McCone and I and the local CIA station chief strongly oppose this course of action," Ray Cline.

**On instructions from Averell Harriman**.... The orders that ended in the deaths of Diem and his brother originated with Harriman... When President Kennedy learned of the murders, William Corson said, he was as "angry as I ever saw him, absolutely shaken." By 1963, according to Corson, **Harriman was running "Vietnam without consulting the president or the attorney general.**" In 1963 James Angleton was worried about Averell Harriman and had begun a highly secret counterintelligence investigation code name DINOSAUR. "There was a strong circumstantial case that Harriman was at least an agent of Soviet influence and maybe much worse," Angleton said. Angleton believed that the Vietnamese assassinations were designed to throw American policy in that country into chaos. [259] (This was a pretty gutsy move on Harriman's part, to ignore the wishes of a President. Harriman's gutsy bold move came on the same day that President Kennedy was in Chicago where the first assassination attempt was thwarted, and this also came just weeks before President Kennedy's assassination in Dallas. Notice how Ray Cline said he had strongly opposed the assassination of the leader of Vietnam.)

Following the Kennedy assassination, as the year 1965 began, President Johnson began a search to replace McCone, the Director of the CIA, who had resigned. One faction within the CIA supported Richard Helms; another faction supported Lyman Kirkpatrick, the Executive Director/Comptroller. McCone told Ray Cline, the Deputy Director for Intelligence, that he had recommended Richard Helms, Lyman Kirkpatrick, and Ray Cline. It's clear then, that the CIA was plumping for an intelligence professional, and preferably one who had worked his way up through the ranks. Johnson shocked everyone by abruptly announcing that the new Director of Central Intelligence would be Admiral William F. Raborn, a fellow Texan and prominent Johnson supporter.

Cline would collide once too often with the Admiral Raborn, and in 1966 he went to Helms and asked for a station overseas. Helms, who in 1966 exercised unprecedented control over the Agency as DDP, arranged for Cline's appointment as chief of station in Frankfurt, Germany. But before he left Washington, Cline went to see Clark Clifford at the President's Foreign Intelligence Advisory Board and told him that Raborn had to go. He told McGeorge Bundy the same thing. In June of 1966, the first intelligence professional to work his way up through the ranks to the top, Helms was given the job. [260]

The Deputy Director for Intelligence, Ray Cline was to the CIA what Knute Rockne was to Notre Dame -- coach, good old boy, and role model. [261]

Ray Cline left the CIA in 1969, and from 1969 to 1973, Ray Cline was director of the State Department's Bureau of Intelligence and Research under Henry Kissinger. <u>Terre Haute Tribune- Star, Mike McCormick, April 25, 1999</u>

Henry Kissinger called Ray Cline "one of our nation's most distinguished intelligence experts."

Cline usually returned to his hometown twice each year. Terre Haute lawyer Morris Blumberg, a classmate at Wiley and Harvard, remained a close friend. In 1972, Ray dedicated the Freedom Shrine at Terre Haute South Vigo High School. <u>Terre Haute Tribune-Star, Mike McCormick, April 25, 1999</u>

I was there. I attended South Vigo my Junior and Senior years. I remember walking down the hallway and running into the dedication ceremony that took place in the hallway near the front office of South Vigo. I remember leaning over to someone I knew that was standing next to me and saying, "Who are these old guys?" We were kind of irreverent back in those days, stupid too. I guess over time Ray Cline showed me just who the hell he was.

Ray Cline said, "Strategic intelligence is the thing that gets the shield to the right place at the right time. It is also the thing that stands ready to guide the sword." [262]

Ray Cline's association through WACL and the China Lobby and their association with names such as Clare Booth Luce, E. Howard Hunt, Lucien Conein, Guy Banister, the Gehlen spy network and numerous real original German Nazis is interesting, if not scary.

Ray Cline was a strong anti-communist. Harry L. Power is shown in the public record as a communist. Had Ray Cline been assassinated in the Terre Haute House, if there was ever any such plan to begin with, perhaps this would have resulted in the perception of the American people and the world that the assassination of Ray Cline was further proof of a wider communist/Castro conspiracy. Was there a plan? The CIA operative Robert Morrow said so when he said, "The Mob, the leaders of our nation, and our government's intelligence agencies **conspired together to assassinate very important people** [perhaps the CIA's Ray Cline?], including the President.

Were there others who would not have been to disappointed with the sudden demise of Ray Cline? The DDP, Deputy Director of Plans, side of the house contained the CIA's Richard Helms, Tracy Barnes, David Atlee Phillips, William Harvey, James Jesus Angleton, and E. Howard Hunt. Although the Deputy Director of Plans was supposedly reporting his activities, so that Ray Cline could have what the CIA termed "the wider view" of things. Requiring the DDP side to report to the DDI so soon after the Bay of Pigs fiasco might have seemed to the adults of the DDP like they were being treated like children who were now being required to tell mommy everything that they were doing. Would the DDP, side of the house miss reporting what they were doing to Ray Cline, the DDI? I don't think so. Add to this the simmering resentment of Angleton and of Plans toward Cline's having won the debate about what to do with the Khrushchev speech, which seems petty to us, but Angleton was still ranting about it years later.

If the guys in Plans planned the Kennedy assassination, who would have thought that the CIA would take out one of their own?

I haven't seen any evidence that Ray Cline knew how close he may have possibly come to being assassinated, but you can see how incredibly ironic the following story is:

In September 1977 Ray Cline, the former CIA Director William Colby, and David Atlee Phillips accepted invitations to a public discussion held at the University of Southern California. Following this event, Ray Cline, Phillips, and Colby had dinner with their host, Donald Freed. Freed reports that they ended up discussing when it was appropriate to assassinate someone. Ray Cline basically stated that "it was acceptable to kill anyone at any time if it seemed like a good idea at the time," or, as Cline would say, "if it was essential and served what he considered to be the national interest." [263] (Ray Cline might not have held this opinion had he known how close he may have come to being such.)

# RAY S. CLINE AND WILLIAM KING HARVEY

So, here we have two CIA agents, both from Terre Haute, Indiana, both graduates of Wiley High School. William Harvey graduated in 1931. Ray Cline graduated in 1935. From that point on they each took quite opposite approaches to life. It is not known whether they knew that they had each attended the same high school, or even knew that they were from the same town. William Harvey's wife C.G. knew Ray Cline personally and said to Mike McCormick, "if Bill knew that Ray Cline was from Terre Haute and had attended Wiley High School, he didn't share it with me." I have seen many comments by Ray Cline about Harvey, yet none of them reference the hometown connection that they shared, which leads me to believe that Cline didn't know either. I wonder if anything would have been any different had they known, or not known?

Both men were nearly exact opposites. Both men rose to the top in their careers and the very top of the CIA. Both were very intelligent. Both had very different skill sets. In researching this story, it absolutely amazed me that out of the thousands of CIA employees and with hundreds if not thousands of books written about the CIA, how many stories and situations came up that dealt with William King Harvey and how many times quotes and explanations came up referencing Ray Cline. Bill Harvey made history and was sworn never to explain it. Ray Cline primarily analyzed and explained history, but also had a hand in making it. It made me wonder if anyone else besides these two were even doing anything productive at the CIA of any significance or relevance.

Cline appears to be more the scholar, and the historian who stepped back and analyzed the information in an attempt to determine what was reality and how to deal with it. Bill Harvey was reality, the go to guy for the tough stuff. The guy who rolled up his sleeves and caused things to happen. Bill Harvey was also the guy who could quote poetry from memory, for hours on end to his daughter. Both were very intelligent and giants in their field. Both found their way through life, Bill Harvey without a father and Ray Cline from the humblest of beginnings.

Bill Harvey was among the first three intelligence agents to take on Soviet spies in the U.S. for the FBI. Hoover turned to Bill Harvey to try and demonstrate the FBI's ability to catch Soviet spies when Hoover was hoping to turn the FBI into the nation's international intelligence service. Hoover apparently initially relied on Bill Harvey as his eyes and ears in the CIA. Harvey's tunnel, or "Harvey's Hole" as it is often referred to, generated tons of information for Ray Cline to analyze. When Berlin was the hot spot, Harvey was there. When the pressure was on the CIA concerning Cuba, Harvey was there. When the dirty job of assassinations came about, he was there. Harvey and his operation played a significant role in gathering evidence concerning the missiles going into Cuba. Bill Harvey requested the U-2 photos of the suspected missiles in Cuba and Ray Cline presented the results to the President. As regards the Kennedy assassination, the questions are, was William King Harvey involved, not involved, or setup to look like he was involved?

One thing can be said, no one ever questioned the loyalty and dedication of William King Harvey, or of Ray S. Cline, to their country. Something that cannot be said for many of the other power-hungry characters in this story whose only interest appears to be their own selfish self-centered interest.

## HARRY POWER AND/OR THE RIFLE, EITHER ONE SIGNIFICANT?

Harry L. Power and Lee Harvey Oswald, as you have seen, have a lot of similar characteristics in the public record, nearly a page and a half of them. Richard Case Nagell said that the guy who left a rifle in Terre Haute was significant.

Keep in mind that apparently most all players in the spy business are on a need-to-know basis. Here is an example: Bill Harvey enlisted Ted Shackley [the head of JM/WAVE] for the drop-off of weapons to mobster John Rosselli as part of the effort to kill Castro. Shackley later asserted: "I knew virtually nothing of substance concerning Harvey's relationship with Rosselli. I never met the gangster—not even when I accompanied Harvey to the parking lot. Bill simply asked me to obtain a shopping list of weapons. I had no need to know," Shackley explained. [264]

Ted Shackley once said, "Back in Berlin it had taken me nearly two years to learn about the tunnel that engineers, under Harvey's direction, had driven into the Soviet sector. If I didn't need to know about something, I wasn't told." [265]

Straight-and-true Company officers did not ask why. They respected the cherished principle of compartmentalization: only those who need to know are told the details. "Unless you were a fool," said Shackley, "you did not ask questions of Bill Harvey." [266] (My point being: If someone told a young intelligence agent to show around a card and claim that it was a "Young Communist League" card, or to leave a rifle in a hotel in Indiana, well they might not know all the ramifications. None of us would, especially a young twenty-year old on a need-to-know basis.)

Oswald appears to have been an intelligence operative of some kind, Harry does too. The CIA admitted losing some 37 documents on Oswald and they opened his 201 file a full year after his defection to the Soviet Union in Angleton's CI/SIG division. The creation of the 201 file did not occur in the Soviet Russia Division of the CIA, were many CIA employees suspect it would have been, or should have been created.

It appears from the evidence presented that Bobby Kennedy was running the show and that included operations to get Castro. Following the assassination, Bobby Kennedy reportedly picked up the phone, made a call to anti-Castro Cuban Harry Williams, and said, "one of your guys did it." We might draw from this that it is possible that Bobby Kennedy recognized who Lee Harvey Oswald was and who, or what, he might have been involved with. If the allegation from both Nagell and Rosselli is true, that an operation that Bobby Kennedy was running to get Castro flipped and got his brother and given that Lee Harvey Oswald is the only confirmed person in the assassination story who might have flipped and gotten President Kennedy, then Oswald would have to have been a part of Bobby Kennedy's operation. Bobby Kennedy might have recognized the name Harry L. Power for the very same reasons.

If it is true that the Kennedys were involved in the dirty business of killing people, then I hope that efforts were not made to save the Kennedy family name at the expense of the American people's trust of their government, but I'm afraid that it was.

If Harry L. Power was a part of this operation and playing a similar role as Lee Harvey Oswald, then it would stand to reason that we might find artifacts of information like the possibility that a person whose name sounded like ~~Ower~~ Power might have had contact with Luisa Calderon. If

Oswald and Power were playing similar roles, then it would be logical that they would appear in the public record very similarly. Nagell who had been sent into the field to check on Oswald and the Cubans said that **Harry Power and the rifle that was left in a hotel in Terre Haute, Indiana was significant**.

I am sure in Harry Power's mind, as evidenced in his statement in the first two paragraphs of this book, that whatever Harry was doing was far removed from what might appear on the surface and how lucky he was back then, that those who might have jumped to conclusions didn't come to know what was placed in the public record and later revealed about him. Because back then people were looking for a shooter for the knoll, combined with Harry's alleged Cuban intelligence connections, and his alleged association with Oswald and that it might appear that he came to Terre Haute to get the CIA guy Ray Cline, combined with an intelligence operative Richard Case Nagell who said, "that Harry was significant," well let's just say Harry is very lucky that what had been placed in the public record and now known about him was not better known back then.

The rifle left in Terre Haute certainly does fit in so many ways, the length, the description, etc. It fits so much better than the old rusty Italian rifle on size alone, let alone everything else that we have seen. What did Dial Ryder say, "if he put a scope on a rifle for a guy named Oswald it was an Argentine rifle." What did the Select Committee choose to picture in their twelve-volume study to represent a German Mauser? The answer: A German Mauser Argentine 1891 rifle. The same rifle as was left in Terre Haute, Indiana, only the Select Committee's picture showed one that was unmodified, or un-sportsterized.

If it someday turns out that the rifle was left as a warning, either Harry L. Power and/or the rifle had to be significant.

# QUESTIONS

**When I began this quest, my questions where:**

- Was this incident in Terre Haute related to the Kennedy assassination?

- Was Harry L. Power a real person, or was someone using an alias?

- Was the rifle and or Harry Power of significance?

- Why Terre Haute?


**Now the questions become:**

- Did William King Harvey plan, or participate in, the assassination of President Kennedy?

- Was William King Harvey an innocent bystander who had nothing to do with the assassination of President Kennedy? But Harvey's past assets were used.

- Was William King Harvey framed to look guilty by Philby and/or Angleton and/or the Boys from the Guatemalan Coup/Bay of Pigs?

## WHO WAS JAMES JESUS ANGLETON?

Just a few more words about James Jesus Angleton and Kim Philby. Angleton was sometimes called "the Black Knight," "the Cadaver," and "the Poet." When he was in the field he went by the name of Hugh Ashmead. Helms would call Angleton a "strange, strange man." Angleton was a strange, twisted fellow, whose drinking problem description matched and then surpassed that of William King Harvey. Angleton is reported to have gotten to the point where he couldn't even bend over and tie his own shoes.

In Anthony Summers' book about J. Edgar Hoover, *Official and Confidential*, Summers showed how Meyer Lansky, a top Mafia figure had blackmail power over J. Edgar Hoover through possession of a photo showing Hoover and his associate Clyde Tolson together sexually. [267]

Angleton had the same photos and claimed they had been taken around 1946.

Angleton was known to have bugs all over town. Indeed, just about everyone in the Agency who knew Angleton came to fear him and to avoid crossing his path. Angleton was called "no-knock" because he had unprecedented access to senior agency officials. He wouldn't knock, he would just walk right in.

Angleton always came alone and had this aura of secrecy about him, something that made him stand out—even among other secretive CIA officers. In those days, there was a general CIA camaraderie, but Jim made himself exempt from this. He was a loner who worked alone.

Angleton knew that knowledge was power. So not only

would he go to extraordinary lengths to obtain such, but he would also lord his knowledge over others, especially incoming CIA directors. He was utterly contemptuous of the chain of command. He was a master at waiting to see the new director alone—on his own terms and with his own agenda. [268]

**Angleton's most powerful patrons were Allen Dulles and Richard Helms.** There was often a significant failure of executive control over Angleton's activities. Actions were performed without bureaucratic interference. The simple fact is that if Angleton wanted something done, it was done.

Counterintelligence was a unit that conducted operations, not just research. For that reason, the CI staff resided inside the Directorate of Plans (DDP) and not on the analytical side of the agency. In addition to counterintelligence, Angleton oversaw the FBI - CIA liaison relationship, and he had the sole control of the intelligence relationship with Israel and its intelligence service, the Mossad. [269]

Angleton's power within the CIA was enormous. Angleton's power outside the CIA was equally impressive given his connections.

Staff D was an enigma within the DDP. Was Angleton's counterintelligence involved with Bill Harvey's infamous Staff D? The answer is yes and can be found in Joseph B. Smith's book, *Portrait of a Cold Warrior*. Smith wrote he was given Staff D clearance by the CI staff. "No one got a Staff D clearance unless Angleton's people were satisfied. Not only did Staff D attempt coups, but Staff D also attempted assassinations."

In HSCA testimony, the CIA's Whitten said that Angleton was involved with the Mob:

The Department of Justice asked the CIA to help provide the

true names on numbered bank accounts in Panama because the Mafia was depositing money there...skimmed off the top from Las Vegas. "And we [CIA] were, indeed, in an excellent position to do this and told them so, whereupon Mr. Angleton vetoed the idea and said that is the Bureau's business." "I told J.C. King this and he smiled a foxy smile and said 'Well, that's Angleton's excuse. The real reason is that Angleton himself has ties to the Mafia and he would not want to double cross them...'"

Whitten went on to say: "I do believe that I have heard that Angleton was one of those several people in the Agency who were trying to use the Mafia in Cuban operations."

Angleton developed a fearsome reputation within the agency. He was known to deliberately expose agents he no longer trusted, even when exposure could cost the life of the agent. [270]

Could Angleton have planned or been involved in the assassination? ZR/RIFLE was supposedly a pet project of Angleton's. If anyone should have known about Oswald and his defection to the Soviet Union it should have been the CIA's head counterintelligence officer, James Jesus Angleton.

Angleton was extremely close to Kim Philby. Philby trained him in counterintelligence in England early in his career and he was constantly with Philby when Philby was posted here in the United States. That is, up until the time that Bill Harvey exposed Philby as a Soviet spy and accused Angleton of the same. As we saw in the affidavit from the two investigators in Banister's office, Philby was reportedly working with Robert Kennedy leading up to the assassination.

Angleton was told that Philby was a communist, a year before Bill Harvey figured it out. Think of the damage Philby would have been able to do in that length of time. This alone raises serious questions about Angleton's loyalty.

Was Philby well positioned to manipulate Angleton psychologically? I think so.

In a note to Robert Crowley, Angleton wrote, "There was not an hour that I did not think of the damage he [Philby] could do after he defected." For Angleton, the paranoia was heightened by the death of the President and by Philby's betrayal. **Angleton later said, "I came to believe that the events that would lead to my own downfall at the CIA and the successful cover-up of <u>the Soviets' involvement in the Kennedy murder was orchestrated by Philby</u>."**

Okay, let's stop right there. So now we have Angleton, Jack Martin, and David Lewis all on record as having said that Kim Philby "orchestrated the assassination of President Kennedy" and Frank Sturgis has said that "his theory was that the assassination itself involved groups of agents in Russia's KGB, Cuban intelligence and the CIA."

Rufina Philby, who married Kim Philby in Russia, years after the assassination, wrote a book in 1999 detailing her husband's continued contact with Soviet intelligence officials until his death on May 11, 1988. In her book, Rufina Philby reveals that Kim Philby was subject to close scrutiny rather than being revered by the Russians. It appears they feared he might divulge significant state secrets. [271]

James Jesus Angleton requested and then was put in charge of the CIA portion of the Warren Commission investigation.

Angleton seems to be the one running around trying to keep everything in check. Examples include Mary Meyer was one of President Kennedy's mistresses and Mary Meyer had also been married to the CIA's Cord Meyer. Mary supposedly knew too much and was murdered. Newspaperman, Ben Bradley caught Angleton attempting to break into Mary Meyer's studio following her murder in search of her diary. Mary Meyer was Ben Bradley's sister-in-law. Ben Bradley later found the diary and turned it over to Angleton. When the CIA's Mexico City Station Chief, Win Scott suddenly died, Angleton immediately flew to Mexico City and demanded from Scott's family the contents of Win Scott's safe. Win Scott had just finished a draft of a book about events surrounding Lee Harvey Oswald from when Lee was in Mexico City.

Gordon Novel participated in "the most patriotic munitions burglary in history down in New Orleans." Gordon Novel apparently had ties with both 544 Camp Street, and the CIA. Gordon Novel said that in 1967 when he was suing District Attorney Jim Garrison, J. Edgar Hoover wanted him to drop the suit and the Johnson administration, and the CIA wanted him to pursue it. Novel claims that Angleton showed him sexually compromising pictures of J. Edgar Hoover with his assistant Clyde Tolson, so that Novel could use this knowledge as leverage on Hoover. **The point I want to make here is Angleton's involvement and association with Gordon Novel.** I have also read that the Nixon White House later talked to Novel about the possibility of Novel working with them to erase the recording tapes involved in the Watergate scandal.

Angleton continued to rant years later concerning Ray Cline following the Khrushchev speech argument, which Cline won, and Angleton lost.

E. Howard Hunt detailed the existence of a small CIA assassination team in an interview with the *New York Times* while in prison in December 1975 for his role in Watergate. The assassination squad, allegedly headed by Col. Boris Pash, was ordered to eliminate suspected double agents and low-ranking officials. Pash's assassination unit was assigned to Angleton.

During the Warren Commission, Angleton met regularly with a member of the commission-Allen Dulles. Dulles briefed Angleton about the direction of the investigation. Angleton in turn briefed his closest aide, Raymond Rocca who was the CIA's official liaison with the commission. [272]

At the time of Angleton's forced retirement there were more than forty 1,000-pound safes located in the Counterintelligence section of the CIA. Much of their contents had not been shared with the CIA's main filing system.

The team who replaced Angleton found little to no evidence of the recruitment of foreign agents, did not find any active counterintelligence operations, and no penetration of the opposing side. What they did find in one of the safes was what turned out to be twenty outstanding leads on GRU agents being run by the Soviets throughout the world, which the FBI had turned over to Angleton years earlier. What did Angleton do with them? He sat on them for up to ten years and did nothing. [273]

Angleton had even smuggled out and delivered to the Soviet defector Golitsyn enough classified CIA records to fill a couple of station wagons.

Both William Harvey and Claire Petty suspected Angleton at one time or the other of having crossed over to the dark side, the Soviet side. Both Bill Harvey and Claire Petty had proven track records for spotting Soviet spies. It would not surprise me at all if Angleton and Philby had a hand in planning and coordinating the assassination of President Kennedy and attempted to set William King Harvey up for the fall. On the other hand, it would also not surprise me if Angleton called upon Bill Harvey to help in the operation. [274]

One high-ranking SDECE (French Intelligence) officer,

Leonard Houneau said, "Angleton was a madman and an alcoholic. He was trying to set us against one another." [275]

Angleton made a bizarre statement to the *New York Times* on Christmas Eve 1974, regarding the secrets that he possessed. "A mansion has many rooms and there were many things going on ... I'm not privy to who struck John." When asked, what he meant by that statement, Angleton volunteered, "It had nothing, the 'John' does not refer to John F. Kennedy." Angleton had not been asked if it did. [276]

One nagging little detail that bothers me is how on the 26th of November 1967, almost exactly four years after the assassination, James Jesus Angleton was reported in a CIA document as having bumped into William King Harvey and Johnny Rosselli at a hotel in Washington. In 1967 Rosselli was pressuring the CIA to intervene in the U.S. Government's attempt to deport him. Either this meeting is an amazing coincidence, or Angleton felt compelled to be involved in yet another suspicious incident, for some reason.

It was Angleton who ran the false defector program. The Church Committee concluded that counterintelligence was the "focal point" of Oswald's employment with the CIA. [277]

Judyth Vary Baker claims to have been romantically involved with Lee Oswald and appears to have been seeing Lee Harvey Oswald when Lee was in New Orleans. Judyth Vary Baker said in her book, *Me & Lee,* Lee Oswald told her "He believed the odds of his leaving Russia alive were about 50/50. And, if he did make it out, his own boss might have him arrested." Lee said his name was "Jesus," letting the irony speak for itself. Judyth spells it out for us in her footnotes saying, **"One of Lee's CIA handlers when he went to the USSR was James "Jesus" Angleton."** [278]

Reports on Oswald were going to several different locations within the CIA. Who in the CIA had **access to all the**

**reports on Oswald**? The answer: **Angleton's CI/SIG** which, in conjunction with the Security Office, had all the pieces to the Oswald puzzle. [279]

The *Sunday News Journal*, August 20, 1978, by Joe Trento and Jacquie Powers reported seeing a 1966 CIA memo that placed E. Howard Hunt in Dallas Nov. 22, 1963, the day of the assassination. The memo was initialed by Richard M. Helms, former CIA director, and James J. Angleton, former counterintelligence chief. As evidenced by the memo, three years after the assassination (1966) apparently Helms and Angleton felt it necessary to discuss covering up the fact that Hunt had been in Dallas. Helms and Angleton felt that a cover story, giving Hunt an alibi for being elsewhere the day of the assassination, "ought to be considered." E. Howard Hunt was in Dallas the day of the assassination.

Author Lisa Pease take on Angleton's motive at the time of the release of this memo, "the noose was closing in on Angleton and his counterintelligence group in relation to Oswald. The more people dug into Oswald's past, the more often Angleton and his associates kept appearing. I believe Angleton was feeling the pinch, and possibly fearing that the assassination was about to be pinned on himself, moved to show that **the assassination's chain of conspirators went even higher, to Helms himself**." [280]

During a *Spotlight versus Howard Hunt* deposition, Richard Helms was asked, if it was "reasonably possible that Mr. Angleton could have either engineered the Kennedy assassination or set the wheels in motion to cover it up, or withhold information as a vest-pocket operation, that is without the knowledge of you as director or his immediate superior?"

Helms's reply is not a ringing denial, nor did he answer the questions. He said, "I don't believe it is likely that Mr.

Angleton (a) would have wanted to assassinate President Kennedy, or (b) that he would have taken off from the agency and done this without anybody's being aware of it." This is not a denial by Helms of Angleton's involvement. (a) Angleton might not have wanted to assassinate President Kennedy, but he and Dulles and Helms could have been forced into doing it, given other's knowledge of their past, especially concerning the Nazis (which I will get to later) and (b) if Allen Dulles or Richard Helms had been aware of the operation, then Angleton would not have acted alone and the second part of Helms statement would also be true. In other words, Angleton didn't embark on this on his own.

The most consistently prominent players in the assassination saga continues to be James Jesus Angleton and his counterintelligence staff. They held a file on Oswald predating the assassination by at least three years. After the assassination, Angleton and his closest associate, Ray Rocca, served as the gatekeeper between the Warren Commission and the CIA. If anyone was in a position to move Oswald around prior to the assassination and control the cover-up afterwards, it was Angleton. [281]

Angleton's actions had a significant impact on the operations of the Central Intelligence Agency, effectively bringing it to a halt. If this had been the goal of the Soviet's, then they certainly succeeded.

Two men, who had headed the CIA Soviet Bloc Division at different times, would make the same point. "If I were to pick a Soviet agent at the Agency [a mole], it would be Angleton for all the harm he has done. Everything that had gone wrong could be traced to Angleton. He is the guy who is perfectly placed." **The Soviets had penetrated the counterintelligence operations of the British with Kim Philby (close friend of Angleton's)** and of the Germans with Heinz Felfe. **Why not the CIA with James Jesus Angleton?**

The defection of Anatoliy Golitsyn, who refused to cooperate with anyone other than Angleton, adds to the suspicion surrounding Angleton. It appears the KGB had specifically targeted Golitsyn for Angleton's use, resulting in many ruined CIA careers, the paralysis of the espionage operations against the Soviet Union and straining relations with friendly intelligence services.

Angleton's handling of other defectors, such as Nosenko, also raised concerns. Despite Nosenko's providing some fifty leads, Angleton simply dismissed them as false and referred to them as "giveaways." "Giveaways" are less important spies that one side is willing to give away in order to protect a very valuable asset from being discovered. "If Nosenko was giving away this many throwaways in order to protect something much bigger," a senior CIA officer commented, "then this mythical character would have to be pretty damn big," implying it was Angleton. Some members of the CIA believed that these fifty some leads were genuine and could have potentially led to significant discoveries and should have been pursued.

Angleton made a crucial mistake by assigning Claire Petty, one of his counterintelligence officers, to investigate Soviet moles and penetration of the CIA. Petty's comprehensive examination of CIA records and history led him to believe that Angleton himself was working for the Soviets. Petty concluded that Angleton had ceased genuine counterintelligence activity after 1962, monopolizing the resources and attention of the CIA's counterintelligence and Soviet Division. This resulted in a stagnation of operations, a halt in recruitment efforts and inaction on valuable leads that ended up hidden away in Angleton's personal safes, unshared with anyone in the CIA.

Claire Petty had a notable track record for identifying spies, having previously uncovered Heinz Felfe as a major Soviet penetration of West German intelligence. Of course, Bill Harvey was the first to suspect Angleton way back in 1951. Petty has said, "I think Bill Harvey found it very difficult to believe that Angleton did not understand what Philby was up to."[282]

Angleton was safe while Helms was Director, but the war in Vietnam was rapidly altering the face of the Agency, the gathering political faction for détente were beginning to undermine the foundations of Cold War suspicion upon which Angleton's empire was built.[283]

William Colby became director of the CIA in 1974. Colby was not a fan of Angleton and given that Colby was an experienced intelligence officer, having worked in Vietnam; he was not easily misled by Angleton.

On December 22, 1974, the New York Times published a major article identifying Angleton—as the mastermind of a massive and illegal spy campaign against antiwar and civil rights activists. The source for the story was William Colby.

When the story went public, Colby summoned Angleton to his office and told him he would have to leave the agency. He also summarily fired Ray Rocca, Scotty Miler, and other Angleton loyalists within Counterintelligence. It was at this moment that Angleton made one of his most famous statements: "A mansion has many rooms…I'm not privy to Who Struck John." The comment itself was recorded in the *New York Times.*

Later in a court of law, under oath Angleton was asked what that phrase meant, Angleton said, "The 'John' does not refer to John F. Kennedy." But, as Mark Lane has pointed out, "He had not been asked if it did." It is possible that Angleton was firing a shot across Colby's and the CIA's bow as to knowledge of the CIA's role in the assassination. The implication appears to be, "Take me down, and I will take you with me." [284]

Angleton did not clear out his desk, climb into his black Mercedes, and drive away from Langley until almost a year after his resignation. According to Robert Crowley, "Angleton arranged with a handful of trusted friends, including Crowley, to carry the most important counterintelligence files he possessed away from Langley in their briefcases." By the time Angleton's successors took possession of his office, the counterintelligence files in the special room next door had been sanitized. [285]

CIA Director Colby claimed that he did not think that Angleton was a Soviet spy. However, Colby did fire Angleton because he felt Angleton was doing more harm than good. Angleton's top aides, Rocca, Miler, and Hood also left.

Colby might be right; Angleton might not have been a Soviet agent. In the book *Ratlines, How the Vatican's Nazi Network Betrayed Western Intelligence to the* Soviets, the authors Mark Aarons and John Loftus wrote: "There was what Moscow called a 'useful idiot' in the CIA, not a witting Communist agent, but a person who helps his enemy without realizing it. His name was James Jesus Angleton." [286]

Angleton's resignation was announced at the morning staff meeting. Angleton casually lit a cigarette, and then spoke about what some called his "nature of the threat" speech—dire predictions, grim warnings, and suspicion of détente. [287]

It is interesting to note that Soviet leader Nikita Khrushchev's immediate impression following the assassination of President Kennedy was, "that the enemies of détente had succeeded in undermining their initiative." [288]

James Jesus Angleton said, "I realize how I have wasted my

existence, my professional life. Do you know how I got to be in charge of counterintelligence? I agreed not to polygraph or require detailed background checks on Allen Dulles and 60 of his closest friends. They were afraid that their own business dealings with Hitler's pals would come out. They were too arrogant or had no choice but to hope that the Russians wouldn't discover it all. The real problem, there was no accountability. Fundamentally, the founding fathers of U.S. intelligence were liars. The better you lied and the more you betrayed, the more likely you would be promoted. These people attracted and promoted each other. Outside of their duplicity, the only thing they had in common was a desire for absolute power. I failed to protect the CIA, because there was no real desire to secure the place from the Soviets. I never understood the great advantage the Russians had over us.... As Americans we just hold no real value in secrecy. God, it was such a simple explanation." [289]

Angleton died of cancer on May 11, 1987.

## WHO PLACED BILL HARVEY IN THE PUBLIC RECORD

We know a lot about the CIA's William King Harvey and James Jesus Angleton as a result of the book: "*Wilderness of Mirrors*" written by David C. Martin. In the forward of his book David Martin says: "It was from Angleton, that I first heard some of the more colorful stories about Bill Harvey. **Angleton served as the source of information about Harvey.** Harvey always hung up on me when I called, although I did manage a brief conversation with his wife some months after he died."[290]

Author David Martin wrote a letter dated June 19, 1977, to a prospective CIA source indicating that, "the book *Wilderness of Mirrors* was initially intended to be specifically 'about Bill Harvey.'" According to a Security Analysis Group, CIA memo dated July 14, 1977, it says "retired CIA employee **David Atlee Phillips appears to be working with the author David Martin**, resulting in the book '*Wilderness of Mirrors*'" (which firmly placed William Harvey in the public record. David Atlee Phillips was a master of deception, misdirection, psy-ops, he was at the time of the Bay of Pigs the propaganda chief and had been involved in the CIA's Guatemalan Coup of 1954.)

**This conscious effort by the CIA's David Atlee Phillips and James Jesus Angleton to put Harvey in the public record** via the book "*Wilderness of Mirrors*" is more than just interesting it was deliberate. Someone who I believe knows intelligence work once said to me: "If it is published, it is published for a reason." Did you notice how Phillips's and Angleton's role unfolded in this story? It leads me to ask: What might have been Phillips's and Angleton's motive for helping to shine the spotlight on William King Harvey? In fact, we might find it very helpful to ask on what dates in time did information concerning the Kennedy assassination come to light (particularly in 1967). Far more effort seems to have gone into placing the blame on various people and various organizations, to make them appear to have been involved in the assassination, with far lesser effort required for the assassination itself.

The book *Wilderness of Mirrors* is the book, which all books written about Angleton and Harvey draw from heavily, including this one. The main source of information on Harvey came from Angleton and David Phillips. In the book William King Harvey ends up being portrayed in a less than flattering light when it came to his drinking and weight. My point is that Angleton and others in intelligence work are masters at disinformation and media manipulation and the book *Wilderness of Mirrors* was probably an attempt on Angleton's and Phillips's part to portray Harvey in a less than favorable light, or to shine some light on Harvey who otherwise would have been an obscure, if not invisible character in history. The author David C. Martin, did however, manage to relate an excellent story despite what Angleton and Phillips might have intended.

In the book "Conspiracy," by Anthony Summers on page 528, there is a section entitled: "Who planned the assassination." Writes Summers: In the closing stages of the Assassinations Committee's (HSCA) mandate, some staff members felt that, while Mafia marksmen may have carried out the assassination, it could only have been orchestrated by someone in American intelligence, someone with special knowledge of Oswald's background. Investigators gave renewed attention to the senior CIA officer who coordinated the CIA-Mafia plots against Castro-William Harvey. [291]

Anthony Summers did not know about the rifle that was left in Terre Haute. I think that information might have reinforced his theory.

Gerry Hemming may have given us the answer to some of the mysteries of the assassination. The CIA furnished a picture it claimed was of Oswald outside of the Cuban Embassy at a time when Oswald was in Mexico City, however the individual in the picture is not Oswald. Hemming identified the Mexico City mystery man shown in the picture as German born Mario Tauler Sague, recruited for the CIA by Bill Harvey while Harvey was the Berlin station chief. Sague was involved in one of the earliest attempts on Castro's life, said Hemming. [292] (Hemming was a singleton for Angleton, so once again this information offered up by Hemming may be another attempt to tie Bill Harvey into the assassination story. Guilt by association.)

The release of this picture of German born Mario Tauler Sague outside the Cuban Embassy strikes me as interesting and significant. "A," the CIA, as a hard and fast rule that generally protects its agents and operatives from exposure. Why would they release a picture of one of their own operatives? And "B," you would think that they would recognize the picture of one of their own operatives and not mistakenly declare him to be Oswald. The CIAs David Atlee Phillips releasing the picture of one of William King Harvey's operatives. Was this a deliberate attempt by Phillips to point a finger at Bill Harvey, or an attempt to frame Bill Harvey, by insinuating that Bill Harvey may have been involved with what was going on down in Mexico City?

In April of 2007, Andy Alderton called me and told me about that month's Rolling Stone magazine and on page 52, E. Howard Hunt's son, St. John Hunt, relates how his dad had written out for him who was involved in the assassination.

At the top of the list was **Lyndon Johnson** followed by **Cord Meyer, David Atlee Phillips** (both CIA, at the time of the assassination Cord Meyer was head of Covert Actions in the CIA Plans Division, Phillips had been involved in Guatemalan Coup and the Bay of Pigs. When Lee Harvey Oswald visited Mexico City, Phillips was stationed there. Cuban assassin **Antonio Veciana** (who is also on Hunts list) has now come out and said that Phillips, aka Bishop, introduced him to Oswald in Dallas prior to the assassination. Oswald's New Orleans girlfriend, Judyth Vary Baker says that Lee Oswald told her that Phillips was his contact in the field. Phillips admitted to his brother that he was in Dallas on the day JFK was killed. At the time Phillips may have been in charge of ZR/Rifle.) Also on the list: **William K. Harvey**, **Frank Sturgis** (CIA/Mafia connections. Sturgis ended up in jail as one of the Watergate burglars. Sturgis is quoted as saying Watergate was a part of the JFK cover-up, Sturgis thought the KGB, DGI, and CIA were all involved in the assassination), **David Morales** (CIA, had been posted in Germany and worked under William Harvey and Ted Shackley out of the Miami JM/WAVE station as the chief of paramilitary operations. Additionally, Morales was a part of the Guatemalan Coup of 1954 and Bay of Pigs operation), and finally on the list a French gunman.

St. John explained in the article that LBJ connected with Cord Meyer, Cord Meyer recruited David Atlee Phillips, who brings in William Harvey and Antonio Veciana. Veciana meets with Oswald in Mexico City... Then Veciana meets w/ Frank Sturgis in Miami and enlists David Morales in anticipation of killing JFK in Miami.

World Exclusive: E. Howard Hunt: JFK Assassination Revelations –P1 from YouTube (InfoWars.com). "You have said that David Phillips apparently meets with Oswald in Mexico City?" Hunt: "Yeah. Before the assassination." "You have said that Bill Harvey may very well have recruited French or Corsican gunmen?" Hunt: "Yeah." "To shoot and you have also said that Cord Meyer had a motive in that his wife Mary Meyer was having an affair with John F. Kennedy?" Hunt: "I heard from Frank [Sturgis?] that LBJ had designated Cord Meyer Jr. to undertake a larger organization while keeping it totally secret."

Hunt contends in the YouTube video that William Harvey did this for LBJ, because LBJ would then be able to advance William Harvey's position in life, however, I would doubt this, as there is no evidence following the assassination that LBJ did anything for Bill Harvey. As we have seen Bill Harvey is forced out or asked to retire from the CIA and E. Howard Hunt supposedly retires from the CIA and ends up working for President Nixon. On the other hand, David Phillips, Ted Shackley-head of the JM/WAVE Miami Station, Desmond Fitzgerald, and Richard Helms careers advanced quite nicely. E. Howard Hunt was a part of the Guatemalan Coup and Bay of Pigs operations of which Bill Harvey was not a member. E. Howard Hunt was also very close to Allen Dulles and Richard Helms. The plan by this group was probably to pin the blame on Bill Harvey. Especially since Bill Harvey slighted the Guys from Guatemala/Bay of Pigs when he took over the Cuban operations and cut them out of the picture.

Hunt: "He **[Harvey] had been a deputy to Angleton** and very deeply involved in counter-espionage activities." (Note how Hunt doesn't mention that Bill Harvey pretty much reported to Richard Helms, not Angleton. Interesting how Hunt leaves Helms out of the picture.)

"Do you think that it is possible, that while he [William Harvey] was in Rome that he might have recruited a Corsican assassin to kill Kennedy?" Hunt: "Yes! It is possible. It is one thing to set yourself up in splendid isolation [Rome] and it is another thing to use that isolation as a tool so that you're not an immediate suspect in the case of a capital crime." (This is an important point. Where was Bill Harvey in the period leading up to and during the assassination? As we saw earlier, CIA Officer Mark Wyatt has said, "I was actually running the office most of the time [in Rome], while he [Bill Harvey] was off ... some place..." C.G. Harvey herself complained about her experiences while living in Italy, she said, "Bill was in Washington. He left me to deal with the rats and the Communists." And there seems to be some confusion as to where Bill Harvey was exactly on the day of the assassination. C. G. Harvey said, "Bill was actually in Sicily, talking to the Mafia..." The CIA has yet to release Bill Harvey's travel records from summer of 1963 through November 1963.)

On YouTube E. Howard Hunt seemed to spend the most time talking about William King Harvey. E. Howard Hunt was not a buddy to William King Harvey, he was buddies with Allen Dulles, Tracy Barnes, Richard Helms, and David Atlee Phillips.

E. Howard Hunt in my opinion was still pushing the party line right up to his death, in his attempt to focus in primarily on William King Harvey as the primary source of the assassination, as seen on YouTube.

## HOUSE SELECT COMMITEE'S INTEREST

Please note what information the House Select Committee on Assassinations (HSCA) was interested enough in that they voted for a subpoena on August 15, 1978. Listed are five items of information wanted from the CIA. **Three out of the five items listed below relate to what we have been interested in, in this story**. The subpoena lists:

- Copies of "mug books" shown to AMMUG-1 [or A-1] (A-1 of course was the Cuban intelligence agent that defected from Cuba and said that **Luisa Calderon** had received a love letter from a young American whose name sounded like "Ower.")
- All files and file references to **William Harvey**, including but not limited to personnel and security office files, for the period 1959 through 1966.
- All debriefing memoranda, which reflect or relate to information sought or obtained from a **Cuban defector known by the cryptonym AMMUG-1 [or A-1].**
- The three-volume history of the CIA Mexico City station operations prepared by **Ann Goodpasture** in 1969-1970. (**Goodpasture was Division D, which links her to Harvey's Division D and she links to David Atlee Phillips and the Guatemalan Coup in 1954.**)
- All files and file references to Maria Teresa Proenza pertaining to events and transactions involving her between September 1, 1963, and January 31, 1964.

Notice how what we have been interested in, in our Terre Haute related investigation, is what the House Select Committee was also zeroed in on, namely William King

Harvey and Louisa Calderon.

# WILLIAM KING HARVEY, POST ASSASSINATION

During his time in Rome, Bill Harvey reportedly engaged in some troubling activities. It is said that he encouraged Colonel Renzo Rocca, an officer in the Italian Intelligence Agency (SIFAR), to orchestrate bombings targeting the offices and newspapers of the Christian Democratic Party. The intention was to falsely attribute these acts of violence to left-wing groups. F. Mark Wyatt, Harvey's deputy in Rome, was shocked when he heard Harvey suggest recruiting Mafia hitmen to assassinate Italian Communist officials. Wyatt objected and Harvey flew into a rage. [293]

For a while, the situation in Italy seemed to improve. Bill Harvey managed to carry out a few operations that, although not remarkable, proved to be useful. This modest success gave him a glimmer of confidence. However, his colleagues noticed a concerning pattern: Harvey began relying heavily on alcohol, starting early in the morning. As the day progressed, his demeanor deteriorated. By noon, he was no longer himself. Colleagues learned to avoid conducting business with him in the afternoon since he appeared drowsy and not alert, although not necessarily intoxicated.

During a visit to the Yugoslavian border, a local carabinieri colonel took Harvey on a tour of checkpoints. However, Harvey spent most of the trip in a drunken slumber. On another occasion, when he visited his former Berlin base in Berlin, witnesses were dismayed by his behavior. One agent who had great fondness for Harvey described the experience as dreadful. Harvey nearly fell out of an elevator on his way to the base's office and he was walking around with his suit torn at the knee, completely oblivious to his bloody knee and his appearance. On this occasion, he also was seen carelessly twirling his revolver around in public.

During an emergency meeting called by U.S. Ambassador Frederick Reinhardt, Harvey in a state of intoxication, slumped over the arm of his chair and eventually fell asleep. In the process, his gun slipped from its holster and clattered to the floor. Exasperated, Reinhardt snapped, "Who sent him to this town, for Christ's sake?" Joe Widlmuth, who had served alongside Harvey in Berlin, sadly recalled the last time he saw Harvey was in Rome. According to Wildmuth, Harvey appeared pale, slightly diminished and utterly defeated.

CIA headquarters began hearing rumors of Harvey having walked into a glass door and that he had run over a roadside kiosk.

Bill Harvey suffered a heart attack, and two CIA Doctors from Germany were dispatched to look after him. They told him that he should stop drinking and smoking.

His gun went off in his office and the secretaries were afraid to open the door for fear Harvey had killed himself. When they finally opened the door, there sat Harvey as if nothing had happened. [294]

Said CIA Executive Director, "Red" White, "Bill Harvey got to be a problem in Rome. He developed quite a reputation." Harvey's drinking had become a big problem. Desmond FitzGerald the CIA's Deputy Director of Plans had been getting reports and hearing rumors, so he went over to investigate. FitzGerald determined that Bill Harvey needed to be relieved of his command. [295]

McCone left the CIA in April 1965. President Johnson appointed fellow Texan, Vice Admiral William Raborn as the

Director of the CIA. Helms became Deputy Director Central Intelligence (DDCI) in April 1965 and later the Director of CIA in June 1966.

Prior to Bill Harvey's arrival back in Washington, Richard Helms called a meeting to determine what to do with Bill Harvey. In attendance, Richard Helms, Desmond FitzGerald, Jim Angleton, Tom Karamessines and Lawrence "Red" White. "Red" White was given the responsibility of supervising or overseeing Bill Harvey. [296]

Bill Harvey returned to Langley in 1966, and then took a special assignment to survey the vulnerability of CIA installations to technical coverage. Bill studied possible techniques that could be used to thwart electronic surveillance attempts against the United States." <u>SSCI</u> 157-100004-10138

At about this time the career of one of Harvey's old Berlin officers appeared to get sidetracked because Angleton had falsely suspected that the agent might be a mole. The agent decided that the man who could best advise him was his old boss from Berlin base, Bill Harvey. The agent was obviously out of the loop because he had no idea that Harvey's own career had plummeted. He went to CIA Headquarters in Langley and, searched the building for Harvey. He heard rumors from Helm's staff that Harvey's mind was gone, that he had left the CIA and joined a Washington law firm. In an out-of-the-way corner, the agent finally tracked down his old chief, still employed by the CIA. "He was in an office," the agent recalled, "...just a big broom closet. He's a big bulky guy sitting at this little, tiny desk. I went in and sat down and said, 'Bill, I don't know what the fuck is going on. This is some kind of weird scenario. Nobody will tell me what's happening. Really, I am not coming to you to tell me what's going on. I am coming to ask you what I should do about it.' And he looked at me for maybe 10 or 15 seconds and said, 'I can't help you.' That was the end of it." Looking back, the agent later realized that "Harvey was powerless to help anyone: Angleton was involved all the time in trying to destroy him…. Bill knew that." [297]

"So," said 'Red' White, "I took charge of Bill Harvey, and I talked to him immediately." I said, "Bill you've got a wonderful reputation, and you've got a drinking problem. You and I have never had any supervisory relationship, but starting right now we have a clean slate." [298]

"It wouldn't be long before Bill would show up at some meeting just crocked. I sent for him. He'd come in the door apologizing, every time. After about the third or fourth time, he said 'If I ever embarrass you or this Agency again, I'll retire.' It wasn't a month until he did, and he came in and said, 'I made a promise to you, and I'm here to live up to it.' I said, 'Bill, I hate to see your career end this way, but I guess that's the way it has to be.' I said, 'You've got some sick leave coming, why don't you take that?' So, he did, and he hung around town for about six months before he actually retired." [299]

According to the FBI, around May 6, 1967, Bill Harvey applied for retirement from the CIA.

In the meantime, the men and women whom Harvey had trained and brought up through the ranks fanned out to all parts of the world, playing larger and more important roles. Especially in Southeast Asia, where Harvey's JM/WAVE station chief Ted Shackley played a major role in the Vietnam War.

## HARVEY'S AND ROSSELLI'S POST ASSASSINATION ACTIVITY

In 1967 Johnny Rosselli, to try and get himself out of trouble with the law, started talking about the CIA, Robert Kennedy and the Mafia's activity to assassinate Castro, and how that operation might have flipped and gotten President Kennedy. Notice the flurry of activity that ends up being triggered in 1967, starting with Rosselli. It is interesting to note that Bill Harvey and the CIA parted company around May 1967, reason: on "sick leave pending retirement."

FBI memo dated May 4, 1967, the day after the CIA cut all official contact with Rosselli, says: "the CIA IG told the Bureau liaison officer that CIA has instructed Harvey to avoid contact with subject if possible. CIA realizes that Rosselli may force a contact and it will be impossible for Harvey to evade the subject.... If contact is made, Harvey is to furnish the results, which will be passed on to the Bureau.... Harvey is on sick leave [pending] retirement.... CIA is in an extremely vulnerable position."

A CIA memo dated 10/4/1967, entitled: "Luncheon Meeting with William K. Harvey," said: The CIA's Howard Osborn reports, "I asked him point-blank what the nature of his relationship with 'Johnny' was since it seemed totally inconsistent to me with his desire to re-enter law practice in the district." He agreed with this and said that he didn't give a damn; that he would not turn his back on his friends; and that 'Johnny' was his friend." <u>CIA</u> 104-10122-10208

He went on to say that it was his opinion that "it would be the worst thing he could do for himself or the Agency, to turn his back on 'Johnny' at this time." He seemed to want to establish clearly with me the fact that it will be his neck if our use of 'Johnny' comes out in the open, since he believes that the Agency could not, or would not, admit involvement. *CIA* 104-10122-10208

Harvey then said that he felt very uncomfortable about the entire situation and fully realized its implications to the Agency if it ever surfaced publicly. He said that he felt sure 'Johnny' would never "pull the string" on us unless he was absolutely desperate, but that **his concern was that Senator Robert Kennedy knew all about the operation.** *CIA* 104-10122-10208

CIA memo dated 11/20/1967, entitled: "Telephone Conversation with William K. Harvey." It says: Harvey plans to see Rosselli during his visit and it is highly probable that Rosselli will stay with Harvey as he has in the past. Harvey is going hunting on the 21$^{st}$ of November on the Eastern Shore and will not be back in town until late Wednesday, 22 November. *CIA* 104-10106-10628 (November 22$^{nd}$, interesting timing four years to the day that President Kennedy was assassinated, William King Harvey and Johnny Rosselli are getting together.)

The author of the memo, Howard Osborn, Director of Security, writes: "I do not trust Harvey. However, irrespective of our distrust of Harvey, I believe it important to keep in touch with him as long as possible as a window into Rosselli's plans and intentions. *CIA* 104-10106-10628

CIA memo dated December 12, 1967, entitled: "Meeting Between William K. Harvey and Johnny Rosselli." Excerpt from memo: Harvey was in contact with Johnny on Sunday, the 26$^{th}$ of November when Johnny called to let him know he had arrived in Washington and was staying at the Madison Hotel. He claims he had a three-hour session with him. **At one point in their Monday meeting, they "bumped**

**into" Jim Angleton** and Harvey introduced Johnny as "Mr. Ralston." (**What a coincidence, they bumped into Angleton at a hotel**.) On Tuesday, 28 November, Harvey spent eleven hours with Johnny at the Bethesda Country Club. They chatted from 11:30 am until nearly midnight. <u>CIA</u> 104-10059-10142

Harvey says that Johnny will maintain his trust unless he is convicted, and the threat of deportation arises. Harvey feels the Agency must exert influence to have the indictment "killed." <u>CIA</u> 104-10059-10142

Toward the end of our discussion, I asked Harvey if he was sure that his involvement with Johnny wasn't more than just to protect the Agency's interest. He became highly indignant at this and said that Johnny has no hold on him in the past or in the future. He added that he would never do anything to hurt Johnny. <u>CIA</u> 104-10059-10142

It is difficult to assess Harvey's role in this affair. Despite his protestations to the contrary, I cannot help but feel that there is something in his relationship with Johnny that he is concealing. <u>CIA</u> 104-10059-10142

According to CIA records, Bill Harvey left CIA for "medical reasons." He practiced law for a while in Washington D.C. before returning to Indianapolis, Indiana to work at the Bishop Private Investigative Service. Bishop Service was comprised mostly of former CIA agents. Eventually Bill Harvey moved to the Publisher, Bobbs-Merrill in Indianapolis a company owned by ITT. <u>Mike McCormick's interview with C.G. Harvey</u>

According to the FBI's Sam Papich, Bill Harvey was very bitter about the manner in which he had been forced out of the CIA and **seemed to focus his attention on the Director Richard Helms as the point of his resentment.**

In a CIA memo, Howard Osborn reported that he has a very uncomfortable feeling that Harvey would not hesitate to use his knowledge of the Johnny operation as a handle on the Director, or the Agency, if he thought he could benefit from it.

For his part, Richard Helms advised the FBI's Sam Papich on October 31, 1967, that he mistrusted Harvey and that he was not going to permit himself, or CIA, to be blackmailed by anybody; and he has no fear of threats, which may emanate from subject.

In 1971, Johnny Rosselli was again facing possible deportation and prosecution for illegal gambling activities that occurred back in 1967. To try and pressure the CIA into pressuring the Immigration and Naturalization Service to discontinue their efforts to deport him, Rosselli again went public. But this time he included the name of William King Harvey. *HSCA* Vol. 10 Page 155 & 182

June 18, 1971, Monday. *The Washington Merry-Go-Round, The Washington Post*, by Jack Anderson.

The article broke the news that the CIA had attempted to kill Castro on six different occasions. This appears to be news to the ex-CIA Director John McCone who vigorously denied that the CIA had ever participated in any plot on Castro's life. Asked whether the attempts could have been made without his knowledge, he replied, "It could not have happened."

The article tells how the CIA enlisted Robert Maheu, a former FBI agent with shadowy contacts, who had handled undercover assignments for the CIA in the past, and it explained how Maheu had recruited John Rosselli.

Then **the article discloses** how the CIA assigned two of its most trusted operatives, **William Harvey and James O'Connell** to the hush-hush murder mission.

The article also puts forth this theory, that there is a suspicion that Castro became aware of the U.S. plot upon his life and somehow recruited Oswald to retaliate against President Kennedy.

C.G. Harvey told Mike McCormick that it was not until Jack Anderson article came out in January 1971 that Bill Harvey's mother, a professor at Indiana State University, learned that her son worked for the CIA. She had always thought that he had worked for the State Department. Bill Harvey knew how to keep a secret. *My Interview with Mike McCormick*

In an affidavit, dated June 17, 1971, Leslie Whitten (who worked with Jack Anderson) verified that Harvey did not talk. "As a part of my investigation, I twice called William K. Harvey, a retired Central Intelligence Agency official, now of Indianapolis."

On my first call, in January, wrote Leslie Whitten, I asked Harvey if it were not true that he had personally intervened with the Justice Department to mitigate the government's prosecution of Rosselli on the basis that Rosselli had done a formidable service for his country. Harvey said, "This is a long story...I don't think it ought to be printed." I asked him whether it was not true that he had a high regard for Rosselli. "I still do," he earnestly replied.

"In pursuing the story further, I called Harvey again in Indianapolis in February," says Whitten, "and asked him whether he could comment on our story about Rosselli, which by now had been published widely in the United States. He declined to comment. But he twice reaffirmed his 'high regard' for Rosselli. I advised him I was making an affidavit on Rosselli's behalf, and he expressed concern for Rosselli, asked his present status and said he would 'follow up' on Rosselli's behalf from his end."

In 1975, Harvey was summoned to testify before the Senate Select Committee on Intelligence. To the committee's surprise, Harvey displayed a remarkable willingness to share his information. Some staff members initially feared that Harvey might be less than forthcoming, given Harvey's reputation for being tough character and super secretive. One staff member recalled, "As it turned out, we could hardly shut him up."

Some of the Select Committee staff thought that they detected a subtle whispering campaign by the CIA designed to undermine Harvey's credibility as a witness. The staff was inundated with stories about Harvey's penchant for three or four martini lunches, which led them to think that they might have to discount Harvey's testimony. However, Harvey's extraordinary ability to recall details from events that took place thirteen years ago stood in stark contrast to many of the committee's witnesses whose inability to remember, strained credibility.

One committee member commented, "All these big shots from the Kennedy administration came slinking in, worried about their reputations, and **then came Harvey-the assassin himself-saying, 'Yeah, I did it, and I'd do it again if so ordered.'**"

The senators, after hearing various accounts about Bill, couldn't resist asking Bill if he was still carrying a gun. "No," replied Harvey, but he was carrying a device that would erase their taping of his testimony, as he reached into his pocket and slapped the device down on the table. The stunned room feel silent until Bill broke the tension by chuckling and slowly removed his hand to reveal a cigarette case.

Senator Frank Church then posed the ultimate question: "Isn't it true, Mr. Harvey, that you were assigned to assassinate Fidel Castro?" Harvey's response, "Senator, if I had accepted the assignment to assassinate Castro, Castro would be dead now, and we wouldn't be having these hearings!"

Said David Belin, attorney for the Warren Commission and the Rockefeller Commission, "Some witnesses lied to the Church committee, some witnesses did not. Among those who told the truth was William King Harvey."

The impact Harvey made on one senator was profound, with the senator stating that, "Bill Harvey left the greatest impression on him of any man he had ever met."

Harvey managed to avoid having his picture taken during the hearings. When asked about this, G.G. Harvey responded, "There are things still living."

And what did Bill think about the hearings? He said, "They didn't ask the right questions!"

In May 1975, Rosselli testified behind closed doors before the Senate Intelligence Committee. Senator Frank Church later said, "He gave us a good deal of detail."

Angleton said "Bill Harvey called me not long before it happened. I warned Bill that Giancana would not appear before the Senate." Was this a veiled warning to Bill Harvey concerning his own testimony? And how the hell would Angleton know this if he were not a part of it?

The news of Sam Giancana's murder, in his home, in Chicago, caused quite a stir at the offices of Bobbs-Merrill in Indianapolis. Suddenly, everyone noticed a bulge in Bill Harvey's jacket, Bill Harvey had begun to carry his gun for protection.

Richard Case Nagell, our man that knows a lot, believed that the CIA was responsible for the deaths of Giancana, Hoffa and Rosselli. [300]

I noticed that Captain Bradley Ayers book *The War That Never Was*, was published by Bobbs-Merrill in 1976. It is a book that has been referenced in this work and was about training the anti-Castro Cubans down in Florida and the conducting of raids on Cuba. It's a book that not only mentions Rosselli's involvement with the Cuban raiders, but it also mentions Robert Kennedy's visits and involvement down in Florida with the anti-Castro Cubans. I wonder if Harvey had a hand in editing *The War That Never Was*? The book illustrates Bobby Kennedy's and Rosselli's direct involvement with the anti-Castro Cubans down in Florida. It put their actions in the public record.

On the morning of June 7, 1976, Bill Harvey had another heart attack. C.G. Harvey told Mike McCormick, "Bill underwent open heart surgery without any anesthetic. His doctor said he was the bravest man he had ever met." (So, he was one tough son-of-a-bitch, after all!) *Terre Haute Tribune-Star, Mike McCormick, May 23, 1999*

Dr. Jack Hall, Methodist Hospital, "He was very alert and very sharp and one of the most effective decision makers I had ever seen. You know he made decisions exceedingly well and I was amazed at this." [301]

Bill Harvey died the next day at Methodist Hospital in Indianapolis with his devoted wife, C.G. Harvey by his side. He was 60 years old.

"Bill Harvey died of a heart attack shortly before Rosselli's murder and weeks before Bill Harvey was scheduled to testify once more in Washington. That autumn, Harvey's widow told a journalist: "Up to his last breath Bill told me never to talk to anyone." Her Indianapolis home was subjected to two attempted break-ins shortly after Harvey's death. "They're after his papers," Mrs. Harvey said. "But I burned everything." [302]

In Bill Harvey's eulogy, which C.G. Harvey read to Andy Alderton, it mentioned his service to America, Germany, **Japan**, and Italy. He served in America, Germany, and Italy, but I haven't seen anything on the record about him serving in Japan. Why, I wonder was Japan listed, unless he was posted there for a time, and it's not been made public? Oswald of course was posted at Atsugi, Japan around 1957-1958, prior to his defection. Military Intelligence Agent, Richard Case Nagell and Oswald knew each other from having both been in Japan at this time. Details of Bill Harvey's career abroad between 1952 and 1959 are being withheld by the CIA.

There was almost nothing that Bill Harvey didn't tell C.G., that was because C.G. was also CIA. <u>Alderton tape</u>

At the funeral home beside the casket C.G. was heard to say, "Few men were blessed with the opportunity to serve their country, as he had been. Unfortunately, I cannot talk about many of the things that he had really done." Then she tearfully stated, "It was unfair to leave Bill stranded in the public record as the CIA's hit man." To quote one CIA official "He was asked to do things that nobody should have been asked to do." [303]

September 7, 1976, *Washington Post,* Jack Anderson and Les Whitten, article entitled, "Behind John F. Kennedy's Murder." (Interesting to note this came out almost exactly three months after William K. Harvey died and a few weeks after Johnny Rosselli was murdered. Also, of interest is how soon after Bill Harvey's death came Johnny's demise.) The following is a brief summary of the article:

Before he died, Rosselli hinted to associates that he knew who had arranged President Kennedy's murder. It was the same conspirators, whom he had recruited earlier to kill Cuban Premier Fidel Castro. (So here Rosselli is saying that the people that he knew and recruited are the same people who killed President Kennedy. Who would that be? I don't know, maybe Giancana, Trafficante, perhaps Oswald, I don't know about Harry, the CIA/Guys from Guatemala, the Mafia, or the three-man team that supposedly went into Cuba?)

The article continued: Castro learned ... that President Kennedy was behind the plot. The Cuban leader, as the supreme irony, decided to turn the tables and use the same crowd to arrange Kennedy's assassination. To save their skins, the plotters lined up Lee Harvey Oswald to pull the trigger.

The Cuban underworld elements were supposedly under the loose control of Florida's Mafia chieftain, Santos Trafficante. Trafficante had been lodged for a period of time in a Cuban jail [when Castro first took over Cuba].

It has also been established that Jack Ruby, indeed, had been in Cuba and had connections in the Havana underworld. One CIA cable, dated November 28, 1963, reported that "an American gangster type named Ruby" had visited Trafficante in his Cuban prison. <u>HSCA</u> VOL. 10 Page 160 (Trafficante was released from jail shortly after Ruby's visit and Trafficante then returned to Tampa, Florida. Speculation is that Trafficante cut a deal with Castro, having to do with trafficking in narcotics and that Trafficante then became aligned with Castro interests from that point forward. Trafficante is believed by some to have been warning Castro all along about each of the attempts to assassinate him.)

The article goes on to say that Jack Ruby was ordered to eliminate Oswald.

If Trafficante was a double agent, working with the CIA but was actually supplying information to Castro, then another scenario emerges. It is then logical to assume that Castro knew of the CIA-organized crime operations from their inception. Trafficante could have received sanctuary and assistance in smuggling contraband [drugs in exchange] for such information. *HSCA* Vol. 10 Page 185

Two weeks after having had dinner with Santos Trafficante, August 1976, John Rosselli's butchered body was found stuffed inside an oil drum, which was floating in Key Biscayne Bay, Fla., shortly after his testimony before the SSC regarding the CIA-organized crime plots. *HSCA* Vol. 10 Page 186

## HARVEY ALLUDES TO RUMORS

Bill Harvey said to the Senate Select Committee in 1976, that after he left the Cuban Operation and went to Italy, that "he knew nothing about plots to assassinate Castro coming out of Guantanamo, any involvement of **Barker, Sturgis, or any first-hand knowledge of the Cubela plot**, although he later learned of it. *SSCIA* 157-10004-10136

Belin: Anything else you wish to add on the record? *Rockefeller Commission* 178-10002-10324

Harvey: One point please. **There have, as you know, been some unfortunate and in my opinion distorted allegations about that, that have surfaced publicly since then**, but I have had **no official connection** with any **Cuban operation** of any kind since June—probably May would be more accurate—at the very latest—of May of 1963. And from the time that I left the Cuban task force in the early months of 1963—to the best of my recollection around March—I have in no sense attempted to keep current or involve myself in it in any sense whatever. *Rockefeller Commission* 178-10002-10324

Of course, Bill Harvey saying that he had nothing to do with Cuban operations is not the same as saying that he had nothing to do with the Kennedy assassination and it bothers me a little bit that he said he had "no official connection." That is not exactly the same as saying I had no connection of any kind. However, the opposite of "no official connection" is an "informal connection." Did Bill Harvey involve himself, unofficial, as a participant in the planning and execution of the assassination?

C.G. Harvey was upset about how they tried to portray Bill Harvey after he left CIA. She wanted to write a book about what had happened but was told they would cut off her pension. *Mike McCormick/C.G. Harvey interview*

In a CIA memorandum dated January 22, 1971, Howard J. Osborn, Director of Security wrote about Bill Harvey, "I am inclined to believe Bill Harvey. He has a form of professional integrity of his own."

## WHO WAS BILL HARVEY?

Who was William King Harvey? One of his former lieutenants said, when asked about all the speculation by people as to who Bill Harvey really was. The lieutenant responded, "at what point did they know him, he changed throughout his career." [304]

The CIA's John Whitten said of Bill Harvey, "He was a really hardboiled, unsubtle, ruthless guy...a very dangerous man."

CG Harvey told author Bayard Stockton, "The CIA told me that the Agencies files on Bill would absolutely not be accessible until 2063? Why did the CIA tell Bill Harvey's wife this? Why that particular year, exactly one hundred years after the assassination of President Kennedy? [305]

G. Robert Blakey, chief counsel of the House Select Committee on Assassinations once wrote concerning Bill Harvey: "The committee staff people who looked into him swear that he was involved."

Bill Harvey's calling card. It is possible that William King Harvey planned the assassination, or was asked or ordered by someone like Angleton, Helms, or Dulles to help. If anyone was capable of running an invisible operation and could keep his mouth shut and details off of paper, it was Bill Harvey. You could trust him to do that. Bill Harvey did go up against Bobby Kennedy, who obviously had the power of the executive branch of the United States Government and Harvey lost, big time. But Harvey by virtue of his experience, skill, and connections had a lot of power of his own in what has been termed the Invisible Government and with the Mafia through Rosselli. Art Thurston, CIA Retired said, "Harvey was a pretty tough guy, blunt, outspoken, and a man you wouldn't want to fool around with." Bill Harvey was familiar with the key players and organizations and many if not all the players in the field were at one time or the other, Bill Harvey's assets, or had worked with him. But there were some who appear as key players in this story that were not likely to invite Bill Harvey to join their team, nor would they rush to be on his team. Unless they saw it as an opportunity to really stick it to Bill Harvey. In the book *Wilderness of Mirrors*, Angleton and Phillips saw to it that Bill Harvey was placed in the public record as, "absolutely hating Bobby Kennedy's guts, with a purple passion." C.G. Harvey even said it; Bobby Kennedy and Bill Harvey "were absolutely enemies. I mean absolute enemies."

Author Dick Russell reports in his book *On The Trail of the Assassins*, that he spoke with the CIA's Sidney Gottlieb (Dr. Death) and **as they talked about William King Harvey**, Gottlieb said, "My view, as somebody who was as close--or not so close--to it all as I was, it's a thing out of the whole cloth. I don't think anything like that ever happened. I don't think the CIA ever had a role..."

His voice trailed off momentarily. "In what?" I asked.

"In the Kennedy's assassination," Gottlieb said.

Says Dick Russell, "I had not yet broached that subject." [306]

Interesting where Gottlieb's mind went when the subject of William King Harvey was being discussed. It went to the Kennedy assassination and the possibility of the CIA's role in it.

Like Mrs. Harvey, Bill Harvey's coworkers also became aware of Harvey's fast-growing bond with Rosselli. An assistant CIA chief of station who worked directly under Harvey noted, "Bill was proud of his friendship with Rosselli. He bragged about it. These were guys that got things done, and that appealed to him." [307]

What if the rifle in Terre Haute, Indiana was a calling card for William King Harvey? William King Harvey absolutely hated Bobby Kennedy's guts and had suffered a great deal of abuse and public humiliation at the hands of Bobby Kennedy. What if leaving a rifle in Terre Haute, Indiana was Harvey's way of saying to Bobby Kennedy, "I killed your brother, you little fucker." A rifle is left in Terre Haute matching the description of a rifle used in the assassination of the President. Terre Haute, why Terre Haute, who was from Terre Haute?

I find it particularly disturbing the year in which Bill Harvey was asked to leave the CIA was 1967. 1967 is the year that things started heating up, when Bill's good friend Johnny Rosselli started to hint at his knowledge of the Kennedy assassination, and this is also the year that District Attorney Garrison began his investigation into the Kennedy assassination. If Bill Harvey was a major force behind the assassination, or brought about the assassination, his departure may be a clue that the CIA recognized this fact and recognized the embarrassment they might experience if Bill was still on the payroll.

Was Bill Harvey this gutsy? Who was it that placed himself behind a .50-caliber machine gun, in a tunnel at the border between East and West Germany, and faced down the approaching Russian troops? Who was the one who always took the tough jobs in service to his country and generally got the job done? Who was the one who said no and stood his ground firmly against some of the stupid assassination and covert ideas from the lunatic fringe? Who was the one who underwent open-heart surgery without any anesthetic? Who was the only one who never talked, but when he was compelled to testify, he was the only one who was supposedly honest and told the truth? Who was the only one who had the guts to tell the Kennedys to their face, what he really thought? Who was the one who paid the price for being honest? Who was the one who was very good at playing his cards close to his vest, leaving no trails or traces?

Bill Harvey certainly knew or had connections with most all the people and organizations suspected in this story of possible involvement in the conspiracy to murder President John F. Kennedy. There is absolutely no question that Bill Harvey and Johnny Rosselli were really tight. It bothers me to think, but I cannot imagine Johnny Rosselli meeting with Bill Harvey in June of 1963 and not telling Harvey about the project that Rosselli was surely involved in to assassinate President Kennedy. On the other hand, there is no guarantee as to how Bill Harvey might react to the thought of murdering the President of the United States. However, if the facts presented to Bill Harvey indicated a threat to the United States and national security and suspected treason, we know which side Bill Harvey would have come down on.

Robert Morrow has written, "Bill Harvey met regularly with John Rosselli, Santos Trafficante, Sam Giancana, Robert Maheu, and Eladio del Valle, through whom I originally met Harvey." Del Valle although in Miami is said to be working with 544 Camp Street. Del Valle and Ferrie supposedly worked together, and both died on the same day when it became known that District Attorney Garrison was interested in them. Banister, Maheu, Win Scott (CIA head Mexico City) and Harvey were all former FBI agents. Harvey and Rosselli were very close. Rosselli is said by one Mafia family to have been in Banister's office checking out Oswald, and by another Mafia family as having been the triggerman in the storm drain in Dallas, Texas on the day of the assassination.

What did James Jesus Angleton say, "Fundamentally, the founding fathers of U.S. intelligence were liars. The better you lied and the more you betrayed, the more likely you would be promoted. These people attracted and promoted each other. Outside of their duplicity, the only thing they had in common was a desire for absolute power."

Bill Harvey was not a member of this club. Bill Harvey was not afraid to tell the truth to a superior. Said attorney David Belin of the Rockefeller Commission, "Some witnesses lied to the committee, some witnesses did not. Among those who told the truth was William Harvey."

So why the whispering campaign about Bill Harvey prior to his testimony before the Senate Select Committee on Intelligence? Why did Angleton warn Bill Harvey before his testimony that Giancana wasn't going to make it? Why did David Atlee Phillips and James Jesus Angleton work to spotlight William King Harvey and his career in the book *Wilderness of Mirrors*?

Bill Harvey told the Church Committee that, "I have never done anything unauthorized, freewheeling or in any way outside the framework of my responsibilities and duties as an officer of the agency."

Was William King Harvey involved in the assassination planning? Bill Harvey was most probably only involved, "if so ordered" or asked to participate by Richard Helms or James Jesus Angleton, and even then, they surely had to offer up a pretty damn good reason, something like our democracy, or nation, is at risk.

To me the most damning evidence that Bill Harvey might have been involved in the planning of the Kennedy assassination came from C.G. Harvey herself who said that "Bill was in Washington. He left me [in Italy] to deal with the rats and the Communists." The CIA is currently still withholding Bill Harvey's travel records for the time leading up to the assassination.

Ray Cline also felt the need to make this same point: **According to Ray Cline**, "In January 1961, when preparations for the invasion were at their peak, Bissell ordered William Harvey, a veteran station chief, to set up a 'standby capability' for what was called euphemistically 'Executive Action,' a capability for assassinating foreign leaders as a 'last resort.' Harvey was a colorful figure, a former FBI man who always carried a pistol when posted abroad, something unique among the CIA officers. I am sure he believed that it was patriotic, even moral, to kill a foreign ruler **when ordered to do so by his superiors** for reasons of U.S. security. Many of the romantic so-called 'cowboy' types of covert action officers would have accepted this proposition, in 1960-1961."

Was Ray Cline trying to tell us something here? Ray Cline's job, is information, is knowing. Surely if anyone had heard any rumors about Bill Harvey it would have been Ray Cline. Was Ray Cline trying to tell us that if Bill Harvey was involved, he was under orders from his superiors?

Bill Harvey, by all accounts was not an accepted member of the club. He was the odd man out regarding the upper echelon CIA clique. Even though he was intellectually superior, was renowned for his decision-making ability, loved by those who served under him, and seemed to exhibit better judgment than most, one example being his non-use of AM/LASH.

Bill Harvey was proud of his country, proud of his roots, and proud to be who he was. He refused to be like them, he refused to be something he was not. He was reluctant to poor mouth anyone. Bill Corson said, "Bill Harvey could hold his own intellectually with anybody. And so, in an attempt [by Harvey's CIA contemporaries] to not feel inferior, because they really were, they had to play like they were socially superior."

If Bill Harvey really did plan the assassination, or even participated in it, then Bill Harvey was very, very good about covering his tracks, because other than Bill Harvey's having had associations with nearly all the parties shown in this story I have yet to find any evidence of anyone directly saying Bill Harvey did this or did that regarding the assassination of President Kennedy. Everything has been this past operative of his did this or did that, resulting in a kind of guilt by association.

Bill Harvey loved his work. Bill Harvey lived for his work. Bill Harvey returned from Italy a man whose spirit had been totally crushed. He had been able to standup to the entire world of communism, but he could not stand-alone.

There is one thing for certain, if there was real evidence that real harm was being done to this country, a country that Bill Harvey obviously loved so much and fought so hard for, and if he had been called upon once more, you know he would have been there.

C.G. Harvey, Bill Harvey's widow, contends her husband strongly resisted the cold-blooded murder of foreign leaders. [308]

What else did Mrs. Harvey say? She said, "Few men were blessed with the opportunity to serve their country, as he had been."

Here is the real contrast in this story: Allen Dulles and the ruling elite inside and outside of the CIA were all about their own self-interests, self-enrichment, self-preservation, their power and prestige and they used the resources, sweat, and blood of this country to acquire it, protect it, and attempt to hide their activities from the world. They were out and out deceitful liars. **My impression of William King Harvey,** on the other hand is that **he looked out for his country more than he looked out for himself.** That is the real contrast in this story.

There are two who standout in this story whose loyalty and patriotism were never in question and were above reproach, the two Hoosiers from America's Crossroads, America's Heartland: William King Harvey and Ray S. Cline.

At the funeral home beside the casket C.G. was heard to say that "she could not talk about many of the things that he had really done." Then she tearfully stated that "It was unfair to leave her husband stranded in the public record as the CIA's hit man." To quote one CIA official "he was asked to do things that nobody should have been asked to do."

And then came Harvey-the alleged assassin himself-saying, "Yeah, I did it, and I'd do it again <u>if so ordered</u>," or would he say, "How on earth can I convince these idiots that this is so wrong?"

## THE DARK FORCES

Despite the earlier account of how Bill Harvey and Jim Angleton began their relationship on a very contentious competitive note, back in 1947, most of the accounts about Harvey and Angleton's relationship reflect an air of mutual respect. You get the impression that they would walk into any room or situation side by side, Angleton quiet but deadly, Harvey physically dominant and deadly serious, both confident in each other's ability and ready to take on anyone, or anything. Together they surely were a force to be reckoned with. They appeared to regularly share a drink, compare notes, consult, and bounce ideas off of each other.

On the other hand, Angleton may have been practicing the age-old adage "keep your friends close and your enemies closer." After witnessing Bill Harvey's singlehanded destruction of his close friend Kim Philby and knowing Bill Harvey's fanaticism, zeal, and doggedness in the pursuit of commies and their stooges, well the closer you stand to an elephant the hard it is to see the whole thing. If Angleton had anything to hide, or if he was the mole incarnate, keeping Bill close was his only hope in hell.

Was it the intention of Allen Dulles, James Jesus Angleton, Richard Helms, David Atlee Phillips, E. Howard Hunt, Kim Philby, and Tracy Barnes to plant evidence and put things in the public record about Bill Harvey, in an attempt to set him up as the ultimate fall guy in the assassination, if needed? Yes, there is evidence of this.

The evidence:

- There was a picture released around the time of the assassination of a Mario Tauler Sague allegedly one of Bill

Harvey's operatives outside the Cuban Embassy in Mexico City that was falsely labeled as Oswald and released by David Phillips and identified as one of Bill's operatives by Gerry Hemming whose loyalty was to Angleton.

- James Jesus Angleton and David Athlee Phillips put Bill Harvey in the public record by supplying the information that appeared in the book Wilderness of Mirrors. Including such quotes as "Bill Harvey hated Bobby Kennedy's guts with a purple passion" and "everyone felt that Bill Harvey had been shafted by the Kennedys."

- E. Howard Hunt's revelations to his son, published in April 2007 concerning who was involved in the assassination, with Hunt's greatest focus and or emphasis being placed on William King Harvey, even though LBJ was at the top of the list.

- The use of many of Bill Harvey's former operatives in the field, like Josh Plumlee, Johnny Rosselli, David Morales, Mario Tauler Sague, and perhaps even Lee Harvey Oswald.

- And maybe, just maybe, the appearance three days after the assassination, in Bill Harvey and Ray Cline's hometown, of one Harry L. Power and one German Mauser Argentine 1891 rifle. The effect of which got at least this author to look and wonder.

There appears to be far more evidence that the Guys from the Guatemalan Coup/Bay of Pigs/Ivy League Set were involved in the assassination. Far more evidence than there is for Bill Harvey having been involved, other than Bill Harvey knew most of the alleged players. When Bill Harvey took over the Cuban operation, according to Harvey he may have offended the GFGC when he asks and was allowed to cut them out of the Cuban operation. I can't imagine that they would feel a need to ask Bill Harvey for his help in any operation that they were running. I can imagine that they would be really motivated to demonstrate to Mr. Harvey just how good they really were. I don't think that the Guys from Guatemala, nor Kim Philby would have hesitated at a chance to make Bill Harvey the fall guy.

E. Howard Hunt (GFGC) in his 1990's revelations to his son St. John Hunt in a recording on U-Tube focused most of his time talking and pointing the finger at Bill Harvey, when in fact many whom he named where considerably higher up the command chain then Bill Harvey. I think Hunt was still following the game plan and trying to hang this on their designated scapegoat.

If "The Guys from Guatemala" or the "Bay of Pigs," were involved in the assassination, as they very much appear to be, and if they were not pleased that William King Harvey had snubbed them when he took over their failed Cuban operation after the Bay of Pigs fiasco, and if we believe that there was a conspiracy, as the House Select Committee has said that there probably was, and we believe that whoever planned this thing sure paid attention to the details, especially when it came to confusing the issue through the use of patsies, scapegoats, and pinning the blame on others. Well, wouldn't it be logical for the planners, if they were sane, to want to be doubly sure that they achieved their objective of killing the President of the United States? So, wouldn't they logically have more than one sniper, and wouldn't it be logical to have more than one patsy for each sniper, and wouldn't there be more than one rifle, and wouldn't it be logical and easy to hang the planning all on a man who was on record, courtesy of Angleton and Phillips, as having declared that he absolutely hated the little fucker Bobby Kennedy? A man whose career was destroyed by the Kennedys, at a time when many of his peers said he should have been singled out for praise for having discovered the missiles in Cuba. And the man who got one of their own by delivering a staggering blow to Kim Philby.

Could Soviet master spy Kim Philby and Jim Angleton still be working and collaborating with each other? **Could Philby be pulling some strings behind the scenes as Martin and Lewis and Angleton say he was?** If it is conceivable that Philby is working with Bobby Kennedy, then it is even more conceivable that he would be able to work with Angleton. Philby was surely motivated to even the score with his arch nemesis Bill Harvey, who had totally ruined his career and his life eleven years earlier. Kim Philby may have taken great delight in having caused this Terre Haute thing to happen in order to do unto Harvey as Harvey had done unto him, ruin him and his passion - his career. Philby even said as much in his book, he said about Bill Harvey, "**I do not like letting provocation go unpunished.**" Might Philby have made a study of Bill Harvey enough to know what Harvey's hometown might be? If Philby was communicating and working with Angleton, then Angleton and the CIA's knowledge might have been Philby's knowledge, which might have included that Ray Cline was going to take a little time off to go speak at his high school alma mater's 100-year (centennial) celebration in Terre Haute, Indiana on November 29, 1963. Wouldn't it be delicious to create a disturbance in Terre Haute, Indiana that appears to be related to the Kennedy assassination that might draw everyone's attention to what Bill Harvey had been doing, or better yet let's make it appear like Bill Harvey could have done, after all Angleton knows everyone, Bill has ever been involved with. Wouldn't it be fun to hang the Kennedy assassination on the once proud Bill Harvey and finally ruin his career after all these years?

How better to even the score with Bill Harvey than to hang the murder of an American president around Bill Harvey's neck! Martin and Lewis would not have had a clue concerning the significance of their revelation about Kim Philby and how it might relate to what went on in Terre Haute, Indiana and Terre Haute's association to William King Harvey. Provided that Harry L. Power and/or the rifle is or was significant. People who, at the time, may have been made cognoscent of what went on in Terre Haute would surely have asked the same questions that I asked. Why Terre Haute? If Bobby Kennedy or Ray Cline were to have heard about the rifle, they might have asked themselves. Why Terre Haute? What is the significance? And if Bobby were to discover that Bill Harvey was from Terre Haute, wouldn't you think that he might wonder if perhaps he messed with the wrong guy? Had Ray Cline learned about Harry and/or the rifle and their proximity to himself in a hotel days after the assassination, wouldn't that make him think how close he might have come? Wouldn't it seem like a warning to Ray Cline and his boss the CIA Director, John McCone to be careful and watch your step concerning matters that you might become involved in because these people can reach out and touch you? The real question here is who might be sending the message? Is it Bill Harvey, and/or others who have built layer upon layer of misdirection, setting up patsies, scapegoats and whole organizations or countries for their own protection? Bill Harvey surely was gutsy enough to leave this calling card and at this juncture in his life he may have felt he had nothing to lose and with the right encouragement everything to gain. Was Bill Harvey made to look guilty by incorporating peripherally his lower-level operatives such as Plumlee, Rosselli, Morales, and Mario Tauler Sague? Haven't we seen throughout this story how the club consistently dumped on Bill Harvey? Why wouldn't they have continued to do what they had always done? Which was to set Bill Harvey up for the possibility of failure and ruination.

Rosselli might have had a line into Bill Harvey to tell him what was going on, but Rosselli's true loyalty would have been to the mob and their objectives.

If Philby was to get even with and punish Bill Harvey, what was it that Bill Harvey loved the most? Bill Harvey lived, loved, and took pride in his work and his personal protection of the United States. Philby was forced out of his major formal role in the spy business by America's James Bond. Likewise, Bill Harvey was forced to resign from the CIA not too many years after the Kennedy assassination. Did Philby have the motive, means, and the opportunity to commit or coordinate this crime? I think we have seen evidence that it is a very distinct possibility.

Once again, here is James Jesus Angleton who comes right out and tells us what was going on: Angleton said, "I came to believe that the events that would lead to my own downfall at the CIA (and perhaps Bill Harvey's) and the successful cover-up of <u>the Soviets' involvement in the Kennedy murder was orchestrated by Philby</u>."

# SO, WHAT COULD HAVE MOTIVATES THEM?

What would possibly motivate someone connected with the CIA to be involved in murdering a President?

Was it blackmail or in service to their friends? Who was Allen Dulles, James Jesus Angleton, in bed with and perhaps to a lesser extent Richard Helms and Tracy Barnes?

## *The Period Leading Up To World War II*

Fascism came into fashion with many of the leading corporate families in America leading up to and during World War II. The Dulles brothers were deeply involved with American interests that supplied the funding for the rise of Hitler and represented many of the bankers and businesses located in Nazi Germany.

The authors John Loftus and Mark Aarons have written that Allen Dulles was one of the worst traitors in American history, an economic version of Benedict Arnold. He was [one of the men] who sold his country out for money, blackmailed presidents, and helped to fund Hitler.

The financing for Adolph Hitler's rise to power was handled through the J. Henry Schroeder Bank with branches in Frankfurt, London, and New York. Chief legal counsel to the J. Henry Schroeder Bank was the law firm whose senior partners included John Foster and Allen Dulles.

Dulles knew many of the central players in the secretive Swiss financial milieu because he and his brother had worked with them as clients or business partners before the war. The Dulles brothers' Wall Street law firm, was at the center of an intricate international network of banks, investment firms, and industrial conglomerates that rebuilt Germany after World War I.

America's wealthiest families, only believed in one thing: making money. It is not an exaggeration to say that they funded both Hitler and Stalin.

On December 1, 1958, John Foster Dulles is quoted as saying, "The United States of America does not have friends; it has interests." This statement becomes much clearer when you substitute the words "business or financial interests." Sounds pretty cold if you don't understand that this is coming from a "Dulles perspective" of reality. In other words, in their view "The U.S. does not have friends; it has business interests." For a Dulles it was all about the money, power, arrogance, and an unapologetic sense of superiority. And they got away with it. [309]

## *Germany Lost The War, But Did The Nazis Lose?*

During the war, Allen Dulles worked for the U.S. Office of Strategic Services (OSS) the wartime intelligence service. Allen Dulles insisted on being posted in Bern, Switzerland the home of secret bank accounts and the ability to secretly move money and assets.

As an American Intelligence Officer, Allen Dulles, used his position in the OSS to protect himself and his clients from investigation for laundering Nazi funds back to America. [310]

During the war Dulles used Vatican couriers with diplomatic immunity to move communications back and forth across the Nazi and Allied lines.

There came a point during World War II when it became

abundantly clear to the Nazis that they were losing the war and they began working with their foreign financial and business contacts, with people like Allen Dulles, to escape from Germany with all of their war loot. [311]

Back in 1930, Allen Dulles first met Hugh Angleton, the father of James Angleton, while Dulles was on a business trip to Italy. Hugh Angleton was an American, living in Italy, who was the European representative for National Cash Register. Hugh Angleton became a longtime business agent for Allen Dulles.

Hugh Angleton believed in fascism. Before the war he praised the efficiency of Italian "corporatism" and denounced President Roosevelt as a "socialist."

Hugh Angleton went to work for the OSS during World War II in Italy.

According to an OSS memo dated September 25, 1943, Hugh Angleton pulled some strings to get his son James Jesus Angleton on with the OSS.

The person who trained James Jesus Angleton in espionage and counterintelligence work during the war in England was Kim Philby, prior to Angleton's posting with the OSS in Italy during the war. The move to Italy put father and son together working for the OSS.

Allen Dulles helped German industrialists and various individuals to launder and move Nazi money, gold, and war booty out of Germany during and after the war. All engineered in large part by Allen Dulles and his corrupt protégé, James Jesus Angleton and his Fascist father, Hugh Angleton. Jim Jesus Angleton and Allen Dulles also helped setup, in conjunction with the Vatican, the "Ratlines" or escape routes through Italy, which enables countless Nazis and war criminals to escape from Germany following the war. [312]

The genius who thought up the whole recruitment of Nazi war criminals for underground guerilla networks to be used behind the Iron Curtain after the war was Kim Philby.

Allen Dulles fell for Philby's story, hook, line, and sinker. Allen Dulles and Jim Angleton helped Philby to smuggle Nazis into America, Canada, Australia, and South America, to be trained for Cold War espionage. Only problem was many of them were communist intelligence agents.

Following World War II, Kim Philby helped the KGB to take over the Vatican's network of ratlines. The Soviets were only too glad to help the Catholic Church smuggle Nazis into every Western nation gullible enough to take them. The KGB must have been amused that the Vatican was smuggling Soviet agents along with the Nazis into western countries.

It is estimated that the CIA experienced a 98% fatality rate behind the Iron Curtain, as every operation was betrayed by Kim Philby. Kim Philby played Allen Dulles and Jim Angleton like a fiddle.

One ex-CIA officer insists that it was Hugh Angleton who personally arranged for the Nazi gold to be trucked to Italy and his son James Angleton who would later block every investigation of it as the head of the CIA's Counterintelligence unit. [313]

During the war, an enormous amount of stolen gold was exchanged by the Nazis, through Switzerland and the Bank of International Settlement (BIS), to pay for war materials used in the war. Additionally, a great amount of wealth that had been accumulated by the Nazis during the war seemed to have just vanished by the end of the war. Although the Germans lost the war, the Nazis, because of their connections to and knowledge about the network of worldwide bankers, financiers and businessmen were able to escape with much of their assets intact.

The CIA's Richard Helms also worked for the OSS during World War II. Richard Helms's grandfather Gates W. McGarrah from 1930 to 1933 was head of the Bank of International Settlements (BIS), which formed originally to help facilitate Germany's World War I war reparations payments, but BIS soon morphed into a conduit for moving funds in and out of Nazi Germany. Which may explain how Richard Helms was able to get a prized interview with Adolf Hitler back in 1936 when Helms was working with United Press as a writer for the Indianapolis Times Publishing Company. [314]

At the end of the war Allen Dulles and those who had traded with the enemy, and or who had developed economic relationships with German and/or Nazi bankers and industrialists volunteered their services, or the services of their proxies, for the administration of post war Germany and Italy. Not out of patriotism, but to suppress and hide the evidence concerning their dealings with the Nazis and to preserve their relationship with those still in the possession of enormous wealth. [315]

It is estimated that the escaped Nazis set up over 250 front corporations worldwide.

Immediately following the war, the Nazi spy organization run by Reinhard Gehlen sold itself as America's answer to countering the Soviets and jumped right in bed with the CIA. Another bargaining chip for Gehlen, you can be pretty sure, was that he was aware of Allen Dulles's and all his American business buddy's relationship with Nazi Germany over the years. Dulles probably had to bring Gehlen's group into the CIA in order to help keep hidden all of his and his friend's misdeeds and treason.

It is now obvious that it was not in the best interest of the United States to give a Nazi spy organization the incentive to trump up the Soviet threat during "the cold war," but that is exactly what was done. The bigger and scarier the Soviet Union could be made to appear by the Gehlen organization, the more funding and power for the Gehlen spy organization.

Supreme Court Justice Arthur Goldberg served in U.S intelligence during World War II and collected information on the Dulles boys' activities over the years. He told the authors of The Secret War Against The Jews in an interview, "The Dulles brothers were traitors." [316]

Roosevelt entrusted the post-war probe of American financial collaboration with the Nazis to Henry Morgenthau, his Secretary of the Treasury. Morgenthau initiated Operation Safehaven, a program to trace Nazi flight-capital back to the western investors. Morgenthau's original files escaped Dulles's shredder and can be found in the wartime State Department Post Files. The Switzerland Post files of Operation Safehaven accused Dulles of laundering money for the Nazis. The Safehaven files were stolen by Eleanor Dulles and given to the Zionist intelligence service. They then blackmailed Nelson Rockefeller into pressuring the Latin American nations to supply the extra votes needed in the UN for the creation of the State of Israel.

Navy Lieutenant Commander Richard Nixon oversaw reviewing, at the Brooklyn Navy Yard, captured German financial documents, some of which, according to legend, involved the Dulles brothers and their clients. It is interesting to note that later the Dulles brothers financed Richard Nixon's first run for Congress and then later persuaded Eisenhower to select Richard Nixon as his Vice President. [317]

Then one day I picked up on the fact that in the time

leading up to the assassination, President Kennedy and Nikita Khrushchev were in the process of talking in the backchannel and in letters to one another concerning what to do about the flashpoint between the two sides in Germany and in particular the Berlin problem. This preliminary discussion came on the heels of the narrowly avoided nuclear conflict between the two sides over Cuba and was an attempt by the two leaders to possibly defuse tensions over Berlin. Khrushchev suggested in one of his letters the permanent division of Germany.

The eventual reunification of Germany was most certainly a goal and a dream of the Gehlen organization and of all good Germans everywhere. President Kennedy and Khrushchev were working the backchannel, exploring a possible solution to be applied to the "German fatherland." As we have seen, many of the players from the CIA on down were partnered with the Nazis to the point of taking huge risks even while the war raged around them.

By 1962 the West German government had grown anxious about the fact that President Kennedy might someday pull U.S. troops out of Germany, leaving the country defenseless against the Soviets.

In this assassination story, two of the leading organizational candidates for having pulled off the assassination, the CIA, and the Mafia, and we have seen how in bed they were back then. Well, if that is believable then equally believable is the possibility that many powerful people inside and outside of the CIA had a very longstanding relationship with the real original Nazi brotherhood. Pressure and even blackmail might especially have come to bear if the "Fatherland" was being threatened by the thought of a permanent division of Germany, or even worse, an abdication of defense against the Soviet Union through the withdrawal of American forces from Germany.

At the very moment of the assassination [of President Kennedy] General Maxwell Taylor and the Joint Chiefs of Staff were meeting in the Pentagon's Gold Room with the commanders of the West German Bundeswehr (Germany's Federal Defense Force, its military). [318]

Reminder, Angleton said, "Do you know how I got to be in charge of counterintelligence? I agreed not to polygraph or require detailed background checks on Allen Dulles and 60 of his closest friends. They were afraid that their own business dealings with Hitler's pals would come out. They were too arrogant to believe that the Russians wouldn't discover it all." (Please note Angleton's last sentence. He is indicating that the Soviets had figured it out and knew all about Dulles's past dealings with the Nazis. Therefore, the Soviets had the ability to blackmail Dulles and 60 of his closest friends, in addition to the power of blackmail already possessed by the Nazis of old.)

Over his lifetime Allen Dulles jumped in government service with the State Department then into private enterprise, back into government service with the OSS, out into private enterprise, then back into public service with the CIA. Was it in service to the nation, or was it in the best interest of Allen Dulles?

## DEALING WITH BERLIN

An assumed intelligence asset once said to me: "I know it was a sad day in America when the President was killed. There is no doubt about that. For two reasons: that somebody would do it, and two **they never got a chance to figure out what he was going to do**, but it is an unfortunate set of circumstances. I think it is important for people to know what could have happened and let them make their own decisions."

What was it that the American people never got a chance to figure out, that President Kennedy was going to do?

Well one possibility: The secret agreement between Kennedy and Khrushchev to end the Cuban Missile Crisis had gone beyond removing the missiles in exchange for a U.S. pledge not to invade Cuba. **Kennedy and Khrushchev had also agreed to deal with Berlin** and with the entire issue of East Germany. [319]

Following the Cuban Missile Crisis, Khrushchev was under tremendous pressure and criticism in his own country and from communist China who was pushing for more radical measures and challenging for the leadership of the global communist movement. Khrushchev appears to have determined that the best way to strengthen the Soviet standing and or his own standing was to establish closer relations with the United States. Khrushchev and Kennedy were definitely moving toward détente and working together as evidenced by their letters, President Kennedy's speech to American University and their signing of the nuclear test ban treaty.

Here is further evidence concerning Germany. On October

26, 1962, in recorded conversation at the White House during the Cuban missile crisis the following was said by Douglas Dillon: "This Turkish thing [the withdrawal of US missiles in Turkey] has got to be thrown, you're quite right, Mr. President, into the overall European context; **and you can bring in Berlin**, I think it's fine." (1:28:53) "The Turkish proposal opens the way to a major discussion toward relaxed tensions in Europe, **including Berlin**." (1:29:52) One participant (unidentified) reacts: "**If you mention that, you've lost the Germans**." (1:30:09) [320]

October 29, 1962, the day following the end to the Cuban Missile Crisis, President Kennedy was recorded expressing the hope that we can use this moment to initiate a "decent deal in Berlin" since it is our most "paralyzing" problem. (1:13:45) [321]

Kennedy and Khrushchev exchanged at a minimum 120 different letters as can be found in the book *The Kennedy-Khrushchev Letters*. Khrushchev can be seen in his letters pushing for a German peace treaty the purpose and outcome of which appears to be, as **Khrushchev is proposing, the official recognition of two sovereign German States**. I can see why the escaped Nazis of old and any good Germans in general would not like this possibility, as I am sure their ultimate desire would be the re-unification of their country, not the formal recognition that they should be permanently divided.

### Nazis Seriously? Didn't They Lose The War?

I once exclaimed when putting this story together, "you wouldn't believe how close the CIA and the Mafia was back then." Well, you wouldn't believe how close a faction of the State Department, and Allen Dulles was with the surviving, and some might say thriving German Nazis whom Allen Dulles and James Jesus Angleton helped in their escape through the ratlines, following the war. [322]

I know what you might be thinking, Nazis, that's crazy! That is the same thing I first thought when I read that Jack Ruby wrote in a letter from jail, "The old war lords are going to come back. S.A. [South America] is full of these Nazis! They will know that it is only one kind of people that would do such a thing...that would have to be the Nazis and that is who is in power?"

The last thing I focused on was the Nazis from World War II. I had seen what Jack Ruby had written in a letter while in prison about Nazis. Ruby wrote, "This man [Lyndon Johnson] is a Nazi in the worst order." And I said to myself, that's just crazy; Jack Ruby must have lost it. I had also seen where the New Orleans District Attorney had pointed at the Nazis as relates to the assassination, but Garrison pointed at one time or the other at just about everybody except the Mafia, so I discounted this, thinking that he surely meant Americans who espoused Nazi beliefs. Every group imaginable seems somehow to have been made to look peripherally associated with the assassination. It never occurred to me that we might be talking about the real Nazis from World War II. After all everyone knows that they were defeated in World War II, right?

In my studying I read a story published out on the internet, which came from *Confession To Conspiracy To Assassinate JFK* written by Sondra London based on her interviews with Kerry Thornley, which was shown on TVs "A Current Affair." That interview really kept working on me over the years. In 1959, Kerry Thornley served in the Marines with Lee Oswald. Thornley talked in this interview about these two guys he used to meet with in New Orleans a year or so preceding the assassination of President Kennedy. One called himself Gary Kirstein or was referred to as "Brother-in-law." Years later when Watergate rolled around Kerry Thornley saw a picture of E. Howard Hunt in the newspapers and seemed pretty sure that this was the same guy calling himself "Brother-in-law" back in 1962.

Brother-in-law would serve Thornley awful tasting coffee and over the years Kerry began to remember things that had occurred and were said during these get togethers. Making it sound like he had been drugged and perhaps hypnotized as if he might have been a part of the CIAs MK/ULTRA Program. I would also add that Kerry professed but did not explain the fact that he had traveled to Mexico City around the same time that Oswald was supposedly there. This is perhaps just another example of another young American male trying to get into Cuba at about this time.

According to Joan Mellen in the book *A Farewell to Justice*, the leaflets handed out by Lee Harvey Oswald in support of the Fair Play for Cuba Committee were ordered and picked up by Kerry Thornley who called himself Lee Osborne. Additionally, there were a number of people who witnessed Lee Oswald and Kerry Thornley together in the New Orleans, in the summer of 63. [323]

"Brother-in-law" professed to Thornley that he was a Nazi and as a side note he seemed to use a lot of Mafia slang and exhibiting a lot of knowledge in that area as well. But the thing that "Brother-in-law" said that really kept turning over and over in my mind was that he said, something like "Kerry, you know, **the Germans lost the war, but the Nazis were actually winning economically.**" What? Now wait a minute, I thought, I mean didn't we wipe out the Nazis in 1945? Well, read on.

Lee Oswald's newfound friend in Dallas, George de Mohrenschildt was suspected by the FBI and British intelligence of being a spy for the Nazis in this country, during World War II. [324]

Clay Shaw is believed to have participated in "Operation

Paperclip." Operation Paperclip was the U.S. operation that grabbed as many German scientists as we could and brought them to the United States at the end of World War II.

How might Bill Harvey have felt about the possibility of a compromise on West Berlin and a watering down of western military forces there? I can't speak for big Bill Harvey, but once again here is what C.G. Harvey had to say about Berlin: "Bill always believed that one person could make a difference. And he did. He made a difference in Berlin … He held Berlin for the west. There were only seventy-five of us up there. But those of us who were there, the seventy-five, held Berlin for the west. Knowing that, you and your husband spent your whole life fighting to have the downfall of Communism, so that they couldn't blow us up and rule the world. The only way to be safe is to be strong." *Andy Alderton/C.G. Harvey Interview*

# HINTS AND GLIMPSES

CIA hints and rumors following the assassination seemed intent on pointing the finger at William King Harvey, as the renegade CIA officer who brought about the assassination of President Kennedy, but I think it goes much deeper. If Bill Harvey was involved in the assassination of President Kennedy he certainly did not act alone, nor was he the originator, nor did he have the power, or the authority to put such an action in motion. On the other hand, there is no doubt that William King Harvey was fully capable of pulling off such an operation, while leaving no evidence, trace, or hint of his involvement.

Yes the Mafia participated in the assassination, they pretty much have admitted that over the years and the CIA Guatemalan Coup/Bay of Pigs guys most definitely appear to have been involved in activities surrounding the assassination. But for the bigger picture one need only focus in on what Madline Brown told us about a party the night before the assassination. In attendance: rich Texas oil guys, Vice President Lyndon Johnson, J. Edgar Hoover, Richard Nixon, and the big tip off: John J. McCloy.

LBJ's mistress, Madeleine Brown, reports in her book "Texas in the Morning" that, "Thursday night, Nov. 21, 1963, the evening before the assassination, I attended a social gathering. It was a tribute honoring **FBI Director J. Edgar Hoover**. The guest list included **John McCloy** [later on the Warren Commission], **Richard Nixon**, and oilmen such as **Clint Murchison and H.L. Hunt. Vice President Lyndon Johnson** made an unscheduled visit, and the group immediately went behind closed doors." A short time later Lyndon Johnson re-appeared and whispered in his mistress's ear "After tomorrow those goddamn Kennedys will never embarrass me again - that's no threat - that's a promise." She then says that "Johnson went to the night club 'The Cellar' where many of President Kennedy's Secret Service detail partied until four in the morning."[325]

I had heard of everyone else at the party, but who the hell was John J. McCloy?  John J. McCloy was an attorney by profession, from the United States, who among other things shared a box with Adolph Hitler at the 1936 Olympics in Germany.  He worked closely with many German companies beginning after World War I.  McCloy was an attorney for Farben the big German chemical monopoly and one of Hitler's biggest suppliers.  McCloy in his lifetime was chairman of Chase Manhattan Bank, chairman of the Ford Foundation, trustee of the Rockefeller Foundation, Council on Foreign Relations, president of the World Bank, had a close relationship with the Rockefeller family, served during World War II as Assistant Secretary of War, and was the U.S. High Commissioner for Germany after the war. **As U.S. High Commissioner for Germany** immediately following World War II he oversaw the creation of the Federal Republic of Germany and **he conducted a campaign of wholesale pardoning and commuted the sentences of many Nazi war criminals**, including those of the prominent industrialists Friedrich Flick and Alfried Krupp, and Martin Sandberger, the son of an IG Farben industrialist. **John McCloy, months later following this party, would serve on the Warren Commission with his good friend Allen Dulles**!

Allen Dulles, James Jesus Angleton, and Richard Helms appear to me to be the ones who would have been capable of overseeing and coordinated all the elements involved in the Kennedy assassination, one of the elements might have been Bill Harvey.  Why would Allen Dulles, James Jesus Angleton, and Richard Helms orchestrate the assassination of President Kennedy? It must be understood that Allen Dulles, early on was a Wall Street attorney who was dedicated to his constituents and dedicated to keeping many of their international and domestic activities a secret. Some of the constituents for whom Dulles and Angleton served would have their own specific reasons for wanting to stop, or reverse President Kennedy's policies, direction, and initiatives.

I noticed how tight Allen Dulles and others had been with German business interests prior to, during, and after World War II. Plus, Allen Dulles and Jim Angleton are said to have helped a number of Nazis to escape after the war through the ratlines along with helping to facilitating the transfer of their war loot through the international banking system. [326] It is my goal to show how Dulles's and Angleton's German friends might have called on them, or had a handle on them, or blackmailed them, to stop President Kennedy from negotiating with Khrushchev the permanent division of Germany.

Although Allen Dulles was no longer in charge of the CIA at the time of the Kennedy assassination, I think it is important to understand that "the old man" as his functionaries in the agency affectionately called him, continued receiving direction from him. Allen Dulles retained his power and had the clout to steer the direction of the CIA, via the loyalty of Richard Helm, James Jesus Angleton, Tracy Barnes and E. Howard Hunt. Allen Dulles power to still direct the CIA came in part from Angleton and Helms knowledge and recognition that Dulles was the nexus, the connection, the link to the wishes of a very rich, powerful, and well-connected crowd.

David Talbot, author of *The Devil's Chessboard* writes. Following Allen Dulles's dismissal from the CIA, Dulles's brick house on Q Street became a boiling center of anti-Kennedy opposition. The actively retired spymaster maintained a busy appointment calendar, meeting not only with retired CIA old boys like Charles Cabell, but with a steady stream of top-rank, active-duty agency officials such as Angleton, Helms, Cord Meyer, and Desmond Fitzgerald. More surprisingly, Dulles also conferred with midlevel officials and operational officers such as E. Howard Hunt, James Hunt (a key deputy of Angleton, and no relation to Howard), and Thomas Karamessines (Helms's right-hand man). McCone, too, routinely checked in with his predecessor, dining with him and sending him cordial notes. E. Howard Hunt during this time could often be found working with Dulles. Hunt was a prolific author churning out spy novels. In 1962 E. Howard Hunt assisted Allen Dulles in writing his book *The Craft of Intelligence.*

Following on the heals of the Bay of Pigs, E. Howard Hunt became a personal assistant to Allen Dulles. It is a fact that E. Howard Hunt worked with Allen Dulles to write his memoirs following Dulles's dismissal from the CIA.

Allen Dulles was in Dallas Texas between October 25 and 29, 1963 speaking to the Dallas Council on World Affairs. Writes the author of *The Devil's Chessboard*, "Dulles often used speaking engagements and vacations as covers for serious business, and his detour through Texas bears the markings of such a stratagem. His stopover in Texas stood out as an anomaly in a book tour otherwise dominated by appearances on the two coasts." Dulles of course had a long-standing relationship with Texas oil. "With the Kennedy trip to Texas just weeks away, the president was surely a hot topic in these local circles."

David Talbot further writes: In the weeks leading up to the assassination of President Kennedy the flurry of meetings at Dulles's home intensified and on the weekend of the assassination. Even though he had been removed from the agency two years earlier, Dulles hunkered down from November 22$^{nd}$ through November 24$^{th}$, for unexplained reasons, at a top-secret CIA facility in northern Virginia known as "the Farm. [327]

Dulles reportedly worked hard to get President Johnson to appoint him to the Warren Commission. He was so active on the Warren Commission that some said it should have been called the "Dulles Commission."

Additionally, it appears that the prospect of a loss of power, position, privilege, survival, and prestige can be very motivational for some when backed into a corner. **Examples of being backed in a corner at the time of the Kennedy assassination:**

- Lyndon Johnson's very real possibility of being dropped from the ticket by the Kennedys in the next Presidential election and his political career ended.

- The Mafia from the extreme pressure and harassment being applied to the Mafia by Bobby Kennedy.

- The animosity between the Kennedys and J. Edgar Hoover of the FBI.

- The threat of assassination made clear to Fidel Castro.

- President Kennedy's threatened revocation of the "oil depletion allowance" which was saving the oil industry millions in taxes.

- Kennedy's blocking of nuclear weapons to Israel and Israel's assured survival.

- A potential agreement between Kennedy and Khrushchev to permanently divide Germany, which any good German or Nazi would oppose.

- The embarrassment of being fired and having your career ended and your reputation tarnished by the Kennedy's, which Dulles, Bissell, Cabell, and William Harvey got to experience and which Richard Helms surely would have experienced had Bobby Kennedy's learned that Helms was still using the Mafia to try and assassinate Castro.

And what message did the termination of William King Harvey, Dulles, Cabell, and Bissell at the hands of Kennedys send to the members of the U.S. intelligence community? Any excuse and you are gone. What is the one thing that really made Bobby Kennedy mad in this story? Bobby Kennedy got really mad when he learned that the CIA was using the Mafia in attempts to assassinate Castro. Bobby Kennedy gave instructions that he was to be informed of such in the future and was led to believe that the Mafia involvement was a thing of the past, when in fact the Mafia's involvement had not been terminated. William King Harvey and Richard Helms did not curtail this activity; even after learning that this made Bobby Kennedy mad. By working with the Mafia, the CIA had in effect helped to immunize the Mafia from prosecution. It was the Mafia's get out of jail free card. This would have been excuse enough for Bobby Kennedy. Knowledge of this and heads would have rolled, especial vulnerable, Richard Helms.

Richard Helms and William King Harvey both have demonstrated a certain contempt for authority. Richard Helms was in fact later convicted of perjury before Congress, which he declared "a badge of honor."

If the CIA's perception of themselves, or their institution, was one of a patriot and a guardian, when personally backed into a corner what might their reaction have been to the threat issued by the Kennedys to smash their institution into little pieces, to cut off their unvouchered funding and diminish their power? They would probably be looking for any excuse, real or imagined, to justify the elimination of the threat to the game they had going and the game that they loved to play. Bill Harvey has been reported as saying that "some of the acts of the Kennedys bordered on treason."

## ALLEN DULLES, JAMES JESUS ANGLETON, & RICHARD HELMS

Allen Dulles and Jim Angleton's history traces back to World War II and in particular their joint effort to facilitate the escape of the Nazis and their war loot. [328]

Allen Dulles appears to be more loyal to his business interests and devoted to keeping his and his associate's past history hidden, than he was loyal and devoted to his country. You don't have to take my word for it, again, Allen's brother Foster Dulles spelled it out for us when he said: "The United States of America does not have friends; it has interests." In other words, Allen Dulles was not as much a friend to his country, as much as he and his brother Foster had business interests and those business interested needed protection. Sadly, this protection of foreign assets was provided for by the U.S. Military and later by the CIA, at the expense of the American taxpayer and at the expense of the lives of American's sons and daughters.  This claim is based upon their interest in United Fruit in Guatemala in 1954 and in Standard Fruit in Cuba at the time of Castro's confiscation of those assets and upon their need to hide their business dealings with the Nazis leading up to, during, and following the war.  There was the ongoing need to keep theirs and others past traitorous business activities from exposure.  Consider the blackmailing capability of those, like the Nazis, who possessing evidence of their business activities leading up to, during, and after the war.  We would be pretty naive if we believed that Reinhard Gehlen and his Nazi spy organization didn't have all kinds of documents, knowledge, and proof of the complicity throughout the war of the Dulles brothers and many other prominent American and European families. Remember even the CIA's Richard Helms worked with Allen Dulles and the OSS during World War II. Helms's grandfather, Richard McGarrah, is another who is said to have done business with Hitler.

Is it overreaching to suggest that the Nazis had the power to blackmail Dulles and other prominent American families? We only need to look to the book *The Secret War Against The Jews* page 167 where it says that the Jewish nation of Israel and Prime Minister Ben-Gurion "blackmailed the hell out of Nelson Rockefeller" to get the votes needed in the United Nations for the creation of the State of Israel. The book describes how Ben-Gurion knew all about what the Dulles brothers and Nelson Rockefeller had done in regard to the Nazis and in regard to garnering natural resources in South America during the war. My point, if Ben-Gurion and Israel had the power to blackmail this group then the Nazis would have had an even greater knowledge and capability to blackmail and/or to be able to call upon this little group of longtime friends to do their bidding.

At what points in history might the Nazis have used subtle pressure, or levered the power that they possessed, or simply took advantage of the bond they shared with Allen Dulles and his business associates? Some possibilities come to mind: the transferring of their wealth through the international banking system leading up to the end of the war, their escape from Germany toward the end of the war, their escape from prosecution (enter John McCloy), their establishment of some 250 companies worldwide after the war and the ability to keep their original German companies intact after the war, the matriculation of Gehlen's Nazi spy organization into the CIA, and finally in addressing the potential threat that President Kennedy and Soviet leader Nikita Khrushchev might have posed in settling on the permanent division of the German fatherland.

Here is the ultimate irony of ironies: If Allen Dulles and Jim Angleton and their many Nazi interconnections did help to bring about the demise of President Kennedy and thus the demise of President Kennedy's opposition to the development of nuclear weapons by Israel, how ironic is that? The Nazis may have facilitated, or brought about the demise of President Kennedy, thus opening the door for the nuclear defense of the Jewish State of Israel!

On the other hand, if the Israelis believed that their survival was dependent on their acquisition of a nuclear deterrent, which President Kennedy was doing all that he could to block and they helped to bring about the President's demise, how equally ironic is that? The Israelis may have helped the Nazis of old, by preventing the permanent division of the German fatherland!

In the book *Final Judgment*, author Michael Collins Piper states on page 57 that "it is his thesis ... that Ben-Gurion, in his final days as Prime Minister, ordered Israel's Mossad to orchestrate the assassination of John F. Kennedy." Kennedy was blocking nuclear development in Israel, refused to sign a security treaty with Israel, and on November 20, 1963, two days before the assassination, President Kennedy's delegation to the UN called for further movement on the Palestinian issue. The Israelis had connections to the Mafia's Meyer Lansky, to the French Secret Army Organization (OAS) whose Jean Souetre may have been one of the assassins, and they had a handle on Allen Dulles and Jim Angleton based on their knowledge of past Dulles/Angleton/Rockefeller activity.

I seriously doubt, because I haven't seen any proof, that the State of Israel had a hand in the assassination of President Kennedy, but I have little doubt that Angleton was involved in the assassination. We have seen how Bill Harvey and

Angleton avoided using Sicilian assassins for the fear of implicating the Mafia in the attempts to assassinate Castro. So why on earth would the Israeli's use a French assassin associated with the OAS? They wouldn't for the same reason, the OAS and its support from Israel would be too easy to trace and would result in Israels possible implication in the Kennedy assassination. Jack Ruby, aka Jack Rubenstein, was Jewis as well. The Israelis would not be dumb enough to use an OAS assassin, nor Jack Rubenstein. Although the Israelis obviously had enough on Dulles and Angleton to blackmail them concerning their Nazi history, I don't think that the Israelis would erect a monument commemorating a man, Jim Angleton, following his death, as Israel did, if Angleton's recognized service to Israel was based upon his having to be coerced or blackmailed. Rather you would erect a monument commemorating a man who went above and beyond what was asked of him. It would not surprise me if Angleton played a very important role in Israel's getting nuclear weapons, but I haven't seen any convincing evidence of Israeli's involvement in the Kennedy assassination.

Who coordinated the assassination, the misdirection, and the cover-up? My opinion, it had to be Allen Dulles, James Jesus Angleton, Richard Helms, David Athlee Phillips, Tracey Barnes, and E. Howard Hunt. Why did they do it? Because they had to. Their main motivation, to keep their past deeds hidden. We can see how certain groups, who knew back then what we know now, could easily have blackmailed this proud, smug little group.

What did they have to hide? How about a continuous partnership with the Nazis beginning in the 1930s? Partnering with the Mafia. Using taxpayer dollars and sacrificing America's sons and daughters to protect their foreign business interests.

Is blackmail beyond belief? We have been told that

blackmail, based upon knowledge concerning the Nazis insured the votes necessary for the creation of the State of Israel. Angleton himself said they [Dulles and company] were foolish to think that the Soviets wouldn't figure everything out. In other words, Angleton is telling us the Soviet's KGB and Leonid Brezhnev had figured out their dirty little Nazi secret and had a handle on this smug little group.

Nixon appears to have secured his financial backers based upon his knowledge of the Americans who helped bring Hitler to power and continued to trade with Nazi Germany throughout the war.

The escaped Nazis and Gehlin's spy organization knew all about Germany's relationship and history with these fellows.

Jim Angleton advised, "rely on your instinct, because the facts are so easy to manipulate."

## SO, WHAT'S YOUR INTEREST IN IT?

I was once asked: "So, what's your interest in it?" My interest began with my loyalty to Terre Haute and a mysterious story that sparked my imagination and interest. A story that hardly anyone had ever heard before.

Some authors might be tempted to wrap things up at this point and declare that Bill Harvey planned the assassination and reaped his revenge, and he may have. Bill Harvey certainly had connections to many if not all who appear to be involved. My heart, however, goes out to Bill Harvey. It may be because he is from Terre Haute, and I don't want to hang this on him. But I suspect that I feel for Bill Harvey because standing back from our viewpoint we have seen what Dulles and his following did to him. Bill Harvey's situation at the CIA reminds me of junior high school where you had your "clique", and you had your "in crowd." Bill Harvey was never really accepted by the ruling elite in the CIA, even though the people who worked under him in Germany raved about him and even though he appears to have been intellectually superior to most and was doggedly dedicated to his mission of beating back communism. The truth be told, the ruling elite probably laughed at him behind his back for taking this all so seriously. Didn't he understand that the real game was not really about fighting communists, it was all about personal self-interest, personal enrichment, money, wealth, power, manipulating world events, garnering and controlling the worlds natural resources, and hiding or covering up what they had done to get it? They weren't in their positions to serve their country; they were positioned to serve themselves and their friends. On top of this, I am sure it did not endear Bill Harvey to Allen Dulles when he pointed out that Kim Philby, son of Dulles's lifelong friend Jack Philby, was spying for the Soviets. This had to be embarrassing for both Allen Dulles and for Jim Angleton.

The pattern leading up to the assassination is that this elite group, led by Allen Dulles basically dumped on, or dumped everything on Bill Harvey. They dumped both the dirty work and the high-risk operations, all on Bill Harvey. So, if this proud group, which includes those who planned the Guatemalan Coup of 1954 and the Bay of Pigs fiasco, had a hand in the assassination, which I think we have seen that they probably did, why should we assume that they would suddenly include, feel the need to include, or even trust Bill Harvey as a part of their operation, unless it would be to continue the pattern of setting him up for a fall? I think the plan was to make things look like Bill Harvey did it in part by involving Bill Harvey's past operatives and associates. The plan that E. Howard Hunt was still pushing in taped interviews up to his death, where his primary focus of blame was pointed at Bill Harvey, even while Hunt listed Vice President Johnson as the lead member in his list of conspirators.

Ray Cline once said something along these lines, "It is probably not in the nation's best interest to continue to harass the CIA forever, let's get it out and get it over with."

So, that's my rendition of the story. For my sake, I hope you like it Harry, wherever you are.

---

If you wish to see copies of the following, I have scanned and placed them in an ebook with the title: Documentation

Supplement America's Crossroads. Here is a list of the documents that it contains:

- Terre Haute Police reports
- San Antonio's reply to the Terre Haute Police
- Terre Haute Police's Letter to Earl Warren, Warren Commission
- Redlich's memo at the Warren Commission
- FBI reports on Harry L. Power
- Signature cards from the Terre Haute House for 11/23/1963 – 11/30/1963 the period before, during and after Harry L. Power made his appearance. (In case you want to see if something additional might have been going on in the Terre Haute House, like meetings.)
- Copies of the Terre Haute House Register for the month of November 1963.

---

# CITATIONS

[1] Russell, Dick. *The Man Who Knew Too Much*, Carroll & Graf Publishers, 1992, P. 408-410 and Garrison, Jim. *On The Trail of the Assassins*, Warner Books, 1988, P. 214 and 216 and Morrow, Robert D. *Betrayal*, Henry Regnery Company, 1976. P. 122.

[2] *Final Report Of The Assassination Records Board*, P. 133 and HSCA 1801002510111 and Russell, Dick. *The Man Who Knew Too Much*, Carroll & Graf Publishers, 1992, P. 55-56, 408-410 and Garrison, Jim. *On The Trail of the Assassins*, Warner Books, 1988, P. 215 and Russell, Dick. *On The Trail Of The JFK Assassins*, Skyhorse Publishing, 2008, P. 192

[3] Russell, Dick. *The Man Who Knew Too Much*, Carroll & Graf Publishing, 1992. P. 572.

[4] News piece that was broadcast on WTWO, Terre Haute, done by Mark Edwards.

[5] Russell, Dick. *The Man Who Knew Too Much*, Carroll & Graf Publishing, 1992. P. 572-573.

[6] Kantor, Seth. *Who Was Jack Ruby?* Everest House, 1978, P. 86, 89, 156-157. and www.spartacus.schoolnet.co.uk/JFKredlich.htm and Shenon, Philip. *A Cruel and Shocking Act*, Henry Holt and Company, 2013, P. 126 and P. 141

[7] Pease, Lisa. *The Assassinations*, Feral House, 2003, P. 181-182

[8] Russell, Dick. *The Man Who Knew Too Much*, Carroll & Graf Publishers, 1992, P. 568, 585 and La Fontaine, Ray & Mary. *Oswald Talked*, Pelican Publishing Company, 1996, P. 374

[9] Affidavit by Buell Wesley Frazier and Frazier's testimony before the Warren Commission

[10] McCormick, Mike. *Terre Haute Queen City of the Wabash*. Arcadia Publishing, 2005, P. 127-126

[11] Mike Lunsford, Tribune-Star, August 25, 2019 and McCormick, Mike. Terre Haute Queen City of the Wabash. Arcadia Publishing, 2005, P. 127-126

[12] Mike Lunsford, Tribune-Star, August 25, 2019 and McCormick, Mike. Terre Haute Queen City of the Wabash. Arcadia and Mark Bennett, Tribune-Star, July 3,, 2009

[13] Wikipedia – Sin City and https://brisray.com/th/sincity2.htm Terre Haute Sin City and McCormick, Mike. Terre Haute Queen City of the Wabash. Arcadia Publishing, 2005, P. 135

[14] Rockefeller Commission 178-10002-10324 & Terre Haute/Mike McCormick & Indiana University

[15] FBI 124-90092-10021and Terre Haute Tribune-Star/Mike McCormick

[16] McCormick, Mike and the Terre Haute Tribune-Star

[17] Indiana University and Terre Haute Tribune-Star/Mike McCormick

[18] Harvey, C.G. Wife of William King Harvey

[19] Indiana State University

[20] Alderton, Andy - Interview with C.G. Harvey

[21] FBI 124-90092-10021 & Rockefeller Commission 178-10002-10324 and Indiana University

[22] Lamphere, Robert. The FBI-KGB War, Random House, 1986, P. 61 and Ganis, Major Ralph P., USAF, Ret., The Skorzeny Papers: Evidence for the Plot to Kill JFK, 2018, Skyhouse Publishing, Kindle Version

[23] Wikipedia on the Internet and Martin, David C. Wilderness of Mirrors, Harper & Row, 1980. P.23-24 and Stockton, Bayard. Flawed Patriot, Potomac Books, 2006, P. 15-16 and Trento, Joseph. The Secret History of the CIA, Random House/Forum, 2001, P. 42-43.

[24] FBI memo dated July 15, 1947, FBI memo dated July 23, 1947, and Martin, David Wilderness of Mirrors, Harper & Row, 1980. P.32-34 and Stockton, Bayard. Flawed Patriot, Potomac Books, 2006, P. 17-19 and Riebling, Mark, Wedge, Simon & Schuster/Touchstone, 1994, P. 89-90.

[25] Trento, Joseph. The Secret History of the CIA, Random House/Forum, 2001, P. 76.

[26] Martin, David. Wilderness of Mirrors, Harper & Row, 1980. P.37 and Stockton, Bayard. Flawed Patriot, Potomac Books, 2006, P. 25 and Trento, Joseph. The Secret History of the CIA, Random House/Forum, 2001, P. 77 and Riebling, Mark, Wedge, Simon & Schuster/Touchstone, 1994, P. 91 and Martin, David C. The CIA's Loaded Gun, The Washington Post Outlook, Sunday, October, 1976.

[27] Philby, Kim. My Silent War. Grove Press, Inc., 1968. P.163

[28] Martin, David. Wilderness of Mirrors, Harper & Row, 1980. P.65,23 and Riebling, Mark, Wedge, Simon & Schuster/Touchstone, 1994, P. 90-91 and Stockton, Bayard. Flawed Patriot, Potomac Books, 2006, P. 22,25,27 and Trento, Joseph. The Secret History of the CIA, Random House/Forum, 2001, P. 77.

[29] Cochrun, Tom. Indiana's James Bond. VideoIndiana Inc., 1986 (WTHR), Dispatch Printing Co.

[30] Cochrun, Tom. Indiana's James Bond. VideoIndiana Inc., 1986 (WTHR), Dispatch Printing Co.

[31] Burton, Hersh. The Old Boys, Tree Farm Books, 1992, 2002, P. 174

[32] Burton, Hersh. The Old Boys,Tree Farm Books, 1992, 2002, P. 174

[33] Burton, Hersh. The Old Boys,Tree Farm Books, 1992, 2002, P. 174

[34] Pease, Lisa, The Assassinations, Feral House, 2003. P. 137

[35] Buckley Jr., William F. Spytime, Harcourt, 2000. P. 9-10

[36] Loftus, John and Mark Aarons. The Secret War Against the Jews, St. Martin's Griffin, 1994. P. 87 and Trento, Joseph. The Secret History of the CIA, Random House/Forum, 2001, P. 35 and Mangold, Tom. Cold Warrior, Touchstone/Simon & Schuster, 1991. P. 38

[37] Martin, David C. Wilderness of Mirrors, Harper and Row Publishers, 1980. P. 12 and Luftus, John and Mark Aarons, The Secret War Against the Jews: How Western Espionage Betrayed

The Jewish People. St. Martin's Griffin, 1997. P. 87 and Mangold, Tom. Cold Warrior, Touchstone/Simon & Schuster, 1991. P. 41

[38] Pease, Lisa. The Assassinations, Feral House, 1991. P. 139

[39] Pease, Lisa. The Assassinations, Feral House, 2003. P. 137 and Mangold, Tom. Cold Warrior, Touchstone/Simon & Schuster, 1991. P. 31-33, 42-44 and Martin, David C. Wilderness of Mirrors, Harper and Row Publishers, 1980. P. 11-19

[40] Ganis, Major Ralph P., USAF, Ret., The Skorzeny Papers: Evidence for the Plot to Kill JFK, 2018, Skyhouse Publishing, Kindle Version and Martin, David. Wilderness of Mirrors, Harper & Row, 1980. P. 34-35 and Trento, Joseph. The Secret History of the CIA, Random House/Forum, 2001, P. 78.

[41] Philby, Kim. My Silent War. Grove Press/Dell Publishing, 1968. P. 164 and Corson, William and Trento, Susan and Trento, Joseph. Widows, Crown Publishers, Inc, 1989, P. 72 and Trento, Joseph. The Secret History of the CIA, Random House/Forum, 2001, P. 36-37, 39, 79. and Mangold, Tom. Cold Warrior, Touchstone/Simon & Schuster, 1991. P. 64

[42] Lamphere, Robert and Shachtman, Tom. The FBI-KGB War, Random House, 1986. P.329-230 and Martin, David. Wilderness of Mirrors, Harper & Row, 1980. P. 46-48

[43] Burton, Hersh. The Old Boys, Tree Farm Books, 1992, 2002, P. 176

[44] Martin, David. Wilderness of Mirrors, Harper & Row, 1980. P.57 and Corson, William and Trento, Susan and Trento, Joseph. Widows, Crown Publishers, Inc, 1989, P. 73 and Trento, Joseph. The Secret History of the CIA, Random House/Forum, 2001, P. 82.

[45] Luftus, John and Mark Aarons, The Secret War Against the Jews: How Western Espionage Betrayed The Jewish People. St. Martin's Griffin, 1997. P. 211 and Martin, David. Wilderness of Mirrors, Harper & Row, 1980. P.57 and Trento, Joseph. The Secret History of the CIA, Random House/Forum, 2001, P. 80.

[46] Philby, Kim. My Silent War. Grove Press/Dell Publishing,

*1968. P. 197*

[47] *Trento, Joseph. The Secret History of the CIA, Random House/Forum, 2001, P. 83.*

[48] *Luftus, John and Mark Aarons, The Secret War Against the Jews: How Western Espionage Betrayed The Jewish People. St. Martin's Griffin, 1997. P.21, 24, 39*

[49] *Trento, Joseph. The Secret History of the CIA, Random House/Forum, 2001, P. 83.*

[50] *Corson, William and Trento, Susan and Trento, Joseph. Widows, Crown Publishers, Inc, 1989, P. 71-73 and Mangold, Tom. Cold Warrior, Touchstone/Simon & Schuster, 1991. P. 346 and Martin, David. Wilderness of Mirrors, Harper & Row, 1980. P. 210-211 & 213.*

[51] *Wyden, Petter. The Wall: the Inside Story of Divided Berlin, Simon & Schusteer, 1989. P. 94*

[52] *Martin, David. Wilderness of Mirrors, Harper & Row, 1980. P. 63, 68*

[53] *Martin, David. Wilderness of Mirrors, Harper & Row, 1980. P. 66 and Trento, Joseph. The Secret History of the CIA, Random House/Forum, 2001, P. 93, 94*

[54] *Stockton, Bayard. Flawed Patriot, Potomac Books, 2006, P. 38, 47-48 and Trento, Joseph. The Secret History of the CIA, Random House/Forum, 2001, P. 130.*

[55] *Burton, Hersh. The Old Boys, Tree Farm Books, 1992, 2002, P. 174 and Martin, David. Wilderness of Mirrors, Harper & Row, 1980. P. 66-67 and Stockton, Bayard. Flawed Patriot, Potomac Books, 2006, P. 56.*

[56] *Martin, David C. The CIA's Loaded Gun, The Washington Post Outlook, Sunday, October, 1976 and Powers, Thomas. The Man Who Kept The Secrets. Alfred A. Knopf, 1979. P. 156*

[57] *Martin, David C. The CIA's Loaded Gun, The Washington Post Outlook, Sunday, October, 1976 and Ganis, Major Ralph P., USAF, Ret., The Skorzeny Papers: Evidence for the Plot to Kill JFK, 2018, Skyhouse Publishing, Kindle Version and Stockton, Bayard. Flawed Patriot, Potomac Books, 2006, P. 43-44, 61 and Murphy, David E. and Kondrashev, Sergei A. and Bailey,*

George, Battleground Berlin. Yale University Press, 1997. P. 153. And Thomas, Evan. The Very Best Men, Touchstone/Simon & Schuster, 1995, P. 131 and Martin, David. Wilderness of Mirrors, Harper & Row, 1980. P. 65. and Trento, Joseph. The Secret History of the CIA, Random House/Forum, 2001, P. 97.

[58] Cochrun, Tom. Indiana's James Bond. VideoIndiana Inc., 1986 (WTHR), Dispatch Printing Co. and Stockton, Bayard. Flawed Patriot, Potomac Books, 2006, P. 59-64.

[59] Stockton, Bayard. Flawed Patriot, Potomac Books, 2006, P. 68 and Thomas, Evan. The Very Best Men, Touchstone/Simon & Schuster, 1995, P. 132 and Trento, Joseph. The Secret History of the CIA, Random House/Forum, 2001, P. 97, 121-124

[60] Cochrun, Tom. Indiana's James Bond. VideoIndiana Inc., 1986 (WTHR), Dispatch Printing Co.

[61] Cochrun, Tom. Indiana's James Bond. VideoIndiana Inc., 1986 (WTHR), Dispatch Printing Co.

[62] Cochrun, Tom. Indiana's James Bond. VideoIndiana Inc., 1986 (WTHR), Dispatch Printing Co.

[63] Cochrun, Tom. Indiana's James Bond. VideoIndiana Inc., 1986 (WTHR), Dispatch Printing Co.

[64] Cochrun, Tom. Indiana's James Bond. VideoIndiana Inc., 1986 (WTHR), Dispatch Printing Co.

[65] Cochrun, Tom. Indiana's James Bond. VideoIndiana Inc., 1986 (WTHR), Dispatch Printing Co.

[66] Cochrun, Tom. Indiana's James Bond. VideoIndiana Inc., 1986 (WTHR), Dispatch Printing Co.

[67] Cochrun, Tom. Indiana's James Bond. VideoIndiana Inc., 1986 (WTHR), Dispatch Printing Co.

[68] Thomas, Evan. The Very Best Men, Touchstone/Simon & Schuster, 1995, P. 131 and Martin, David. Wilderness of Mirrors, Harper & Row, 1980. P. 67.

[69] Cochrun, Tom. Indiana's James Bond. VideoIndiana Inc., 1986 (WTHR), Dispatch Printing Co. and Martin, David. Wilderness of Mirrors, Harper & Row, 1980. P. 67

[70] Murphy, David E. and Kondrashev, Sergei A. and Bailey, George, Battleground Berlin. Yale University Press, 1997. P.

229-231 and Trento, Joseph. *The Secret History of the CIA*, Random House/Forum, 2001, P. 145. and yard Stockton, *Flawed Patriot*, Potomac Books, 2006, P. 87-91 and Martin, David C. *The CIA's Loaded Gun*, The Washington Post Outlook, Sunday, October, 1976

[71] Martin, David. *Wilderness of Mirrors*, Harper & Row, 1980. P.87-88 and Stockton, Bayard. *Flawed Patriot*, Potomac Books, 2006, P. 93 and Trento, Joseph. *The Secret History of the CIA*, Random House/Forum, 2001, P. 145 and Martin, David C. *The CIA's Loaded Gun*, The Washington Post Outlook, Sunday, October, 1976

[72] Helms, Richard and Hood, William. *A Look Over My Shoulder: A Life in the Central Intelligence Agency*, Presidio Press, 2004, P.137 and Murphy, David E. and Kondrashev, Sergei A. and Bailey, George, *Battleground Berlin*. Yale University Press, 1997. Picture after P. 262 and Trento, Joseph. *The Secret History of the CIA*, Random House/Forum, 2001, P. 146. and Stockton, Bayard. *Flawed Patriot*, Potomac Books, 2006, P. 92.

[73] Burton, Hersh. *The Old Boys*, Tree Farm Books, 1992, 2002, P. 353-355 and Winks, Robin W. *Cloak & Gown*, William Morrow and Company, 1987, P. 412-413 and Martin, David. *Wilderness of Mirrors*, Harper & Row, 1980. P. 90.

[74] Burton, Hersh. *The Old Boys*, Tree Farm Books, 1992, 2002, P. 355.

[75] Burton, Hersh. *The Old Boys*, Tree Farm Books, 1992, 2002, P. 355.

[76] Burton, Hersh. *The Old Boys*, Tree Farm Books, 1992, 2002, P. 355.

[77] Martin, David. *Wilderness of Mirrors*, Harper & Row, 1980. P. 90.

[78] Cline, Ray S. *The CIA Reality vs. Myth*, Acropolis Books, 1982, P. 187.

[79] Pease, Lisa. *The Assassinations*, Feral House, 2003. P. 162 and Trento, Joseph. *The Secret History of the CIA*, Random House/Forum, 2001, P. 191-192 and Martin, David C. *The*

CIA's Loaded Gun, The Washington Post Outlook, Sunday, October, 1976.

[80] Bardach, Ann Louise. The Washington Post, The Sugar King of Havana. Sunday, August 15, 2010. Internet: http://www.washingtonpost.com/wp-dyn/content/article/2010/08/13/AR2010081302364.html

[81] Cohen, Rich. The Fish That Ate the Whale: The Life and Times of America's Banana King, Farrar, Straus and Giroux, 2012. P. 186-195 and Ayala, Cesar J. American Sugar Kingdom, The University of North Carolina Press, 1999.

[82] Strodes, James. Allen Dulles, Master of Spies, Regnery Publishing, 1999. P. 504.

[83] New York Times, CIA: Maker of Policy, or Tool?, April 23, 1966 and Morrow, Robert D. The Senator Must Die, Roundtable Publishing, 1988, P. 71-72, 76, 86, 124-125, 151.

[84] Thomas, Evan. The Very Best Men, Touchstone/Simon & Schuster, 1995, P. 223 and Hersh, Seymour M. The Dark Side of Camelot, Back Bay Books-Little, Brown and Company, 1997. P. 186-187 and Stockton, Bayard. Flawed Patriot, Potomac Books, 2006, P. 147.

[85] Becker, Ed and Charles Rappley. All American Mafioso. Doubleday, 1991. P. 225

[86] Powers, Thomas. The Man Who Kept The Secrets. Alfred A. Knopf, 1979. P.157

[87] Thomas, Evan. The Very Best Men, Touchstone/Simon & Schuster, 1995, P. 206

[88] Martin, David C. The CIA's Loaded Gun, The Washington Post Outlook, Sunday, October, 1976 and Hersh, Seymour M. The Dark Side of Camelot. Back Bay Books/Little, Brown and Company, 1997. P. 192

[89] Stockton, Bayard. Flawed Patriot, Potomac Books, 2006, P. 114

[90] Trento, Joseph. The Secret History of the CIA, Random House/Forum, 2001, P. 195.

[91] Russell, Dick. On the Trail of the JFK Assassins, Skyhourse Publishing, 2008, P. 268-269

[92] Piper, Michael Collins. Final Judgment, The Wolfe Press, 1995, P. 100.

[93] Russell, Dick. On the Trail of the JFK Assassins, Skyhourse Publishing, 2008, P. 266, 273, 274-276

[94] Martin, David. Wilderness of Mirrors, Harper & Row, 1980. P. 120-121.

[95] Cochrun, Tom. Indiana's James Bond. VideoIndiana Inc., 1986 (WTHR), Dispatch Printing Co.

[96] Corn, David. Blond Ghost. Simon & Schuster, 1994. P. 48

[97] Cochrun, Tom. Indiana's James Bond. VideoIndiana Inc., 1986 (WTHR), Dispatch Printing Co.

[98] Cochrun, Tom. Indiana's James Bond. VideoIndiana Inc., 1986 (WTHR), Dispatch Printing Co.

[99] Cochrun, Tom. Indiana's James Bond. VideoIndiana Inc., 1986 (WTHR), Dispatch Printing Co.

[100] Wright, Peter. Spy Catcher. Stoddard Publishing, 1987. P. 146-162 and Trento, Joseph. The Secret History of the CIA, Random House/Forum, 2001, P. 195-196.

[101] Russel, Dick. The Man Who Knew Too Much. Carroll & Graf Publishers, 1992. P. 581

[102] Russell, Dick. The Man Who Knew Too Much, Carroll & Graf Publishing, 1992. P. 245, 247 and Martin, David. Wilderness of Mirrors, Harper & Row, 1980. P. 128 and Trento, Joseph. The Secret History of the CIA, Random House/Forum, 2001, P. 207 and Martin, David C. The CIA's Loaded Gun, The Washington Post Outlook, Sunday, October, 1976.

[103] Russell, Dick. The Man Who Knew Too Much, Carroll & Graf Publishing, 1992. P. 245 and Martin, David C. The CIA's Loaded Gun, The Washington Post Outlook, Sunday, October, 1976 and Martin, David. Wilderness of Mirrors, Harper & Row, 1980. P. 137

[104] Shackley, Ted and Finnery, Richard. Spymaster, Potomac Books, 2006, P. 50 and Hersh, Seymour M. The Dark Side of Camelot, Back Bay Books-Little, Brown and Company, 1997. P. 268.

[105] Weiner, Tim. Legacy of Ashes, Doubleday, 2007. P. 273. and

Hersh, Seymour M. The Dark Side of Camelot, Back Bay Books-Little, Brown and Company, 1997. P. 268.

[106] Weiner, Tim. Legacy of Ashes, Doubleday, 2007. P. 273. and Hersh, Seymour M. The Dark Side of Camelot. Back Bay Books/Little, Brown and Company, 1997. P. 269

[107] Hersh, Seymour M. The Dark Side of Camelot. Back Bay Books/Little, Brown and Company, 1997. P. 278

[108] Russo, Gus. Live By The Sword, The Secret War Against Castro and the Death of JFK, Bancroft Press, 1998. P. 450

[109] Thomas, Evan. The Very Best Men, Touchstone/Simon & Schuster, 1995, P. 297 and Martin, David. Wilderness of Mirrors, Harper & Row, 1980. P. 134 and Hersh, Seymour M. The Dark Side of Camelot. Back Bay Books/Little, Brown and Company, 1997. P. 278-279

[110] Martin, David. Wilderness of Mirrors, Harper & Row, 1980. P. 134.

[111] Corn, David. Blond Ghost, Simon & Schuster, 1994. P. 82 and Martin, David. Wilderness of Mirrors, Harper & Row, 1980. P. 135.

[112] Talbot, David. Brothers, Simon & Schuster. P. 104 and Corn, David. Blond Ghost, Simon & Schuster, 1994. P. 82.

[113] Martin, David. Wilderness of Mirrors, Harper & Row, 1980. P. 130 and Trento, Joseph. The Secret History of the CIA, Random House/Forum, 2001, P. 211.

[114] Corn, David. Blond Ghost, Simon & Schuster, 1994. P. 82 and Martin, David. Wilderness of Mirrors, Harper & Row, 1980. P. 135 and Trento, Joseph. The Secret History of the CIA, Random House/Forum, 2001, P. 212.

[115] Morrow, Robert D. First Hand Knowledge, S.P.I. Books/Shapolsky Publishers, Inc., 1992. P. 146, 349

[116] Hersh, Seymour M. The Dark Side of Camelot. Back Bay Books/Little, Brown and Company, 1997. P. 286 and Russo, Gus. Live By The Sword, The Secret War Against Castro and the Death of JFK, Bancroft Press, 1998. P. 65.

[117] "The CIA: America's Secret Warriors," The Discovery Channel, 1997.

[118] *Russo, Gus. Live By The Sword, The Secret War Against Castro and the Death of JFK, Bancroft Press, 1998. P. 82.*
[119] *Russo, Gus. Live By The Sword, The Secret War Against Castro and the Death of JFK, Bancroft Press, 1998. P. 80*
[120] *Stockton, Bayard. Flawed Patriot, Potomac Books, 2006. P. 128*
[121] *Powers, Thomas. The Man Who Kept The Secrets, Alfred A. Knopf, 1979. P. 161. and Russo, Gus. Live By The Sword, The Secret War Against Castro and the Death of JFK, Bancroft Press, 1998. P. 81.*
[122] *Mahoney, Richard D. Sons & Brothers, Arcade Publishing, 1999. P. 174. and Corn, David. Blond Ghost, Simon & Schuster, 1994. P. 82-83.*
[123] *Hersh, Seymour M. The Dark Side of Camelot. Back Bay Books/Little, Brown and Company, 1997. P. 272*
[124] *US CONARC Participation in the Cuban Crisis, 10/63, P. 8; CINCLANT Historical Account of Cuban Crisis, 4/29/63, P. 39; Department of Defense Operations during the Cuban Missile Crisis, 2/12/63, P.2*
[125] *CINCLANT Historical Account of Cuban Crisis, 4/29/62, P. 40*
[126] *Cochrun, Tom. Indiana's James Bond. VideoIndiana Inc., 1986 (WTHR), Dispatch Printing Co.*
[127] *Cochrun, Tom. Indiana's James Bond. VideoIndiana Inc., 1986 (WTHR), Dispatch Printing Co.*
[128] *Cochrun, Tom. Indiana's James Bond. VideoIndiana Inc., 1986 (WTHR), Dispatch Printing Co.*
[129] *Fursenko, Aleksandr and Naftali, Timothy. One Hell of a Gamble, W.W. Norton & Company, 1997. P. 193-194.*
[130] *Codevilla, Angelo. Informing Statecraft, The Free Press, Maxwell Macmillan International, 1992. P. 201-202.*
[131] *Martin, David. Wilderness of Mirrors, Harper & Row, 1980. P. 142.*
[132] *Corn, David. Blond Ghost, Simon & Schuster, 1994. P. 88.*
[133] *Trento, Joseph. The Secret History of the CIA, Random House/Forum, 2001, P. 216 and Corn, David. Blond Ghost,*

Simon & Schuster, 1994. P. 90-91 and Martin, David. Wilderness of Mirrors, Harper & Row, 1980. P. 141-142

[134] Cline, Ray S. The CIA Reality vs. Myth, Acropolis Books, 1982, P. 220.

[135] Cline, Ray S. The CIA Reality vs. Myth, Acropolis Books, 1982, P. 220.

[136] Cochrun, Tom. Indiana's James Bond. VideoIndiana Inc., 1986 (WTHR), Dispatch Printing Co.

[137] http://www.hpol.org/jfk/cuban/

[138] Hersh, Seymour M. The Dark Side of Camelot, Back Bay Books-Little, Brown and Company, 1997. P. 375 and Russo, Gus. Live By The Sword, The Secret War Against Castro and the Death of JFK, Bancroft Press, 1998. P. 81.

[139] Hersh, Seymour M. The Dark Side of Camelot, Back Bay Books-Little, Brown and Company, 1997. P. 375 and Russo, Gus. Live By The Sword, The Secret War Against Castro and the Death of JFK, Bancroft Press, 1998. P. 81 and Thomas, Evan. The Very Best Men, Touchstone/Simon & Schuster, 1995, P. 291 and Martin, David. Wilderness of Mirrors, Harper & Row, 1980. P. 144 and Trento, Joseph. The Secret History of the CIA, Random House/Forum, 2001, P. 251.

[140] Thomas, Evan. The Very Best Men, Touchstone/Simon & Schuster, 1995, P. 291 and Martin, David. Wilderness of Mirrors, Harper & Row, 1980. P. 144-145.

[141] Shackley, Ted and Finnery, Richard. Spymaster, Potomac Books, 2006, P. 68-69 and Martin, David. Wilderness of Mirrors, Harper & Row, 1980. P. 144-145 and Russo, Gus. Live By The Sword, The Secret War Against Castro and the Death of JFK, Bancroft Press, 1998. P. 81.

[142] Jones, Milo and Silberzahn, Phillippe. Constructing Cassandra: Reframing Intelligence Failure at the CIA, 1947-2001, Stanford Press, P. 141 and https://archive.org/stream/CIA McCone-DCI-History/McCone-DCI-History_djvu.txt and Martin, David. Wilderness of Mirrors, Harper & Row, 1980. P. 144

[143] Shackley, Ted. Spymaster, My Life in the CIA, Potomac

Books, Inc, 2006, P. 69

[144] Stockton, Bayard. Flawed Patriot, Potomac Books, 2006, P. 234-235.

[145] Thomas, Evan. The Very Best Men, Touchstone/Simon & Schuster, 1995, P. 297 and Hersh, Seymour M. The Dark Side of Camelot. Back Bay Books/Little, Brown and Company, 1997. P. 377

[146] Twyman, Noel. Bloody Treason, Laurel Publishing, 1997. Kindle E-Book and Stockton, Bayard. Flawed Patriot, Potomac Books, 2006, P. 183.

[147] Martin, David. Wilderness of Mirrors, Harper & Row, 1980. P. 146 and Trento, Joseph. The Secret History of the CIA, Random House/Forum, 2001, P. 251

[148] Martin, David. Wilderness of Mirrors, Harper & Row, 1980. P. 183.

[149] Stockton, Flawed Patriot, Potomac Books, 2006, P. 236.

[150] Stockton, Bayard. Flawed Patriot, Potomac Books, 2006. P. 236

[151] Summers, Anthony. Conspiracy, Paragon House, 1989, P. 529.

[152] Stockton, Bayard. Flawed Patriot, Potomac Books, 2006. P. 237

[153] Mellen, Joan, A Farewell To Justice, Skyhorse Publishing, 2013. Kindle Edition.

[154] Guy Johnson interview with Bernard Fensterwald, August 24, 1967, Assassination Archives and Research Center, Washington, D.C. and National Archives transcribed 6/5/67

[155] Martin and Lewis Affidavit and Russo, Gus. Live By The Sword, The Secret War Against Castro and the Death of JFK, Bancroft Press, 1998. P. 148 & 150

[156] http://mcadams.posc.mu.edu/weberman/nodule24.htm

[157] Martin and Lewis Affidavit and Russo, Gus. Live By The Sword, The Secret War Against Castro and the Death of JFK, Bancroft Press, 1998. P. 150

[158] Baker, Judyth Vary. Me & Lee. Trine Day, 2010. Location 3802 in Kindle Version

[159] *Summers, Anthony. Not In Your Lifetime. Marlowe & Company, 1998. P. 233*

[160] *Russell, Dick. The Man Who Knew Too Much, Carroll & Graf Publishers, 1992, P. 408-410 and Garrison, Jim. On The Trail of the Assassins, Warner Books, 1988, P. 214 and 216*

[161] *Baker, Judyth Vary. Me & Lee. Trine Day, 2010. Location 6810 in Kindle Version*

[162] *Mellen, Joan, A Farewell To Justice, Skyhorse Publishing, 2013. Kindle Edition.*

[163] *DiEugenio, James and Lisa Pease. The Assassinations, Feral House, 2003. P. xxii*

[164] *Baker, Judyth Vary. Me & Lee. Trine Day, 2010. Location 9166 in Kindle Version*

[165] *Marchetti, Victor. True Magazine, April 1975 and Morrow, Robert D. First Hand Knowledge, S.P.I. Books/Shapolsky Publishers, Inc., 1992. P. 286-287*

[166] Martin and Lewis Affidavit and Russo, Gus. Live By The Sword, The Secret War Against Castro and the Death of JFK, Bancroft Press, 1998. P. 148, 150

and Scott, Peter Dale. Crime and Cover-Up, Open Archive Press, 1993. P. 15 and Summers, Anthony. Conspiracy, McGraw-Hill, 1980. P. 579-580 and <u>HSCA</u> VOL. 10 Page 110 and <u>My notes from Jim Garrison investigation, New Orleans Library Microfilm, conversation between Richard Davis and author investigator, Harold Weisberg Jan. 24, 1968</u>

[167] *DiEugenio, James and Lisa Pease. The Assassinations, Feral House, 2003. P. xxii*

[168] *Summers, Anthony. Conspiracy, McGraw-Hill, 1980. P. 579-580*

[169] *Waldron, Lamar and Hartmann, Thom. Ultimate Sacrifice, Constable & Robinson Ltd, 2005, Kindle Version and Waldron, Lamar. Watergate, The Hidden History, Counterpoint Berkeley, 2012. Kindle Apple iBook and Simkin, John, David Morales biography at the British educational website www.spartacus.schoolnet.co.uk, see also Larry Hancock, Someone Would Have Talked (Southlake, TX:*

JFK Lancer, 2006), many passages; Wayne Smith commnts on BBC "Newsnight" report 11-20-06; Eric hamburg, JFK, Nixon, Oliver Stone, and Me (New Yourk: Public Affairs, 2002); David Corn, Blond Ghost (New Your: Simon & Schuster, 1994), 85.

[170] Malone, William Scott. The Secret Life of Jack Ruby, New Times, 23 January 1978.

[171] Waldron, Lamar and Hartmann, Thom. Legacy of Secrecy, Counterpoint, 2008 and Waldron, Lamar. Watergate: The Hidden History, Counterpoint, 2013 and Waldron, Lamar and Hartmann, Thom. Ultimate Sacrifice, Counterpoint, 2008, Apple iBook and Kindle Versions and https://kennedysandking.com/john-f-kennedy-articles/maurice-bishop-documents and https://kennedysandking.com/john-f-kennedy-articles/maurice-bishop-was-david-atlee-phillips and https://en.wikipedia.org/wiki/David_Atlee_Phillips

[172] Morrow, Robert D. First Hand Knowledge, S.P.I. Books/Shapolsky Publishers, Inc., 1992. Page xi & Page 204-205

[173] Marchetti, Victor. True Magazine, April 1975 and Morrow, Robert D. First Hand Knowledge, S.P.I. Books/Shapolsky Publishers, Inc., 1992. P. 286-287

[174] Hancock, Larry. Someone Would Have Talked. JFK Lancer Productions & Publications, 2010.

[175] Baker, Judyth Vary. Me & Lee. Trine Day, 2010. Location 12021 in Kindle Version

[176] DiEugenio, James and Lisa Pease. The Assassinations, Feral House, 2003. P. xxii

[177] Martin and Lewis Affidavit and Microfilm from New Orleans Library/Jim Garrison's Papers and Russo, Gus. Live By The Sword, The Secret War Against Castro and the Death of JFK, Bancroft Press, 1998. P. 148.

[178] Russo, Gus. Live by the Sword. Bancroft Press, 1998. P. 422

[179] Piper, Michael Collins. Final Judgment, The Wolfe Press, 1995, P. 123 & 243 and Ganis, Major Ralph P., USAF, Ret., The Skorzeny Papers: Evidence for the Plot to Kill JFK, 2018,

Skyhorse Publishing, Kindle Version

[180] DiEugenio, James and Pease, Lisa. The Assassinations, Feral House, 2003. P XXIV.

[181] Stockton, Bayard. Flawed Patriot, Potomac Books, 2006, P. 221.

[182] Furiati, Claudia. ZR Rifle, The Plot to Kill Kennedy and Castro, Ocean Press, 1994. P. 162

[183] Dankbaar, Wim. Files On JFK, Wim Dankaar, 2007-2008. P. 137 and Internet: http://educationforum.ipbhost.com/index.php?showtopic=5793 and http://www.jfkmurdersolved.com/toshfiles.htm

[184] Dankbaar, Wim. Files On JFK, Wim Dankaar, 2007-2008. P. 137 and Internet: jfkmurdersolved.com/TOSHTRANS1.htmTosh

[185] Russo, Gus. Live By The Sword, The Secret War Against Castro and the Death of JFK, Bancroft Press, 1998. P. 304 and Stockton, Bayard Flawed Patriot, Potomac Books, 2006, P. 208-209 and Talbot, David. The Devil's Chessboard, HarperCollins Publisher, 2015. P. 476.

[186] Stockton, Bayard. Flawed Patriot, Potomac Books, 2006. P. 225

[187] Talbot, David. The Devil's Chessboard, HarperCollins Publisher, 2015. P. 477.

[188] Anderson, Jack. Peace, War, and Politics, A Forge Book, 1999. P. 115 & 116

[189] Summers, Anthony and Robbyn Summers, "The Ghost of November," Vanity Fair, December 1994, 109; also Washington Post, 20 November 1983 or 17 April 1981 and Talbot, David, Brothers . Simon & Schuster, 2008. P. 10. and http://www.maryferrell.org/pages/JFK_Assassination_Quotes_by_Government_Officials.html?search=One%20of%20your%20guys%20did%20it.

[190] Russo, Gus. Live By The Sword, The Secret War Against Castro and the Death of JFK, Bancroft Press, 1998. P. 165

[191] Adrian Alba interview with W. Scott Malone, 2-27-93 Alba repeated the story to Gus Russo and Waldron, Lamar and

Hartmann, Thom. Ultimate Sacrifice, Constable & Robinson Ltd, 2005, Kindle Version and Russo, Gus, Live by the Sword, Baltimore: Bancroft Press, 1998), p. 551;

[192] Russo, Gus. Live by the Sword. Bancroft Press, 1998. P. 141-142

[193] Mellen, Joan, A Farewell To Justice, Skyhorse Publishing, 2013. Kindle Edition and HSCA per DiEugenio, James. The Assassinations, Feral House, 2003. P. 235 and Summers, Anthony. Conspiracy, Paragon House, 1989. P. 338.

[194] Mellen, Joan, A Farewell To Justice, Skyhorse Publishing, 2013. Kindle Edition.

[195] Mellen, Joan, A Farewell To Justice, Skyhorse Publishing, 2013. Kindle Edition and CIA memo from Jerry Brown to chief, Security Analysis Group, June 11, 1976; NARA, JFK files, RIF 1993.06.29.15:26:50:400280 and NARA, JFK files, NIS (3 boxes) 1994 release. Memo from deputy chief, Operational support Division to chief, Support Branch, February 2, 1962. Subject: Hemming, Gerald Patrick and File no. 29 229 and Newman, John. Oswald and the CIA. Carroll & Graf Publishing, 1995. P. 101 & 251 & 253 & 254.

[196] Mellen, Joan, A Farewell To Justice, Skyhorse Publishing, 2013. Kindle Edition.

[197] Russell, Dick. The Man Who Knew Too Much, Carroll & Graf Publishing, 1992. P. 409 and Jones Harris memo to Jim Garrison (March 1, 1969).

[198] Local TV WTHI or WTWO and Harding, David. New York Daily News, Sunday, November 10, 2013, 12:36 and Christopher Bucktin. Mirror News November 10, 2013

[199] Mellen, Joan, A Farewell To Justice, Skyhorse Publishing, 2013. Kindle Edition.

[200] Source: text of documents given in *Flawed Patriot* Page 155.

[201] U.S. News & World Report, 2/19/1962 and Hersh, Seymour M. The Dark Side of Camelot, Back Bay Books-Little, Brown and Company, 1997. P. 247-250, 254-255 and Fursenko, Aleksandr and Naftali, Timothy. One Hell of a Gamble, W.W.

Norton & Company, 1997. P. 252.

[202] Summers, Anthony. Conspiracy, Paragon House, 1989, P. 528.

[203] Argosy Magazine, April 1977 and Newman, John. Oswald and the CIA. Carroll & Graf Publishing, 1995. P. 104-105.

[204] George T. Kalaris memo, subject: "Lee Harvey Oswald," dated September 18, 1975. See NARA, JFK files, RIF 1993.07.02.13:52:25:56030 and Newman, John. Oswald and the CIA. Carroll & Graf Publishing, 1995. P. 171 & 176.

[205] Morrow, Robert D. First Hand Knowledge, Spi Books A division of Shapolsky, 1992. P. 170-172.

[206] Francis Gary Powers with Curt Gentry, Operation Overflight: The U-2 Pilot Tells His Story for the First Time (New York: Holt, Rinehart and Winston, 1970). See also, L. Fletcher Prouty, The Secret Team: The CIA and Its Allies in Control of the U.S. and the World (Englewood Cliffs, N.J.: Prentice-Hall, 1973) and "The Sabotaging of the American Presidency – The U-2 Debacle." See also Michael R. Beschloss, MAY-DAY: Eisenhower, Khrushchev and the U-2 Incident (New York: Harper and Row, 1986) and Lawrence R. Houston in Periscope: Journal of the Association of Former Intelligence Officers XI (Summer 1986): 11. See also obfuscating statements of Dino Burgioni. and Mellen, Joan, A Farewell To Justice, Skyhorse Publishing, 2013. Kindle Edition.

[207] Trento, Joseph. The Secret History of the CIA, Random House/Forum, 2001, P. 229.

[208] Baker, Judyth Vary. Me & Lee. Trine Day, 2010. Location 3019 in Kindle Version

[209] Trento, Joseph. The Secret History of the CIA. Forum/Prima Publishing, 2001. P. 221

[210] Fursenko, Aleksandr and Naftali, Timothy. One Hell of a Gamble, W.W. Norton & Company, 1997. P. 323, 325

[211] Trento, Joseph. The Secret History of the CIA, Random House/Forum, 2001, P. 257, 260, 262, 266, 477

[212] Waldron, Lamar. Watergate: The Hidden History, Counterpoint, 2013, Apple iBook.

[213] Martin, David. *Wilderness of Mirrors*, Harper & Row, 1980. P. 152-153 and Trento, Joseph. *The Secret History of the CIA*, Random House/Forum, 2001, P. 262.

[214] Russell, Dick. *The Man Who Knew Too Much*, Carroll & Graf Publishing, 1992. P. 426-427.

[215] Philby, Rufina. *The Private Life of Kim Philby, The Moscow Years*, Fromm International, 1999 and Trento, Joseph. *The Secret History of the CIA*, Random House/Forum, 2001, P. 478.

[216] Fonzi, Gaeton. *The Last Investigation*, Thunder's Mouth Press, 1994. P. 79

[217] Riebling, Mark. *Wedge*, Touchstone Simon & Schuster, 1994. P. 174 and Newman, John. *Oswald and the CIA*. Carroll & Graf Publishing, 1995. P. 427-429

[218] Neman, John. *Oswald and the CIA*, Carroll & Graf Publishers, 1995. P. 400 and the "thirteenth appendix" to the HSCA Report, known as the "Lopez Report."

[219] Lane, Mark. *Plausible Denial, Was the CIA Involved in the Assassination of JFK?* Thunder's Mouth Press, 1991. P. 103

[220] Ayers, Bradley E. *The Zenith Secret*. VoxPop, 2006. P. 175

[221] Fonzi, Gaeton. *The Last Investigation*, Thunder's Mouth Press, 1994. P. 380, 382-383, 390, 388-389, 390 and Ayers, Bradley E. *The Zenith Secret*. VoxPop, 2006. P. 187

[222] Mahoney, Richard D. *Sons & Brothers*, Arcade Publishing, 1999 P. 166

[223] Fonzi, Gaeton. *The Last Investigation*, Thunder's Mouth Press, 1994. P. 386, 387

[224] Ganis, Major Ralph P., USAF, Ret., *The Skorzeny Papers: Evidence for the Plot to Kill JFK*, 2018, Skyhorse Publishing, Kindle Version

[225] Ganis, Major Ralph P., USAF, Ret., *The Skorzeny Papers: Evidence for the Plot to Kill JFK*, 2018, Skyhorse Publishing, Kindle Version and Piper, Michael Collins. *Final Judgment*, The Wolfe Press, 1995, P. 123 & 243

[226] Pease, Lisa. *The Assassinations*, Feral House, 2003. P 181 and Trento, Joseph. *The Secret History of the CIA*, Random House/Forum, 2001, P. 277.

[227] *Whitten deposition, P.73.*
[228] *Whitten deposition, P. 113.*
[229] RIF #104-10004-10199, "Report on Oswald's Stay in Mexico," by John Whitten, 12/13/63, P. 19.
[230] *Alba: interview with Anthony Summers, 1978; reported in affidavit of private researcher Ian MacFarlane, Decemver 23, 1975; Dallas Morning News, August 7, 1978; (HSCA comments) HSCA Report P. 193- and 146, Reily: the Garrison Case: A Study in the Abuse of Oower by Milton Brener (Clarkson N. Potter, New York, 1969), P. 47, FBI failure: (to use Cuban Section) HSCA Report P. 128.*
[231] *Cline, Ray S. The CIA Reality vs. Myth, Acropolis Books, 1982.*
[232] *Cline, Ray S. The CIA Reality vs. Myth, Acropolis Books, 1982. P. 72.*
[233] *Cline, Ray S. The CIA Reality vs. Myth, Acropolis Books, 1982. P. 79.*
[234] *Cline, Ray S. The CIA Reality vs. Myth, Acropolis Books, 1982. P. 128.*
[235] *Cline, Ray S. The CIA Reality vs. Myth, Acropolis Books, 1982. P. 133.*
[236] *Cline, Ray S. The CIA Reality vs. Myth, Acropolis Books, 1982. P. 184.*
[237] *Cline, Ray S. The CIA Reality vs. Myth, Acropolis Books, 1982. P. 185.*
[238] *Cline, Ray S. The CIA Reality vs. Myth, Acropolis Books, 1982. P. 125.*
[239] *Cline, Ray S. The CIA Reality vs. Myth, Acropolis Books, 1982. P. 154-155.*
[240] *Cline, Ray S. The CIA Reality vs. Myth, Acropolis Books, 1982. P. 155.*
[241] *Cline, Ray S. The CIA Reality vs. Myth, Acropolis Books, 1982. P. 192.*
[242] *Cline, Ray S. The CIA Reality vs. Myth, Acropolis Books, 1982. P. 165-166.*
[243] *Cline, Ray S. The CIA Reality vs. Myth, Acropolis Books,*

1982. P. 183.

[244] Ranelagh, John. The Agency, Simon & Schuster, 1986. P. 504.

[245] Cline, Ray S. The CIA Reality vs. Myth, Acropolis Books, 1982. P. 177-178.

[246] Cline, Ray S. The CIA Reality vs. Myth, Acropolis Books, 1982. P. 195.

[247] Cline, Ray S. The CIA Reality vs. Myth, Acropolis Books, 1982. P. 196.

[248] Marchetti, Victor and John D. Marks. The CIA and The Cult of Intelligence, Dell Publishing, 1974. P. 65

[249] Cline, Ray S. The CIA Reality vs. Myth, Acropolis Books, 1982. P. 209-211.

[250] Cline, Ray S. The CIA Reality vs. Myth, Acropolis Books, 1982. P. 211.

[251] Cline, Ray S. The CIA Reality vs. Myth, Acropolis Books, 1982. P. 218.

[252] Bundy, McGeorge and William Bundy. The Color of Truth, Simon & Schuster, 1998. P. 234.

[253] Wise, David and Ross, Thomas B. The Invisible Government, Random House, 1964. P. 234, 236, 238, 239.

[254] Cline, Ray S. The CIA Reality vs. Myth, Acropolis Books, 1982. P. 221-222.

[255] Cline, Ray S. The CIA Reality vs. Myth, Acropolis Books, 1982. P. 231.

[256] Cline, Ray S. The CIA Reality vs. Myth, Acropolis Books, 1982. P. 225.

[257] Cline, Ray S. The CIA Reality vs. Myth, Acropolis Books, 1982. P. 230.

[258] Cline, Ray S. The CIA Reality vs. Myth, Acropolis Books, 1982. P. 222-223.

[259] Cline, Ray S. The CIA Reality vs. Myth, Acropolis Books, 1982. P. 223 and Trento, Joseph. The Secret History of the CIA, Random House/Forum, 2001, P. 334-335.

[260] Powers, Thomas. The Man Who Kept The Secrets, Alfred A. Knopf, 1979. P. 190-191, 194-195.

[261] Hinckle, Warren and William Turner. *Deadly Secrets*, Thunder's Mouth Press, 1981 & 1992. P. xxxii
[262] Cline, Ray S. *The CIA Reality vs. Myth*, Acropolis Books, 1982. P. 12.
[263] Lane, Mark. *Plausible Denial*, Thunder's Mouth Press, 1991. P. 85-86
[264] Corn, David. *Blond Ghost*, Simon & Schuster, 1994. P. 78
[265] Shackley, Ted and Richard Finnery. *Spymaster*. Potomac Books, 2006. P. 56
[266] Corn, David. *Blond Ghost*, Simon & Schuster, 1994. P. 78.
[267] Pease, Lisa. *The Assassinations*, Feral House, 2003. P 140.
[268] Pease, Lisa. *The Assassinations*, Feral House, 2003. P 142.
[269] Pease, Lisa. *The Assassinations*, Feral House, 2003. P 143.
[270] Pease, Lisa. *The Assassinations*, Feral House, 2003. P 163.
[271] Philby, Rufina. *The Private Life of Kim Philby, The Moscow Years*, Fromm International, 1999.
[272] Trento, Joseph and Powers, Jacquie. Sunday news Journal, August 20, 1978.
[273] Mangold, Tom. *Cold Warrior*, Touchstone/Simon & Schuster, 1991. P. 340-341.
[274] Corson, William and Trento, Susan and Trento, Joseph. *Widows*, Crown Publishers, Inc, 1989, P. 71-73 and Mangold, Tom. *Cold Warrior*, Touchstone/Simon & Schuster, 1991. P. 346 and Martin, David. *Wilderness of Mirrors*, Harper & Row, 1980. P. 210-211 & 213.
[275] Mangold, Tom. *Cold Warrior*. Simon & Schuster, 1991. P. 133
[276] *The New Your Times*, March 1975 and Lane, Mark. *Plausible Denial*, Thunder's Mouth Press, 1991. P. 171
[277] Mellen, Joan, *A Farewell To Justice*, Skyhorse Publishing, 2013. Kindle Edition.
[278] Baker, Judyth Vary. *Me & Lee*. Trine Day, 2010. Location 4389 & 4571 in Kindle Version
[279] Newman, John. *Oswald and the CIA*. Carroll & Graf Publishing, 1995. P. 396.
[280] Pease, Lisa. *The Assassinations*, Feral House, 2003. P 197.

[281] Pease, Lisa. The Assassinations, Feral House, 2003. P 172.
[282] Corson, William and Trento, Susan and Trento, Joseph. Widows, Crown Publishers, Inc, 1989, P. 71-73 and Mangold, Tom. Cold Warrior, Touchstone/Simon & Schuster, 1991. P. 346 and Martin, David. Wilderness of Mirrors, Harper & Row, 1980. P. 202, 205, 207, 210-211 & 213.
[283] Wright, Peter. Spy Catcher, Stoddart Puvlishing Co., 1987. P 308.
[284] Pease, Lisa. The Assassinations, Feral House, 2003. P 194 and Lane, Mark. Plausible Denial, Thunder's Mouth Press, 1991, P. 171.
[285] Trento, Joseph. The Secret History of the CIA, Random House/Forum, 2001, P. 410-411.
[286] Aarons, Mark and Luftus, John, Ratlines. Mandarin, Octopus Publishing, 1991. P. 235 and Aarons, Mark and Luftus, John, Unholy Trinity, St. Martin's Press, 1991. P. 235.
[287] Martin, David. Wilderness of Mirrors, Harper & Row, 1980. P. 214.
[288] Fursenko, Aleksandr and Timothy Naftali. One Hell of a Gamble W.W. Norton & Company, 1997. P. 339
[289] Talbot, David. The's Chessboard, HarperCollins Publisher, 2015. P. 620 and Trento, Joseph. The Secret History of the CIA, Random House/Forum, 2001, P. 478
[290] Martin, David C. Wilderness of Mirrors, Harper and Row Publishers, 1980. P. xiii
[291] Summers, Anthony. Conspiracy. Paragon House, 1989. P. 528
[292] From Google Groups: alt.assassination.jfk by Gerry Simone or Tim Gratz on the internet sounds like he may have talked to Hemming.
[293] Willan, Philip. Puppetmasters: The Political Use of Terrorism in Italy, Authors Choice Press, 2002. P. 38 and Talbot, David. The Devil's Chessboard, HarperCollins Publisher, 2015. P. 475.
[294] Martin, David C. The CIA's Loaded Gun, The Washington Post Outlook, Sunday, October, 1976 and Stockton, Bayard.

Flawed Patriot, Potomac Books, 2006, P. 241.and Martin, David. Wilderness of Mirrors, Harper & Row, 1980. P. 183, 188, 186 and Trento, Joseph. The Secret History of the CIA, Random House/Forum, 2001, P. 253.

[295] *An Interview With Former CIA Executive Director Lawrence K. "Red" White, Central Intelligence Agency web page, by James Hanrahan* https://www.cia.gov/library/center-for-the-study-of-intelligence/csi-publications/csi-studies/studies/winter99-00/art3.html

[296] *An Interview With Former CIA Executive Director Lawrence K. "Red" White, Central Intelligence Agency web page, by James Hanrahan* https://www.cia.gov/library/center-for-the-study-of-intelligence/csi-publications/csi-studies/studies/winter99-00/art3.html

[297] *Trento, Joseph. The Secret History of the CIA, Random House/Forum, 2001, P. 405.*

[298] *An Interview With Former CIA Executive Director Lawrence K. "Red" White, Central Intelligence Agency web page, by James Hanrahan* https://www.cia.gov/library/center-for-the-study-of-intelligence/csi-publications/csi-studies/studies/winter99-00/art3.html

[299] *An Interview With Former CIA Executive Director Lawrence K. "Red" White, Central Intelligence Agency web page, by James Hanrahan* https://www.cia.gov/library/center-for-the-study-of-intelligence/csi-publications/csi-studies/studies/winter99-00/art3.html

[300] *Hersh, Seymour M. The Dark Side of Camelot. Back Bay Books/Little, Brown and Company, 1997. P. 189-190 and Martin, David. Wilderness of Mirrors, Harper & Row, 1980. P. 219, 221 and Russell, Dick. The Man Who Knew Too Much, Carroll & Graf Publishing, 1992. P. 581-582*

[301] *Cochrun, Tom. Indiana's James Bond. VideoIndiana Inc., 1986 (WTHR), Dispatch Printing Co.*

[302] *Martin, David C. The CIA's Loaded Gun, The Washington Post Outlook, Sunday, October, 1976 and Russell, Dick. The Man Who Knew Too Much, Carroll & Graf Publishing, 1992. P.*

582.

[303] Martin, David. *Wilderness of Mirrors*, Harper & Row, 1980. P. 222.

[304] Cochrun, Tom. *Indiana's James Bond*. VideoIndiana Inc., 1986 (WTHR), Dispatch Printing Co.

[305] Stockton, Bayard. *Flawed Patriot*, Potomac Books, 2006, P. 202.

[306] Russell, Dick. *On the Trail of the JFK Assassins*, Skyhourse Publishing, 2008, P. 245-246.

[307] Russo, Gus. *The Outfit*, Bloomsbury, 2001, P. 426.

[308] Andy Alderton/C.G. Harvey Interview and Mike McCormick/C.G. Harvey Interview

[309] Martin, James and Miller, Mark, *All Honorable Men*. Open Road Media, 2016. P. 51 and Quigley. P. 433 and Allen, Gary and Abraham, Larry. *None Dare Call It Conspiracy*, Concord Press, 2013, P. 85 and Still, William T. *New World Order*, Huntington House Publishers, 1990, P. 139-141 and Marrs, Jim. *The Rise of the Fourth Reich*, Harper, 2008, P. 8-12 and Luftus, John, *America's Nazi Secret*. Trine Day, 2010. Kindle Edition, Footnote 20 and Luftus, John and Mark Aarons, *The Secret War Against the Jews: How Western Espionage Betrayed The Jewish People*. St. Martin's Griffin, 1997. P. 55 and Talbot, David. *The Devil's Chessboard*, HarperCollins Publisher, 2015

[310] Luftus, John, *America's Nazi Secret*. Trine Day, 2010. Kindle Edition, Footnote 8: From the Treasury Department investigation, codenamed Operation Safehaven which is described in detail in J. Luftus and M. Aarons, *Unholy Trinity* and *Ratlines*.

[311] Lernoux, Penny, *In Banks We Trust*, Doubleday, 1984. P. 189 and Aarons, Mark and Luftus, John, *Unholy Trinity*, St. Martin's Press, 1991. P. 237-240, 277, 279 and Luftus, John, *America's Nazi Secret*. Trine Day, 2010. Kindle Edition and Luftus, John and Mark Aarons, *The Secret War Against the Jews: How Western Espionage Betrayed The Jewish People*. St. Martin's Griffin, 1997. P. 80, 82, 85 and Aarons, Mark and Luftus, John, *Ratlines*, Mandarin, 1991.

[312] *Luftus, John, America's Nazi Secret. Trine Day, 2010. Kindle Edition and Luftus, John and Mark Aarons, The Secret War Against the Jews: How Western Espionage Betrayed The Jewish People. St. Martin's Griffin, 1997. P. 77, 80, 82, 83 and Aarons, Mark and Luftus, John, Unholy Trinity, St. Martin's Press, 1991. P. 237-240.*

[313] *Luftus, John and Mark Aarons, The Secret War Against the Jews: How Western Espionage Betrayed The Jewish People. St. Martin's Griffin, 1997. P. 84 and Aarons, Mark and Luftus, John, Unholy Trinity, St. Martin's Press, 1991. P. 217 and Aarons, Mark and Luftus, John, Ratlines, Mandarin, 1991. P. 217 and Luftus, John, America's Nazi Secret. Trine Day, 2010. Kindle Edition*

[314] *Trento, Joseph J. Prelude To Terror, The Rogue CIA and the Legacy of America's Private Intelligence Network. Carroll & Graf Publishing, 2005. P. 4*

[315] *Luftus, John, America's Nazi Secret. Trine Day, 2010. Kindle Edition*

[316] *Luftus, John and Aarons, Mark, The Secret War Against the Jews: How Western Espionage Betrayed The Jewish People. St. Martin's Griffin, 1997, P. 71 and Yeadon, Glen and Hawkins, John. The Nazi Hydra in America, Progressive, 2008 Kindle Version and Talbot, David. The Devil's Chessboard, HarperCollins Publisher, 2015. P. 29.*

[317] Luftus, John and Mark Aarons, The Secret War Against the Jews: How Western Espionage Betrayed The Jewish People. St. Martin's Griffin, 1997 and Luftus, John, America's Nazi Secret. Trine Day, 2010. Kindle Edition

Lernoux, Penny, In Banks We Trust, Doubleday, 1984. P. 189 and Aarons, Mark and Luftus, John, Unholy Trinity, St. Martin's Press, 1991. P. 237-240, 277, 279 and Luftus, John, America's Nazi Secret. Trine Day, 2010. Kindle Edition and Luftus, John and Mark Aarons, The Secret War Against the Jews: How Western Espionage Betrayed The Jewish People. St. Martin's Griffin, 1997. P. 80 & 82 and Aarons, Mark and Luftus, John, Ratlines, Mandarin, 1991.

Luftus, John, America's Nazi Secret. Trine Day, 2010. Kindle Edition, Footnote 8.

[318] *Bamford, James. Body of Secrets, Random House/Anchor Books, 2002, P. 131 and Manchester, William. The Death of a President: November 20-November 25, 1963, Hachette Book Group, Little, Brown, 2013 and Luftus, John and Mark Aarons, The Secret War Against the Jews: How Western Espionage Betrayed The Jewish People. St. Martin's Griffin, 1997. P. 290*

[319] *Trento, Joseph. The Secret History of the CIA, Random House/Forum, 2001, P. 255.*

[320] *Wyzant/Resources: www.wyzant.com/resources/lessons/history/hpol/jfk/cuban/missilecrisis13*

[321] *JFK Library release notes prepared by Sheldon M. Stern and http://www.wyzant.com/help/history/hpol/jfk/cuban prepared by Jerry Goldman and Giel Stein.*

[322] *Aarons, Mark and Luftus, John, Unholy Trinity, St. Martin's Press, 1991. P. 237-240 and Luftus, John, America's Nazi Secret. Trine Day, 2010. Kindle Edition and Luftus, John and Mark Aarons, The Secret War Against the Jews: How Western Espionage Betrayed The Jewish People. St. Martin's Griffin, 1997. P. 80 & 82.*

[323] *Mellen, Joan, A Farewell To Justice, Skyhorse Publishing, 2013. Kindle Edition.*

[324] *Article: Oswald Friend Labeled CIA Informant in Memo. Dallas Times Harold, July 27, 1978.*

[325] *Brown, Madeleine Duncan. Texas In The Morning, A Harrison Edward Livingstone Book/The Conservatory Press, 1997, P. 166.*

[326] *Lernoux, Penny, In Banks We Trust, Doubleday, 1984. P. 189 and Aarons, Mark and Luftus, John, Unholy Trinity, St. Martin's Press, 1991. P. 237-240, 277, 279 and Luftus, John, America's Nazi Secret. Trine Day, 2010. Kindle Edition and Luftus, John and Mark Aarons, The Secret War Against the Jews: How Western Espionage Betrayed The Jewish People. St. Martin's Griffin, 1997. P. 80 & 82 and Aarons, Mark and Luftus, John, Ratlines, Mandarin, 1991.*

[327] *HSCA Deposition of E. Howard Hunt (November 3, 1978) Prt II, p. 6:10-17 and Talbot, David. The Devil's Chessboard, HarperCollins Publisher, 2015. P. 449, 487-488, 545-547.*

[328] *Lernoux, Penny, In Banks We Trust, Doubleday, 1984. P. 189 and Aarons, Mark and Luftus, John, Unholy Trinity, St. Martin's Press, 1991. P. 237-240, 277, 279 and Luftus, John, America's Nazi Secret. Trine Day, 2010. Kindle Edition and Luftus, John and Mark Aarons, The Secret War Against the Jews: How Western Espionage Betrayed The Jewish People. St. Martin's Griffin, 1997. P. 80 & 82 and Aarons, Mark and Luftus, John, Ratlines, Mandarin, 1991.*

# ABOUT THE AUTHOR

## Kevin Barr

Kevin Barr, is third generation Terre Haute, Indiana. Had he not lived in Terre Haute he would not have been able to see and connect so many dots concerning the Kennedy Assassination. His book, America's Crossroads, The Public Record takes you on a journey as it explores a German Mauser that was left in the Terre Haute House three days after the Kennedy assassination by a young twenty-year-old from San Antonio, Texas.

Two major CIA guys were from Terre Haute, William King Harvey, who headed the Mafia and anti-Castro Cuban attempts to assassinate Castro. Bobby Kennedy ruined Harvey career. Was the rifle a calling card from Bill Harvey to Bobby Kennedy? Or did master spy Kim Philby, who Bill Harvey exposed eleven years earlier arrange for the rifle in Terre Haute to make Bill Harvey look guilty? Ray Cline, our second CIA guy was in charge of the Intelligence wing of the CIA and may have come close to being shot in the Terre Haute House.

Also see what clue Oswald left as to who was behind the assassination.

# BOOKS BY THIS AUTHOR

## America's Crossroads The Public Record

The day of President Kennedy's assassination, the Dallas Police discovered a rifle on the sixth floor of the Texas School Book Depository, they identified the rifle as a German Mauser rifle.

Three days after President Kennedy's assassination a young twenty-year-old named Harry L. Power walked into the Terre Haute House, in Terre Haute, Indiana. He had no luggage, although he did carry a long paper package and according to FBI reports, a Young Communist League Card in his wallet. He registered at the hotel giving a San Antonio, Texas address. Two days later the maid found that he had left behind a 7.65 Argentine German Mauser Rifle, Model 1891.

At the time, there were two very prominent CIA guys who were from Terre Haute. William King Harvey oversaw the Mafia and the anti-Castro Cubans trying to assassinate Castro. Bill Harvey's Cuban agents discovered the missiles going into Cuba. Harvey should have been hailed as a hero, but unfortunately Bill Harvey and Robert Kennedy were not getting along and Harvey's career and position in the CIA suffered greatly as a result. William King Harvey is on the record as saying he, "hating Bobby Kennedy's guts with a purple passion." Some speculate that Bill Harvey was responsible for the assassination of President Kennedy. Was this rifle left in Terre Haute as a calling card from Bill Harvey to Bobbie Kennedy? Or, did Kim Philby, the Soviet spy who Bill Harvey unmasked eleven years earlier, arrange for the rifle to come to Terre Haute to call attention to Bill Harvey, in an effort to make Bill Harvey look guilty?

Our second CIA guy, Ray Cline, was the Deputy Director of Intelligence at the CIA, second only to the Director of the CIA. Ray Cline may have come close to being shot in the Terre Haute House while making a speech to his and William King Harvey's old high school alma mater, Wiley High School, at Wiley's 100 Year Centennial Celebration in the Terre Haute House.

Oswald left us a clue as to who was behind the assassination, this story will reveal the clue.

# BOOKS BY THIS AUTHOR

## Documentation Supplement America's Crossroads

The book: Documentation Supplement America's Crossroads is a complementary supplementary book for the book: America's Crossroads, The Public Record.

The book: Documentation Supplement America's Crossroads contains copies of the Terre Haute Police Reports, San Antonio Police Reports, Terre Haute Police Letter to Earl Warren, Warren Commission Response, FBI Reports on Harry L Power, copies of Signature Cards from the Terre Haute House, copies of Terre Haute House Guest Register for November 1963, Jack Martin and David Lewis Affidavit, CIA AMUG Report and FBI Report - Dr. Penabaz.

www.ingramcontent.com/pod-product-compliance
Lightning Source LLC
Jersburg PA
0058170426
CB00014B/2382